LINKING RINGS

LINKING RINGS

William W. Durbin and the
Magic and Mystery of America

JAMES D. ROBENALT

The Kent State University Press ■ Kent & London

Frontis: W. W. Durbin (1932). Author's collection.

© 2004 by The Kent State University Press, Kent, Ohio 44242
ALL RIGHTS RESERVED
Library of Congress Catalog Card Number 2004000138
ISBN 0-87338-808-9 (paper)
ISBN 0-87338-820-8 (cloth)
Manufactured in the United States of America

08 07 06 05 04   5 4 3 2 1

Photo of Francis Durbin at the 1940 Democratic Convention reprinted by
special permission of the *Chicago Sun-Times* ©2003.

LIBRARY OF CONGRESS CATALOGING-IN-PUBLICATION DATA
Robenalt, James D., 1956–
Linking rings : William W. Durbin and the magic and mystery of America / James D. Robenalt.
p.   cm.
Includes bibliographical references (p.   ) and index.
ISBN 0-87338-808-9 (pbk. : alk. paper) ∞
ISBN 0-87338-820-8 (hardcover : alk. paper) ∞
1. Durbin, William W. (William Warner). 2. Politicians—Ohio—Biography.
3. Democratic Party (Ohio)—Biography. 4. Ohio—Politics and government—1865–1950.
5. Kenton (Ohio)—Politics and government—20th century. 6. United States—Politics and
government—1865–1933. 7. United States—Politics and government—1933–1945.
8. Magicians—Ohio—Kenton—Biography. 9. Kenton (Ohio)—Biography. I. Title.
F496.D87R63 2004
977.1'043'092—dc22
2004000138

British Library Cataloging-in-Publication data are available.

To Margaret Durbin Robenalt,

a magician's granddaughter, with love.

We inherit much from our ancestors—why not their memories?

HENRY RIDGELY EVANS
The Linking Ring

CONTENTS

PREFACE AND
ACKNOWLEDGMENTS

I did not start off to write a book. I was doing what a lot of people do at times of generational transition: trying to find out more about my family. The trigger was my mother's death in 1990.

Very quickly I knew that this was a story that had to be told. Franklin Roosevelt, Warren Harding, Harry Blackstone, Woodrow Wilson, John Brown, Harry Houdini, George Remus, the "King of the Bootleggers," and William Jennings Bryan all converged in the person of William Warner Durbin, my mother's grandfather. He flew below the historical radar screen, but what if he had never lived? There were so many links, so many contingencies, conspiracies, discoveries, and inexplicable twists and turns to the drama of his life that it almost seemed like fantasy.

So how to tell of the life of a magician whose vocation was politics? A simple biography was out of the question. All of the hard research led to an idea. Why not travel back in time for one night to meet the old wizard himself in a car ride that actually did take place at the end of his life? Once there, he could tell his story directly to one of his descendants—a transference of family memories that just may have had national significance. Surely a magician could accomplish such a meeting.

The ride takes place in italics. Most of the quotes from Durbin have a source in his notes, letters, and published articles. Everything in a normal typeface is real history, mined and researched over ten years across libraries, magic studios, and archives from the FDR Library in Hyde Park to David Copperfield's home in Las Vegas.

I am indebted to several people in the magic world for their help and support. David Copperfield and his archivist, Leo Behnke, provided encouragement, research assistance, and comments on the ideas for this book. David Price opened up Egyptian Hall for me, copied materials, commented on drafts, and continually reminded me to avoid exposing the secrets of magic. Mike Caveney, who bought the Price collection along with George Daily, was always willing to share photos and materials from the collection. Ted Carrothers introduced me to Harry Blackstone Jr.; Harry Blackstone Jr. introduced me to David Price; and the late Bob Lund looked at drafts and let me have copies of his Durbin file.

John Sears, who was the executive director of the Franklin and Eleanor Roosevelt Institute, gave me his thoughts on drafts of the book and has always been willing to introduce me to people or answer questions. John is currently the associate editor of the Eleanor Roosevelt Papers.

My friends Mark Gamin and Neil Evans were wonderful editors. Special thanks to Michael Ruhlman and Philip Jackson, both of whom gave me an author's perspective. Joanna Hildebrand Craig of the Kent State University Press was willing to take a chance on a first-time author. Kathy Method has been a superb editor.

My wife, Beth, and my children, Jim, Meg, and John, went with me to some pretty obscure places to do research. They all showed endless patience with my obsession and provided love, support, and humor throughout the writing process. Beth in particular kept this project going with her constant encouragement. My two Durbin aunts, D. D. Childers Root and Sally Wolfer, told me stories, read my drafts, and always sent "love and prayers." My assistant Gail Motley cheerfully helped with word processing and had insightful comments.

Thanks to all.

PROLOGUE: WASHINGTON, D.C.

Tuesday, August 1, 1933

Magic is a powerful thing.

"For years Washington has felt the need for a magician," the *New York Evening Post* reported in the first week of August 1933. "This has especially been true since the depression began."[1]

So it was that a strange gathering packed the house on August 1, 1933, in the Treasury Department to witness an extraordinary event on a suffocating Tuesday afternoon in the nation's capital. Temperatures were expected to flirt with the upper nineties.

The "ever-resourceful Roosevelt Administration" had found a magician to take one of the top jobs in the United States Treasury. Dean Acheson, the undersecretary of the Treasury, was there to administer the oath of office. Suspense hung in the air as the old wizard—the man they all came to see—rose from his seat to be sworn in by Acheson. The group bustled and buzzed while Acheson shuffled nervously, seeming to brace himself as the old man approached.

Acheson was hardly a man of shaky disposition. Tall, dashing, with bushy eyebrows and a carefully manicured mustache, he had an imperial air and looked more like a fine English gentleman than the American son of an Episcopal bishop from Connecticut. A graduate of the Reverend Endicott Peabody's Groton, he attended Yale before enrolling in the Harvard Law School. Cole Porter had been his roommate at Yale and briefly at Harvard before he dropped out of law school to pursue music. Acheson was deeply influenced during his time at Harvard by his young law professor, the brilliant Felix Frankfurter, and upon graduation Acheson became the private

PHOTOGRAPH BY GEORGE P. HIGGINS FOR THE AMERICAN MAGAZINE

HERE is William Warner Durbin, Register of the Treasury of the United States, demonstrating one of his famous flashing finger-tricks. He's president and founder of the International Brotherhood of Magicians and a past master of black art. As Register of the Treasury, appointed by President Roosevelt, he keeps track of billions of dollars' worth of United States bonds. But when the day's work is done he turns to his magic. Puts on a show several times a year in his own house of magic in Kenton, Ohio, his home town. Born there 67 years ago. At nineteen he studied law and ran the Democratic County Committee in Kenton—before he was old enough to vote. A few years later, "Presto!" he pulled a Democratic governorship (James M. Cox) out of the clutches of Republican Ohio. Since then he has done 2,000 other tricks—almost as unusual.

II Interesting People

secretary to Justice Louis D. Brandeis, the first Jew appointed to the Supreme Court in American history.

No affection existed between FDR and Acheson. Within three months of
this hot August morning Acheson would resign his post, following what he
called a "spectacular row" with FDR over the president's policy of setting
the price of gold every morning from his bedroom in the White House.
Acheson was lured back to the administration as the assistant secretary of
state, despite his personal dislike of FDR (he found it especially annoying
that FDR called everyone by their first name), and he would play a crucial
role in 1940 in helping to devise an embargo on Japan so stifling in its range
and effect that the Japanese military machine was able to use it to convince
Japan's political leaders that the only recourse was to attack Pearl Harbor.

Later, he became Harry Truman's towering secretary of state and credited himself with the creation of a new world order out of the chaos and
disaster of World War II. *Present at Creation* was the title of Acheson's not-
so-self-effacing autobiography, covering his years in the State Department.[2]

Still, there was something unsettling even to Acheson about the ceremony
over which he had come to preside. There was a weird electricity in the
room; he had a hard time putting his finger on the feeling. The old man to
be sworn in as the register of the Treasury looked like any other well-dressed
businessman or politician. He wore a nicely tailored, dark, three-piece wool
suit. He was tall but stooped-shouldered, bespectacled with wire-rim glasses,
and he flashed a kind, easy smile as he strode through the standing-room-
only crowd to the front of the room.

But Acheson was on his guard. He knew that this old man was none
other than the current president of the International Brotherhood of Magicians. In magic circles, he sported the stage name "The Past Master of the
Black Art."

He was also known as a politician of fire, a lone wolf from Ohio, who
lately had been written up in the newspapers as "Wild Bill" because of his
proclivity to start fights with foes and friends alike.[3]

No one in the room knew what to expect, and the old sorcerer liked it
that way.

"It's fun to be fooled," he would say to reporters immediately after the
ceremony. Mystery was his friend.[4]

The aging prestidigitator's name was William W. Durbin, but he usually
went by W. W. Durbin. By almost any measure he was the polar opposite of

Facing page: Durbin performing tricks in the register of the Treasury's office (1934).
Courtesy *American Magazine.*

Acheson. He was not the product of elite Eastern schools; indeed, he never finished high school, although he completed night courses at the National Law School in the 1880s when he worked in Washington as a common clerk for the Treasury Department during Grover Cleveland's first administration. He distrusted the Eastern establishment and "the interests," as he called them. He was a rural populist, a self-proclaimed disciple of the Great Commoner, William Jennings Bryan. An unshakable Democrat, he had grown up in a town of eight thousand souls located in the flat, fertile farm country of western Ohio. He disliked jazz; his musical taste tended toward Wagner's *Tannhäuser*, waltzes, and marches.[5]

Where Acheson counted among his lifelong friends the urbane W. Averell Harriman, son of a railroad tycoon and later ambassador to the Soviet Union during the Cold War, Durbin knew the bumpkin Warren G. Harding as a neighbor from a nearby town. Harding and his superstitious wife—the Duchess, as Harding liked to call her—were magic aficionados, attending every one of W. W. Durbin's magic shows given in Harding's hometown of Marion, Ohio. Usually, the couple took up seats in the very front row.[6]

In contrast to Acheson, Durbin liked it that Franklin Roosevelt called him by his first name. Durbin would write affectionately about a telephone call he took in his room at the Palmer House Hotel in Chicago placed by FDR sometime after four o'clock in the afternoon at a crucial moment in the 1932 Democratic National Convention. Durbin had taken a stand for Roosevelt in a nationally broadcast proceeding in the wee hours on the first night of balloting as the governor of New York listened anxiously in his office in Albany.

"Is that you, Bill?" Roosevelt yelled over the hissing phone line, "your voice sounded mighty good this morning."[7]

Bemused, if not fascinated, by the makeup of the group that had gathered to see Durbin become the register of the Treasury, Acheson surveyed the faces. Several of Washington's most prominent women were there. Acheson had just sworn in Mrs. Blair Banister, sister of Senator Carter Glass of Virginia, as the assistant treasurer of the United States, the first woman to hold such a position. She remained in the room to watch the Durbin ceremony. Mrs. Trenholm Abrams, representative of the League of Nations, was also in attendance, as was Altrude Grayson, wife of the personal physician of the late Woodrow Wilson.[8]

By far, though, the most distinguished spectator in the audience was the grand dame of the Democratic Party, Edith Wilson, widow of the president. Edith was Woodrow Wilson's second wife, introduced to him in March 1915, just eight months after Wilson's first wife Ellen died in the White House.

Altrude Grayson and her husband became close confidants of the Wilsons, and the friendship continued between the two women long after Wilson died in 1924.

Edith had "been to the mountaintop" with her husband at the end of the Great War and had beheld sights few mortals would ever witness. She traveled with Wilson to Europe in 1918 to attend the extended Paris Peace Conference and observed firsthand one of the greatest outpourings of emotion ever showered on any world leader. Hailed as the savior of mankind in Paris and London, Wilson kept Edith close by his side as stupendous crowds greeted their appearance. She was also with him a half year later when it all came apart in one of history's most spectacular falls, as he was buffeted by a series of strokes, perhaps visited upon him by angry gods offended by the hubris of a man who thought he could change the world and end all wars.

Wilson fell first during a whirlwind train trip across the country to gain support for his doomed League of Nations. The day before his attack, he had spoken in Pueblo, Colorado, when suddenly he lost his words and began to cry. Hoping to clear his mind, Dr. Cary Grayson suggested a stroll in the Colorado countryside, stopping the train a few miles outside Pueblo, where Wilson, Edith, and Grayson alighted and took a walk in the September twilight. Secret Service agent Edmund Starling followed the three closely. When they spotted a sickly looking soldier in uniform sitting on a porch, Grayson and Wilson climbed over a fence to greet the man and his family. Later that night, Wilson suffered a grave headache that could not be soothed. When he awoke, the left half of his face had fallen and he mumbled and slurred his words. He was rushed back to the White House where, a week later, he collapsed while attempting to shave. This time the stroke was more serious. His left side was paralyzed; his life hung in the balance.

Incapacitated, Wilson depended on Edith's protection for the last year and a half of his presidency. She carefully controlled access to him and most likely made many of his decisions. Few doubted that she was, de facto, the first woman president of the United States.[9]

Seated near Mrs. Wilson in the overflow crowd in the Treasury Department was Judge Timothy Ansberry, an Ohio lawyer and politician who was long a Durbin ally. Ansberry was the man who put the young Franklin Roosevelt's name in nomination for the vice presidency a dozen years earlier at the 1920 Democratic National Convention in San Francisco. Durbin and Ansberry worked behind the scenes to convince Ohio's governor, James Cox, the man the Democrats nominated to succeed Wilson, to accept the thirty-eight-year-old Roosevelt as his running mate.[10]

"It was an audience to inspire the artist—and W. W. Durbin is an artist to the tips of his toes, a master magician who has entertained millions of people here and abroad,"[11] a news service reported, taking, appropriately enough, artistic license with the facts (Durbin had never been abroad and, although he entertained for a wide public, he had hardly performed for millions).

Inspiration was something Durbin believed in. It was his stock-in-trade, and not just as a performing artist. According to his philosophy, everything important in the world was revealed through inspiration. In the spring of 1934 he wrote about this idea in a magazine he published and edited for magicians only, *The Linking Ring*. "When the good Lord made this world," he wrote about the invention of new tricks and illusions, "he put all knowledge here and from time to time it is revealed through His chosen servants."[12]

He found abundant evidence to support this proposition. "This is true in the world of science, art, and also in the world of magic," he explained. "That two or more persons may hit upon the same idea at the same time is revealed by looking at the records of the United States Patent Office where it will be found that a person in Maine and one in Texas hit upon the same idea about the same time."

To Durbin it was natural to believe that a Supreme Being, in the very moment of creation, had impregnated the world with all knowledge and that over the course of history a plan would be unveiled through designated servants. After all, he had witnessed the well-known phenomenon that people were "struck" by their most important ideas and had heard that inventors and artists often dreamed of their creations. He also had seen great and small leaders rise up from the people, promoting carefully reasoned programs, only to discover that their actions were governed mostly by intuition, visions, apprehensions, and moments of sudden lucidity.

He believed it was the destiny of America to be the great engine of progress for all mankind, empowering the drive toward the ultimate revelation of a divine plan. And since he knew that nature wasted nothing, perhaps he believed that memories themselves were passed down through posterity as a means of facilitating the long-term process of the uncovering of the truth behind existence. A true Progressive, Durbin believed that history was going somewhere. Did he conceive that the meaning and purpose of life could be found over time in the accumulated memories of mankind?

Was the discovery of all knowledge nothing more than the totality of generation after generation *remembering* the instant of creation? And was there such a thing as inherited memories?

His friends in the magic world wrote about this very idea—that of in-herited memories—in the 1920s. Magic historian and scholar Henry Ridgely Evans, whose publications Durbin supported as a patron, suggested that the earthly success of the master magician Harry Houdini could be ac-counted for as the result of his ability to tap into his own ancestral memo-ries. This explained, for example, Houdini's achievement in finding his way out of the labyrinth of a Russian prison he had never before visited.

"We inherit much from our ancestors," Evans wrote, "why not their memories?"

The claim Evans made was intriguing and even mysterious. "To a certain extent," he observed about ancestors, "they live again in us."[13]

Durbin followed his own inspiration in magic and politics. It occurred to him, for example, that magicians should band together in an international brotherhood and should meet yearly to share secrets in a festival of legerde-main. He felt, in a similar mystical way, that William Jennings Bryan, Woodrow Wilson, and Franklin D. Roosevelt should be presidents of the United States.

"Let it be understood that Bill Durbin is no ordinary magician," the *New York Evening Post* editorialized. "He is so good, in fact, that he visioned the Roosevelt bandwagon far ahead of the other astute Buckeye politicians."[14]

Durbin now stood directly opposite Acheson because of his predictive powers, his reliance on inspiration, and his trust in the American mission.

That he was also a master of diversion could be appreciated from the fact that exactly one year ago to the day he had faced an Ohio jury that found him guilty on criminal charges. Despite this, he was positioned to become the guardian of the nation's debt. Another magician and Durbin friend, Harry Kellar, was widely quoted on the subject of a good magician's facility for using distraction as his most important tool. "If you could thoroughly engage a man's attention," Kellar often said, "a herd of elephants might pass before him and he would not notice what was transpiring."[15]

Misdirection, Durbin understood, played a powerful role in magic as well as politics.

The room grew quiet as Acheson took the Bible in his left hand and with trepidation raised his right hand to start the ceremony. Durbin placed one hand on the Bible and lifted the other with a motion so quick and smooth that everyone sat forward to see what was happening. According to the news-papers, the audience "expected to see him pluck a rabbit from the pockets" of Acheson as the oath was administered. Would he do it? Perhaps some-thing even more spectacular?

"I, William Warner Durbin, do solemnly swear," Acheson began, an eye twitching, glancing sidelong to see if his wristwatch was still there. Everyone held their breath.

"I, William Warner Durbin," the old conjurer repeated, "do solemnly swear . . ."

A broad smile spread across his face. He recognized the moment for what it was: he had once again outwitted his opponents.

⇒ 1 ⇐

AND THINGS ARE NOT
WHAT THEY SEEM

February 1, 1937

Three and a half years after W. W. Durbin was sworn in as register of the Treasury, he faced a crisis. His daughter-in-law, Agnes, was dying of ovarian cancer. Durbin reacted to the news of her imminent demise by calling his chauffeur, Delbert Krock, to drive from Washington, D.C., back to Ohio.[1]

Durbin was my great-grandfather; Agnes was my grandmother. My mother, Agnes's oldest, told me of those terrible days in February 1937. Mom was just thirteen years old then, but the events of this time were seared into her memory. She told me of her grandfather, too, the magician and politician. Stray portraits of Franklin Roosevelt and Woodrow Wilson populated some of the nooks and crannies of our basement; they were silent artifacts and occasional reminders to me that something special had taken place in my family history.

Just what had happened and the extent of the story were quite unclear. While I knew of Durbin and had an inkling that he was part of extraordinary events, virtually all of his papers and documents and all of his magic programs, apparatus, and paraphernalia were lost to the family, either sold or thrown out. I started making my own inquiries in the early 1990s, and like some great magic show, strange but wonderful things began to happen. I have often wondered if this was because Durbin was a magician or because he was a Democrat.

More and more the focus kept coming back to that fateful night in early February of 1937, just after FDR had been sworn in for his second term. What was it about that night that so transfixed me? "And things are not what they seem," Durbin proclaimed in one of his magic programs that I found in my search, and so it became for me. I was transported to the blustery and dark late afternoon of February 1, 1937. A curtain was coming down.

"We have so little time," he says to me as the chauffeur loads some bags in the trunk of the car.

I know there is little time, and I have to take a big breath to pace myself. I also know I have to studiously avoid gawking at the man who stands next to me.

"You got any grips?" the chauffeur asks me.

"Grips?"

"Yeah, bags, suitcases?"

"No . . . no, I don't." I ask the older man in a manner that I hope suggests an unforced casualness: "How did I get here?"

"Just a moment," he waves off the question, distracted by something. "Deb," he says to the chauffeur, "I forgot the papers on my desk, in that pile on the right side of the desk."

"Right." The chauffeur hurries back toward the building, but diverts his trot and comes over to me to make his introduction first. "Delbert Krock," he says, tipping his cap with his left hand, "glad to know you."

Delbert Krock, here was someone I had been told was Durbin's chauffeur. He and I had never met; I could only imagine him, until a magician who read some of my early chapters told me of an article that had appeared in *The Linking Ring* in 1957.[2] Delbert's wife, Hazel Krock, appeared on the cover of the magazine on the occasion of her retirement from her duties as treasurer of the International Brotherhood of Magicians. Hazel had been Durbin's secretary; she married Delbert in 1943. The article therefore contained side-by-side photos of Delbert and Durbin. Strange indeed for me to see the faces of these two together after I was deep into my writing of a trip with them.

Delbert disappears into a massive neoclassical building that, above its Corinthian columns, proclaims itself as the Bureau of Engraving and Printing.[3] I look around and see a street sign that says we are on Fifteenth Street. There are lots of old cars passing. Across a sloping lawn, I see some dormant Japanese cherry trees, a tidal basin, and what appears to be the Jefferson Memorial, flickering as if it is moving in and out of time. Slowly, the memorial and the tidal basin dim and vanish.

The car we are standing next to is a Studebaker, a four-door, top-of-the-line model from the President's Series.[4] It has a long narrow grill slanting jauntily toward the front bumper. The side panels are graced with horizontal louvers, and a flying goddess stands as a mascot on the hood. It is a huge, humming machine.

Delbert Krock and Durbin pictured in *The Linking Ring* (1957). Courtesy *The Linking Ring*.

Delbert reappears from the building and scurries on the double-quick back to the car, holding a file in his hand that he gives to his boss. The older man opens the file to inspect its contents, thumbs through it, and looks satisfied.

"Okay," he utters to Delbert, "let's get on our way."

"You want to take the old National Road?"

"Yes," Durbin tersely replies, still reading a paper in the file. So this is William W. Durbin, my mother's grandfather, the great magician.

But did my involvement in the car ride actually take place? I confess that even now I have trouble resolving this question with anything approaching certainty. A mystery surrounds it all.

The old National Road, the highway Durbin routinely used for his travels between Ohio and Washington, was the first great national highway constructed over the Appalachians to the west. Congress passed legislation in 1806 launching the National Road, or the Cumberland Road as it was called, and Jefferson picked three commissioners to lay out the appropriate route. The path chosen followed ancient Indian trails that probably started as portage routes from the headwaters of the Potomac River near Cumberland, Maryland, to the Monongahela River south of Pittsburgh. From there, a traveler on boat could hook up with the Ohio and navigate into the Ohio country.

The road eventually ran from Baltimore to the Mississippi. The cause of many battles in Congress, the road was built in stages. It ran over the ridges of the Alleghenies to the "Big Crossings" of the Youghiogheny, across the intervening hills and Laurel Mountain, right by Fort Necessity, where Washington surrendered to the French in 1754, up through Uniontown, Pennsylvania, to "Old Red Stone Fort" at the head of the navigation on the Monongahela at Brownsville, Pennsylvania, and across the panhandle of Virginia (today West Virginia) to the Ohio River near Wheeling and then across the center of Ohio through Columbus.

When Andrew Jackson came over this road to be inaugurated as president in 1829, he is supposed to have been caught in a snowstorm on the west slope of Meadow Mountain at Tomlinson's Tavern, where he waited it out by playing a card game called "Old Sledge" with his friends. Henry Clay made innumerable journeys on this road to and from his home in Lexington, Kentucky. A busy highway of commerce before the advent of the railroad, it was one of the nation's most important thoroughfares.

"It continued to flourish," one writer said, "with its host of stage-drivers, wagoners, blacksmiths and hostlers, its six-horse teams, Conestoga wagons, Concord coaches and private carriages, its numerous taverns and landlords, its stone paved way, its stone culverts, arches and bridges, its curious triangular stone mile-posts and oddly constructed toll houses, its manners and customs, its usages and traditions and all its busy traffic, until the [eighteen] fifties when the railroads came."[5]

In Durbin's day, the National Road was called Route No. 1. Later it would be renamed U.S. Route 40, and today it has been partially replaced and enveloped by Interstate 70.

To pick up Route No. 1 from Washington, Durbin would have driven out of town north on the old Seventh Street Pike to Olney and then to Ridgeville, Maryland, where he would have picked up the great road.

Durbin recommended that magicians coming from Maryland or Pennsylvania to the 1927 IBM convention in Kenton, Ohio, should "take Route No. 1, the Old National Road, which runs out of Washington through Frederick, Cumberland, Maryland, and then down over the mountains through Uniontown and Washington, Pennsylvania, and down to Wheeling, West Virginia, where they should cross the Ohio River and follow this Route No. 1 through Bridgeport, St. Clairsville, Cambridge, Zanesville into Columbus. From there they can either go by Route No. 4 to Marion, Ohio and then cross over on Route No. 10 (Harding Highway), or they can take Route 21, which is a straight line through Marysville to Kenton."[6]

"You know where we're going, don't you?" Durbin solicits.

" I think so."

"Well then, we'll talk about how you got here later. What is important is that we get underway. Get in."

Agnes Kelly Durbin with my mother, Margaret Morgan Durbin, in her lap (1925). Author's collection.

The car has frosted windows, and for the first time I notice how cold it is outside. The sun has already begun to fall behind the thick clouds, so it appears to be getting dark even though Durbin's watch reads half past three.

Delbert jumps in and revs the motor. Durbin carefully climbs into the backseat, and I join him there. The car smells of leather from the seats, which are shiny and smooth, and the sparseness of the dashboard surprises me. There are no fancy dials, no radio.

Our trip to Ohio figures to be a sad journey. With death slowly closing in on my grandmother, Durbin's thoughts of his own mortality cannot be far from his mind. He has had a special relationship with Agnes over the years. She was beautiful, with thick auburn hair (she once cut it in a "flapper" style in the 1920s in a fit of feminism) and a stately Irish look. Over the last year, though, she had wasted away; now she weighs no more than eighty or ninety pounds and is bedridden.

Like many, my interest in the genetic milieu from which I sprang was not awakened in earnest until one of my parents died. In my case it was my mother's death in the summer of 1990. After she died, I found that I was drawn to her grandfather, not recognizing what I was getting into. I did not start off to be obsessed by him, the process sucked me in; the old man seemingly provoked, incited, and energized the encounter. The odyssey I embarked upon actually began one evening when I found a box in a storage bin of a condominium my parents owned. The box was cluttered with photos, letters, old magazines, and newspapers. Out of this jumble of papers and documents, one newspaper in particular presented itself, as if someone had pushed it to the top.

In it was an article dated June 26, 1936. The crumbling and yellowing remnant of the newspaper contained a picture of my mother grasping the Ohio standard at the Democratic National Convention, which was held that year in Philadelphia, the city where the nation was born. During this convention, FDR delivered one of his best-remembered lines. Like so many of his speeches, this one contained word-magic, for what he said that day could not have been more true or prophetic for my mother and her generation. "There is a mysterious cycle in human events," he said to the crowd of over one hundred thousand adoring followers in Franklin Field. "To some generations much is given," Roosevelt bellowed as he held precariously to his wind-blown speech. "Of other generations much is expected. This generation of Americans has a *rendezvous with destiny*."[7]

My mom was twelve when she was brought to the City of Brotherly Love to see and participate in the grand spectacle of her first national convention. She had accompanied her father and grandfather as an initiation rite of sorts in her political education.

I read the old article and something deep inside was triggered in my soul. I had to find out more.

> Margaret Durbin is only 12 but she is going to be the first Congress-woman from Ohio, declare both she and her father, Francis Durbin, delegate from Ohio and manager of Senator A. Vic. Donahey's successful 1934 Ohio campaign. So in order to prepare her for her future political activities, Delegate Durbin brought her from Lima, Ohio, to attend the Democratic national convention.
>
> Margaret's grandfather is William W. Durbin, register of the treasury in Washington and manager of the William Jennings Bryan campaign in 1896.

Margaret thinks the convention is "just grand" and isn't missing a single activity. Her favorite affair was the William Jennings Bryan breakfast, because her granddaddy was a friend of Bryan and he used to be a frequent visitor to their home.[8]

The writer of the article, a woman, obviously enjoyed her young subject. "Since she has been in Philadelphia, Margaret has met such notables as Secretary of State Cordell Hull, Senator Alben W. Barkley and Marvin McIntyre, President Roosevelt's personal secretary, but she hasn't achieved her heart's desire—to meet a congresswoman!"

My mother never did become a congresswoman, although she would have been a great one. She joined the navy as a Wave in 1943, typed correspondence for some of the navy brass in Washington and, after the war, went to the Ohio State University on the GI Bill. During her time in the service, she started what became a lifelong habit of smoking. She stopped in 1986 after my father had heart bypass surgery, but in 1989 she was diagnosed with lung cancer.

After graduating from college with a degree in education, she worked briefly at a Lima radio station, married my father in 1950, and together they raised five boys and two girls through the fifties, sixties, and seventies. We were the focus of her life. She was strong-minded, opinionated, self-assertive, and active in my hometown—on school boards and on local TV talk shows (where she reviewed books like *Go East, Young Man,* the autobiography of Supreme Court Justice William O. Douglas). She was on the faculty and boards of two community colleges, an Ohio State branch campus, and the Lima Technical College. She was endlessly fascinated with people, always stopping to talk, and it appeared that she knew everyone we met on the street or in the grocery store. She usually knew where someone was from, who their families were, and who their cousins married.

She told us about the Durbins, proselytized at times, cigarette waving in one hand, but I now know what we heard was just the smallest fraction of the story. Like most oral histories, the chronicle came in dribs and drabs over spurts of time, all anecdotal, with huge pieces missing. We frequently suspected that she was making things up. Some of the tales seemed farfetched—an ancestor who fought at Gettysburg, was shot in the head, had a steel plate inserted, and survived. Over time, the accounts began to mix, fade, undulate, and swirl into a confusing soup of information.

I am not sure why I did not ask more questions while she was alive. I suppose it all seemed too unreachable, a dim, distant, dark past that could never be reconstructed or recovered with any accuracy or reliability. There was a

Margaret Durbin, Wave (1944). Author's collection.

time barrier in the past that simply could not be breached. As long as my mother lived, the past was as dead as the people who were buried in the cemeteries I rarely visited. I could no more hope to understand their lives than to resurrect them from their graves.

Yet, after she died, doors began opening. The time barrier was not so insurmountable: old magicians die, it appears, but they never fade away. The more materials that came into my possession, the more my ancestral memories were stirred. My search for validation of these family memories led me across the country. I found them in Hyde Park, New York, in the archives of the Franklin D. Roosevelt Library; in the microfilm collection of the Woodrow Wilson Papers; in Washington at the National Archives and in the Library of Congress.

An ailing judge, Tom Dowd, from Kenton, Ohio, decided to give me a file he kept containing Durbin memorabilia: magic programs, photos, and a Treasury Department scrapbook. Judge Dowd, himself an amateur magician, knew Durbin, and he told me that the Kenton Historical Society would not take the Durbin papers because of his connection with magic. This conservative town wanted nothing to do with magic, something considered "devil's work."

Harry Blackstone Jr. (son of the "Great Blackstone") told me in a phone interview from his home in Redlands, California, of a man named David Price, who maintained a magic museum dedicated to Durbin in a specially built wing of his Nashville home. The eighty-two-year-old Price showed me his museum in 1993.

I found Durbin memories in an environmentally controlled archive room in David Copperfield's warehouse and home (in a secret location) outside Las Vegas. There Copperfield carefully maintained a treasure trove of magic antiques, letters, giant posters, books, and files, some of which started with the fabled Mulholland Collection. Durbin knew John Mulholland, a New York magician who for a time was the editor of the magical publication *The Sphinx.* I saw Copperfield's (or really the Mulholland) file on Durbin in April 1995.

The capstone of my research was finding a York, Pennsylvania, man, George Dailey, who collected and sold magicana. For $1,500 he sold me a complete set of mint-condition magic magazines published for magicians only, *The Linking Ring,* from the first issue in 1922 through 1994. *The Linking Ring* has always been the official organ of the International Brotherhood of Magicians (called the IBM). Shortly after Durbin became president of the IBM in 1926, he also became the editor of this monthly. Within the astonishing pages of these well-preserved magazines, I unearthed hundreds of pieces written by Durbin himself over a twelve-year period in some 116 volumes. There were tales of the IBM, about his life in magic, and even some of our family.

I found never-before-seen photographs of my mother as a child at magic conventions and pictures of her parents, happy photographs taken before the hard times of 1937. I could not put them down. I took them with me to coffeehouses. I read them late into the night. With each turn of a page, I moved ever deeper into the mysteries of magic, closer and closer to the reality of my mother's family and further and further into the maelstrom of some mystical ancestral consciousness.

So here I am at last, meeting the great man. I look outside the car window as we prepare to pull away from the Bureau of Engraving and Printing. Durbin continues to look through the file Delbert retrieved.

He waves to Delbert, who looks back at him in the mirror and nods. We are jolted back in our seats as Delbert releases the clutch and we lurch out, traveling north on Fifteenth Street. If we are where I think we are, the Holocaust

Memorial should be in this same block. There is instead now only a barren lot. At the corner of Fifteenth and Independence, we turn right and then left on Fourteenth, traveling north.

We pull ahead, slowly passing through the Mall, with the Washington Monument pointing heavenward on our left and the United States Capitol down the Mall to our right in the distance.

"I came here when I was a young man, just nineteen," Durbin says. "Grover Cleveland had been elected president, and the local party back in my hometown of Kenton sent me here. It was the reward for my efforts in that presidential campaign. I wasn't even old enough to vote; yet I was taken with politics. I was given an appointment in the Treasury Department as a clerk. Washington was a different town in those days."[9]

Kenton, the town Durbin left in 1886 to go to Washington, was not much bigger than a flyspeck on the Ohio map. Located on the banks of the Scioto River, sixty-three miles northwest of Columbus, it was situated in an area once occupied by the Wyandots and Shawnees.[10] The town was organized in 1833 and was named after the frontiersman and scout Simon Kenton, a companion of Daniel Boone's. Kenton was a grizzled, hulking man and a renowned Indian fighter who had the remarkable reputation of surviving eight runs through the gauntlet. There is no evidence Simon Kenton ever visited Kenton, Ohio, and he never lived there. The local legend is that Simon Kenton was a "warm friend" of one of the founding fathers of the tiny frontier village, and that this is how the town got its name.

Durbin lived his entire life in Kenton, except for his years in Washington. His father was a pioneer physician, itinerant by nature, and a man who had ambled through the thick forests of Ohio on horseback to treat patients during the nineteenth century. Durbin was born in 1866, just after the Civil War. His mother was an immigrant from Germany. Her first husband, a Swiss immigrant, died during the Civil War, one of those who gave "the last full measure of devotion" to the cause of the American experiment in democracy.

Durbin's mother married old Doctor Durbin, who was thirty years her senior. He survived a first wife and was a rare specimen in his day: an available widower in a little town that had a number of war widows.

Will Durbin was the couple's first child; Eliza, his sister, the second and last.

Durbin would make Kenton the center of the rural progressive Democratic movement, an ephemeral moment in political history that has since faded. He also made Kenton the capital of the magic world for a dozen years. There are, however, no memorials or landmarks in Kenton commemorating him for these accomplishments. His house still stands, 87 Resch Street, and is well cared for by its current owners, but it has no marker to indicate it is a place where William Jennings Bryan once visited and was the site of the first convention of the International Brotherhood of Magicians.

The signs welcoming a visitor to Kenton today proudly declare that Kenton was the hometown of Jacob Parrott, the first person to be awarded the Congressional Medal of Honor. Parrott was one of Andrews' Raiders, a group of Union soldiers who volunteered to dress as civilians in order to sneak behind enemy lines to hijack a train near Atlanta, with the idea of destroying bridges and rail lines as they fled north. The train's engine eventually faltered, and all the raiders were captured, including Parrott, the youngest. Some of the raiders were hung in Atlanta as spies (according to accounts, the ropes were too long, so frantic Southern soldiers dug out the earth beneath strangling soldiers to complete the execution), some were exchanged for Confederate prisoners, and some escaped. Parrott was exchanged and picked by Lincoln's secretary of war, Ohioan Edwin Stanton, to be the first to receive the newly created Congressional Medal of Honor in recognition of the valor he had shown when he refused to confess after his capture, though he had been severely beaten.[11]

Ohio was known as the "Presidential State" in Durbin's time.[12] Before the Civil War, presidents came in abundant numbers from Virginia; afterward they came from Ohio. Ulysses S. Grant (1869–77), Rutherford B. Hayes (1877–81), James A. Garfield (1881), Benjamin Harrison (1889–93), William McKinley (1897–1901), William Howard Taft (1909–13), and Warren G. Harding (1921–23) were all claimed by Ohio. The succession of Ohio presidents was only broken by assassination (Garfield and McKinley) or a rare Democrat victory (Cleveland and Wilson).

So common was the myth of Ohio's prowess in the presidential sweepstakes that Chauncey Depew, president of the New York Central and a Republican speaker at the turn of the century, once said: "Some men have greatness thrust upon them, some are born great, and some are born in Ohio."[13]

Unfortunately for Durbin, all of these Ohio presidents were Republicans. As a Democrat in Ohio, Durbin was an upstream swimmer. Marcus A. Hanna, the corpulent Cleveland political kingmaker and senator, symbolized the power of the Grand Old Party in Ohio at the turn of the century. A wealthy industrialist, Hanna raised millions for the Republican Party, ran McKinley's two successful front-porch campaigns, and believed that government existed primarily to help business. He once told the Ohio attorney general, who sued to dissolve Standard Oil, to drop the suit. "Come on," Hanna pronounced, "you've been in politics long enough to know that no man in public life owes the public anything."[14]

Durbin and his friends scrapped and fought, with little or no money, to make significant inroads into the Republican mastery of Ohio. Ohioans began electing Democrat governors after 1900, and Durbin's colleagues turned Ohio away from Republicans in the national elections of 1912 with Woodrow Wilson and in 1932 with Franklin Roosevelt. Securing these election victories was a story of intrigue, charm, determination, strategy, and chicanery. Because world wars erupted during both the Wilson and Roosevelt presidencies, the elections of these two men took on world-changing significance, and Ohio played as important a role as any in their elections.

That Durbin wandered through an important landscape of change in the history of the United States is best underscored by reference to one of the nation's most significant milestones that quietly passed at the end of the second decade of the twentieth century, at the height of Durbin's political influence. America, for the last time, was predominantly a rural nation in 1920. Thereafter, cities gained the balance of power.[15]

Presidents were supposed to have been reared on farms, born full of hope and pluck in log cabins, and young men like Durbin found that coming from a small town was no impediment to a successful national political career. The reality of the dream of the small-town boy raising himself to the highest position in the country, especially one fortunate enough to have been born in Ohio, was no better illustrated than by Warren G. Harding, a boy born not far from Kenton in a village outside Marion, Blooming Grove, at virtually the same time as Durbin.

A friendship between Durbin and Harding was forged through magic.[16] Despite this, they would eventually find themselves in 1920 at the opposite ends of one of the dirtiest presidential campaigns in American history. This clash of these two Ohio country boys was no coincidence.

"Nothing is a coincidence," Durbin imparts. "There is a plan."

He continues to shuffle through the papers in the folder Delbert brought him as the Studebaker picks up speed.

"Goddammit," he mumbles in obvious frustration.[17] He is distracted and, temporarily at least, annoyed. He finds what he is looking for, and gives me one of his magic programs, which declares his show is, "The premier magical entertainment of America, and the great revival of the mystic art, since the days of Houdin, Anderson, Heller and Herrmann." He is billed as "Durbin: The Past Master of the Black Art."

"And you wonder how you got here," Delbert says with a smirk. "Things are not what they seem."

The "Black Art" that Durbin was a past master of first appeared in the 1870s when a magician named Max Auzinger, or "Ben Ali Bey," as he called himself on the stage, discovered that if he dressed in white and stood in a completely black velvet recess with lights directed at the audience, the audience would be partially blinded so that assistants dressed in black (who were therefore invisible to the audience) could make white objects "appear" and "disappear" by pulling off or throwing black cloths over them. Vases and orbs would "float" as the unseen black-clad helpers picked them up and walked them about the stage.

By the time Durbin was in his prime, the Black Art was a not-so-well-kept secret, and magicians had all but abandoned it. He liked the name, though, and he used it all of his career.[18]

Durbin looks at me with great seriousness, as if he is now going to take me into his confidence. "There are rules."

"Rules? . . . What rules?"

"The first rule to be borne in mind by any magical aspirant is this," he says, looking around to see if anyone might be eavesdropping, "never tell your audience beforehand what you are going to do."

"Professor Hoffman," Delbert interjects, talking from the side of his mouth, his gaze straight ahead.

"Professor who?"

"Hoffman," Durbin whispers, still looking over his shoulder. Realizing we are alone, he raises his voice.

"He wrote this in a magic book that I consider one of the pioneering works on the art. It is called Modern Magic, A Practical Treatise on the Art of Conjuring, *and it is one of the first books I read as a student."[19]*

"Professor Hoffman," Delbert says, "was the pen name used by Angelo John Lewis, an attorney in London, who wrote several 'how to' magic books fifty or sixty years ago. Harry Houdini used to say he was 'one of the brightest stars in the firmament of magic literature.'"

"There is a reason for this first rule . . . ," Durbin stresses.

"Yes? . . ."

"If you do tell your audience what you are going to do, you at once give their vigilance the direction that it is most necessary to avoid and increase tenfold the chances of detection."

"I see."

"It follows, as a consequence of this first rule," Delbert yammers from the

front seat as if in competition to show there is more than one authority in this car, "that you should never perform the same trick twice on the same evening."

"Ahem," Durbin huffs.

"The best trick loses half its effect on repetition," Delbert continues, unde-terred, "but besides this, the audience knows precisely what is coming and have all their faculties directed to find out at what point you cheated their eyes on the first occasion." Delbert tugs his cap in self-satisfaction.

"Well, well," Durbin says, "look who's been doing some reading."

On the floor of the backseat of the car is a highly decorated small black enamel chest, a box that Durbin says is a magical apparatus that magicians call a "Japa-nese box" or simply "Jap Box." It is a box from which endless articles and objects can be extracted, he tells me, such as streams of handkerchiefs or flags.

Durbin reaches over and opens the lid, removing a newspaper. It is a copy of the Washington Post, *dated February 1, 1937. He sets the folded newspaper on the seat between us and removes from the box a silver orb. Holding the orb with great care, he slowly pulls his hands away but the orb remains floating between his hands.*

Watching the floating orb for several moments of silence, I ask him how the trick is done.

"The student must cultivate from the outset the art of talking and especially the power of using his eyes and his tongue independently of the movement of his hands. To do this, it will be necessary to prepare beforehand not only what he intends to do but also what he intends to say."[20]

The orb now circles back to its original position between his hands. He is clearly having fun fooling me. He moves his hands around the orb in dramatic fashion to create the illusion that the orb is floating of its own accord.

Now he pulls out a hoop from the Japanese Box and places it over and around the suspended orb to further his point that this is no ordinary trick. "A puzzle for students of physics and psychics, don't you think?" a very sly smile crossing his face.

He returns the hoop to the Japanese Box, and as he does, the orb slowly descends into the box, which he closes once the orb disappears.

"Knowledge and success do not become one's possessions overnight. They are not obtained by the turn of the hand or the toss of a coin. Nor can anyone imagine himself so fortunate that, like the vagaries of a dream, these attributes will steal upon him as he reposes at ease."

I am abundantly fortunate to be here. Not only am I the seeker who has the rare opportunity to meet his subject, I am meeting my direct ancestor, a man who has coursing through his veins ancient blood that I share, the very blood that perhaps encodes in its DNA *the long-forgotten and ancient memories of my family.*

We are now on Pennsylvania Avenue. To our left I see the Treasury Build-ing, and behind it is the White House. Out of his coat pocket Durbin pulls an invitation to the White House and hands it to me. The invitation is for a de-partmental reception to be given at nine in the evening on Thursday, February 4, by the president and Mrs. Roosevelt.[21]

The reception was part of the social season, a standard affair given by the Roosevelts to thank the various departments of Treasury, State, Interior, Agriculture, Post Office, Commerce, and Labor. In previous years Durbin had attended these receptions for which the guest lists included Joseph Kennedy, General Pershing, and William O. Douglas.

He takes off his glasses and rubs his tired eyes. "Looks like I'll miss that reception this year. I'll have to write the president a note."

We drive slowly past the White House. I think of how the Durbins were such avid Roosevelt people.

From my search through the archives at the FDR Library, I have a hand-written note to FDR from Durbin's sister, Eliza Wallace Durbin, a school-teacher who never married and who spent a good deal of her time compos-ing poetry.

Eliza wrote this note on July 20, 1932, a few weeks after the Democratic National Convention in Chicago, where Roosevelt was first nominated for president. She sent along a poem that she said had been composed "in the old days" for William Jennings Bryan, *The Radical.*

"It is rather presumptuous for so humble a democrat to intrude upon your now especially taxed time," Eliza wrote, "yet I feel that representative as I am of hundreds of thousands of small town voters it will not be un-pleasing to you to concede a few moments to reading of the satisfaction of heart and mind your nomination brought to us."

The poem she wrote for Bryan ends with some lines that were porten-tous, both for Bryan in his day, who died unexpectedly from a heart attack at the end of the Scopes trial in 1926, and later for Roosevelt, who at sixty-three, looking like a broken, aged man, succumbed to a massive cerebral hemorrhage in April 1945:

THE RADICAL

Truth's youngest steep he seeks to climb
Nor heeds the jeers below;
Nor cringes from the mud and slime
Rude ignorance doth throw;

He can not breathe the burnt-out air
Shut in crowded creed;
He is God's answer to the prayer
Wrung out from human need;
'Twas he that lured man's vision dim
From cent'ring on grey clod
For eyes upturned to follow him
In time saw past to God;
And he unto the end shall lead
To richer realms of soul;
His heart may break, but hearts that bleed
Mark trails to freedom's goal;
When pointing to the last his view
He drops, his vigor spent,
By blood upon the stones we threw
We seek the way he went.

"In every age," Eliza inscribed, "there have been valiant souls that found the cause of democracy swell within them until it crowded out selfish consideration of personal welfare. Such leaders inspire a fervor that gives the cause strength to live on even in the face of defeat. Such temporary halts are only the price of ultimate victory, and we are sure you, such a leader, are come at the happy time of ultimate victory."[22]

"Such a letter of approval was deeply appreciated by me," Roosevelt responded on August 27, 1932. "Thank you for sending me a copy of the verse that you wrote a great many years ago."[23]

These firmly held beliefs in sacred democracy, the godlike qualities of leaders, and the faith in the "ultimate victory" of which Eliza Durbin wrote—I have wondered about these things as I have studied the Durbins.

I had some exposure to these feelings when I was growing up, but I cannot say I have felt that way since the summer of 1968. In my youth, two Kennedys and Martin Luther King Jr. were murdered in short succession. For a time it felt like most good leaders were marked not for "ultimate victory" but for assassination.

A few weeks after Eliza wrote Roosevelt, Durbin sent FDR a telegram in which he invited John Garner, Roosevelt's Texan running mate, to a barbecue in Kenton to start off the fall campaign: "THE DEMOCRACY OF NORTH-WESTERN OHIO WHICH IS THE GIBRALTER OF DEMOCRACY ARE GOING TO HAVE A MONSTER BARBEQUE AT KENTON TO START THINGS OFF WITH A BANG," he wrote in a Western Union telegram to Roosevelt, delivered to Hyde Park on August 14, 1932.[24]

Nothing was done in a small way with this man.

FDR responded on August 24 in his "never wanting to say no" style, politely sidestepping the request. "Have not answered your telegram of August 14th for two reasons, one being that I have [been] literally swamped, as you can realize, and the other, because I have been waiting to know something a little more definitive about the plans that are being made for my running mate's itinerary."[25]

"I'm glad you're here," Durbin says and pats me on the leg. He seems to have gathered his bearings and is less nervous and distracted.

"I need to talk about Agnes, your grandmother. I need to tell you about her family."

Delbert shifts the car to a higher gear, and we speed up, passing out of Washington.

Durbin will never return here again.

⇒ 2 ⇐

"TIM KELLY WILL NOT SOON BE FORGOTTEN"

June 16, 1844

We have made our way through Washington, and we are driving at a fair clip on the old Seventh Street Pike toward Ridgeville. Once there, we will turn west and head toward New Market and Frederick, Maryland, where we will start to ascend into rocky hills and South Mountain beyond.

"I want to talk to you about the Kellys," Durbin says to me, "your grandmother's family."

I know why he wants to start this journey talking about his daughter-in-law. He so obviously has Agnes deeply in his thoughts and finds some comfort in telling me about her family.

"First, though, you must be limber," he tells me. "You need to expand your mind, loosen it up to unravel the deep unconscious. You must stretch your mind like an athlete stretches his muscles before a competition."

"Watch yourself," Delbert warns from the front seat.

"I want you to sit back and let your mind concentrate for a moment."

I do as he says, but I feel terribly self-conscious.

"Just sit for a moment and let your mind think of one thing only. Clear out everything else."

I close my eyes to concentrate.

"Good. What do you think of when I say the name Timothy Patrick Kelly?"

After a pause for reflection, I say what comes first to my mind, "Marion, Ohio . . . he was Agnes's father, and he was from Marion, Ohio."

"Yes, but what about an image? Conjure an image, find Tim Kelly in your mind, look for his face." He repeats, "Look for his face," slowly, rhythmically, but no image surfaces.

I found Tim Kelly's biography in Columbus at the Ohio Historical Society in the *History of Marion County*. The volume contained an outline of his life, but there were no photographs or likenesses of him. "Tim Kelley [he spelled it Kelly], a native of County Limerick, Ireland, was born June 16, 1844; his parents, Timothy and Ellen Kelley, were natives of the same county and both died there, the former in 1848 and the latter in 1849."[1]

Kelly's parents succumbed to the Great Potato Famine in Ireland, which raged from 1845 onward, the worst year being the infamous "Black '49." With both parents dead from this horrific catastrophe by the time he was five, Tim and his older brother fled Ireland in desperation a few years later. There is nothing to tell me how these boys got out or who paid their way, but it is a good guess that their cross-Atlantic journey was a terrifying and disorienting experience.

"Mr. Kelley, the subject of this biography, in 1852, came to America with his brother, Jeremiah Kelley, and stopped in Queen's County, Long Island; remained there until 1856, then went to Albany, N.Y., and in December, 1861, came to Bucyrus, Ohio, and subsequently to Marion."

Like so many of his Irish kinsmen, Tim Kelly was star-crossed. In December 1861, a survivor of one of the world's most notorious famines, he found himself in a country exploding in civil war. He was seventeen years old, the wrong age, at the wrong time, and in the wrong place.

Finally, after what seems like a long time, I admit my failure to conjure his image.

"Here. Let's try this," Durbin says. He opens the Japanese Box and yanks out a map.

"Now stick with me," he says. "So many people are four-eyed, like me, they have trouble reading the small print." He adjusts his glasses and together we start to pour over the unfolded map. He squints as he struggles to run his finger over the route of the National Road we will be taking. "See here, up through Maryland into Pennsylvania," he says tracing the curving line. His fingers are long and powerful, perfect for coin manipulation.

"There," he says, "where the Potomac River meets the Shenandoah River, do you see it?" He punches his finger into a point on the map at the intersection of Virginia, West Virginia, and Maryland.

"Harpers Ferry?" I say, narrowing my focus to see the name of the location. It is a town south of the National Road.

"That's the place where old John Brown made his raid before the Civil War. Do you know who he was?"

I am under cross-examination.

Durbin practiced law for some years before going full time into business, politics, and magic. He apparently enjoyed questioning witnesses. He wrote in *The Linking Ring* of a trial he once conducted, when some of his political friends were placed under arrest for breaking up a spiritualist meeting in Kenton.[2]

"The spiritualist society in Kenton had at least 25 to 50 members," he remembered, "and one morning a couple of my political lieutenants came to see me in my office and announced they had been arrested before a justice of the peace for disturbing a religious meeting. It seemed that they got into a spiritualist meeting, where the fellow was giving a séance, and they struck matches and caught the fellow with the trumpet up to his mouth talking."

Durbin gleefully agreed to represent his cohorts. "Well, we had a wonderful trial and the spiritualists hired a very able attorney to represent them, and I represented my two lieutenants. I offered to reproduce any of the feats of spirit mediums. I always had a part of my program devoted to the exposure of spiritualistic phenomenon and while I never showed the way I did it, yet I put it into my program to show that this can be accomplished by ordinary means. Well, the trial lasted for about a half a day and I made a good deal of fun out of cross-examining the spirit medium. After the arguments, the justice of the peace discharged my clients."

"John Brown? . . . sure," I say cautiously, "of course I know of John Brown." I stop here, knowing it is best to take my time. Answer just the question posed, never volunteer. "The abolitionist?" I finally venture, breaking my own rule.

"An abolitionist, yes," Durbin says. "But the man was crazy, bughouse right."

"Oh, really?" Delbert says from the front seat.

"My father knew him from his days in the Western Reserve," Durbin snaps. "He used to talk about Brown when I was a boy."

For the moment, he tells me no more of his father's acquaintance with Brown, but he does tell me the story of John Brown's capture at Harpers Ferry just before the Civil War.

"Lying on the engine house floor, bleeding from sword cuts to his head and shoulders, John Brown had already calculated that out of his dismal defeat would come sublime martyrdom."

The story then magically unfolds before me, though Durbin has stopped talking. The phenomenon is that of a large stone rolling down hill, it takes on its own momentum. Before me, the vision opens.

It was October 1859. Col. Robert E. Lee's forces, with the assistance of Lt. J. E. B. Stuart, had stormed and taken the engine house in which Brown and his men held a dozen hostages. They had been under siege for over a day.

One of the hostages was Col. Lewis Washington, great-grandnephew of George Washington. Brown captured Colonel Washington, who lived five miles west of Harpers Ferry, because he coveted a pistol and sword the colonel inherited that had once belonged to George Washington. Brown yearned for there to be a symbolic connection between his raid and the "first" American Revolution.[3]

"When he struck the first blow to free the slaves," an author has noted, "he rather fancied the idea of wearing the sword and brandishing the pistol once owned by the man who led the fight to free the American colonists from a similar kind of tyranny."[4]

Near Brown was one son, Oliver, shot dead, and another, Watson, was slumped, mortally wounded. Governor Henry Wise of Virginia, who had come to take personal command of the situation, was one of the first to confront Brown.

"What was your object in coming?" Wise asked.

"We came to free the slaves, and only that," Brown responded, remarkably alert and vital, despite his wounds and that he had not eaten for over a day.

Brown had been beaten and stabbed into unconsciousness by Lt. Israel Green, the first man in the engine house. "Quicker than thought," Green recounted years later, "I brought my saber down with all my strength on his head." The blow was meant to behead Brown, but the old man's catlike reflexes from years of guerrilla struggle allowed him to avert a direct hit. "He was moving as the blow fell, and I suppose I did not strike him where I intended, for he received a deep saber cut in the back of the neck," Green wrote. "He fell senseless on his side, then rolled over on his back."

"Upon what principles do you justify your acts?" another asked Brown when he revived.

"I pity the poor in bondage, that have none to help them," Brown said in a loud, strong, baritone voice, eyes ablaze. "That is why I am here, not to gratify any personal animosity, revenge or vindictive spirit. It is my sympathy with the wronged and the oppressed, that are as good as you, and as precious in the sight of God."

Governor Wise beheld the old man, his hair and beard matted with blood, and saw "a broken-winged hawk, with a fearless eye, and his talons set for further fight if need be."[5]

John Brown's raid on the United States Armory at Harpers Ferry, Virginia, on October 16, 1859, electrified the country. But the raid was doomed from the start, and some speculate that Brown wanted it that way. He dawdled in the engine house, allowing himself and his small party of raiders to be

surrounded by an angry citizen militia, and later the army, so that no escape
was possible. It was, according to some, the mad act of a troubled terrorist
who first made his mark in "Bleeding Kansas" in the struggle between free-
soil and proslavery forces. There in 1856 Brown had participated in the
Pottawatomie Creek massacre, the brutal nighttime murders of five proslavery
settlers. The victims were found hacked or stabbed to death near the
Pottawatomie Creek in western Kansas, some decapitated.

"Horrible," Durbin says, "just horrible."

The Harpers Ferry raid was the spark that set the conflagration roaring,
spreading the madness from the west to the east. Brown himself predicted
the coming Civil War. As he was led to the gallows from the jail in Charles
Town, Virginia (today Charles Town, West Virginia), he handed a sheet of
paper to one of the guards, and on it were words, connected by puzzling
punctuation:

> I John Brown am now quite *certain* that the crimes of this *guilty, land:*
> *will* never be purged *away;* but with Blood. I had *as I now think: vainly*
> flattered myself that without *very much* bloodshed; it might be done.[6]

"Brown was a righteous man," Delbert blurts out in a high-pitched voice
that sounds very distant and deeply perturbed.

"That's bunk," Durbin firmly responds, just as testily. "This man was in-
sane. Look what his crazy act begot: death, destruction, war." He is fairly spit-
ting his words.

These two have obviously had this conversation before.

Durbin looks at me, upset. "Listen here, son, your own family's blood was
spilled in the Civil War. If you take my driver seriously, you'll have your head
on all twisted. Damn."

In my mind's eye, I now see a minié ball, rotating slowly, twisting but coming
straight toward me. It is a big, heavy, conical bullet, three times encircled at its
base, the kind that used to rip whole sections of bone, arm, or leg in the Civil War.

I know that the war that Brown predicted just before his death caused
my family to spill blood. Tim Kelly had volunteered, and when I was young
I heard from my mother that he had been shot in the head and had survived. I have a vague recollection of her saying that he was wounded at
Gettysburg and that a steel plate was inserted in his head as a result of the
gunshot wound.[7]

After some investigation in the National Archives, it turns out that she
was right about most of the facts, but not necessarily the context. He was

wounded in the head, and he did survive the grisly injury, and he was a participant in the battle of Gettysburg, but he was not shot there. Instead, he was wounded a year after Gettysburg at a place in Georgia, near Dallas, called New Hope Church.

It is fortunate that to this day the National Archives and Records Administration continues to maintain the military and pension records of soldiers from the Civil War. For the ten dollars that I mailed to them in August 1992, they researched and sent me Tim Kelly's files, about sixty pages of materials. These records survived because of post–Civil War pension programs enacted to provide for families of the war dead and those who had been injured or partially or wholly incapacitated by the war. The promise of soldiers' pensions was the big pork barrel of the day. Politicians used the issue not just as a means to respond to the need to care for the war widow and the disabled veteran but also to solidify the Republican hold on the veteran vote.

To document and prove claims, a massive bureaucracy emerged. The task of managing and sorting through claims resulted in the creation, retention, and storage of documents that tell the story of a soldier's military service and his family life after the war.

Tim Kelly's thick file included a copy of his volunteer enlistment, executed on August 16, 1862. He had blue eyes, dark hair, and a dark complexion, the document recited:

I, Timothy Kelly, born in Ireland, aged nineteen years [he lied about his age—he had just turned eighteen in June], and by occupation a farmer, DO HEREBY ACKNOWLEDGE to have volunteered this sixteenth day of August, 1862, to serve as a *Soldier* in the *Army of the United States of America,* for the period of THREE YEARS, unless sooner discharged by proper authority.

I stared at his signature on the enlistment paper for a long time when I first got his file. I tried to discern what he was thinking when he placed his name and made his three-year commitment. Was he scared? Did he feel a burst of patriotism? Was he just following his friends? His writing was highly stylized and laborious. The handwriting suggests that he was not accustomed to writing, but he wrote in large letters, leaving no one to doubt it was Timothy Kelly who enlisted. The National Archive file also contained Tim Kelly's company muster rolls, excerpts of special orders, pay department forms, transportation requisitions, affidavits of soldiers who served with him and casualty sheets of the wounded.

"This man was wounded at Dallas, Ga., as will be seen by reference to the report from which this sheet was made, and not during July," an irritated pension clerk wrote in 1881 while carefully researching Tim Kelly's file in response to an application for pension. My mother was not the only one, apparently, to have the facts about Tim Kelly's wounding a little mixed up.

Kelly was assigned to Company A of the 82d Ohio Volunteer Infantry regiment, part of a unit that served in the Eleventh Army Corps. The regiment was composed of young men from Marion County and the surrounding counties of Logan, Richland, Ashland, and Union. When Kelly first enlisted, a German immigrant and mathematics instructor, Frantz Sigel, commanded the Eleventh Corps. Sigel was succeeded by the one-armed O. O. Howard in the winter of 1862–1863. Howard, who was personally brave (he lost an arm in the Peninsula campaign in 1862), had a dubious war record, to say the least. He was surprised by Stonewall Jackson after Jackson's famous flanking march at the battle of Chancellorsville in the spring of 1863, and part of his Eleventh Corps was routed again by the Confederates three months later on the first day of Gettysburg when they ran back through the town to the safety of a cemetery, which is where they stayed in reserve for the rest of the battle. They were in perfect position to witness the sound and fury of the desperate charge of Pickett on the third day of the battle from their vantage point in the cemetery.

For the 82d, however, there was no shame in their performance at Gettysburg. Called up for emergency relief on the first day of battle, July 1, 1863, they marched a fast and hard ten miles from Emmitsburg, Maryland, with full packs on a sultry and overcast July morning, enduring a brief but heavy shower of rain and arriving within sight of Gettysburg at noon. By then the battle was in full swing on the western side of the town, and the 82d was thrown into the fray in support of a battery. The regiment suffered heavy losses at Gettysburg, starting the day with 22 commissioned officers and 236 men. By day's end 19 officers and 147 men were killed, wounded, or captured, leaving only 3 officers and 89 men.

A few months after Gettysburg, Tim Kelly was detailed to the headquarters of the Eleventh Corps as an orderly to one of its officers, Lieutenant Colonel Asmussen, the inspector general of the corps. The Eleventh Corps was then moved twelve hundred miles to the west to join Grant's Army of the Cumberland in September 1863. In April 1864 the Eleventh and Twelfth Corps were consolidated, forming the Twentieth Corps, under the command of the irascible "Fighting" Joe Hooker. Tim Kelly continued his special duty as an orderly, now on Hooker's headquarters staff. Kelly's "crowded

Lt. Col. C. W. Asmussen (1863). Tim Kelly as orderly reported to him. Courtesy U.S. Army Military Institute (USMHI), Carlisle Barracks, Pennsylvania.

hour," as Teddy Roosevelt would later call his experience on San Juan Hill, was fast approaching.

Only two generations separate me from Tim Kelly—my mother and her mother—yet prior to my request of the National Archives in 1992, I must admit I knew little about him. I did not know his war record; let alone what he did for a living following the war, or where he came from, or who his parents were. I did not know if he had brothers or sisters. Tim Kelly's memory was composed of but a few snippets of information in my mind, half of which turned out to be false.

Durbin again asks me to form an image of Kelly. Kelly's enlistment described him as a farmer who was five feet eight and one half inches tall. I suddenly have a flash of memory of an old portrait that was packed away in a side room in the basement of my childhood home in Lima. I remember studying it when I was young and having no idea who the people were in the photograph.

What I see now is the portrait of a man and a woman in an old silver-colored wooden frame. It is one of those portraits that had been colorized, with both subjects given ruddy cheeks and bright blue eyes, looking by contrast incredibly

Tim Kelly and family (1889). Agnes was not yet born. Author's collection.

pale in complexion. The man has a full beard, a straight thin nose, and a serene look on his face. His noble eyes look directly into the camera. The woman's face is rounder, and her hair is parted in the middle and pulled back tightly around her head. Unlike the man who is square shouldered with the camera, the woman is turned sideways, and she has a more tentative look on her face, eyebrows slightly raised. The dark background gives no clue about when or where the picture was taken.

This must be Tim Kelly and his wife, Nora Keating Kelly. Perhaps this was their wedding portrait.

Durbin appears to be accomplishing his goal. Like any long-forgotten memory, this image was resurrected from its deep burial in my unconscious.

The records of the National Archives contain a marriage certificate created by the pastor of St. Mary Roman Catholic Church in Marion, Father James A. Burns, giving some details of Tim and Nora Kelly's marriage and family. The document, dated November 2, 1892, confirms the couple's nuptials eight years after the war ended (on October 16, 1873) and provides the birth dates of their children who were under the age of sixteen in 1892:

Edward David, born on May 7, 1878; Mary Ellen, May 7, 1880; Margaret, April 25, 1882; Timothy Clement, November 7, 1884; Marcellus Gregory, November 17, 1886; Charles Stephan and John Louis, August 25, 1888; and Honora Agnes Kelly, January 12, 1891. Because William P. and James K. were both older than sixteen in 1892 (and thus not eligible for pension purposes), they were not included in the list.

I tell Durbin of my success in bringing up Tim Kelly's image, and he seems genuinely pleased.

"We are making progress, real progress," he says.

On April 25, 1864, the entire Twentieth Corps of the Army of the Cumberland concentrated in Lookout Valley, Tennessee, to guard the railway and to begin, with the rest of William Tecumseh Sherman's Army, the attack on Joe Johnston's Army of Tennessee on the way to Atlanta.

Sherman, a tall and lanky red-haired Ohioan, said that he was fighting for two reasons: "I believe in fighting in a double sense. First to gain physical results and next to inspire respect on which to build up our nation's power."[8] Sherman's attacks were being coordinated with Grant's campaign in the north against Lee's Army of Northern Virginia. Simultaneous blows were meant to bring an end to the war in the summer of 1864.

The Twentieth Corps commander, Maj. Gen. Joseph Hooker, was a study in hubris. Just a year earlier, Hooker had been commander of the entire Army of the Potomac, appointed by Lincoln in his restless search to find a general who could fight and win. Hooker had been critical of Lincoln and his administration's conduct of the war. What the country needed, Hooker rashly told newspapermen, was a dictator.

Lincoln knew of Hooker's treasonous talk; yet he felt Hooker would fight with self-confidence, a characteristic lacking in Ambrose Burnside, the commander defeated by Lee at Mary's Heights, Fredericksburg. Lincoln sent Hooker a letter on his appointment advising him that he was well aware of Hooker's indiscretions: "I have heard, in such a way as to believe it, of your recently saying that both the army and the government need a dictator. Of course it was not for this, but in spite of it, that I have given you the command. Only those generals who gain successes can set up dictators. What I now ask of you is military success, and I will risk the dictatorship."

Lincoln warned Hooker, though, to avoid overconfidence: "And now beware of rashness. Beware of rashness, but with energy and sleepless vigilance go forward, and give us victories."[9]

On the eve of Chancellorsville, Hooker felt cocky enough to predict victory over Lee: "My plans are perfect. May God have mercy on General Lee for

General Joseph Hooker (tallest standing) and his staff at Lookout Mountain (1864). Courtesy USMHI.

I will have none!" Hooker eventually failed, just as had all his predecessors, the victim of the audacity of Lee and Jackson at Chancellorsville, who boldly divided their army in the face of the enemy, marched around one flank, and attacked from the rear. Hooker was relieved of his command of the Army of the Potomac a few months later on the eve of the epic battle of Gettysburg.

Unlike many of his predecessors, however, Hooker lived to fight again, and in 1864 he found himself in command of the newly formed Twentieth Corps. He continued to have the support of Lincoln, although Sherman disliked him.

When the Twentieth Corps was formed, Special Order No. 4 issued from Hooker's headquarters in Lookout Valley, Tennessee, on April 25, 1864, directing that Private Timothy Kelly of the 82d Ohio Volunteer Infantry be detailed "for special duty at these Headquarters." By command of Major General Hooker, Kelly was to "report to Lt. Col. Asmussen."

Hooker was anxious to redeem himself in this new fight. "He looked forward with pleasure to the coming campaign, even though Sherman was to direct it," a biographer wrote. Dan Sickles, a Union general who had lost his leg at Gettysburg and was at the time visiting Hooker, asked what he considered the highest form of human entertainment. Fighting Joe replied, "Campaigning in an enemy's country."

I suspect that Tim Kelly was infected with this fighting spirit as a witness to Hooker's inner circle, but his life was about to change. In May 1864 the Twentieth Corps of the United States Army was on the move, chasing the Army of Tennessee south toward Georgia. It had been a particularly dry and hot May. Hooker's men took the old route toward Rossville, Georgia, then turned south through the Chickamauga battlefield and crossed the creek at Lee and Gordon's Mills. Sherman's purpose was to turn and outflank Johnston's army in a race to Atlanta. Hit them, recoil, and then go around them, was his plan.

On May 25 Hooker was engaged in a fierce battle near Dallas, Georgia, just northwest of Atlanta. One focus of the fighting was an old Baptist meetinghouse called New Hope Church. Margaret Mitchell described the scene in *Gone With the Wind:* "At New Hope Church, fifteen miles farther along the hotly fought way, the gray ranks dug in for a determined stand. On came the blue lines, relentlessly, like a monster serpent, coiling, striking venomously, drawing its injured links back, but always striking again."[10] Small ravines with dense woods and considerable underbrush marked the battlefield. This was the kind of land that precipitated close-in combat. The dry air held the sweet smell of pine and pinecones.

The battle on May 25 started late and ended because of darkness and a severe thunderstorm that crackled and rumbled at nightfall. The electrical storm was so intense that the men who fought there gave New Hope Church the name the "Hell Hole." Hooker's command remained in front of the church house, and on the morning of May 26 the major action appeared to have passed to their left. Tim Kelly probably did not sleep well in the rainstorm during the night of the twenty-fifth. Flashes of lightning would have played on his Irish superstition, perhaps causing premonitions of an ancient Gaelic wraith who visited and foretold the future.

The affidavits in the National Archives' file actually tell what happened. First, Tim Kelly himself recounted the story in a declaration given in 1879:

Timothy Kelly, aged 35 years, and a resident of Marion County of Marion and State of Ohio, who being duly sworn according to law, declares that he is the identical Timothy Kelly who enlisted in the service of the United States . . . [and] that while in the line of duty as a Soldier, doing duty as an orderly for and under General Joe Hooker at a place called Dallas Woods in the State of Georgia, while in an engagement with the Rebels on the 26th day of May 1864, he received a gunshot wound, the ball breaking the skull and entering the top of the head.

The colonel of the 82d Ohio Volunteer Infantry, James S. Robinson, filed a confirming affidavit in 1892: "[O]n the 26th day of May, 1864, while in the line of duty, the said Timothy Kelly was wounded very severely on the top of his head." Robinson said he "was present when the said Kelly was wounded and saw him fall."

A captain of the 82d, William E. Scofield, also filed an affidavit: "[O]n or about the 26th day of May, A.D. 1864, while in the line of service of the United States, near New Hope Church, in the state of Georgia, the said Timothy Kelly received a severe gun shot wound on the top of his head, said shot came from the rebel lines, that said W. E. Scofield was present when said Kelly was wounded, saw him fall from the effect of said wound, lifted him from the ground and assisted the surgeon in dressing the said wound."

Remarkably Kelly testified that he "was not treated for said wound in any Hospital but was treated for the same by the medical director at Corps Head-Quarters," which explains why his wounding was not initially reported in the usual records. This special treatment might also account for his survival. Perhaps it was in the care of the medical director of the Corps that Tim Kelly had the steel plate my mother spoke of inserted in his skull to replace a piece blown away by a bullet.

The man to whom Tim Kelly reported at Hooker's headquarters, Colonel Asmussen, was so wrought up over the fighting at New Hope Church that a few days afterward he lost his composure when Sherman made a flip remark to Hooker about the Twentieth Corps' heavy losses. Sherman said to Hooker, "Oh, most of 'em will be back in a day or two."

Asmussen was infuriated; he begged a fellow officer for a pistol that he might "shoot the God-damned son of a bitch."

That Kelly's life was spared was miraculous in a time when the simplest wound could easily kill, but he would never be the same. His affidavit said he "could not any longer do duty as a Soldier nor perform any longer the duties of orderly and was (after he became able to do anything) detailed as a servant to do light services for Colonel C. W. Asmussen, Inspector General of the 20th Army Corps."

The *History of Marion County* reports that Kelly continued to serve in the Twentieth Corps until the war's end. "He marched through the Carolinas to Richmond; thence to Washington, D.C., where he witnessed the grand review." When he was discharged in June 1865, Asmussen ordered Kelly to report to the chief mustering officer in Ohio and gave him a rail pass to travel from Washington to Columbus on June 10. Back in Marion, Kelly clerked for a merchant and then started his own grocery, carrying "provisions, tobacco, cigars, foreign and domestic liquors."

His war wound left him in distress the rest of his life. According to an affidavit written on Kelly's behalf, "Ever since receiving said wound he has suffered more or less pain and that it has affected his memory and is therefore an inconvenience to him in matters of business and that he cannot be out in the sun and heat, and when he bends over or stoops, it causes dizziness and pain in the head, making him therefore unable to perform manual labor."

Captain Scofield corroborated the disabling nature of the injury: "The said wound was severe and disabled said Kelly from active service as a soldier. That he [Scofield] has been well acquainted with said Kelly ever since the close of the war, knows that said Kelly has been a constant sufferer from the effect of said wound, being unable to stand excitement or even the heat of the sun without great suffering."

Things got worse. On December 8, 1891, the same day Francis Durbin was born in Kenton (the future son-in-law he would never know), Kelly, now forty-seven years old, signed a declaration for an additional pension. He complained of "continuous head aches" and an "affliction of the ears [that started] about 15 years ago causing a perpetual roaring in the head." He added disturbances he now attributed to his service at Gettysburg. "Claimant is also suffering with palpitation of the heart, heart disease and vertigo," the declaration states, "a result from heat and exertion caused by a double quick march to the battle field and a charge on the first day's battle of Gettysburg, Pa., July 1, 1863." Kelly was receiving in December 1891 a pension of eight dollars per month.

By August 1892 Tim and Nora Kelly had ten children: seven boys, including the twins, and three girls. Nora was pregnant with their eleventh. Their youngest child, Agnes, my grandmother, was barely a year and a half old. Never comfortable in heat, Tim Kelly probably seemed unusually agitated and restless that warm August.

On Thursday evening, August 18, 1892, he suffered a stroke, "apoplexy," the newspaper called it. Two days later, on Saturday, at two in the afternoon, he died, just a few months after celebrating his forty-eighth birthday.

Durbin passes Tim Kelly's obituary to me from the Japanese Box. The newspaper is the Marion Daily Star *of Saturday, August 20, 1892.*

The description of Tim Kelly's last illness tells of the concern of a small town about a beloved neighbor: "His friends had been without hope since learning of his affliction, and yet the attack of fatal illness was so sudden and sad that the end came in the nature of a shock. The physician had given out that there was no possibility of a recovery, that death was but a question of a few hours."

Whether medically correct or not, the newspaper ascribed Kelly's stroke to his war wound. "He was wounded in the head at New Hope Church, which undoubtedly brought on the apoplexy that ended in his death."

TIM KELLEY DEAD, *the headline mourned,* AND MARION LOSES A MOST VALUABLE CITIZEN.

HE NEVER RALLIES FROM HIS ATTACK OF APOPLEXY AND LIFE SLOWLY EBBS. A GALLANT SOLDIER, A TRUE CITIZEN, AN AMIABLE GENTLEMAN.

Durbin tells me to look more closely at the editorial page. I see a tribute to Tim Kelly and then notice why Durbin has directed my attention to this page. The editor and publisher of the Daily Star *is "W. G. Harding."*

Harding's eulogy of Tim Kelly is almost poetic:

> Marion must keenly feel the loss of such men as Timothy Kelly. He was of the class who are an actual benefit to a city. He lived not for himself alone, but ever quietly and unostentatiously doing good for others. He was in closer sympathies of the masses, and his Irish fellow citizens invariably looked to him for advice. To the honor of the man it may be said he never abused the unbounded trust confided in him.
>
> Few men have exercised so unselfish and devoted an interest in public affairs, where there is no other reward than the consciousness of well doing. He served his fellow-men as he did his country, valiantly and faithfully. His charities were beyond estimate, for he relieved the distressed and gave cheer to the discouraged. To the Irish citizens there was but one Tim Kelly, yet he was not clannish. He was useful and energetic in all worthy directions.
>
> Such men do not shine in the fading glamour of ostentatious activity, but endear themselves in the hearts of their fellow citizens so that they live in memory. Tim Kelly will not be soon forgotten. He will be remembered long after the sorrow of his untimely death has faded away.[11]

Harding's prediction that Tim Kelly would not soon be forgotten hit me hard when I first read Kelly's obituary. Tim Kelly's own descendants soon forgot him. How is it such a man could be lost to his own family in such a relatively short period of time?

Lincoln's second inaugural, delivered as John Wilkes Booth stood on a balustrade behind him on the steps of the Capitol, spoke of the imperative "to bind up the nation's wounds; to care for him who shall have borne the battle, and for his widow, and his orphan." This promise took on special significance for Tim Kelly's family that August 1892. He had surely borne the battle, and now his widow survived him with ten children.

Agnes, the youngest, would have no memory of her father, which is why she would always tell Durbin he was the only "Dad" she ever knew, explaining their close bond. Nora Kelly, her mother, was two months pregnant with her last child when Tim Kelly died. An application for an additional widow's pension filed in 1893 states that a "posthumous minor," Francis Patrick Kelly (Pat), was born February 28, 1893. Nora sought an additional two dollars per month to care for this soldier's orphan.

I now recognize that Durbin's limbering exercise with me was more than just a mental game of gymnastics; it was to awaken my own subconscious memories. They have been triggered.

At the time of Tim Kelly's death in 1892, Warren G. Harding was unknown in politics other than being the editor of a small-town newspaper. He had arrived in Marion from the hinterland in 1882, a sixteen-year-old hayseed with slight prospects. Harding claimed he rode into town on a mule from his farm, like Jesus arriving in Jerusalem, though without the same fanfare. Harding recalled that his journey on that warm July evening went entirely unnoticed.

"The evening shades were falling when I reached the vicinity of Roberts' farm," he would recount years later during his presidency, "three or four miles out of Marion. The situation was looking dark to me and I stopped to ask an old fellow, who was smoking his pipe, how far it was to Marion. Without cracking a smile, he replied: 'Well, if you're going to ride that mule, it is a farther distance than you will ever get.' As I neared the town the evening bells were ringing for the mid-week prayer. I do not know that I have ever heard a concert of bells that sounded so sweet."[12]

A family legend has it that Nora Kelly, a seamstress, stitched Florence Kling's wedding dress when she and Warren Harding were married on July 8, 1891, six months after Agnes was born and a year before Tim Kelly died. Florence Kling was a particularly unattractive woman, and she was five years older than the handsome Harding. More shockingly, she was a divorcee and the mother of a son she had given to her overbearing father to raise.

Amos Kling, Florence's father, was appalled at the thought that his daughter would "throw herself away a second time" when she announced her engagement to Harding. Kling, one of Marion's most prosperous men, was infuriated with the match because he believed, as did many in Marion, that

Harding was from mixed blood. In a chilling and locally famous encounter, Kling confronted Harding in the Marion courthouse before the marriage, threatening to "blow his head off," calling him "a nigger." The couple counted their blessings when Kling refused to attend the wedding.

Despite the ostracizing, Harding's marriage was the magical turning point of his life. Florence Kling inherited her father's savvy, and she would ensure that her "Wurr'n" would succeed. How well he would succeed was surely unimaginable even to Florence in 1891, but succeed Harding did.

"She always said I was the only 'Dad' she ever knew," Durbin repeats as if talking to someone not in this car. He appears to be listening, waits for a response, and then nods his head after a moment of silence.

"His soul goes marching on," Delbert says from the front seat.

⇒ 3 ⇐

THE DOCTOR

July 3, 1803

Studying the map that Durbin produced, I can see that beyond Frederick, Mary-land, we crossed over South Mountain, and now we have descended into a valley that is north of the Antietam Battlefield and Harpers Ferry. We are roughly following a route cut by the Potomac River. The Potomac's headwaters are near Cumberland, Maryland, somewhere west of here. To get there, we will be required to drive through Hagerstown and travel through the Narrows, a small gap in Wills Mountain created by Wills Creek. This has been called the "Gate-way to the West," and I suspect that Durbin's father, who was born in Balti-more, probably came over this road in his travels to and from the Western Reserve in Ohio in the first half of the nineteenth century.

The origins of the Western Reserve in Ohio go back to the beginning of the country. The region that now constitutes the states of Ohio, Indiana, Illinois, Michigan, Wisconsin, and the eastern part of Minnesota, a total area of about 265,000 square miles, was once known as the Northwest Territory.[1] Great Brit-ain relinquished its claim to this territory to the United States in 1783 at the end of the Revolutionary War. But questions arose about how to deal with this land. States such as Massachusetts, Connecticut, New York, and Virginia all claimed sometimes conflicting title to parts of this western territory, based on royal charters that extended from the Atlantic to what was then called the South Sea (Pacific Ocean). New Hampshire, Rhode Island, New Jersey, Dela-ware, and Maryland were all bounded and confined to the Atlantic Plain, and Pennsylvania did not extend past the forks of the Ohio River.

This presented a nasty problem for the struggling young republic. The states with defined western borders saw the potential for states that claimed

coast-to-coast boundaries to grow into unwieldy monsters if they retained
all the land from their original colonial charters. Maryland stood up and
insisted that the land between the Allegheny Mountains and the Mississippi should belong to the country as a whole. Maryland refused to accept
the Articles of Confederation until the claiming states surrendered their
"western" holdings. After debate and compromise, most of the area was
ceded by the claiming states to the United States as a whole.

Some of the area, however, was "reserved" for special purposes. Virginia's
reserve in southern Ohio, for example, was used to pay Revolutionary soldiers for their service. Connecticut's was used to raise money for its public
schools and to compensate victims whose homes were burned by the British
in the war (to this day, one area in northern Ohio is still called the "Firelands"
or the "Sufferers Lands"). Connecticut's reserve was an area of approximately
3.5 million acres on the southern shores of Lake Erie from the Pennsylvania
border, extending west into the Ohio territory about 120 miles and south to
the forty-first parallel. The land became known as the "Connecticut Reserve"
or the "Western Reserve." The Western Reserve was settled in large part by
New Englanders. Their pilgrim and puritan heritage, along with Quaker settlers from Pennsylvania, would make the reserve a center of antislavery activity. The abolitionist John Brown made his principal home on the Western
Reserve from 1805 to 1825 and then from 1835 to 1855.[2]

The Ordinance of 1787 (or the Northwest Ordinance), which set up the
territories and the mechanisms for organization and eventual admission of
new states such as Ohio, forbade slavery, although fugitives could be reclaimed
lawfully. The nascent country's deep ambivalence toward slavery can be seen
in the irony that, at almost the exact same time Congress was enacting the
Northwest Ordinance, the delegates to the Constitutional Convention were
formulating a series of compromises on slavery that would allow it to continue until a later time. Although hotly debated in the formation of the Constitution, the document never mentions the words *slave* or *slavery*.

As Lincoln would say, "The thing is hid away . . . just as an afflicted man
hides away a wen or a cancer, which he dare not cut out lest he bleed to death."[3]

The United States had a difficult birth. Only white men who owned land
could vote. This nation of "liberty" eventually became one of the largest
slave empires that the world has ever known. "In number of acres and numbers of field workers it might be compared to Rome itself at the time of
Christ," one scholar has written.[4]

And although slavery was outlawed in the Ohio Territory, Ohio and Indiana came into existence only because of the ruthless and bloody Indian

Wars that culminated in the 1795 Treaty of Greenville. George Washington, as president of the new country, sent General "Mad" Anthony Wayne to Ohio to fight and subdue the people who lived there. The treaty that resulted from this conflict established boundary lines and set up reservations within the Ohio territory, separating Indian lands from those now open to the new Americans. It was only a matter of time before the American Indians were completely displaced, sent to the West.

Durbin's father came to the Western Reserve when he was a young man. There is some suggestion in obituaries that the Durbins first came to Ohio when Durbin's grandfather was appointed by President Thomas Jefferson to serve as an instructor to the Wyandot Indians at their reservation near Marseilles, Ohio, but there is no evidence to substantiate this claim. What is provable through census records is that Durbin's father settled in a township just south of the Western Reserve border line in Columbiana County by at least 1830. His name was William Warner Durbin, and he was a native of Maryland.[5]

He was born on July 3, 1803, when Thomas Jefferson was in his first term. His family seems to have been of some means. William's first cousin and contemporary, Rev. John Price Durbin, became a Methodist churchman and was appointed chaplain of the United States Senate in 1831 during the Jackson administration. He served at a time when Henry Clay, Daniel Webster, and John C. Calhoun roamed the Senate.[6]

One known fact about Durbin's father, the first W. W. Durbin, is that he came to the Ohio frontier to "read medicine," becoming a doctor in an area starved for physicians. According to the 1830 census records, another male between twenty and thirty years old lived in his household in Green Village, perhaps a brother or brother-in-law. The records also mention a female between the ages of twenty and thirty, no doubt a wife, and a female between fifty and sixty years old, a mother or mother-in-law. They were all part of a population explosion that occurred in Ohio after the Treaty of Greenville. In 1800 the Ohio territory had about 45,000 white residents. By 1820 that number had ballooned to over 500,000, allowing Ohio to become a state in 1803.

"My dad became a physician by reading medicine with a doctor," Durbin says to me as we pass near the Potomac, which comes up from the south to meet us and cuts a path through the mountains. The sun has completely disappeared. Frost rings all of the car's windows. The interior light from the dashboard begins to illuminate Delbert's face.

"In his day, few doctors, especially those who ventured into the wilderness, graduated from medical colleges. A man's education therefore was secured

through a preceptor system. The student attended to his preceptor, learning everything he could, from the care of his medicines and instruments to the care of his horses, saddles, and harnesses. Doctors were always traveling the backwoods on horse or in buggies. Long drives gave the student time to discuss medicine with his mentor and to receive personal instruction."[7]

"What was he like, your father?" I ask, and Delbert immediately shoots me a look. This is one man I want to know more about, but Delbert appears to think I have ventured into unsafe territory.

"He was a hell of a man, I'll tell you that," Durbin says. "Imagine what he lived through. Ohio was nothing but unbroken wilderness when he first went there."

"Was he a good man?"

"What the hell kind of question is that?" I hear, but the voice is different, deeper, and raspy. A breeze seems to blow across my face as if a window has been cracked. I feel an extremely odd sensation of electric current and notice the whole energy of the car has changed instantaneously. I look at my great-grandfather's feet and see dusty boots where there were oxfords. Rough cotton breeches have replaced the wool suit pants. The smell is somewhat raw, a combination of chemical powder, alcohol, and horse sweat.

"We all come from dirt, says so in the Scriptures," he says.

Durbin is gone, but there is a man who looks much like him. His spectacles are small round Ben Franklin–looking glasses. He is smaller than Durbin but heavier in the face and has weather-beaten skin. He has a leather neck, wrinkled and creased, and a dark complexion.

"I ought to know," he says, pulling a flask from his vest pocket and taking a quick drink. "For you are dirt, and unto dirt you shall return." He takes a second quick swig.

"Delbert, . . . ah . . . what's going on?"

"Evening, Doc," Delbert says without answering my question.

"That's of course unless one of us medical students didn't get hold of you before you had the chance to turn to dust."

"Hee-hee," Delbert laughs.

"We had a way of resurrecting those that willed themselves to the medical sciences and even some who didn't."

"Nobody ever talked about that, and that's a fact," Delbert responds.

"Mostly not. But I would venture to say I resurrected half a dozen or so, . . . eh, . . . volunteers you might say, when I was a student and later as an instructor myself. You tried to get them out of the quiet country churchyards soon after burial. That way nobody noticed the disturbance much, and you had a good specimen."

"Had to do it during the cold weather, too, didn't you, sir?" Delbert adds.

"Yes, sir. You moved them to a barn loft where your student could dissect them and learn about the anatomy. If you hit a warm spell, you sometimes had to replace your volunteer."

I notice as he talks, the Doctor pyramids his fingers, and they look remarkably like Durbin's. They are long slender fingers, full of strength.

"The student would then clean the skeleton and keep it as the first item of equipment for his future office. A second volunteer would be obtained toward the end of the student's course with his preceptor to carry out a series of surgical operations, mostly amputations at various points."

"I think I have an idea who you are," I interrupt, "but I'm not real sure of anything tonight."

"Yes, of course," he responds. "Permit me to introduce myself to your Excellency," he says with a mocking bow in my direction, "by simply saying that I am a native of Maryland and have been a resident of Ohio the past thirty-nine years. I have resided on the Western Reserve most of that time."

I look over and see that he is reading from a letter. The stationery has a sky-blue color, with small handwriting on it and a small piece of printed material pasted in the top left-hand corner.

He hands the letter to me. "Go on, take a look."

"You'll find that letter in the Library of Congress in your day," Delbert says.

"Probably is the only letter to survive me."

And it is. Finding this letter in the Library of Congress was one of the happy accidents in my research that now seems to have been no accident. In July 1995 I went to the Manuscript Reading Room located in the Madison Building directly behind the Capitol to research the papers of William Jennings Bryan. After several hours of reading I was nearing the time to leave. While I waited for the last Bryan files to be brought out, I idly opened a nearby old-fashioned manual index file drawer, literally killing time. Magic, though, was at work.

I happened to open the drawer precisely to a card that contained the following notation: "Durbin, W. W. [physician and surgeon], Canfield, Mahoning County, Ohio to Hon. H. A. Wise, stating Brown's insanity on subject of slavery and asking for reprieve."

What? Who was this, and what was the reference?

Sure enough, it was Durbin's father. The discovery was significant because I had been unable to gather reliable information on this man. What little published material existed about him seemed flatly contradictory, inconsistent, or implausible. In some local histories he was described as coming to

Ohio to live and work among the Wyandots: "For some years previous to [coming to Kenton] he lived at Marseilles [a village between Kenton and Upper Sandusky, Ohio], having been appointed to the Indian Service on the Indian reservation at that place." Yet a search of the records of the Bureau of Indian Affairs shows no reference to the Doctor's employment as an Indian agent.

"While associated with the Indians, he had learned to speak the Wyandot language. When the Indians departed for the West, Dr. Durbin came to Kenton and made it his home for the rest of his life."

This too seemed at least in part incorrect. *The History of Hardin County* (where Kenton is located) written in 1883 states: "In the decade between 1840 and 1850, inclusive, many physicians came and went—some remaining during their lives, while others soon removed to other fields. Of these, we find that Dr. W. W. Durbin came to this county in 1840–41, locating near Patterson in Jackson Township. . . . Subsequently he went back to Columbiana county, Ohio, where he had read medicine, and also spent a portion of his time traveling, but about 1872–73 he returned to Kenton, where he died a few years later."

These dates too made no sense because I knew the Doctor married and lived in Kenton at the end of the Civil War and had two children there in 1866 and 1869.

Surrounding these mysteries was the troubling question of whether Dr. Durbin had a serious drinking problem.

In the 1883 version of *The History of Hardin County,* the question is not open for debate: "It is said, by old settlers who knew him well, that though a good doctor, he was very intemperate. On one occasion, he had a cholera patient at his house, whom he had brought there for treatment, and when night came on the Doctor got drunk, lay down beside the patient, and woke up in the morning to find the man had been dead for some hours."

In a later edition of the same history, published almost thirty years later in 1910, the reference to drinking was sanitized: "It is said by old settlers who knew him well, that he was a very good doctor. On one occasion he had a cholera patient at his house, whom he had brought there for treatment, and when night came on the doctor lay down beside his patient and woke up in the morning to find the man had been dead for some hours."[8]

Presto!

The shroud of uncertainty wrapped around this ancestor seemed impenetrable until the happenstance discovery in the Library of Congress of a letter written in his own hand in November 1859. This letter contained some important clues to his story.

When I asked to see the letter referenced in the index card, I was given a roll of microfilm and shown to a reading machine. I whirled through to the correct page and found a blurry screen with an illegible document. From surrounding documents, I could discern that the letter was in a collection of letters and affidavits that had been written to the governor of Virginia, Henry Wise, concerning John Brown.

Disappointed in the quality of the copy, I asked one of the staff archivists if anything could be done to help clear up the image. He left for a few minutes and returned with a box. He opened the box and there, neatly filed away with other documents, was the original letter drafted by the doctor on sky-blue stationery.

The fading, almost brownish pencil marks made by the Doctor over a century ago stood out against the odd color of the stationery (the blue background explaining why the letter could not be picked up on microfilm). The handwriting was still difficult and small, but with time and the help of several interested staff members huddled around, we could make it out. Attached to the letter by wax was a scrap of newsprint, which was the Doctor's advertisement from a newspaper: "W. W. Durbin, Physician and Surgeon, Canfield, Mahoning county, Ohio."

The letter written by my great-great-grandfather, dated November 29, 1859, was over 135 years old when it was brought out for my review. I was allowed to hold it in my hands, a very strange yet exhilarating experience. The letter was in good enough shape that the archivists made a copy for me. The full text of the letter is as follows:

Heidlersburg Adams Co Pa Nov 29/59
Hon H. A. Wise
Gov'r of Virginia

Permit me to introduce myself to your Excellency by simply saying that I am a native of Maryland—have been a resident of Ohio for the past 39 years—have resided on the Western Reserve a large portion of that time—have always voted the Democratic ticket—am a physician by profession—am personally acquainted with John Brown under sentence of death at Charles Town Va on Friday next. I am fully satisfied that he is and has been a crazy man for years, perhaps no more so than many others in that benighted region. We have combatted and battled against Abolitionism with the fervor of veterans in the cause of Democracy. We have lived to see the day that a Negro in Ohio has been overestimated. But direct to the question, Brown has been insane for the past ten years to my own knowledge. Is there no possibility that his sanity can be tested or judged by medical jurists? The distinguished position you occupy and the clemency that you can exercise in his case—it is not flattery to say to you that we know Va. wishes to be just and deal righteously.

I am not the apologist of Brown for his crimes or indiscretions but his course in Ohio in 1859 at Cleveland shows him insane. I have no reference to make you as to my assertions except John Rice—Richmond Va.

As the time is drawing close to the Execution and all that I can say or do may have little or no impressment on you in relation to the position we all occupy to an unfortunate crazy fanatic, I think I do not overestimate you when I say I think Virginia has and is merciful even to the fanaticism of Abolitionism. The laws of nature, and the fixed principles of mathematical science will not bend to suit our convenience nor save us from our errors—That you will act accordingly is the prayer of many.

With high regard & esteem,

Yrs Respectfully,

W. W. Durbin, MD[9]

What a blockbuster this letter was, filled with key biographical information, oozing with philosophical statements and beliefs, and ultimately packed with deep and dark mysteries. That I found it through serendipity was enough to let me know that someone was making gestures at the truth, pointing me in a direction, a path that must be followed.

The letter answered some questions but left much unresolved. The Doctor did come from a family in Maryland, transplanted to Ohio in 1820. He had lived on the Western Reserve most of the time since coming to Ohio, though there is no description of his move out to Kenton in the middle of Ohio around 1840 or his alleged work as an Indian agent.

W. W. Durbin Sr. held himself out as a physician and surgeon, and the newspaper clipping suggests that, in 1859 at least, he was making his living back in Canfield, Ohio, in Mahoning County near the Ohio-Pennsylvania border.

His party affiliation—"have always voted the Democratic ticket"—was obviously something he passed on to his son.

What dawned on me over time, however, was that there had to be some significance to the fact that the letter was composed in a town in Pennsylvania named Heidlersburg in Adams County. I had never heard of Heidlersburg. A check of the map opened another set of mysteries. Heidlersburg, it turns out, is a small village about eleven miles north of a crossroads town named Gettysburg. Less than four years after November 1859, when the Doctor wrote his letter seeking clemency for Brown, Gettysburg would explode into a three-day bloody battle, playing one of the key roles in the outcome of the very war John Brown predicted would come as he was led to his death.

A traveler in 1859 to Heidlersburg could hardly have imagined that in such a short period of time Gettysburg, with its 2,500 residents, would be transformed by the clash of two giant armies—100,000 steaming soldiers swarming over its hills—becoming the site of one of the greatest battles in history. The Doctor, though, was clearly inspired near this spot to try to stop Brown's execution. And this in spite of his expressed antipathy for abolitionists.

Why? Did he hear the voices of future ghosts from the nearby fields of Gettysburg, crying in the mist to prevent the coming holocaust? Did he foresee a future in-law, Tim Kelly, running double-quick to the west of town on the first day of battle? Surely not. But what was the Doctor doing in Heidlersburg? Was he traveling to witness Brown's execution or even to meet with an old friend in dire trouble?

Mystery begets mystery.

"Curious, isn't it?" the Doctor says. "I guess there are some things you'll never figure out. Maybe some things you shouldn't ask about, either." The Doctor takes out his flask and takes a big drink. He screws the cap back on slowly, blinking the sting out of his eyes.

John Brown was captured on October 17, 1859, at the federal armory at Harpers Ferry. Despite Brown's severe wounds, Judge Richard Parker started his trial ten days later, on October 27. The whole courtroom drama would last just a little over three days. Brown was brought in on a stretcher, still wrapped in bandages. He had written his wife from his jail cell, "Surely, I can recover all the lost capital occasioned by the disaster by only hanging a few moments by the neck; and I feel quite determined to make the utmost possible out of defeat."[10]

Was Brown crazy as Doctor Durbin opined? There seems little question that his wild scheme to free the slaves by starting an insurrection was a doomed enterprise. But was this exactly what Brown planned?

"It's true," the Doctor, says, "Brown was a crazy man. Nobody paid attention to what I had to say, though."

"Guess they found out the consequences of not listening to you, Doc," Delbert
says.

On the second day of Brown's trial, a court-appointed lawyer for Brown
read a telegram from an abolitionist newspaper editor in Akron, Ohio. The
telegram stated that insanity was hereditary in Brown's family. There was
indeed evidence to support the charge. During and after the trial, scores of
petitioners, including Brown's relatives, asserted that Brown's family was
shot through with madness: three of his aunts, his grandmother, five of his
cousins, one of his brothers, three of his sons, and miscellaneous relations,
all insane or "died insane."

*"There's always a problem when somebody goes around thinking he's God's
instrument, if you ask me,"* the Doctor says.

If the Doctor knew Brown for ten years, as he wrote to Governor Wise, it
most likely would have been during the days Brown and his family lived in
Ohio's Western Reserve between the years 1835 and 1855 and before Brown
made his name hacking proslavery settlers to death in "Bleeding Kansas." Since
the Western Reserve was an intensely antislavery region—an area in which
the Doctor himself asserted that he and other Democrats had been required
to combat and battle abolitionism with all the "fervor of veterans in the cause
of Democracy"—one wonders what relationship the Doctor had with Brown.

Brown was a sheep farmer who lived at various times near Hudson,
Franklin, and Akron, Ohio. Perkins and Brown, the name of his partnership, was a successful venture initially, involved in the raising of rare Saxon
sheep, famous for fine wool that was free of burrs and was snowy white.
Brown modeled himself on the patriarchs of yore. Intensely religious, feeling at times that he was in direct contact with God, he was severe with his
family, relentlessly working his sons, and fathering over a dozen children
through two wives. He tried to organize a cooperative to sell his wool in
England, and he ended up losing everything. Gradually, Brown became
obsessed with the wickedness of slavery, and he came to believe that it was
his destiny to wage a holy war to put an end to the institution.

Perhaps the Doctor had provided medical care to Brown and his family,
and this is how he knew Brown. If so, he would have witnessed the slow
unraveling of Brown, exacerbated by the cruel living conditions of the Ohio
frontier. Brown lost his first wife to an early death, and his second wife,
Mary (she was sixteen when they married), always had children who were
sick with the fever or "the ague." In addition to the five children Brown
brought to his second marriage, Mary bore thirteen sons and daughters.
Only six of these survived childhood. One spring alone, four of the chil-

dren died within days of each other. They all had dysentery. John Brown wrote to one of his older sons: "Four of our number sleep in the dust, and were all buried together in one grave. This has been a bitter cup to all of us indeed, and we have drunk deeply."[11]

The Doctor's cryptic reference in his letter to Governor Wise about Brown's "course in Ohio at Cleveland in 1859" hardly on its face demonstrates, as he put it, that Brown was insane. On the night of March 21, 1859, Brown appeared at Chapin's Hall in Cleveland to raise money and regale a small audience about his involvement in guerrilla warfare in Kansas and Missouri. By then Brown was already known as "Old Osawatomie Brown" because of his association with the antislavery settlement in Osawatomie, Kansas. The hostile governor of proslavery Missouri had placed a $3,000 bounty on his head, and even President Buchanan issued a "standing offer" of $250 for Brown's capture, all believing he and his sons had been involved in the Pottawatomie massacre.

Nevertheless, Brown spoke in Cleveland to a small crowd without being molested. The *Cleveland Plain Dealer* even covered the event.[12] Brown described the border wars in Kansas and Missouri as a justifiable reaction to atrocities perpetrated by the proslavery border ruffians. Brown claimed (disingenuously) that he had never killed anyone in any of his engagements in Kansas. The *Plain Dealer* described Brown as a "medium-sized, compactly-built and wiry man, and as quick as a cat in his movements." Though Brown was "rising sixty," he presented an image of iron and determination. "Turn him into a ring with nine Border Ruffians, four bears, six Injuns and a brace of bull pups, and we opine that the 'eagles of victory would perch on his banner,'" the *Plain Dealer* ventured.

Perhaps Brown's audacity in showing up in Cleveland as a known "outlaw" or maybe his defense of the free-state settlers caused the Doctor to believe that this particular appearance was solid proof of Brown's insanity. Or maybe the Doctor was particularly upset—as was the *Plain Dealer*—with Brown's blatant and cheerful admission of his theft of eleven slaves in Missouri, whom he took to Canada and released to freedom.

"Brown's description of his trip to Westport [just south of Kansas City] and capture of eleven niggers was refreshingly cool," the *Plain Dealer* (a Democratic newspaper) reported, "and it struck us, while he was giving it, that he would make his jolly fortune by letting himself out as an Ice Cream Freezer."

Unapologetic, Brown spoke directly. "He meant this invasion as a direct blow at Slavery. He didn't disguise it—he wanted the audience to distinctly understand it."

But even more, Brown felt his actions were proper, regardless of whether they had been provoked. "On being asked if he would have felt justified in taking these slaves if the people on the Border had behaved themselves, he answered emphatically 'yes.' He considered it the duty of every man to liberate slaves whenever he could do so successfully!"

Despite Dr. Durbin's grim assessment of Brown's mental state, Brown denied he was insane at his trial. "I look upon it," Brown yelled from his cot, "as a miserable artifice and pretext of those who ought to take a different course in regard to me, if they take any at all, and I view it with contempt more than otherwise."[13]

Wrapped in his cover and smelling like a man who had not bathed in weeks, Brown made a fearful presence. "Insane persons, so far as my own experience goes, have but very little ability to judge of their own sanity," he said, "and if I am insane of course I should think I know more than the rest of the world; but I do not think so. I am perfectly *un*conscious of insanity, and I reject, so far as I am capable, any attempt to interfere in my behalf on that score."[14]

The jury deliberated just forty-five minutes before returning a guilty verdict on October 31. "Old Brown himself said not a word," a newspaper reported, "but, as on previous days, turned to adjust his pallet, and then composedly stretched himself upon it."[15]

On November 2, 1859, Brown was sentenced to death. Following the verdict, abolitionists around the country organized an effort to win clemency by seeking a sanity hearing. Dr. Durbin, it turns out, was not the only person to attest to Brown's insanity, but he was one of only two physicians to claim it. For political reasons, the Democratic governor of Virginia, Henry Wise, could not afford to take under advisement pleas for clemency based on an insanity defense. Wise was a hopeful presidential candidate in the upcoming campaign of 1860, and he knew his party would accept nothing short of swift and certain retribution against Brown, regardless of his mental state. This explains the Doctor pointing out his allegiance to the Democratic Party and his statement of hostility toward abolitionists. He wanted Wise to know he was not just another abolitionist Republican dismissing Brown as a lunatic.

Brown sympathizers gathered up nineteen affidavits in Ohio and sent them to Wise on November 23. For some reason, historians have failed to note Dr. Durbin's letter sent a few days later. Indeed, they dismiss the authority of the nineteen affidavits, emphasizing that only one of the affiants was a physician and he was a confirmed abolitionist. In 1971, for example, one scholar, summarizing the question, wrote:

The documents [affidavits] were not objective clinical evidence gathered by doctors who wanted to establish as clearly as possible what Brown's mental disorders were. When the affiants asserted that Brown was insane, they were giving their opinions from a partisan objective. Although many of them doubtlessly believed that their opinions were true, they were still opinions. Except for Dr. Jonathan Metcalf of Hudson, Ohio, none of the affiants was educated in medical matters, and none of them was a psychologist.[16]

Dr. Durbin was no psychologist, or alienist as they were sometimes called back then, nor was he a partisan abolitionist. But he had read medicine, and he personally knew Brown over an extended period of time, and so his letter should have been given some weight by Wise and certainly by historians. Maybe the Doctor's letter went unnoticed by historians because it was so difficult to read on microfilm, and no one bothered to open the box in the Library of Congress to look at the original.

John Brown was hung. From jail he rebuked one of the persons who had sent Governor Wise an affidavit alleging his madness. Brown wrote that he was relieved that he had not been declared a lunatic: "It is a great comfort to feel assured that I am permitted to die for a cause,—not merely to pay a debt of nature, as all must. My whole life before has not afforded me one half the opportunity to plead for the right. In this, also, I find much to reconcile me to both my present condition and my immediate prospect."[17]

On his sanity Brown wrote, "I may be very insane; (and I am so, if insane at all). But if that be so, insanity is like a very pleasant dream to me. I am not in the least degree conscious of my ravings, of my fears, or of any terrible visions whatever; but fancy myself entirely composed, and that my sleep, in particular, is as sweet as that of a healthy, joyous little infant. . . . I have scarce realized that I am in prison, or in irons, at all. I certainly think I was never so cheerful in my life."

"No man ever met his fate with more determination," wrote an eyewitness to the execution on December 2, 1859. "As he passed from the jail to the open air," the observer wrote, "the front of his slouched hat was turned up, and he calmly surveyed the grand array of bristling bayonets with a smile upon his countenance."[18]

The list of those in attendance at the execution is as spooky today as it was prophetic then. Governor Wise, naturally, was there, but so too was Professor Thomas (soon to be "Stonewall") Jackson with his Virginia Military Institute cadets, positioned to put down any last-minute attempt by abolitionists to

John Brown being led to his execution. Courtesy Bettmann/CORBIS.

rescue Brown. Jackson prayed a "fervent petition" for Brown's soul but thought he was likely to be damned to the everlasting fires of hell. A young actor named John Wilkes Booth, who felt intense scorn for Brown, accompanied the First Virginia Regiment from Richmond to watch Brown die.

Assuredly, this gathering of persons knew nothing of the enormity of the tragedy about to befall their country and the leading roles they would play in it.

In a way, the nightmare of the Civil War began on that day, in that place: "Seated on his coffin and surrounded by a thousand troops, he rode to the

place of execution, which was a large and open field. Coolly and calmly he looked upon the military escort and the crowd who were following. On his way he talked to the Sheriff of the beautiful weather and the loveliness of the surrounding country."

"This is beautiful country," Brown is supposed to have said, "I have never had the pleasure of seeing it before."[19]

"Arrived at the place of execution he actively descended from the wagon, and with a firm, unfaltering step ascended the stairs to the scaffold. Within two minutes the cap was drawn over his face and he took leave of the Sheriff and his assistants," a newspaper correspondent wrote of the scene. Despite his request to the sheriff that he not be kept "waiting longer than necessary," Brown stood alone, face covered, for nine minutes before the trap was pulled. The struggle was soon over. "A few convulsive twitches of the arms, and the body hung motionless. After hanging forty minutes it was cut down, placed in the coffin and conveyed to the jail, and thence escorted to [Harpers Ferry] by soldiers, and placed in charge of the friends who had accompanied Mrs. Brown."

"So perish all enemies of Virginia, all such enemies of the Union, all such foes of the human race," a presiding officer declared to the assembled and silent crowd as Brown's body swung from the scaffold.[20]

Like the prophecies from the Hebrew Bible Brown knew so well, his note, handed to a jailhouse guard as he was led away, contained a curse on the nation for its unrepentant ways, averring that "the crimes of this guilty land will not be purged away, but with Blood."[21]

Brown was not alone in this belief. George Mason of Virginia at the Constitutional Convention in 1787 saw clearly the consequences for a nation that was founded on the premise that it was acceptable that some might enslave others. "Slavery," said Mason, would "bring the judgment of Heaven on a country. As nations cannot be rewarded or punished in the next world, they must be in this. By an inevitable chain of causes and effects, Providence punishes national sins by national calamities."[22]

"Does God punish families for the sins of the fathers down to the third and forth generation as suggested in the Bible?" I ask the Doctor.

"Ask me something I can answer," he replies.

For some time, I wondered if the Doctor was in fact on his way to Charles Town to attend John Brown's execution when he wrote his letter from Heidlersburg. Having opened the door, I had to trust that this question would be answered.

"Ask and it will be given to you; seek and you will find, knock and the door will be opened," Delbert says.[23]

As if by clockwork, in the winter of 1998 I found a box in a storage area in a building in downtown Lima that contained daybooks of the Doctor's. These leather-bound books of account probably had survived because they were kept by the Doctor's widow for the purposes of collecting on past-due accounts after his death. Unprotected and rotting in a cardboard box, they were nevertheless priceless specimens of a pioneer country doctor's business records from the middle of the nineteenth century.[24]

They show a physician who moved across Ohio in a time when the state was in its infancy. He traded horses, bought whiskey, purchased lances and blades, mortars and pestles, made his own pills, birthed babies, set broken arms, prescribed cathartics by the score, and even sold hair dye. He recorded that one quart of a solution of opium (called "a tinc. [tincture] of opii") cost him one dollar. He often found it necessary to prescribe vermifuge, a medicine to eliminate intestinal worms. Emetics were given to induce vomiting. Quinine, an antimalarial treatment, was not infrequently needed, evidencing the prevalence of malaria in Ohio in the nineteenth century. Patients would shake violently from the disease, which they called "the ague."

The Doctor was hard to pin down, constantly traveling in Ohio, Pennsylvania, and even a stint in Indiana. He was also perpetually in debt, rarely collecting his fees. In June 1857 there is a reference to payment of jury fees. On January 1, 1858, the Doctor made an assignment of his accounts to his landlord. "I hereby assign to W. B. Dawson any account or accounts hereinafter charged on my books to the extent of my arrearage for rent due him or becoming due against 1 April 1858," he wrote.

Later in the month, the Doctor was clearly strapped for cash. He charged three dollars a day for four days in a row to "24 hour visit and medicines" for one patient.

His steady work seemingly dried up, and big gaps opened in the entries. Nothing was recorded between April and October 1858. On October 11 the Doctor reemerged, charging a whopping ten dollars for a ten-day visit to one patient.

A marginal note next to one entry, perhaps made after an unsuccessful collection effort, states simply: "Gone to Hell."

In October 1859, as John Brown made his final preparations for his Harpers Ferry raid, the Doctor, perhaps alone after the death of his first wife, made a decision to leave Canfield, Ohio. On November 4, two days after Judge Parker sentenced Brown to death, the Doctor's daybook records the unusual contract that would take him from Ohio to Heidlersburg, Pennsylvania:

John Hersh, Heidlersburg, Adams Co., Pa.

To contract to treat a case of Cancer of the lower lip, I am to have fifty dollars to attend the case. Pay $10.00 to Dr. Dorsey out of the $50 and I am to do my best to cure the case in attendance and medicines: $50.00.

Operation to be performed next Monday.

The operation was performed on November 7, and the Doctor attended and dressed the wound for the next eight days.

I suspect he got cash up front.

On November 12 he found another patient on whom he performed some surgery for ten dollars. No doubt he passed some of his time in Heidlersburg reading about the sensational Brown raid, trial, conviction, and the upcoming execution.

He obviously stewed about the implications for his country and felt duty-bound to write the governor of Virginia.

Brown faced the gallows, and the Doctor disappeared into the Pennsylvania backwoods, writing mysteriously in his journal about the treatment of one case of bronchitis for five months and charging fifty dollars. He settled briefly in Pennsylvania, but soon he was on the trail again. This time he moved from Virginia, to Maryland, back to Pennsylvania, through Ohio and then, in November 1860, as Lincoln won the presidential election, he landed in Allen County, Indiana, not far from Fort Wayne.

As if drawn by some gravitational pull, the Doctor moved back to Ohio in 1862, where he practiced for one year in a village called New Stark, just a few miles outside Kenton. In May 1863 he returned to Kenton, after being away for more than twenty years. He was now an old man, sixty years of age.

A thirty-year-old woman named Margaret Born waited in Kenton for news from the war. She was the mother of two little boys, John and Andrew, born in 1857 and 1859, and her husband, Jacob Born, had enlisted in the United States Army, 24th Ohio Volunteer Infantry. His military records indicate he was sick in a hospital in Nashville, Tennessee, in March and April, 1862. Curiously, Dr. Durbin treated a "Jacob C. Born" on June 11, 1863, in Kenton. If it was Margaret's husband home on a short leave, it would be the last time she would see him alive.

"What do you mean that you have lived to see the day that a Negro has been overestimated on Ohio? Why did you fight the abolitionists?"

No answer.

The unsettling question of course, which the daybooks do not answer, is why the Doctor and Democrats of his time abided slavery or, at the least, opposed abolitionists? Having been sent down this road, I had to try to come up with some explanations. With some more poking around, I found guides to perhaps piece together an explanation of the Doctor's views on slavery and abolitionism. The key was reading about the Doctor's first cousin, John Price Durbin, who wrote several books himself and about whom a biography was published in 1889.

Roughly the Doctor's age, John Price Durbin was an active Methodist minister. In addition to being appointed the chaplain of the Senate, he was one of the early presidents of Dickinson College. Remarkably enough, in the 1840s he not only traveled to Europe but also went on a pilgrimage to the Holy Land in the Middle East. One event in his life provides a starting point from which to glimpse into this family and this time long past. As the chaplain of the Senate, John Price was asked in 1832 to perform divine services before both houses of Congress and the Justices of the Supreme Court in celebration of the one-hundredth anniversary of George Washington's birth. There would be no separation of church and state at this event.[25]

In fact, the whole affair took on a distinctly religious tone. Members of Congress desired to take the occasion as an opportunity to further the apotheosis of the father of the country by entombing his remains in the bowels of the newly constructed Capitol.

Chief Justice John Marshall, a man old enough to have worked with Washington, had been invited to speak. Marshall politely declined, although he was overwhelmed by the honor.

"I will not attempt," Marshall wrote, "to describe the impression made on me by this flattering request, and the favorable opinion it implies." However, he went on, "in addition to the pressures of my official duties, which occupy me entirely, and render it impracticable for me to devote so much time to the subject as its intrinsic importance and great interest in the estimation of all would require, I am physically unable to perform the task I would assume. My voice has become so weak as to be almost inaudible, even in a room not unusually large. In the open air it could not be heard by those nearest me: I must therefore decline the honor proposed."[26]

So instead of Chief Justice Marshall, Reverend Durbin was asked to speak. There remained, however, the sticky question of Washington's presence, so to speak, at the birthday celebration.

Henry Clay pointed out that Congress had resolved in 1799, within days of Washington's death, that his remains be disposed of in a public manner and that the widow Washington had given her consent. True enough, Clay conceded, efforts to follow through on the resolution had been unsuccessful, but what better occasion, he noted, than the great man's centennial birth celebration?

Virginia's senators objected, not just because they felt their state had certain rights to the honored dead, but because it was undemocratic, indeed Romish, to consider the worship of a mortal's remains. Moreover, what precedent would be established? "Every age and clime produce great men," Senator Tazewell of Virginia pointed out, "and the last great man, in the opinion of the age, is the greatest."

As a result, "Sir, ten years will hardly pass by, and you will find that some great man is also worthy of a tomb in your splendid dome; a few more years and another great man will be deemed worthy of a place by his side."

The question was obvious: "Will you make the odious distinction between the elder Adams, Thomas Jefferson, and James Monroe, and decree to one a national tomb, passing by the others?" Then, "once commenced, and you will continue to fill the capitol with all the cemeteries it is capable of holding, until the bones of Washington will molder by the side of some— I hope not worthless President."

In the end, Washington rested secure at Mount Vernon, and John Price Durbin rose before the gathered members of both houses of Congress and the Supreme Court to deliver the sermon of his life.

After a short prayer, Reverend Durbin delivered a homily extolling the special blessings that brought about George Washington in a time of national need. Washington was, he said, "the peculiar gift of Heaven to us: the instrument by which God gave us our national liberty and blessings."

His listeners included Clay, Webster, and Calhoun. He was not intimidated, he wrote, by this august assembly. Instead, he was steadied by two great truths about which he was to speak.

The first was that "a special superintending Providence prepared the materials of our national existence and independence, and made George Washington a special gift to us, and His peculiar servant to accomplish this great work."

The second truth was that "our stability as a nation depends upon our national morality which is intimately connected with the reasonable and constant service of God."

John Price Durbin warned of the nation's need to follow a moral path on penalty of national disaster. "The theocracy and history of the Jews as developed in the Old Testament completely establish one fact: that a nation may fill up the measure of its iniquity as well as an individual, and God visits it with national calamities. The history of all nations of the earth which have fallen by great and dreadful evils is luminous commentary on this fundamental principle."

But strangely to me, John Price Durbin did not single out slavery on that occasion as the national iniquity that would bring about a national calamity. Instead, as with so many in his audience, he seemed to assume that slavery had been part of a divine plan. If the nation was divinely inspired and it was created with slavery, it must have been for some providential reason. This notion was confirmed in a speech he gave twenty years later to the Pennsylvania Legislature in 1852 on behalf of the Pennsylvania Colonization Society. The colonization society had been formed to raise funds to pay for the return of African Americans to Africa. Reverend Durbin told the legislature that he saw the colonization movement as the single greatest work of America since the discovery of the continent by Columbus.[27]

Citing Jefferson, Reverend Durbin pointed to the detestable nature of the slave trade but concluded, as Jefferson did, that freedom should be followed by a return of the black race to Africa. "Nothing is more surely written in the book of fate," Jefferson had written and Reverend Durbin repeated, "than that these people are to be free; nor is it less certain that the two races equally free, cannot live in the same government. Nature, habit, opinion, have drawn indelible lines of distinction between them. It is still in our power to direct the process of emancipation and deportation peacefully, and in such slow degrees as that evil will wear off insensibly, and their place be *pari passu* filled by free white laborers."

Here is where John Price Durbin saw what he believed to be the hidden blessing in the whole situation. The full value of the discovery of the American continent had to understood, he said, as having provided the "means of bringing into contact with our race, the dark and benighted race in Africa, in order that they may be taken back again to the land of their ancestors, bearing with them the precious seeds of our blessed Christianity and our glorious liberty and civilization, to elevate, enlighten, and save their countless millions from the barbarism and heathenism which have characterized them from the foundations of the world."

Even Abraham Lincoln came to the conclusion that a divine plan controlled his actions and those of the nation. Ultimately he could find no other way to explain slavery or the war or its length. "Both read the same Bible and pray to the same God," he said in his second inaugural address a month before he was assassinated, "and each invokes His aid against the other. . . . The prayers of both could not be answered; that of neither has been fully answered."

"The Almighty has his own purposes," he said. Then he quoted directly from Matthew: "'Woe unto the world because of offences! For it must needs be that offences come; but woe to that man by whom the offence cometh!'"

Put in the context of his times, Lincoln said: "If we shall suppose that American Slavery is one of those offences which, in the providence of God, must needs come, but which, having continued through His appointed hour, He now wills to remove, and that He gives to both North and South, this terrible war, as the woe due to those by whom the offence came, shall we discern therein any departure from those divine attributes which the believers on a Living God always ascribe to Him?"

"Fondly do we hope—fervently do we pray—that this mighty scourge of war may speedily pass away," Lincoln said.

"Yet, if God wills that it continue, until all the wealth piled by the bondsman's two hundred and fifty years of unrequited toil shall be sunk, and until every drop of blood drawn with the lash, shall be paid by another drawn by the sword, as was said three thousand years ago, so still must be said today, 'the judgments of the Lord, are true and righteous altogether.'"[28]

The silence in the car is now broken by groans from the Doctor, perhaps the labor pains of generational understanding being born.

Or maybe he is drunk again.

Delbert, who has been silently listening to my conversation with the Doctor, suddenly starts to hum the "Battle Hymn of the Republic," trying to drown out the Doctor's groans.

Singing one of its obscure verses, he starts, "They will have to bow their foreheads to their colored kith and kin. They will have to give us house-room or the roof will tumble in! As we go marching on."

An instant later, the Doctor is gone, and Durbin has taken his place.

"Don't worry about him," Durbin says to me. "He comes and goes; he has his ways. He'll be back."

Cumberland is near. Soon we will turn north toward Pennsylvania and climb into the Allegheny Plateau and its mountainous terrain.

⇛ 4 ⇚

MY GOOD OLD MOTHER

September 19, 1863

Zauberei is the German word for magic. Margaret Leibold, Durbin's mother, was born in 1833 in Germany. She grew up in Hintersteinau, a village near Frankfurt. In 1852, when she was nineteen, she came to the United States with her family. Within two years of the Leibolds' arrival in Kenton, Margaret married Jacob Born. I suspect that their courtship was conducted in German, since Jacob was a Swiss immigrant himself. Margaret would have told Jacob of a particularly disturbing experience she had with magic when she was a girl, a story that was Faustian in its details and teachings.[1]

One thing is sure about Margaret Leibold: she hated zauberei; she hated magic.

"Magic always had a fascination for me," Durbin wrote in 1935, "and I worked under many disadvantages, because my mother, who was a very serious woman, thought it was all foolishness, and we were very poor and my mother felt that I wasted my time in fooling with magic."[2]

As she might have said, "*Zauberei ist nur etwas für Narren*" ("Magic is for fools").

"Besides all this," Durbin wrote, "my mother was a German, and the German people thru their folklore which runs thru all generations, had the idea that one sort of bound himself up with the devil when he became a magician." Durbin's mother had to look no further than her own village for confirmation of this proposition. "I had heard stories which were like unto that of Goethe's 'Faust,' of a man who lived in my mother's town in Germany, and who was supposed to be an old wizard, who would sit on a three legged stool at home and milk the cows of other people so that he always had milk altho he had no cows.

"Many wonderful things were ascribed to him, and it was claimed he made a compact with the devil, and one morning the people of the little town were startled to find that he had gotten out of his bed at night and could not be found. A search by all the people of the town was made, and finally my mother with another young girl found the old man who had hung himself in a smokehouse, and the theory of the people of that place was that the devil had come after him in the night and demanded his price."

Durbin's mother was by all accounts a strict and demanding woman. When she died in 1919 at age eighty-six, she was portrayed as a woman of stiff back-bone and strong religious beliefs. Even the trauma she experienced from the fall that fractured her hip several weeks before her death was borne with the grit of a woman long accustomed to life's indignities and hardships. She took everything in the context of her fidelity to a foundational Christian faith.

"Mrs. Durbin never complained," the editor of the *Kenton Daily Democrat* remarked in her obituary, "but bore her suffering with patience and during her last illness she kept ever alive those characteristics that have so marked and rounded out her Christian life."

Her son was fed a strong dose of her brand of religion. He wrote of her requirement that he attend two Sunday school sessions each week, one in German, the other in English. "My mother was a very religious woman," he remembered in the context of his desire to see a circus that came to Kenton on a Sunday in 1876, "and she sent me to German Sunday School in the morning and the Presbyterian Sunday school in the afternoon."[3] Durbin skipped the Presbyterian afternoon session to sneak into the circus. When he got home, he says, his mother did not take it well.

"What I got was plenty," he wrote. "I was sent upstairs to go to bed without any supper."

She was one of Kenton's "pioneer residents" according to her obituary, "one of the County's oldest and most esteemed ladies." A tough, hard German, she carried the responsibility of raising four children from two marriages: Andrew and John Born from her marriage to Jacob Born and William and Eliza Durbin from her marriage to the Doctor. Despite his strict upbringing, Durbin would repeatedly refer to her as his "good old mother" in his writings.

In one letter to FDR in 1931 Durbin wrote about his mother in trying to explain a fight he got into with James Cox, Ohio's Democratic governor during World War I. Cox stirred up anti-German hysteria in Ohio, closing down the German department at the Ohio State University and at one point ordered German books burned. When Durbin complained, Cox dismissed him as soft on the Germans because his mother was German.

"We had some sharp words," Durbin wrote FDR, "in which I told him *my good old mother* was as loyal an American as he was and no one hated the Kaiser more than she did. But Germans resented, especially when they had their boys over in France fighting for America, legislation against their language and their people."[4]

"My mother never complained about her situation in life," Durbin says to me. "We were mighty poor when I was growing up, but we made do."

We are getting close to the Pennsylvania border, climbing Savage Mountain.

Whiz, crack, swish. A small projectile streaks past my head, slowly and then accelerating, ripping the air.

"What's that?"

"What's what?" Delbert says, his words echoing.

Now another very loud crack throws me back in my seat, then a boom. The car begins to fill with smoke. There is great confusion. Yells to get down come from my right. "Fire low!" someone says. "Take good aim." Jesus, I think, what the hell is going on? More cracks, a feeling of heat. More missiles passing within inches of my head. Thuds. Screams.

"Goddammit," I yell, putting my head down and covering it with my hands. I am on grass, with trees everywhere around me. So much smoke surrounds me that I can't see what's happening. There is a hand on my back holding me down. "Delbert?"

"Here they come," a voice says in a heavy German accent. "Sie greifen an. Bleib liegen! Keep down."

I look up and see a red-haired corporal with a sandy complexion in a Union blue uniform. "Who are you?"

"Jacob Born," the corporal replies coolly with a heavy German accent. "Beweg dich nicht. Just stay where you are," he says.

"Where the hell are we?" I say as I put my head back into the dirt. "What's going on?"

"Georgia," he says and then speaks no more. He smells like a man who has been in the field for weeks. He is covered with dirt and dust but his concentration is at its peak. He stands with his rifle, eyes ablaze, pure energy and adrenaline.

Georgia, Jacob Born—of course, Chickamauga.

Margaret Durbin's obituary in 1919 read, "While still a young lady Mrs. Durbin came to this country settling in Kenton in 1852. In 1854 she was united in marriage to Jacob Born. He served in the Northern Army in the Civil War being killed in the battle of Chickamauga."[5]

"Chickamauga" means "River of Death." The Cherokee Indians had so named the winding creek that runs through the heavily wooded area in northern Georgia just south of Chattanooga.

I know why I have been brought here, but I do not want to witness what will—what must—happen.

Although few of us know the circumstances or even recognize the fact, we are all the consequence of the strangest and most unpredictable, sometimes violent, events. More often than not, this includes the untimely demise of someone whom we will never know, someone who lived generations before our own time. Jacob Born is such a person for me.

Jacob Born enlisted in the army on May 18, 1861, at Monroeville, Ohio. He was twenty-nine years old, five feet eight and one half inches tall, with hazel eyes. He had fair red hair that was fine and receding even at twenty-nine. He built barrels, a cooper by trade. He was promoted from private to corporal in Company B of the 24th Ohio Volunteer Infantry. His war records show that he served faithfully and that he spent the spring of 1862 sick in a hospital.

By September 1863, the 24th Ohio Volunteer Infantry was part of the Army of the Cumberland, which was then commanded by an Ohioan named William S. Rosecrans, "Old Rosy" to his men. James A. Garfield was Rosecrans's chief of staff. Two months after the Union victory at Gettysburg, Rosecrans had brilliantly maneuvered the Confederates out of East Tennessee, but he was about to meet an ignominious fate at Chickamauga.

Rosecrans might have been one of the greatest generals of the war. An accident of timing, however, blighted his career. On the second day of the battle of Chickamauga, September 20, 1863, the federal line was momentarily left with an opening when Rosecrans, believing a gap existed in the federal right center, ordered a division already in line to move to the north to close the gap. Instead of closing a gap, this created an opening in the middle of the line. Before the mistake could be corrected, Confederate forces led by Rosecrans's former classmate at West Point, James Longstreet, crashed through the line, cutting the Union position in half. A rout of the federal forces ensued.

The confusion on the field was understandable. The Chickamauga battlefield consisted of a thick forest that was occasionally broken by a few small farms and fields. The woods limited maximum visibility to 150 yards or less. Henry P. Mann, an escort for one of Rosecrans's major generals, Thomas Crittenden, described the confusion on September 20 in his diary: "Sun about an hour high the fight commenced again and there was nothing to be heard but the continual roar of firearms and artillery until about noon when our right give way and the Co. was scattered along the line with drawn sabers to try to stop and rally the men. Gen. Rosecrans was there to doing his best but all that could be said or done did no good."[6]

Charles Dana, the noted journalist who had been appointed assistant secretary of war by Lincoln, was with Rosecrans when the breakthrough occurred. He observed the burly general, a devout Catholic, crossing himself. "Hello," Dana said to himself, "if the General is crossing himself, we are in a desperate situation." Dana overheard Rosecrans say to his staff in a calm voice: "If you care to live any longer, get away from here."[7]

Rosecrans then made the fatal mistake of leaving the field while others, including General George Thomas, stayed on to fight. Thomas became the hero and was thereafter known as the "Rock of Chickamauga." Rosecrans was relieved of his command.

Jacob Born was severely wounded on the first day of the battle, September 19. On the morning of the nineteenth, General Palmer's second division, which included Born's brigade, was ordered to move north five miles to reinforce troops on the federal left. At eight in the morning, Born's brigade commander, Col. William Grose, had his men up and on the road. For two hours, Born marched up and down along La Fayette Road with his regiment until they settled on a little knoll not far from a farmhouse called the Brotherton House. The brigade then moved down Brotherton Road toward the Confederates and took up a position just off the road in the woods.

The battle raged for hours. Around quarter to four in the afternoon the Confederates led by Brigadier General Bate from Tennessee struck the federal line at the angle formed by Grose's brigade. The 24th Ohio, of which Jacob Born was a member, bore the brunt of Bate's attack.[8] According to an eyewitness account, the fighting was furious, and the 24th "stood as if every man was a hero for the space of half an hour."

I am now at that fateful moment. Jacob Born stands and aims his rifle. It is an incredibly reckless act on his part. There is little to describe the fury of the battle that swirls around him. I swear I hear him chuckle, not a nervous laugh, but an almost sinister jeer, as if he is tempting fate itself.

Get down you damn fool, I think, get down. Just as I open my mouth to yell at him, he is hit by a whistling bullet in his left thigh. The bullet enters his leg four inches above the knee and it fractures his femur. The violent impact knocks him to the ground. He falls screaming, "Oh, help me!" The transformation from warrior to prostrated victim is immediate. It is exactly as one Civil War veteran described it: "A moment or two later, I too felt the sting of a bullet, and fell benumbed with pain. It was an instantaneous metamorphosis from strength and vigor to utter helplessness."[9]

Time freezes for Jacob Born as it does for me. He looks at me as he grabs his bleeding leg. I look away. The sounds around us that a split second before were deafening and terrifying become muffled. The rebel-yells now sound as if they were coming from the bottom of a well. For a moment there is complete silence and then he begins to scream in agony. On his belly he turns and drags himself back toward Brotherton Road and the rear of the line, pushing off with his right leg. His blood mixes with the dirt. "We are all from dirt," I think of the Doctor saying to me. I am unable to move, filled with stark terror. There are no litter bearers to be found in this heavy fire, and so, with nothing flowing through his veins but raw determination, Jacob Born pulls himself to his feet, using his rifle as leverage, and he begins to walk to help, ignoring the firestorm behind him.

With a gaping hole in his leg and a badly fractured femur, Jacob Born, as if possessed, walks. I watch him disappear into a line of trees. At first he hops on his good leg, then he begins to almost run, with a horrible limp, on both legs. His hospital records read that he "walked two and one half miles after the reception of the injury" for help. When he finally reached a field hospital, he fainted from the loss of blood. Before he lost consciousness, he noticed how cloudy and unusually cold it was on this mid-September day in Georgia. Everything around him seemed to be a complete confusion of faces, sounds, and noises. Then, darkness.

That night turned bitter cold. Jacob Born would remember the cold and his thirst, but he refused the whiskey offered him. As his doctors would later note, he never liked whiskey. Eventually, he was transported by rail to a hospital in Louisville, where he arrived on September 26, a week after he had been wounded. Despite his injury, his records tell that he "walked up two flights of stairs" when he was admitted to the U.S. Hospital No. 1.

His surgeon, A. G. Watson, thought he could save Born without amputating his leg. The method of healing Watson employed was known at the time as "second intention," a process of waiting for a "benign infection" to produce what was known as "laudable pus."[10] The appearance of pus was considered essential to the healing process. Healing by "first intention," in which the wound healed without infection, was almost unknown. At the same time, Watson also was coming to a crude understanding of what British researcher Joseph Lister was just discovering about the therapeutic value of the use of raw antiseptic methods, such as cleansing the wound with carbolic acid. Jacob Born suffered such "treatments."

Most Civil War doctors thought little of the filth in which they worked. Surgeons particularly were proud of their operating coats or aprons, which were never cleaned and became encrusted with blood and pus, attesting to the surgeon's vast experience.

At first the prognosis was encouraging for Jacob Born. "Simple dressings were applied, case progressing well until October 19th when crepitation was first noticed, discharging large quantities of pus," the hospital records noted. *Crepitation* was the sensation the surgeon felt when placing his hand on the wound in which gas gangrene was present. It was the crackling sensation of gas bubbles generated by the bacteria breaking just below the skin. Still, despite this ominous sign, the doctors hesitated to amputate. Perhaps they knew it was too late.

"On 20 of October extension of limb by weight and pulley applied. Case progressing well until November 5th when the wound commenced bleeding, blood oozing slowly. Bleeding checked by injecting a solution of Persulphate-Ferri. Bromine applied on the 10th November, injected in the cavity."

There was some improvement for a time. Then the infection showed up in another location. "Just beneath the knee joint on the inner aspect of the knee distinct fluctuations were noticed. An incision being made about four ounces of slightly fetid pus escaped interspersed with small blood clots." Evacuations of the newly incised wound were performed but did no good. The infection was too deeply rooted.

"November 15 patient complains of great weakness, pus from original wound healthy, from incision fetid, slight stupor, craves whiskey, which he formerly disliked. November 16 very drowsy, feces passing involuntarily, refuses all nourishment save milk. Discharge from wound healthy, bad odor from breath. November 17 at 9 A.M. about the same as yesterday; at 3 P.M. profuse perspiration. November 18 countenance anxious, tongue whitish coated, breath fetid, had two severe rigors during forenoon and after each rigor emesis [vomiting]. Died at 2 o'clock P.M. of the 18 November 1863."

Corporal Jacob Born was buried in Cave Hill Cemetery in Louisville.

His widow, Margaret, was notified of her husband's wounding by a cryptic telegram that did not describe his wounds but only stated he had been transferred to a hospital in Louisville. I imagine that when news of his death finally arrived, she was so shocked that she might have showed up at the Kenton train depot regularly for a couple of days expecting the return of her husband's body before rereading the telegram, which stated Jacob had been buried in Kentucky. The death notice was cold, written by a semiliterate clerk: "I Sincerely regret to have to inform you of the disease of your Husband Jacob Born of Co. G 24th Ohio Regt. Vols.," the letter began.[11]

I wonder if Margaret Born, who because of Chickamauga would become my great-great-grandmother, ever recovered from Jacob Born's death. With a terrible suddenness, her life was twisted, turned upside down. She received $55.40, the money in Jacob Born's possession when he died, sent by the hospital through the Adams Express Company. "His clothing and the other articles can be forwarded to your address by authorizing by power of attorney anyone whom you may select to transact your business," the clerk wrote. There is no record that Margaret Born ever responded to the letter. His one pair of socks, cotton drawers, flannel shirt, rubber blanket, trousers, and blouse probably were reissued to another soldier.

Margaret was still very much in her childbearing years. She was one of many war widows in Kenton. Old Doctor Durbin's daybooks tell the tale of the start of the relationship between the two. On January 29, 1864, a little over two months after Jacob Born's death, an entry first records the "Widow Born" receiving "cash" of seventy-five cents from the Doctor. On February 17 the Widow Born shows up again for three days of medical attention "for boy" and is charged three dollars "on credit." In March one of her boys is seen by the Doctor again, and she is charged seventy-five cents for the visit. Gradually she too becomes his patient, and occasionally the Doctor loans her money or pays debts on her behalf. On June 10 the Doctor first refers to her as "Margaret Born." His visits to see her increase throughout 1864. He sees her five times in September alone. In October he buys a round trip ticket for her on a train. The destination is not recorded.

In January 1865 something significant clearly is going on. The Doctor pays a seventy dollar invoice on behalf of Margaret, perhaps past-due rent for some period of time.

On February 28, 1865, Margaret Born and Dr. William W. Durbin were married. The entries in his daybook make no mention of the marriage or even suggest that he took the day off. Margaret was pregnant a year later by the beginning of 1866, and William Warner Durbin Jr., their first child, was born on September 29, 1866.

Slowly, the Chickamauga battlefield begins to recede. As it fades, memories wash over me, like a reverse undertow. They propel me back into the Studebaker, where my great-grandfather Durbin has closed his eyes and is resting quietly. As I watch him sleep, I think of how September 19, 1863, the first day of the Chickamauga battle, was such a momentous time for both of us. If Jacob Born had been a little more cautious, less heroic, if a bullet had missed its mark, if General Rosecrans had made different battle plans, we both would have been the figment of some magician's imagination.

The irony of it all was that Durbin's political career began with old General Rosecrans, when Durbin earned a patronage appointment as a messenger boy at the Treasury Department in 1886 after Grover Cleveland was first elected president. Young Durbin's duty was to carry canceled bonds to the register of the Treasury, who was then the elderly General Rosecrans, the very man who unwittingly started the chain of events that led to Durbin's existence.

Unaware of this connection, the newspapers in 1933 only found it noteworthy that Durbin had succeeded Rosecrans as register of the Treasury forty-six years later. "'Now they'll be carrying the bonds to me,' Mr. Durbin said, smiling behind the same desk the general had once sat behind," one newspaper reported.[12]

"It is one of the romances of American opportunity," another newspaper pointed out.[13]

In the car, Margaret Durbin joins us in the front seat. She looks intently at her seventy-one-year-old son. She says nothing. He suddenly opens his eyes and glares at me.

"You forgot about him, didn't you?"

"Forgot about him? . . ."

"Yes, you forgot about Jacob Born."

"I had never heard of Jacob Born."

"He did something few would do," Durbin says. "He knew his options. He didn't have to go to war. He knew the chance he was taking, and he was well aware of his mortal risk, especially on that day in September in 1863. And I'll tell you what, he knew on that day, when he stood in the line of fire, that his actions would have consequences down through the generations. And you and all my descendants have forgotten what he did, as if he meant nothing to you, as if he never existed," he admonishes me, and I see his point.

"But, you see, . . . it's really as if you never existed. He made you possible; he saw you that day in the field, just as plain as he saw the rebels. He made you possible. Don't forget this. Don't ever forget Jacob Born."

Durbin's mother looks at me, then at Durbin. I feel the warmth between the two. His face relaxes as he looks back at her, disclosing a sense of absolute comfort and security. In a moment, she is gone and Durbin again closes his eyes.

On the west side of Meadow Mountain on the National Road, we have come to an area that was once known as the "Shades of Death." Long ago this area was a dense forest of white pine. The cover was so thick that sunlight could not find its way through and highway robbers infested the dark and gloomy byways. Fortunately, those days are long gone. I hope.

≫ 5 ≪

TAKING SECOND MONEY

May 21, 1876

I met a number of magicians around the country when I was following leads to track down Durbin memorabilia. The common trait I found among them was that they all fell in love with magic when they were young, usually around the age of ten or eleven years old. For some reason, magic took hold of them and they couldn't shake it. The same was true of Durbin.

He told and retold the story of his introduction to magic. In February 1920, for example, he sat down with a *Cleveland Plain Dealer* writer to talk about his rise in politics and magic. The interview was given when Durbin was the head of the Democratic Party in Ohio and as he moved into the campaign of 1920. "It has long been a sound educational axiom," the *Plain Dealer* noted, "that a man, to be successful in his vocation, must have an avocation, and W. W. Durbin, who runs the Scioto Sign Co. of Kenton, and whose advertising signs placard the wide world, has two avocations, which some think are one and the same—politics and magic."[1] Durbin told the *Plain Dealer*, though, that he was a magician long before he got into politics. This seemed understandable. "The boy who is not fascinated by magic is not a normal lad," the reporter agreed, "and Kenton's lads were normal."

"Let me begin from the beginning," Durbin says in response to my question of how he got started in magic. A road sign tells me that we are about to leave Maryland, having crossed the bridge at the Little Crossings at Casselman River.

"It was way back in 1876—I was ten years old then—a circus came to Kenton. My father had died a few years earlier when I was just a little fellow."[2]

The Doctor is now back, seated next to Delbert in the front seat. He looks

65

back at Durbin over the top of the high cushioned seat, adjusts his glasses, and turns back to watch the road in front of us.

"Like most country doctors he had a big practice but not much money. He did a lot of work, but a lot of his clients didn't pay him," Durbin says. "After he died, let me tell you, we had a pretty damned hard time of it."

"There wasn't any money for you to go to the circus," Delbert interjects.

"No, sir, there certainly wasn't," Durbin responds rather formally. "Well, it was on Sunday, May 21, 1876, that John Robinson's Circus came to town. The kids, of course, were all there to see them unload. When the circus came in, it was raining, and among other things they had almost two hundred Shetland ponies, which were very little fellows, and there were enough boys to lead the whole two hundred up to the show grounds. I got a pony. Let me tell you that was a thrill."

Remarkably, Durbin is able to extract from his mind the precise date that John Robinson's Circus came to Kenton. It will not be the last time he displays tonight his prodigious memory, an aptitude that must have served him well in his political and magical endeavors.

"I'd been to Sunday school in the morning, and I was supposed to be there again in the afternoon, but I played hooky. I had on my best suit of clothes and my shoes were shined, and I wish you could have seen that suit and those shoes after I got through taking the pony from the tracks to the circus grounds in all the mud."

Delbert screws up a sour face, as if he just bit into a lemon.

"What was just as bad, I got home late. It was my job to bring in the damn cow every night, and when I got home the cow hadn't been taken care of, and the mud was all over me. I heard plenty about it from my mother. She told me I didn't get any money to go to the circus the next day, and she usually meant what she said. She did this time too. But I was determined to see that circus. The next day, I snuck out to the grounds, and pretty soon I saw a man sitting in an open tent."

"Want to see the circus, Bud?" *Delbert growls out in a low gravely voice.*

"I told him I sure did. So he told me if I'd get him a bucket of water, he'd let me in. Then he asked me to get him some wood so he could boil some coffee. I got him some wood, and I helped him make a fire."

The Doctor points to something in the dark in front of us, and Delbert begins to slow the car. Off in the distance I see what appears to be a small fire behind some white tents in an area just in front of Negro Mountain, supposedly named for a black man who, as part of Captain Thomas Cresap's company of trailblazers, defended a white settlement from Indian attacks and was killed in the process. Delbert turns off the main road and drives toward the tents.

"Right here will be fine," the Doctor says to Delbert, as we come to a stop near the fire. Two figures sitting near the fire look up but pay us no mind.

Delbert turns off the car but leaves on the lights. Durbin motions me to the car door, inviting me to jump out. I open the door and we both get out. Delbert and the Doctor follow around the car. The smell of the firewood burning and a tangy smoke odor fills the air.

"That's the guy I was talking about," Durbin says, pointing to the roust-about, a man wearing a vest and a light tan slouch hat with a dark handlebar moustache. Sitting next to him on his haunches is the young Durbin grinding coffee in a wooden grinder with a metal crank. In the background are other, much larger tents, a band chariot, many cages with animals in them, and a few painted tableau cars hitched to ponies.

The John Robinson Circus claimed that it was fifty-four years old in 1876, when Durbin was ten.

True to Durbin's memory of his epiphanic experience that spring, I found the circus's advertisement announcing a visit to Kenton on May 21 on microfilm in Kenton's public library. The ad was a full-page treatment in the *Hardin County Democrat* ("A Family Journal—Devoted to Literature, News, Agriculture and the Dissemination of Democratic Principles").[3] The allure and excitement of the circus must have been intense to an adventuresome boy like Durbin. The circus ad included woodcuts of exotic animals and promised "60 Cages, Vans, Dens, Chariots, Carriages, Tableau Cars, &c., &c."

According to the publicity, "Old John Robinson inaugurated the First Combined Circus and Menagerie that was ever seen in America." Whether true or not, it made a great story. "The Exhibition, as well as the Nation, was in its infancy then. It was a frail bark, launched upon the turbulent tide of public favor, but each year slowly but surely gaining in popularity. For years John Robinson struggled manfully on, enduring privation and hardships that almost any other man would have sunk under. But he had an iron will: he had put his hand to the plow, and he would not look back!"

The circus was in fairly good shape when Durbin first saw it. Within twenty years, though, it fell into disrepute. Indeed, the order, "Give 'em a John Robinson" became known in the business as a signal to rush and cut a performance. Take, for example, the indignity expressed by the editor of the *Urbana (Ohio) Campaign Democrat* in July 1893: "That notorious, un-consolidated, homogeneous swindle known as the John Robinson Circus has come and gone. Had this paper known of the worthless character of this perambulating robber, its advertising matter would not have appeared in these columns."

"And now for my next swindle," Delbert says, nudging the Doctor.

The Doctor smiles, but his mind is strongly focused on the young Durbin. He knows he is now witnessing an event in his son's life that came after he was gone. He seems more curious than anything else.

Once coffee was set to boil on a hanger over the fire, the circus hand and the young boy walk toward the sideshow. The man lifts up the flap in the tent and holds it long enough for all of us to walk in. On various stages are the curiosities: the fat woman, the giant, the armless man who is writing with his toes. The circus hand, it turns out, is also a lecturer. He jumps up on one of the stages and introduces a magician.

This is the moment Durbin will always remember. The magician pulls out a pack of cards and performs some tricks, including blowing spots onto the cards and then blowing them off. Then he produces a butcher knife and runs it through his arm without losing a single drop of blood. Everyone in the audience winces, some instinctively grabbing their arms as they watch.

"Damn," says Delbert. The young Durbin sits mesmerized, eyes bulging out.

"This set me afire as to how such wonderful feats could be done," the older Durbin says.

Delbert starts a conversation with the fat woman and both begin laughing. The Doctor takes it all in. Without saying anything, Durbin wheels, leaves the tent, and slowly moves back toward the car. Delbert, the Doctor, and I follow, looking backward toward the whole buzzing scene.

"After that show," Durbin says as we all gather around the car, "my guide there took me to a box of snakes—he was also the snake man—and he opened the box and wound snakes all around him."

"Ugh," Delbert grunts.

"Then we went back to the fire, and he poured some coffee and cut the bread. Of course, being a kid, I was always hungry, just like all kids. I'd just got through my dinner at home, but I was hungry anyhow. I just couldn't eat that bread, though. He'd had his hands on the bread, and those hands had just touched the snakes. I did drink some coffee."

We get back in the car, doors slam, and slowly we drive away. Durbin is still looking out the window at the circus as we pull out back onto the National Road, set to climb the highest mountain of our journey.

"I never forgot that magician and the dagger," he says. "All summer long I thought about it. I thought about it all winter. I couldn't forget about the damned thing."

"You were hooked for sure," Delbert says.

"The next spring," Durbin says looking at his father in the front seat, "a neigh-bor of ours was cleaning out the attic, and he threw out a copy of Frank Leslie's Boy's and Girl's Weekly. *In that magazine was an ad about a book on black magic. Well, I knew I had to have that book. A cloth-bound copy cost fifty cents; a paper, thirty. The paper one would be all right. I told my pal Charlie Camper about it, and we decided to get the book."*

I am a little cold as the car warms back up. Durbin is now rubbing his hands together; he feels the hard work in his shoulders, circling them to loosen up, and he re-creates in his mind the joy of anticipating the book's arrival.

"We worked and saved for weeks to get that thirty cents. We collected rags and paper and anything else we could find. If anyone hung out an old rug or piece of carpet on their fence, they'd better beware. Finally we scraped up the money, three shinplasters, which were paper ten-cent pieces. I didn't know how to write a letter for this book, so Charlie and I traded off hoeing potatoes for my older brother, Andy Born, who wrote the letter for us, and we put a stamp on it and took it to the post office. The letter couldn't possibly have gotten to New York and the book come back in less than a week, but we were right at the post office the next day."

Durbin shifts his weight from one side to the other, back and forth, back and forth, almost rocking in obvious happiness in the telling of a favorite childhood memory.

"I think we went to the post office two and three times a day—every time the mail came in—and finally on Saturday at noon it came. We ran all the way home, and we were so afraid somebody might learn the secrets in this wonderful book that we didn't go by way of the street but went down the alleys, and we climbed up in the loft of the barn, and we perused this book for hours. Then we began to practice how to do the various things it taught."

Delbert smiles at his boss's delight in recounting the story.

"I began to study magic then, and I've never stopped. I've been a damned magician ever since," Durbin crows.

The memory brings up Durbin's young pals in magic: Charlie Camper and Preston Stevenson. Charlie was his next-door neighbor growing up. His father had been a Union soldier in the Civil War. Charlie was five years older than Durbin, but the two were inseparable. "My pal Charlie and I were always together, and we had many happy days fishing, swimming, playing baseball, and the many games that boys of those days engaged in, but we devoted the greater part of our time to magic and its mysteries," Durbin wrote after Charlie died. "I remember that Charlie learned from his uncle how to turn his vest inside out without taking it off, and this used to be one of the tricks we did in our shows we gave in Charlie's barn."[4]

Preston Stevenson, Durbin's other sidekick, was a deaf mute whose family moved into a nearby apartment. "He was going to the deaf mute school of Ohio in Columbus and he used to come home along in May of each year during the school summer vacation," Durbin later remembered. "He would come down to Charlie's home and we soon found out he knew many tricks and really could give quite a performance. At first he wouldn't divulge any of his secrets but after a time we were taken in and initiated into the mysteries of the art. In addition to the tricks he could perform, he had a set of Punch and Judy figures, and he was the first person I ever saw perform a Punch and Judy puppet show, although he couldn't speak a word. The whole thing was performed in pantomime."[5]

Stevenson and Camper both died in 1927. Stevenson was the first to go. According to a death announcement in *The Linking Ring*, Stevenson, "a steadfast friend of our worthy president," moved away from Kenton to Findlay, Ohio, "where he held the post of Recorder of Deeds for over forty years."

Camper died at the end of the year, on December 24. "Just as the hands on the clock were pointing to the hour of the anniversary of the birth of the Savior of mankind," Durbin wrote, "Charles E. Camper, IBM. No. 746, took his departure for the other world." He described his old friend as the "first assistant the writer ever had when he embarked on the magic stage." Charlie, according to Durbin, "was a most ingenious and clever mechanic and could make anything he laid his eyes upon. It is unnecessary to say that he was a splendid assistant. To the writer, he was as close as a brother, and a most loyal friend."

"Peace to their ashes," Delbert intones.

The Doctor nods quietly in assent.

Durbin looks at me. I notice that sometimes his eyes vanish from behind his wire-rim glasses; I see only a dim reflection of the gray cushioned interior of the car and occasionally my own image pops up.

The boys collected every book they could on magic. From the Eureka Trick and Novelty Company in New York, they ordered *The Parlor Magician* and *The Fireside Magician*. Durbin's obsession with reading about magic was immediate. Describing his routine of retrieving the family cow from its pasturing every night, he told the *Plain Dealer* reporter that he used every moment to immerse himself in his reading: "He walked with the magazine in one hand and while he read he rattled a pair of bones with the other. . . . His mother's cow usually got home late after that night, and thereafter in every spare moment Durbin might have been found in the hay loft, diligently practicing the ABCs of magic."[6]

Reading, studying, and practicing was one thing; true magicians needed tools of the trade. "We had to get some apparatus made," Durbin later wrote, "and I knew a fellow who worked in a tin store, who was a mighty good tinner, and he made many pieces of apparatus for me. He made the cups for the 'Cups and Balls' trick, a houlette for the rising card trick and made me a set of linking rings. Meanwhile my pal's mother had made us an egg bag. We didn't have so many tricks but we practiced so much that we became pretty skillful in the tricks we did do. Then from the barn we graduated into the country school houses where we used to give performances, my pal doing the Punch and Judy, and Stevenson and I doing the sleight of hand."[7]

Delbert reminds Durbin: "It ain't always smooth sailing when boys perform."

"That's true," says Durbin. "I remember in 1879, for example, we saw a magician perform in one of the traveling circuses that came to Kenton, the Sells Brothers Great European Seven-Elephant Railroad Show.

"This magician performed a trick that entirely puzzled us. He borrowed two hats from the crowd who were mostly farmers. He had a box of oats and two tin cups, one of which he filled with oats. He put the cup filled with oats under one of the hats, which sat on a board laid across two saw horses. Then he took the other tin cup, which was empty, and put it under the other hat.[8]

"He commanded the oats to pass from one cup to the other; and sure enough, when the hats were lifted up, the one that was filled with oats was empty, while the one that was empty was full of oats.

"Then he made it pass back again, and finally the oats vanished and passed back to the large box from which they came."

"Truly magical," Delbert says in drollery.

"Well, it puzzled our heads to know how he did the oats hat trick, and we couldn't work it out any other way except that we would have to have trap doors and someone under them to make the change under cover of the hats. So we proceeded to get a large wood box in which clothing was shipped and hauled it down to Charlie's barn, and we cut trap doors in the box. We used strap hinges, made out of leather, with a button to hold the traps up. The box was so turned that my pal could get in and out readily."

"Then you ran into a hitch," says Delbert, winking his eye at me. The Doctor sits mummy-like, taking no part in this conversation. Something about his skin color gives me a shiver.

"When the show started, I borrowed two hats from the audience of small boys, and the hats were so small, and the traps so large, that they almost fell

through; but Charlie made the exchange. The problem was Charlie always wore hobnailed shoes, and they naturally made a lot of noise.

"So once when we had the show in Charlie's barn, a little fellow sat out in front, and when Charlie got around behind the box and crawled in the box, he made so much noise that the boys began to talk, and they asked me who the 'Professor' was in the box. When Charlie began to change the cups with the oats, he almost let the little hats drop through."

"Oops," Delbert chuckles.

"Then they made a great demonstration and laughed at me so that pretty soon it got to the point where the lie was passed, and the next thing I knew one of the fellows was mixed up with me on the floor and I was taking second money. Well, I called to Charlie for help, and mighty soon he came out, and we showed this fellow a trick that was not on the program; but it broke up the show."

The Doctor suddenly comes out of his coma and lets out an enormous laugh. Delbert jabs his fist at an imaginary adversary. Durbin is pleased. He looks sideways at me without turning his head. He has a self-satisfied grin, always the performer.

I interject: "When you say, 'I was taking second money,' you mean . . . ?"

"He was getting whopped," Delbert cries.

"Never heard that one before, son?" the Doctor asks, his head turning with a mechanical quality.

"Let me tell you, my pal Stevenson was the one they were afraid of. He couldn't speak a lick, but he sure had some hard fists. Maybe that comes from being picked on 'cause he was different. To me he was a magician's magician. He was always looking to find magicians who came to Kenton; yet he always would tell me about it, because he had great difficulty in communicating with them. He could talk to me, and then I could tell the fellow what he was saying."[9]

"You knew sign language?" I ask.

"Sort of," he says. "I remember that a fellow named Boucher, who traveled with the Miles Orton Circus as a magician and ventriloquist, came to our town when I was a boy and stayed a week, and he showed us many things we did not know. Along about that time, Hall the Mesmerist came to Kenton, and he stayed a week too, giving exhibitions of mesmerism, which was nothing more than hiring boys to pretend they were mesmerized. Mesmerism was what is called hypnotism now, but we never got into that."

"By 1881 the boys were ready for their big show," Delbert says.

"We gave many shows in the schoolhouses at night, but Charlie and I always longed for a big tent with banners out in front, such as a sideshow has. We worked at various jobs to get the money to buy a top for a tent. Cotton goods in those days

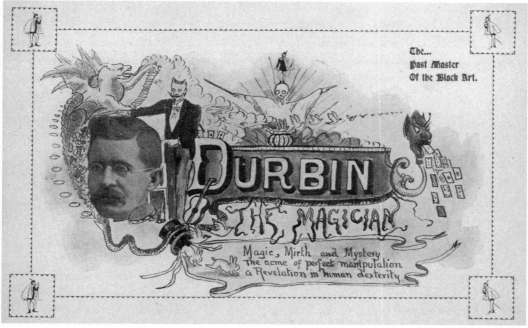

"Magic, Mirth, and Mystery," Durbin magic program (ca. 1900). Author's collection.

were very cheap, and we finally got enough money to buy the canvas for a thirty-foot round tent. Charlie's mother proceeded to make it for us, working every night, and we used to run the treadle for her because it was so hard to sew."

"A good tent is essential," Delbert observes.

"Then we needed poles. First we went out in the woods and cut a hickory sapling and shaved all the bark off and painted it blue and used it for the center pole. Then we needed side poles. There was a cooper shop within a few squares of Charlie's home, owned by old Bill Campbell. Out back in an alley were piled up some poles, just the size we needed. Charlie and I waited until after dark and drove our two-horse wagon down this alley and loaded the poles in the back of the wagon.

"Just about the time we were finishing, we heard old Bill yelling, 'Hey, you fellows, what the hell are you doing?' In the loudest stage whisper I could manage, I urged Charlie to get on the wagon and drive as fast as he could, which he did. Old Bill couldn't catch us. We drove way around the town and unloaded the poles in Charlie's barn."

So, larceny is in my genes—would that that was the worst of it.

"But a sideshow is not complete without banners on the outside. Stevenson was quite an artist and he hunted up one of his friends who was very good at

painting pictures. Every Sunday we went to this fellow's shop and Stevenson would pencil out in chalk or charcoal the pictures he wanted painted. During the week we would cover the canvas with the background. As I remember it, we had a picture of a magician with devils flying through the air. Another banner showed the wonderful mind-reading act, and another displayed a fire-eater, and still another the headless man. Over the door was painted the inscription: 'W. W. Durbin & Company's Great Eastern Museum of Living Wonders.'"

"*An appropriate title of mystery,*" Delbert says.

"*In early March of that year, the weather was balmy and fair, the grass had come out green, and everybody was making gardens. Charlie and I were strolling over the town, and right then and there we decided the show would open up the next Saturday. We went home that night, and with our little printing press, using a lot of pasteboard cards from spool cotton boxes, we printed tickets: ADMIT ONE 5¢.*

"*The next morning we put these into the hands of the various boys who were to help us run the show. By this time the boys and girls in town knew we had a pretty good show and we sold many tickets. Although the show wasn't until Saturday, we loaded up the big wagon on Thursday night and, believe me, we had some load on that wagon.*

"*Friday morning came and everything was fair. We came home for dinner at noon and got back to school at one o'clock, and then it began to snow. It was one of those heavy spring snows. By the time we got out of school, the snow was a foot deep.*"

"*What did you do?*"

"*Well, a council of war was called, and we decided that this show had to go on—rain or shine—and it was agreed that everybody should bring a shovel and a broom. So the next morning at six o'clock we started out for the show grounds with this wonderful show of ours. We drove down the alley to the street. We were not to be deterred.*

"*Charlie was the driver, and I can still hear him say, as he took hold of the lines, 'Geet ep.'*

"*Being one of the proprietors, I rode with Charlie up front, but the other fellows sat wherever they could on the back of the wagon. We were a happy group, and those boys yelled all the way to the show grounds. The people of the town must have thought we were crazy.*"

"*Crazy with happiness,*" Delbert says.

"*When we reached the show grounds, the boys got into action, and you never saw a place cleared so quick. Then Charlie and I went down to the mill and brought up several loads of sawdust, and by nine o'clock the tent was up and everything was ready for the free show, kind of our dress rehearsal.*[10]

"The March winds began to blow, and they never blew so hard as they did that day. We had an awful time to keep the banners up. At ten o'clock the free show was given. I performed the linking rings and my hands were so cold that I had to send one of the boys over to a neighbor's house to get some warm water to put my hands in. By the time he returned, though, old Sol had come out, and the snow began to melt."

"You didn't give 'em a John Robinson, no, sir," Delbert adds.

"We sent our messengers out telling the people the show would go on at one o'clock, and it did. We also had a show in the evening, and, it being a little cold, we had a fire inside and that tent was smoked as black as the ace of spades.

"We had torches that were left over from the presidential campaign of Garfield and Hancock, and these furnished the lights. At half past nine, the tent went down, and everything was packed up, and we drove to Charlie's barn feeling that we were the prize showmen of the earth. We built air castles all night in our dreams of what we were going to be in the show world."

Durbin abruptly stops. He holds one hand up to his head as if the pain is too great, and closes his eyes. Everyone in the car becomes silent. The atmosphere turns pensive. It is as if we are witnesses to an execution and can do nothing to stop it.

That summer of 1881 would be a melancholy one for the nation. President James A. Garfield, a Republican from Mentor, Ohio, was gunned down on July 2, just 120 days after being sworn in as president. He was shot in the back as he walked through the Baltimore and Potomac Depot in Washington by a deranged office seeker, Charles Guiteau. Garfield entered the railroad station unguarded with his Secretary of State James Blaine. Guiteau's first shot grazed Garfield's arm. Dazed, Garfield attempted to turn around to see what was happening when Guiteau got off a second shot, which struck Garfield in his back on his right side, four inches from the spinal column and just above the waist.[11]

One of the first doctors to examine Garfield was pleased to see that he was not paralyzed and could turn over to show his wound. Garfield, however, replied to the physician's encouraging words by saying, "Doctor, I am a dead man."

Guiteau was a lunatic who believed that he had been instrumental in Garfield's election, in return for which he expected a federal job. He was undone when no offer materialized. He had been hanging around the White House for months, gaining access, stealing White House stationery, and begging for a job.

"The Chinese Shuffler," a turn-of-the-century Durbin magic performance. Author's collection.

"Ingratitude is the basest of crimes," Guiteau wrote. He became obsessed with the idea that he needed to "remove" the president.

Garfield, a distinguished Civil War soldier, was a dark-horse candidate who overcame an attempt at the 1880 Republican convention to bring back Grant after he had been out of office during the term of Ohioan Rutherford B. Hayes ("His Fraudulency," as he was nicknamed due to the widely held belief that he had stolen the election of 1876 from Democrat Samuel Tilden). The Grant nomination attempt failed only because the delegates carried the deeply seated American fear of a third-term presidency. The two-term tradition started by George Washington would only be broken (twice) by Franklin Roosevelt.

Garfield lingered all summer. The nation remained riveted by the daily bulletins about his condition. If his doctors had not continually probed his wound to locate the bullet, there is reason to believe he may have survived. Indeed, Guiteau in his murder trial asserted Garfield died from malpractice.

"Therefore, I say he was not fatally shot," Guiteau told the court. "If he had been well treated he would have recovered."

Guiteau lost the argument and his life; he was hung.

Garfield struggled and sweated through the heat in Washington before he was finally moved, mercifully, to the seashore at Elberton, New Jersey, where he died on September 19. He was a few weeks shy of his fiftieth birthday. His body was brought back to Ohio and eventually interred in a great monument in Cleveland's Lakeview cemetery. Chester Arthur succeeded him and presided over a competent but undistinguished administration. To his credit, he did install modern plumbing in the White House and a civil service system in the government.

"The stage was set for the election of 1884," Delbert says, "and Mr. Durbin's entrance into the world of national politics."

The Doctor is concocting something with a mortar and pestle. He mixes his chemicals and takes out a canteen to pour a cup of water. Into the water he dissolves the powder and hands the glass to Durbin.

"This will help."

In a codicil to his last will and testament, the Doctor wrote: "[Margaret Durbin] may manufacture and sell medicines from my recipes or formulas that are favorite medicinal agents and do all she may deem proper for the welfare of both children without partiality or distinction."[12]

Durbin drinks the potion and scowls but dutifully finishes it.

"You'll get through it," the Doctor says.

On the other side of Negro Mountain we will come to the Great Crossings of the Youghiogheny River. Fort Necessity, the site where George Washington surrendered to the French in 1754, is just beyond the Youghiogheny and Flat Rock. A year after Washington's defeat, the British sent another expedition to throw out the French, this one led by the British General Edward Braddock. Washington was Braddock's aide-de-camp.

The army Braddock brought with him cut a military road in 1755 through the wilderness, roughly following an Indian trail that Washington had also used. Braddock's goal was to defeat the French at Fort Duquesne (Pittsburgh), but his army was turned back, and he was fatally wounded. According to lore, he was hastily buried by his troops in the middle of the road they had just built to disguise his remains from the French. No one knows for sure where Braddock was buried.

I notice the old stone obelisk mile markers we pass, assuring us that we are indeed on the National Road.

⇒ 6 ⇐

OUR FIERY TRIAL

April 1896

Durbin's parents—my great great grandparents—lived through times of immense change and uncertainty. They took for granted that their lives were precarious. They survived the bizarre and seemingly uncontrollable illnesses of the pioneer days in Ohio and faced a great civil war. Durbin's time, although better, was itself filled with such dangers and hazards that a person was left grateful at day's end simply to have survived it unscathed. When he was a child, accidents and falls were among the leading causes of death. Durbin's mother, who lived into her eighties, would die as the result of a chain of events brought on by a fall (a broken hip led to killer pneumonia).

The Champion Iron Works, where Durbin took a job as an iron core maker when he dropped out of high school, was a typical manufacturing facility of the time, a steaming hothouse where life and limb were constantly at risk. The foundry, like so many structures of its time, was completely destroyed in a catastrophic blaze in 1902 that could not be controlled, despite calls to fire departments from all the nearby towns. In Durbin's youth, sickness and illness held the dread prospect of complete disablement or sudden death. Both the unlucky and the weak were culled.

Being a magical performer made life even more dangerous.

Take the case of Lester Lake, professionally known as "Marvelo."[1] Lake was one of those magicians who would slide into obscurity, but in his time he knew how to grab a headline and how to scare the bejesus out of a crowd. He used to say that a good subtitle to his magic act would be, "Or why I expect to be confined to a padded cell within the next few years." Lake was a darling of

Lester Lake making flowers grow (ca. 1930). Courtesy Mike Caveney's Egyptian Hall.

the early International Brotherhood of Magicians in the 1920s and 1930s. His act was to be "buried alive" or "burned alive" or, on a good day, both.

"Lake, while in a cataleptic state," a writer for the *New Philadelphia (Ohio) Daily Times* reported, "permitted his assistants to lock him in a casket and bury him in a grave, dug to a depth of six feet in the hillside, and then cover him with several feet of earth. There he remained for a period of twenty-five minutes." He was then dug up and found in fine shape, none the worse for the wear.[2]

Not to be seen as a one-act wonder, later in the day, Lake was burned alive:

Again in the evening, Lake was placed in a metal box where he remained while his assistants built a huge bon fire around the impris-

oned man. For ten minutes wood and oil were heaped and poured on the roaring inferno and then Lake emerged from the casket unhurt despite his experiences. It was one of the greatest exhibitions of magic ever staged in this city.

The members of the IBM were impressed. "Lake is fast becoming a wonderful attraction for parks and fairs and outside shows," one editor, perhaps Durbin himself, wrote in *The Linking Ring*. They hoped Lake would come to the IBM's annual convention in Fort Wayne in 1930. "He is a splendid performer, and we hope to have him at Fort Wayne with us to give the 'Buried Alive,' which was cut out at [the 1929] Lima [convention] because of the rain."[3]

"What about old Lester Lake?" I ask Durbin, who has regained his strength. The headache seems to have passed.

"With magicians it's all fun and games until someone gets hurt," Delbert interrupts. Durbin, who looks a little surprised at the conversation, shakes his head and scowls at Delbert.

"Lester was testing his luck, no doubt about it," Delbert says, not to be deterred.

In Canton, Ohio, in the summer of 1932, Lake's fiery performance went terribly wrong:

He was placed in the metal box around which was heaped excelsior soaked in gasoline. This was ignited, new fuel added and the flames roared about the box. Above the crackling, bystanders heard a pounding and surmised something was wrong. With considerable difficulty they pulled the box from the flames and opened it. Lake was in a semiconscious condition with blood flowing from his nose and mouth and his hands bleeding from pounding against the side of the box.

The heat had expanded the air in the box until the pressure became unbearable. Lake was taken to the emergency hospital at the park and was still there today.[4]

I look over at Durbin. He is nonplussed. "We don't believe in performing these dangerous feats, and magicians would do well to cut them out of their performances."

"Fat chance," Delbert answers under his breath.

"We have had numerous occasions to warn magicians against these dangerous feats," Durbin wrote in *The Linking Ring* after the Lester Lake mishap. "It has not been so very long ago that a magician in Louisville, Ky, was drowned in a large milk can filled with water. All remember the tragic fate of Chung Ling Soo (Billy Robinson) who was shot and killed in a London theatre in performing the catching the bullet stunt. One of our good friends in Canada swallowed about four dozen needles, or rather put them in his mouth and then sneezed, and the surgeons were many hours with the magnets removing them from his mouth and throat.[5]

Danger lurked everywhere for the performing magician. In Quebec in 1936 a magician was stabbed by an excited spectator. "George LaLonde, 28 year old circus performer, was brought to the hospital in serious condition today after being stabbed in the back with his own sword by a spectator who 'couldn't see a woman being cut in two.'" The attacker got away despite efforts by the crowd to stop him.[6]

"Tell me about Billy Robinson."

"I knew Billy Robinson very well," Durbin says. "He was Alexander Herrmann's assistant."

Billy Robinson, the mysterious Chung Ling Soo, did indeed start his career as Alexander Herrmann's assistant. Alexander Herrmann was from the magical Herrmann family of Hanover, Germany. His much older brother, Carl, started the family tradition in magic in Europe in the middle of the nineteenth century, playing for royal patrons such as Emperor Franz Josef I of Austria, King Ludwig of Bavaria, and Queen Isabella II of Spain. Carl came to the United States in 1861 and performed in the East Room of the White House for Lincoln and a group of military officers and cabinet members. When he tried to get Lincoln to shuffle a deck of cards, Lincoln handed them to Simon Cameron, his secretary of war, saying: "This gentleman shuffles the cards for me at present."[7]

The Herrmanns were the first to cast the character of magician as the devil in formal attire. They were slender, smooth with large, dark eyes and continental in manner. Their trademark was their Mephistophelian moustaches and goatees. They always performed in full dress tails. Carl could hurl playing cards to all parts of the house with superb accuracy. He included in his act a demonstration of "second sight" in which he would, while blindfolded, intuit what an assistant in the audience was holding up.

Alexander was twenty-seven years younger than Carl, and he "assumed his mantle" with his own remarkable productions when Carl retired. He became the leading box office attraction of his time. "He loved to do magic and would perform amazing impromptu feats of sleight of hand on the streets, in restaurants and wherever he went," one historian of magic wrote about Alexander. "It was good advertising."

Alexander Herrmann, "Herrmann the Great" (ca. 1890). Courtesy Mike Caveney's Egyptian Hall.

Durbin met Alexander in person in April 1896. He first saw him perform on stage ten years earlier. "I first saw Alexander Herrmann when he played at the New National Theatre in Washington in the winter of 1886–87 while I lived in Washington," Durbin wrote in *The Linking Ring.* "He performed the old time tricks in a manner not equaled by any of his contemporaries. In his hands old tricks were invested with the new charms. To see him walk out on stage was almost worth the price of admission. He looked all the world like Mephisto in Faust. And those wonderful hands—what a study. It seemed like everything his long fingers touched vanished instantly. There was a finesse in his performances you cannot describe in writing."[8]

Durbin admired everything about Herrmann. "Herrmann always stuck to the old school of magic," he wrote, "and always used articles borrowed from the audience, and you can depend upon it that any magician who does this is always remembered when he is gone from a community because the tales of what any magician did with a borrowed half dollar, ring, watch, handkerchief, or anything borrowed from the audience, never lose anything in being retold and are always magnified so that the magician stands out as a real miracle worker."

"You want to know more about Billy Robinson," Durbin says to me, "let me demonstrate."

He leans forward to pull a heavy red velvet curtain closed across the back of the front seat. Delbert and the Doctor disappear behind the curtain as Durbin drags it the length of the seat.

"See you later, kid," Delbert peeps.

The car powers through the countryside just as we come to the Big Crossings of the Youghiogheny in the frosty Pennsylvania night. This triple-span stone arch bridge, made from locally quarried sandstone, will be completely submerged in 1944 when the river was dammed and made into a reservoir lake. The stone bridge was not destroyed and, occasionally, when the water level recedes in the winter or in times of drought, its ghostly remains rise again to the light of day.

Durbin and I are alone.

Suddenly, with a wave of his hand, bright lights outline the edges of the curtain as it comes alive and billows. The brilliance behind the curtain comes up like old-time theater gas footlights; they have a piercing quality. I feel the excitement of a performance coming on.

"When Billy Robinson worked for Herrmann, he was skilled enough to dress up as Herrmann and run a show when Herrmann wanted a night off," Durbin says. "Billy was a skilled metal worker, and he invented many of Herrmann's illusions. He lived with the Herrmanns like family. When Alexander died, his

nephew, Leon, and his widow, Madam Herrmann, continued the Herrmann line and, for a while, Billy stayed with them. But Billy eventually went out on his own, taking up as Chung Ling Soo in England, responding to Europe's demand for Chinese magic."

Durbin wrote that Billy Robinson had perfected the death-defying bullet catching act with Herrmann. "Billy and Alexander Herrmann put on the act where soldiers would shoot bullets at Herrmann, who caught them in his mouth and spit them out on a plate, and Billy reproduced this in his program as Chung Ling Soo." The bullets were marked by someone in the audience and then loaded in rifles and shot at a plate Herrmann or Robinson held over their hearts. Robinson must have performed this trick hundreds of times in his career. It was a staple of his show and became especially popular when he played in England during World War I.[9]

Durbin now leans over and opens the red curtain, and I am temporarily blinded by the glittering gas burners. Delbert and the Doctor are gone, and instead we are looking in at a theater stage.

"It is the night of March 23, 1918," Durbin says, "and this is the stage of the Wood Green Empire Theatre in London."

From one side of the stage Chung (or Billy) emerges resplendent in his Chinese warrior costume. Years ago Robinson had shaved his head and moustache to take on a Chinese Mandarin look. He is mysterious, Eastern, and wildly popular. Along with his wife, little Dot Robinson, they amassed a small fortune playing to capacity houses in England, Australia, and around the world.

Two assistants come from the other side of the stage. They are dressed as soldiers, a common sight in London during the war. Dot takes two bullets down into the audience to have them marked by spectators, and the marked bullets are then put in a cup. The spectators happily take part in this sensational trick.

Dot returns to the stage with the marked bullets, which the soldiers take from the cup and load into the two rifles.

Chung takes two steps forward to center stage. He holds in his hands a plate that he now brings up to his chest as the soldiers raise their rifles and point them at Chung. The suspense begins to make people's blood rush.

During the earlier performance on this Saturday night, the rifles were shot, and a faint click on the plate was heard as women gasped and looked the other way. Cheers erupted when it was seen that Chung had caught the two bullets on the plate, containing the very marks made by the audience members.

In this the second performance—the last act of the night—Chung looks as if he is bracing for a shock. The tension grows unbearable as the soldiers aim their rifles. A drum roll gives the whole affair a grim military air.

Chung Ling Soo (Billy Robinson) (ca. 1910). Courtesy Mike Caveney's
Egyptian Hall.

They fire.

*"My God," Chung spurts as he pitches forward, "I've been shot. Close the
curtain."*

*He falls on his face, the plate crashes, as his stunned assistants stand frozen,
lowering their rifles. The crowd starts to applaud thinking this all part of the
act. Dot Robinson knows better and runs from across stage. "Billy, Billy," she
cries. Blood oozes from both the front and back of his jacket. The theater curtain is used to mop up the blood. The audience quiets, realizing something is*

wrong. The curtains close, and a screen is lowered to show a movie that was scheduled to follow the magic show.

"She rubbed his feet in the ambulance on the way to the hospital because he said they were cold," Durbin says. "He died on Sunday morning, a bullet through the right lung. Fifty-six years old."

More people now fill the stage and frantically buzz around the fallen Chung. Durbin leans forward from our back seat and pulls the curtain in the car closed. "Peace to his ashes."

Was Chung murdered, did he commit suicide, or was it an accident? Magicians have debated these questions since 1918.[10]

An inquest was opened at the Wood Green Town Hall on March 28. The East Middlesex coroner, A. M. M. Forbes, presided. Chung, it was discovered, prepared the rifles before each of his performances, leaving nothing to chance. Dot Robinson testified she knew of no irregularities on the night of the shooting. Between the first and second performance, though, Dot was asked by Billy to come back later because he was talking with a mysterious visitor, a man in uniform. She assumed the visitor was a magician, and she knew that Billy loved talking shop or comparing notes. The two assistants who fired the guns that evening testified they did not know the secret of the trick.

So what happened?

"He was murdered all right," Delbert's voice announces from behind the curtain. "There's no doubt about that."

"I've seen enough," the Doctor says. He opens the curtain and pushes his head through, looking square at us. "I'll see you fellows later," he says disappearing while allowing the curtain to close.

The coroner's jury felt otherwise. "Death by misadventure" was its verdict.

Durbin never seemed to think Billy Robinson was murdered or that he would take his own life. "I knew Billy Robinson very well," Durbin wrote, "and he had learned from Herrmann the art of doing a trick with everything he could put his hands on, and I remember when he came to my house and I took him into my theatre, that it didn't make any difference whether it was cards, dice or a lump of coal, he could do something with it, and he learned this, he told me, from the talented Alexander Herrmann. Now both Herrmann and Billy are gone to the Great Beyond and we have no doubt but that they are the same old pals over there that they were here on earth."

I saw the rifle that fired the fatal shot that night in the Wood Green Empire Theater in a special room in David Copperfield's warehouse home outside Las Vegas when I visited him in 1994. The rifle was displayed on a table beneath framed posters of Chung Ling Soo, Thurston, and Houdini, not far from a treasured group of handwritten letters between Houdini and Harry Kellar.

Durbin, as president of the International Brotherhood of Magicians, constantly warned magicians against taking needless risks for a few extra dollars. In one issue of *The Linking Ring,* for example, he made sure to publicize the untimely deaths of two magicians, both IBM members, killed while performing dangerous stunts.

The first was a South African named Charles Rowan (professionally "Karr the Magician"), who was killed when he was hit by a car after securing himself in a straitjacket and directing the driver of the automobile to speed straight at him, ramping up to forty-five miles per hour from a distance of two hundred yards away.[11]

One pressure-packed moment was left for the escape.

"A ghastly death befell a traveling magician named Karr here this afternoon," the Reuter's news agency reported, "when his oft-repeated stunt of allowing himself to be strapped in a straitjacket and charged by a motorcar failed." According to the account, "the affair took place in front of the Springfontein Town Hall, and a large crowd, including numerous small children, who saw a car dash into Karr and kill him." A local doctor had "begged Karr not to proceed with the performance, but he insisted."

"He seemed to be just a fraction of a second too late in getting out of the way of the oncoming motor car, and he was struck by the right wheel, which almost severed one of his legs."

Karr read a prepared statement before the event, "exonerating the driver of blame in the event of an accident."

The second IBM'er to go down was Gilbert Genestra, a Kentucky wizard, who died a few weeks later in Frankfurt, Kentucky, after being trapped in a barrel of water while performing an escape-artist act.

"One of Genestra's acts," the *Cleveland Plain Dealer* reported, "was to have himself locked in a water barrel after announcing he would extricate himself in two minutes. Last night he failed to emerge after the set time, and stage hands broke open the barrel." Frantic attempts to save Genestra were unsuccessful.

"He appeared to be lifeless, but a physician partially revived him by means of artificial respiration. He was taken to a hospital where efforts to save him proved futile. Before he died he said it was the first time he had failed to free himself."

Durbin took the occasion of this double tragedy to remind magicians of the dangers of certain tricks. "Magic has so many things that are wonderful," he wrote, "they do not require risking of one's life. It seems to us foolish to risk those very dangerous feats which sooner or later result in tragedies like the above. Once before this we wrote in *The Linking Ring* against these dangerous experiments but we presume that those who do not value life are continuing to risk it for a few paltry dollars and a little cheap applause. We have never indulged in these ourselves and we do not advise others to."[12]

Durbin was not a risk-taker in magic. He set up his magic stage with notes on tables to remind him of how to perform a trick or illusion. He would go in a set order from trick to trick, carefully following a prearranged order to his presentation. Everything was thought out in advance.

This same quality, the ability to organize and plan, proved to be the basis for Durbin's quick rise in politics. Organizing people was his gift.

His beginnings in politics came when he left school, because the Doctor had died, and he needed to work to help feed and provide for his family. I found an article in the *Washington Sunday Star* in 1934 that traced the young Durbin's transition from childhood experiments in magic to the working world: "The world of magic with its triumphs and fanfares about that time had to break ground before the unwelcome pronouncements of reality. Young 'Bill' Durbin had to abandon the suave dexterity of the amateur in favor of an apprenticeship as a coremaker in an iron foundry. He wasn't enrolled at the foundry a week before he instigated a new style of 'magic' in that establishment—a reading club of workers who spent a part of the noon lunch daily listening attentively to what Bill read from carefully selected publications."[13]

A local lawyer and judge named Johnson took Durbin into his law office when the iron foundry was temporarily shut down in 1884. The lawyer happened to be the Democratic Party's nominee for mayor of Kenton that year, and he let the eighteen-year-old Durbin run his campaign. "I didn't figure I had much of a chance of being elected," the lawyer later remembered, "and so that may account for the fact that I gave the boy a free rein."

Durbin was in his element. "But I soon discovered," the judge wrote, "he had an amazing genius for organization and propaganda. He had the office swarming with party workers; he wrote statements for me for the newspapers and had them printed without consulting me; he organized meetings and rallies; he would hand me speeches to deliver; he had 'Johnson-for-Mayor' clubs going in every ward. And when I was elected by 45 votes, I and all the other heads readily admitted his brains and tireless energy had done it."[14]

Durbin remembered: "Then I became the Mayor's secretary and began to mix more in politics, and I ran the county campaign in 1885 when I was but nineteen years of age and did so well that the leaders of the Democratic Party secured for me a position in Washington, where I went on July 1, 1886, as a laborer at $620 a year. I was a messenger and carried the bonds from the Loans and Currency Division of the Public Debt to the Register's Office when General W. S. Rosecrans was Register of the Treasury."[15]

Durbin went to Washington when Grover Cleveland was first elected president. Cleveland's election was a rare Democratic victory, and so Durbin's job was a rare plum.

The *Washington Sunday Star* expounded on Durbin's time in Washington: "Later, Mr. Durbin secured a Government job as a laborer in Washington, attended National Law University at nights, and through a Civil Service examination he eventually secured a post as an examiner in the Treasury Department. In the next four years he put himself through law school, took a postgraduate course, aided in support of his mother and sister back in Ohio and saved $1500."[16]

When Durbin returned to Kenton in 1890 he brought a spouse, Mary Danaher of Washington. She had lived around the corner from the house in which Durbin boarded, and they met in a candy store in their neighborhood where she worked. They were married on March 25, the same day he quit his job at the Treasury.

"If everything else fails," he told Mary, "I'll go around exhibiting myself as the only man from Ohio who ever resigned a political job."[17]

Six years later in 1896, when Durbin was thirty, two events helped to define him. The first was his meeting with Herrmann in Findlay, Ohio, in April 1896. Later in the summer, he became chairman of the State Central Committee of the Ohio Democratic Party and met William Jennings Bryan.

"The last time I saw Herrmann," Durbin wrote, "was in 1896 in April of that year. He died in December. I never saw Herrmann to know him before this. At that time he traveled in a railroad car that was built for Mrs. Lillie Langtry, the great actress, who was called the 'Jersey Lily.' It was a beautiful car and I was shown all over by Madam Herrmann, and I saw the bedroom in the car, which was the same one in which Herrmann died in December after that."[18]

Durbin's introduction to Hermann was arranged by a magic dealer from Philadelphia: "I had a letter from the late Tom Yost of Philadelphia, with whom I had dealt, and who made me a great many fine pieces of apparatus. Madam Herrmann introduced me to Herrmann when he came out, after I presented my letter to her, and he received me most kindly. Then he asked to see my hand, and he measured his hand—putting his little finger on my thumb and then having me stretch out my hand so that he could see how far I could span. He was much pleased with my hand, that it would span as far as his."

Herrmann seemed to enjoy the enthusiastic magician from Ohio. Durbin wrote, "I can always remember him saying, 'Well, well, well, now what can you do?' And then, I showed him a few little sleights I could do with coins and right away he began to tell me about a trick which I have used ever since, with a ring."

The two spoke for some time: "He showed me many things and invited me to stay for dinner, but I had another engagement and could not stay. I did go into the drawing room to sit down while he played on the piano. He was not only a magician but a musician, and a good one. That was evidenced by the wonderful music he had in his performance, and let me say right here, that every amateur would do well to have the right kind of music in his performance. There comes a time when we don't want any music at all, but then there are other times when it comes in mighty handy to break a creak or sound, which otherwise might show you up. And then it's mighty nice when you have to go off stage, to have the music playing some beautiful air or waltz and keep that attention of the audience. I learned this long ago and always paid particular attention to the kind of music I had with my performance, and never any of your 'jazz.'"

Durbin always had fond memories of Herrmann and his shows.

"One of the funniest things he did in the show was he borrowed three or four watches and brought someone from the audience up on the stage to help him," Durbin wrote in 1933. "I don't remember exactly how he disposed of the watches, but at any rate, he sat the fellow from the audience in a chair and gave him a pistol in each hand to defend himself with, and then Herrmann brought forward a big pistol, which he fired right at the fellow and instantly, there dropped from the chair, by their chains, three of the watches, which had been borrowed.

"The watches were taken off to the audience and identified by their owners, but one remained lost. After looking around quite a little while, Herrmann would turn the fellow around, his back toward the audience, and there was the lost watch, hooked to his back. This always got great applause."[19]

"I shall never forget," Durbin says to me, "Herrmann's illusion of borrowing a silk hat from someone in the audience. He sent down his colored servant to borrow the hat, and when the servant got back up on the platform, he stumbled and fell, with the hat under him, and he smashed it.

*"Then ensued a quarrel as you never heard, in which Herrmann berated
the poor colored fellow in French, German, and other languages and ended by
kicking him off stage.*

*"Then he motioned to his other assistant to bring in his cannon. Thereupon,
they rolled onto the stage a large cannon, and then Herrmann proceeded to put
the powder in, then took the crumpled hat and tore it all to pieces, stuffed it down
the cannon, and a large cannon ball was rolled in and put in the cannon. And
then the comedy commenced."*

*"The crowd ducked for cover," Delbert says, cringing himself and crouching
behind the wheel, his big ears protruding.*

*"One of the assistants handed Herrmann a gas lighter, but before he touched
off the cannon, he motioned to the galleries and the balconies with his arms. I
can still see them getting out of their seats and moving back, and in the middle
of it all he touched off the cannon, from which a rubber ball went sailing way
up into the gallery.*

*"And there, clear up at the top of the ceiling was the silk hat, hanging, fully
restored. Then Herrmann ran down into the audience, took his pistol, fired at
the ceiling, and down came the hat, which was handed to its owner, with many
thanks."*[20]

When Herrmann died in December 1896, Durbin heard from Billy Robinson that smoking was the cause: "Herrmann was an inveterate cigarette
smoker and he always had his cigarette tray on each side of the stage so that
as he went off, he could get a 'puff' between times. Herrmann died of heart
failure. Billy Robinson always claimed to me that it came from the smoking
of too many cigarettes."[21]

*Taking my hand, Durbin shows me how Herrmann measured the span of
his hand and in the process takes my measure also. "He was a man with a
generous heart," he says of Herrmann, "and was always giving performances
for charity. His great delight was to entertain at hospitals, asylums, and other
places for the sick and afflicted. The day before he passed away was spent in
entertaining crippled children at Rochester, New York. He was at the zenith of
his power when he passed on, and magic lost a wonderful character the like of
which will never be seen again."*

Herrmann was only fifty-two. He started the age of modern magic performances in the United States with his use of large illusions. By 1896, however, a new face was already challenging his place as the preeminent magician of the time. His name was Harry Kellar.

"Will Durbin, who has been in the Treasury Department at Washington
several years," the Kenton newspaper noted in March 1890, "has resigned and

Durbin ca. 1890. Author's collection.

returned to his home. He brought a beautiful wife with him, and will begin the practice of law in this city and reside here permanently."[22] Mary Durbin was fretful about her move to Ohio. She was menaced by visions of a frightening wilderness where wolves roamed and ghostly Indians still attacked settlers.

A year after their move back to Kenton, Francis, my grandfather, was born.

In time, when my mother was born to Francis and Agnes, she would touch the hand of her grandfather, who touched the hand of Alexander Herrmann, who touched the hand of Carl Herrmann, who in his time touched the hand of Lincoln.

In an obscure book, *History of Conjuring and Magic,* published in 1928 by magic historian (and Durbin friend) Henry Ridgely Evans, there is an appendix containing a series of photographs of hands, "Hands of Famous Magicians." I found this book in the rare books collection of the Cleveland Public Library. The hands featured include those of Blackstone, Thurston, "Mysterious" Smith, Cardini, and Durbin.[23]

Durbin's hands are long and slender as opposed to, say, the more meaty hands of Blackstone. But Durbin's photo is different from the others in a disquieting, almost troubling way. The other photos are of hands only. In the Durbin photo, his hands are held palms open to the camera's eye, but his face, shrouded by some sort of fine mesh screen, is visible in the background.

"It is time to meet Mr. Bryan," Durbin says in a commanding voice. I am transfixed by his hands.

"See here," Delbert says trying to divert my attention, "nothing up my sleeve."

"Sixteen-to-one," Durbin sings out, "sixteen-to-one!"

We have reached Fort Necessity. The ghost of General Braddock calls out for his aide, Washington. This night, as every night, he falls again in battle and slips back to his unsettled grave under the National Road.

⇒ 7 ⇐

A CROSS OF GOLD

July 1896

We are passing through an area called the Great Meadows, the widest clear expanse in the Alleghenies. We are just east of Uniontown, Pennsylvania, which lies beyond Laurel Hill and Chestnut Ridge. If we can get over the mountain ahead, it will be a steep dive into Uniontown.

But for now, the road stretches out ahead, and white paint on the base of the utility poles lining the road flicker by, aiding Delbert's night driving.

In 1896 Durbin began his career in national politics with a figure who became known as the Great Commoner. William Jennings Bryan was the white paint on the base of the utility poles along the national road for the Democratic Party, showing the way.

Durbin was a Bryan devotee. Newspapers variously described him as "the first chairman of the William Jennings Bryan campaign for the Presidency in 1896," and "a political figure of the Bryan school."[1]

Durbin's affinity for Bryan seems natural. Bryan was an odd mixture of populist and social conservative, evangelical Protestant, and radical economist. Like Durbin he came from the rural Midwest, where people believed in the inherent goodness of democracy and where many were growing increasingly resentful and suspicious of the well-to-do and the powerful who hoarded the fruits of the labors of workers and farmers.

Durbin was as volatile and irascible as Bryan. They both fought with the intensity and righteousness of religious warriors. Causes sometimes were hard to distinguish from personal grudges. Each could leave friend and foe alike dumbfounded. The message often was the fight and the fight alone.

William Jennings Bryan on the stump (1908). Courtesy Ohio Historical Society.

Tactics aside, Bryan was beloved by his followers and he was nominated three times by his party to run for president of the United States.

Like Moses, Bryan never made it to the promised land, but he brought his people to the border. His influence can be glimpsed in a note Woodrow Wilson wrote to him in 1913 as Wilson was readying himself for his March 4 inauguration. Wilson asked Bryan to be his secretary of state, and pundits predicted that the egos of the two men would clash and not survive long together in an administration.

"How contemptible the efforts of the papers are, the last few days," Wilson wrote from his home in New Jersey, "to make trouble for us and between us,—and how delightful it is—to me, as I hope it is to you—to know, all the while, how perfect an understanding exists between us! It has been to me, since I saw you, a constant source of strength and confidence."[2]

Wilson knew as he wrote these words that he owed much to the pioneering efforts of Bryan. Bryan blazed the trail, built the party, championed "the Democracy," and gathered from across the country loyal followers who "fought the good fight" in the campaigns of 1896, 1900, and 1908 (New York judge Alton B. Parker was the nominee in 1904). Bryan gave form to Progressive ideals and molded the arguments against money, privilege, and "the interests."

"I had nothing in particular to write to you about today," Wilson concluded his handwritten note. "I have written these few lines merely by impulse from the heart."

Impulses from the heart led Durbin into politics. Nothing, however, would come easy as a Democrat in Ohio. The Ohio in which Durbin cut his political teeth was firmly in the grasp of the Republicans. Ohio was a powerful, corrupt state, filled with its share of gutter fighters and warring chieftains. Cincinnati had Boss Cox and Fire Engine Joe Foraker; Cleveland had Marcus Hanna.

Even Warren Harding spawned his "Ohio Gang" with the nefarious Harry Daugherty, his attorney general, and Jess Smith, Daugherty's weasel companion. Bootlegging, illegal distribution of fight films, oil deals, Senate investigations, buying and selling public lands—these were staples of the Harding administration.

Graft was a high art form in Ohio politics. The Democrats of course were no better and could claim no monopoly interest in virtue and morality. The party was in fact quite inept, except in the South, and it was all but shut out in the presidential sweepstakes following the Civil War. Stephen Grover Cleveland of New York was the lone exception before Wilson.[3] Cleveland was the most unlikely of political heroes, a "meteor in the political skies." Two hundred and sixty pounds and bull-necked, he was a prosaic lawyer in Buffalo and a bachelor. He built a steady but fairly unremarkable career until 1882 when he was elected as a reform mayor of Buffalo. One year later, due mainly to political quirks, Cleveland was elected governor of New York, and with the same dumb luck he was elected president of the United States one year later in 1884 when the Republicans, too long in power, fell apart under the leadership of a scandal-ridden candidate, James Blaine of Maine, the arrogant "plumed knight of the Grand Old Party."

The only thing the public knew for sure about Cleveland in 1884 was that he refused to deny the charge that he was the father of an illegitimate child. When the story broke during the campaign, Cleveland wired his managers: "Whatever you say, tell the truth." They did, and although his handlers admitted that Cleveland had had "an illicit affair," they were quick to point out that it was not certain that Cleveland was the father of the child. Others had been involved. Cleveland, they contended, took the honorable course by assuming responsibility. The principle then and now is immutable: in politics, as in magic, there is something to be said for the value of mystery.

Durbin's job as an examiner in the Treasury Department during the first Cleveland administration gave him the opportunity to dive deeply into the money question, which would dominate the national political discussion for the next generation.[4]

He was given a top-secret assignment for the secretary of the Treasury, the famous Daniel Manning. Manning asked Durbin to type up highly confidential handwritten reports from an agent sent to study the money question in Europe. Durbin described his assignment for Manning in a political brochure he drew up for his run for the Senate in 1930:

> Secretary Manning, some months before, had sent a trusted friend to Europe to study the money question. The friend made reports in the form of long, confidential letters to the Department.
>
> Congress began asking Manning for all sorts of information on national and international finances. The confidential letters were a gold mine of information.
>
> "I want these letters typewritten but the work should be done by a tried and true Democrat," said Manning one day to a subordinate.
>
> Bill got the job. It not only educated him on the money question, then coming to the fore as a political issue, but it also brought him to the favorable notice of Secretary Manning.

The United States had long been tied to the gold standard and the conservative view was that a sound money policy required money growth to correspond with an appropriate gold reserve, generally believed to be a surplus in excess of one hundred million dollars. The people most hurt by this restrictive policy were wage earners and the farmers.

There was simply not enough money in circulation to keep pace with their increased production in the factories and the fields. With money scarce, wages and prices were depressed, and farmers in particular had difficulty repaying loans. One solution was to allow the free and unlimited coinage of silver to support an increased volume of currency flow.

By the time Durbin returned to Kenton in 1890, the disparity between the rich and poor in the United States had become so pronounced that the country was threatened with revolution. Although the national wealth exceeded $65 billion, the average family lived on $380 a year.[5] Due to high protective tariffs, most of which had existed since the Civil War, the United States took in more money through the payment of import duties than it could spend. The result was that the United States Treasury had a surplus of gold that burgeoned to the breaking point, making up nearly one-twelfth of the total money in circulation. This meant that money was tied up in the nation's vaults at the expense of the consumer, who had to pay more for duty-laden commodities and artificially protected domestic products. High tariffs, tight money, and the growth of monopolies were choking the average American.

In 1888 Cleveland was defeated for reelection by Benjamin Harrison, an Ohioan by birth and the grandson of William Henry Harrison. Harrison was a senator from Indiana and was described as an uninspiring "frigid little general," who was "utterly wanting in the power to rouse popular enthusiasm." He benefited, however, from Cleveland's self-inflicted wounds. In late 1887 Cleveland, without consulting party leaders, took on the high protective tariff, believing it to be the prime cause of the swelling federal surplus. The Republicans jumped on the issue, and though Cleveland won the popular vote by one hundred thousand votes, Harrison carried the Electoral College, 233–168.[6]

Republicans interpreted their success as a mandate to raise the duties on imports, resulting in the McKinley Tariff Act of 1890, named after the congressman from Ohio. They also set out to spend the excess surplus through the passage of a generous pension law for veterans and their dependents known as the Dependent Pension Act of 1890.[7]

Congress then passed the Sherman Silver Act of 1890, which authorized the Treasury to purchase silver in large quantities and to issue notes, which were redeemable in either gold or silver. Silver was coined at a set price of sixteen ounces to one ounce of gold. Because silver notes were redeemable in gold, holders routinely took their payment in gold. The consequence was a dramatic outflow of gold from the Treasury. The loss of these reserves helped bring about the economic panic of 1893, which threw the country into one of its deepest depressions.

While the depression was in its preliminary stage, Cleveland returned to the White House by defeating the lackluster Harrison in 1892, making Cleveland the only president to serve in two nonconsecutive terms. Within weeks of Cleveland's inauguration, full panic hit, and he struggled to come to terms with it. He argued for the repeal of the Sherman Silver Purchase Act to try to stem the tide of gold rushing out of the Treasury, but his party was deeply divided on the question. The new western states, with their farmers and silver mining interests, pushed for silver, generating the conflict that would set the stage for Bryan, then a congressman from Nebraska.[8]

In Kenton, Durbin had established himself in a law partnership with Phil Crow, "a boyhood chum." With some of the money he saved in Washington, he and Mary built "a little cottage" on the outskirts of Kenton, on Resch Street. The home would be their residence for the rest of their lives, which they remodeled and expanded over the years.[9]

In 1895 Durbin built a little magic theater in the backyard of the house on Resch Street. His brother, Andy Born, hatched the idea for the theater and helped with most of the carpentry. Andy had an ulterior motive for suggesting the magic hall: "My brother and his wife were great dancers and many times they would go to a dance two or three times a week and never get in until early in the morning—but still they went; and so I think there was method in his madness in suggesting the hall, because they thought they could have dances in it—but believe me, they only had one dance and that was when it was first completed."

Meanwhile, Durbin continued to monitor the money question, building on the base of knowledge he acquired when he "studied under it under the Old Masters in the Treasury Department in Washington." Silver became an obsession. Durbin's Senate campaign literature from the 1930 campaign tells the story:

> Down in Congress, William Jennings Bryan of Nebraska, "Silver Dick" Bland of Missouri, John Lentz of Ohio and others were talking themselves hoarse about free silver, while back in Ohio, Bill Durbin, like a John the Baptist, was going everywhere he was invited, telling the rank and file what it was all about.
>
> By 1895, Bill was the Secretary of the Democratic State Silver Committee which had been organized to fight for a free silver delegation from Ohio to the National Convention the following year. . . . This fight brought Bill into contact with many of the big silver leaders of the nation, particularly Bryan, and a bond of friendship was formed between the two that lasted to the day of Bryan's death a few years ago.[10]

As the presidential election of 1896 approached, silver became the main show. Silver was being found and mined in vast quantities in the West, and the glut on the market caused its steady decline in price.[11]

As if to emphasize the undue influence Wall Street maintained over the country, Cleveland was forced to turn to the New York banking house of J. P. Morgan when the Treasury was unable to sell sufficient bonds in return for gold to replenish the government's stock. Morgan held the upper hand in the negotiations and demanded a substantial profit for his agreement. The United States stood helpless before one man from Wall Street.

The seedlings of the New Deal, planted firmly in the Western plains, were being germinated. Bryan and others in his party saw the need for a government-managed currency, relief from the gold standard, governmental pump-priming through spending on public works, a banking system that distributed reserves among leading banks in every state, and a graduated income tax that helped redistribute concentrated wealth.

"Like a John the Baptist, you went out to tell the rank and file about silver?" I say to Durbin.

"I was the chairman of the county central committee, and we were on fire for silver," he says.

"Mr. Durbin sent his partner Phil Crow to Chicago in 1896 as the delegate from his district, and he had one directive," Delbert says, "and that was to vote for the free coinage of silver."

"Come now, let's see what's here," Durbin says, opening the Japanese Box on the floor. A rectangular shaft of light, like sunlight, shines up from the box, and Durbin reaches in. He pulls up the top of a ladder and adjusts it.

"Observe," he says, and he contorts himself around, placing his feet into the box and onto the ladder. He descends, completely disappearing through the car floor. The car, however, continues to speed down the National Road. This is the area where the United States militia marched to put down the Whiskey Rebellion in 1794. I am beginning to think I am under the influence of the corn whiskey that was bootlegged in great quantities around here. Watching a seventy-year-old work his way in the back seat of a car to climb out through the floor is enough to set my head spinning.

"Come on then," I hear Durbin yell from below.

Delbert looks over his shoulder and raises his eyebrows. "I believe I'd be careful if I were you," he says, mock trepidation filling his eyes.

"Thanks for the advice," I respond, and just as I lean over the box a few road stones skip up through the opening into the car and careen off the ceiling and back window, landing on the seat next to me. This does not seem like a good idea by any stretch. "Can you slow down or something?"

"No can do," Delbert says. "What are you, chicken? Go on."

Everything screams that this is not smart, even on a night like tonight, but the challenge has been laid down. I close my eyes and position myself on the top of the ladder, and as I begin to descend the roaring air shoots up around my ankles. It is cold and biting. "Here goes nothing," I say gritting my teeth and hoping no more stones zip by. The transition through the floor of the car into the road that whizzes underneath is heart stopping. I have this sense that I am going to be ground to bits, but instead I literally melt into the asphalt and then through it. The noise is deafening once my head slips just below the speeding car, and my hair is blown, as though I am caught in a whirlwind. And then, suddenly, sunlight and fresh air are all around. Everything comes to a screeching halt, and all I see above me is the ladder. Durbin stands below, dusting himself off, looking much younger. We are on the side of a steep and expansive hillside dotted with row after row of white crosses in green lawns.

The view is commanding; off in the distance is the White House itself. We appear to be standing in the middle of a cemetery. Suddenly Delbert climbs down the ladder and stands next to us.

Beautiful; I guess someone else is driving the car. Delbert shrugs his shoulders and gives Durbin a sheepish grin.

"This is the Arlington National Cemetery," Durbin says. Turning in a semicircle, he points and says, "This is the final resting place of William Jennings Bryan."

In front of us is a headstone the size of large ottoman. On the back of the headstone are inscribed the simple words: "He kept the faith." An enormous tree shades the entire area. "His remains were brought here from Dayton, Tennessee, where he died following the conclusion of the Scopes trial," Delbert says. "You know, the monkey trial," he says flopping one arm over his head in simian imitation, "the one involving the teaching of evolution."

"They laid him away in a forest of flowers," Durbin says, looking trancelike at the headstone.

Bryan was buried in Arlington a week after the Scopes trial in Tennessee. His opponent, Clarence Darrow, had mercilessly grilled Bryan after coaxing him to take the stand on the question of the literal truth of the Bible. Darrow, once a Bryan adherent, said Bryan resembled a "wild animal at bay" on the stand. At the conclusion of the trial, Bryan died in his sleep while taking a noonday nap. Although never definitely determined, it is generally believed he died of a heart attack. Darrow, still raw from the trial, said, "He died of a busted belly."[12]

It was peculiar that Bryan, a renowned pacifist, chose a soldiers' graveyard as his final resting place. Arlington took him because of his service in the Spanish-American War.

"I came upon the widow," a minister from Dayton wrote about his encounter with Mrs. Bryan on the day of Bryan's death.[13] "I found her sitting in her chair, with an occasional tear. She wondered why a great man such as Mr. Bryan had to go now with so much work to be done. I said, 'Mrs. Bryan, workmen die, but their work must go on.' She said, 'But I wonder who will take his place. Where is the man?'"

"Where is the man?" Durbin repeats, reading my thoughts, as we both stand before the burial place. "Where is the man?"

"I tell you, brothers, the time is running out," Delbert adds as he joins us. "From now on, let those having wives act as not having them, those weeping as not weeping, those rejoicing as not rejoicing, those buying as not owning, those using the world as not using it fully. For the world in its present form is passing away."[14]

"Beautiful," Durbin says, expressionless, and then he wheels and motions to both of us to follow. He walks over to Bryan's headstone and shuffles close to the tree nearby. At first I think he is head-bowed in deep respect or prayer, but as I look closer, he seems to have pulled a key or wire from his person, and he appears to be breaking a lock, Houdini-like, of what looks to be a door in the tree.

I don't know whether to expect Lazarus to arise, Bryan to come walking on the water of Galilee with Jesus by his side, or both. I know one thing: I don't want any part of this.

Delbert, sensing my fear and reluctance, puts his strong arm around my shoulder and pushes me toward what is clearly an open door in the tree. Durbin has succeeded in picking the lock, and the door is flung open.

A great cheer arises from within as the door opens in front of me: an unbelievable vista, far above and over the heads of screaming voices and tumult. So surprising is the experience that it sends painful shocks of electricity jolting up and down my spine.

The convention hall!

Banners stream from the high vaulted ceiling; great posters with the likenesses of Jefferson, Jackson, and Tilden drape down the sides of the hall, and they flutter above the people. Flags and bunting are everywhere. Crowds of conventioneers mill about, pushing and shoving; everyone is going in a million different directions; everyone's talking and shouting, hands flying. State standards rise and fall, pumped and jostled around the convention floor. Twenty thousand jam this hot, sweltering hall. We walk onto a balcony, which provides a panoramic view. Delbert shuts the door behind us.[15]

Durbin looks back at me, holding the railing, and he is beaming. He starts to hoot and yell at the crowd. He laughs a great belly laugh as he points to a group

of delegates who have started a fight in the center of the convention floor: swing-
ing wild punches that never land, engaging in wrestling holds where the protago-
nists tumble over, on, and about each other. I can hardly take it all in.

"This," *Durbin roars over the chaotic clatter,* "this is the Chicago Coliseum,
the largest permanent exhibition building in the world. And these are the Democrats of 1896. Look," *he says with a broad sweep of his hand.*

I look for but cannot find any public address system. Not invented yet: no
loud speakers, no microphones. With twenty thousand people crammed into
this massive structure, I cannot comprehend how anyone possibly could be
heard, especially by those like us peering down from the uppermost galleries.
Then I see that most people have fashioned rolled-up newspapers into ear trum-
pets or cones, and they are straining to hear some wildly gesticulating orator.
The delegates, who number about nine hundred, spread out fan-shaped, be-
fore the speaker's platform. This semicircle is about 125 feet deep, with the rest
of the hall filled to capacity with spectators. The people around us are perspir-
ing and flushed but jumping and shouting with excitement.

"There's nothing like a convention," *Durbin howls.* "Nothing like a damn
convention," *he says, slapping Delbert on the back.*

The crowd, with high fever on this hot July day, is shouting down the cur-
rent speaker.

"Organized wealth was sucking the country dry through monopoly prices,
extortionate railroad rates, and tariffs," *Durbin yells at me.* "The farmers were
suffering the most. Seemed like every time they had a bumper year, their prices
sank."

"In God they trusted, in Kansas they busted," *Delbert recites.*[16]

"The country was trying to grow, but there wasn't enough money to support the growth. The money power kept it that way with the gold standard. If
the money supply was tied to one metal like gold, bankers in the East could
count on their loans not being diluted by inflation, but the damn farmers
couldn't get a loan because there wasn't enough money in circulation."

"The country was in a pickle in 1893," *Delbert adds as if he is Durbin's echo.*

"But the money interests didn't want Mr. Bryan," *Durbin says.* "They created the panic to stop silver, but this awakened the public to the potency of
these favored few, and in 1896 the masses of the nation were in a revolutionary
frame of mind."

"Sixteen-to-one!" *Delbert yells at the speaker.* "Free silver!"

The hall is a tumultuous whirlwind.

Young Bryan is about to change everything. Durbin points him out next to
the speaker's stand. Bryan had been traveling the country talking on the silver

issue. He has a large folksy face, a slightly receding hairline, and a black silk bow tie. He is stocky and has an air of confidence, standing with his hands clasped in front, a smile on his lips. He surveys the auditorium, bouncing slowly back and forth on his heels. A simple two-term congressman from Nebraska, he represents the West against the East and all of its privileges. Bryan has developed a reputation as a speaker, with a warm, melodious voice and strong lungs. He enjoys extraordinary vocal carrying power, a distinct advantage in a large hall of this size.

Years after this day, Bryan would say that as he faced this mob, he felt a weakness in the pit of his stomach, "as I always do just before a speech of unusual importance." He wanted to lie down, he said, but this being impossible in the convention, he had gotten a sandwich and a cup of coffee and devoted himself to these as he waited for the debate to begin. "Webster says," Bryan would later write, "that the essentials for a successful speech are eloquence, the subject and the occasion. I felt that I had at least two-thirds of the requirements."[17]

Now was his time. He takes the platform two steps at a time. All around the hall, thousands of people surge to their feet with deafening applause and cheers. The balcony shakes rhythmically as the crowd begins to add foot pounding to the ovation. Bryan stands and waits, thrusting his chin out and nodding as if to say, "just wait." The silver delegates begin to return to their seats, leaning forward in anticipation. The crowd then quickly and remarkably quiets down.

"The excitement of the moment was so intense," Bryan later said, "that I hurried to the platform and began at once. My nervousness left me instantly and I felt as composed as if I had been speaking to a small audience on an unimportant occasion. From the first sentence the audience was with me. My voice reached to the uppermost parts of the hall, which is a great advantage in speaking to an assembly like that."

"Mr. Chairman and gentlemen of the convention," he begins, speaking rapid fire. "I would be presumptuous, indeed, to present myself against the distinguished gentleman to whom you have listened if this were a mere measuring of abilities; but this is not a contest between persons. The humblest citizen in all the land, when clad in the armor of a righteous cause, is stronger than all the hosts of error. I come to speak to you in defense of a cause as holy as the cause of liberty—the cause of humanity."

Bryan has hit the chord, that mystic chord of memory that binds the nation to its past, the cause of liberty, the cause of humanity.

"I shall never forget the scene upon which I looked," Bryan would recall. "I believe it unrivaled in any convention ever held in our country. The audience seemed to rise and sit down as one man. At the close of a sentence it would rise and shout, and when I began upon another sentence, the room was as still as a church. There was inspiration in the faces of the delegates."

His voice now begins to rise to the challenge. He speaks now to those who have argued that gold was essential for business.

"The man who is employed for wages is as much a business man as his employer; the attorney in a country town is as much a business man as the corporation counsel in the great metropolis. The merchant at the crossroads store, the farmer who goes forth in the morning and toils all day, who by application of his brain and muscle to the natural resources of the country creates wealth, is as much a business man as the man who goes upon the board of trade and bets upon the price of grain!

"Ah, my friends, we say not one word against those who live upon the Atlantic coast, but the hardy pioneers who have braved all the dangers of the wilderness, who have made the desert to blossom as the rose—the pioneer way out there [pointing to the West], who rear their children near to Nature's heart, where they can mingle their voices with the voices of the birds—out there where they have erected schoolhouses for the education of their young, churches where they praise their Creator, and cemeteries where rest the ashes of their dead— these people, we say, are as deserving of the consideration of our party as any people in this country. It is for these that we speak. We do not come as aggressors. Our war is not a war of conquest; we are fighting in defense of our homes, our families, and posterity. We have petitioned, and our petitions have been scorned. We have begged, and they have mocked when our calamity came. We beg no longer; we entreat no more; we petition no more. We defy them!"

He had told his wife, Mary, the night before, "I will make the greatest speech of my life tomorrow. . . . I will be at my best."

The delegates erupt. Delbert waves his cap and is now jumping up and down. Durbin gives him a sidelong glance.

"You come to us and tell us that the great cities are in favor of the gold standard; we reply that the great cities rest upon our broad and fertile prairies. Burn down the cities and leave our farms, and your cities will spring up again as if by magic; but destroy our farms and the grass will grow in the streets of every city in the country."

Durbin likes the reference to magic. Nice touch, his expression confirms.

The audience is acting, as Bryan would later say, "like a trained choir." There are farmers in abundance in the crowd, and they were being classed as businessmen. They go berserk with each step of Bryan's argument. Grown men slap coats against seats in front of them, some crying, others standing silently enraptured. Hats fly in the air.

"In fact," Bryan said later, "I thought of a choir as I noted how instantaneously and in unison they responded to each point made."

Now to the conclusion. Can there be any more energy in this crowd?

"If they dare to come out in the open field and defend the gold standard as a good thing, we will fight them to the uttermost. Having behind us the producing masses of this nation and the world, supported by the commercial interests, the laboring interests, and the toilers everywhere, we will answer their demand for a gold standard by saying to them: You shall not press down upon the brow of labor this crown of thorns [here Bryan has raised both his hands to the sides of his head, moving his fingers slowly downward to his temples, as the imaginary thorns dig into his brow and blood trickles down], you shall not [he says, pausing and holding his arms aloft and spread as if on a cross] crucify mankind on this cross of gold!"[18]

Silence. Complete and utter silence. I look at Durbin; tears streak his face. Bryan stands in the position he had assumed, crucified, for five seconds. He lowers his arms slowly to his side, takes two steps back, and begins to walk to his seat. It is only now that the crowd begins to shake and rock.

A madness lets loose, a volcanic eruption—pandemonium! From one end of the convention hall to the other, everything that can be waved or thrown into the air finds flight—handkerchiefs, hats, canes, newspapers. The sounds are frightening; pure emotion finds expression without restraint.

"It all started right here," Durbin says, "the modern Democratic Party was born right here, right now."

"The nomination of William J. Bryan for President by the Democratic Convention in Chicago," the *Kenton Democrat* reported on July 16, 1896, "was hailed with outbursts of enthusiasm by the Democracy of this city. In the evening the Second Regimental Band was secured and an enthusiastic crowd began marching through the streets, shouting for the nominee of the Convention. The DEMOCRAT office was tendered a serenade and W. W. Durbin and D. Flanigan, editor of the paper, made brief remarks." The paper headline read that the impromptu meeting in Kenton was the result of Democrats "jollifying" over the Bryan nomination.[19] "The crowd also visited the home of Judge Johnson, who responded to the call for a speech. W. W. Durbin's home was next visited, and there he made another eloquent speech which raised the enthusiasm to a high pitch."

It was the beginning of the Democratic Party as the refuge of the downtrodden, desperate, and disadvantaged. Out of the stranglehold of tight money emerged a social gospel, deeply rooted in Bryan's religious beliefs and his views on American democracy. In an industrialized, corporate society, Bryan would challenge the privileged to reconcile the nation's democratic traditions with its growing concentration of wealth. If the nation were to remain committed to the principle of majority rule, with the rights of the ordinary people to participate in their government, economic policy had to follow. Legislating to make the well-to-do more prosperous was a hold-up, keeping the country from growing. Legislate to make the masses more prosperous, Democrats began to argue, and their prosperity would find its way through every class.

Somehow, Durbin, a thirty-year-old from a rural county, found himself as the chairman of the State Central Committee during the summer of 1896. "We traveled throughout Ohio in trains with Mr. Bryan," Durbin wrote years later. "We were in the small towns and the large towns. Everywhere there was a crush to hear him and to shake his hand. His voice grew hoarse but he always had some remarks for them. In August, the small towns would turn out 500 people, but by the September, fifty to sixty thousand people came out to hear him in Columbus."

Perhaps in recognition of Durbin's efforts, Bryan visited Durbin's county twice during the campaign. His first trip was to a little hamlet just north of Kenton called Dunkirk. "The train carrying Mr. Bryan reached Dunkirk a few minutes before nine o'clock," the Kenton newspaper noted on August 13, 1896, "and made a few minutes stop. W. W. Durbin, Chairman of the State Central Committee, went to Lima Sunday and came over to Dunkirk on the train with Mr. Bryan. As soon as the train stopped Mr. Durbin appeared on the steps of the car and introduced the distinguished gentleman as the next President of the United States."

A month later, Bryan returned, this time to Durbin's Kenton, to an incredible reception. The city was "in gala attire, almost every home being decorated." Pictures of Bryan were everywhere and the "streets were brilliant with a display of the national colors in every form." The town was filled to capacity. Wagons and buggies lined the public square "as far as the eye could see." At the train depot, six thousand people, "amid the thunder of cannon and uproarious cheering," greeted Bryan and Durbin. They were "escorted to the Reese House for dinner by a throng of which a monarch might well be proud, for 99 per cent of them were sunburnt farmers or sooty, black-clothed mechanics."

In Columbus the crowds swelled to such massive proportions that Bryan had to move from one side of the speaker's platform to the other so that he could address the entire group of people in from all around central Ohio. "It was impossible for all to hear him at once in the Columbus statehouse yard," the newspaper reported, "so he spoke to them in sections from four different sides of the platform erected in front of the Ohio Capitol building."

Durbin escaped from the politics in Columbus to see a magician perform. "I was the chairman of the Democratic State Committee in Ohio," Durbin wrote, "and naturally you would expect me to be at Bryan's meeting. But I heard a magician, Imro Fox, the 'Comedy Conjurer,' was at the Grand The-ater in Columbus, and as I was to be with Bryan for several days, I waited until Bryan's speech started in the statehouse yard, and I slipped away to the theater where Fox had a mighty slim crowd, due to the political meeting. Fox did the money catching in the air, and he created a riot when he got down in the audience, taking the coins off the heads of people and from elsewhere."[20]

"Bryan scared the hell out of the privileged class," Delbert says. "he was the incarnation of demagogy, the apotheosis of riot, destruction, and carnage."

"They called him a 'mouthing, slobbering demagogue whose patriotism was all in his jawbone,'" Durbin says.[21]

"A lot of conservative Democrats left the party," Delbert grins.

Bryan now stands next to us in the gallery. He is, as journalist Ray Stannard Baker described him, "young, tall, powerfully built, clear-eyed, with a mane of black hair which he occasionally thrusts back with his hand." He eventually would lose his hair and grow quite rotund, but in 1896 Bryan was a striking figure of youth and vigor.[22]

Having heard Delbert's comment about the loss of conservative Democrats, Bryan says: "Now, my friends, of course we always hate to lose anybody."[23] Bryan places his hand on Durbin's back. "But of course, if we have to lose anybody, I know of no set of men on earth I would rather lose than those men we have lost. All the people we have lost have been called themselves 'big people.' But there is one great advantage about losing that kind of people, because ev-ery time one of these great big Democrats breaks into the Republican Party, he makes a hole so big that about sixteen little Republicans slip out."

Delbert and Durbin both laugh. All four of us turn away from the human hoard that is the convention and return to the door from which Delbert, Durbin, and I came. Durbin grabs the doorknob and turns back to Bryan.

"We almost did it," he says.

Bryan nods.

"The problem was Hanna, McKinley, and their powerful backers; they bought the election."

"McKinley only carried his home state of Ohio by fifty thousand votes," says Delbert. "A bitter blow for him in his own state, especially considering the work and cost by which he got that much."

"It shows conclusively that, if the threats, frauds, force, and purchase had not been resorted to, Ohio would have gone for Bryan on the merits of the

issue," Durbin sneers. "*I had just $2,700 to spend in Ohio, while the Republicans poured it out of barrels like water.*"[24]

Marcus Hanna, McKinley's manager, in fact raised over $4 million for McKinley's national war chest, an astounding sum given that newspapers in those days sold for a penny.

"The Republican committee had an unlimited amount of funds at its command," the *Kenton Democrat* editorialized at election's end, "and they were used unstintingly. Yet their majority is greatly short of their expectations. The Democratic management of the State campaign was excellent. It could be no better."[25]

Durbin was given much of the credit: "With but little campaign funds to work with, it perfected an excellent organization and did grand work in the State. Mr. Dan McConville, chairman of the executive committee, and W. W. Durbin, chairman of the Central committee, had personal charge of the campaign of the State and have shown themselves to be remarkable organizers, and no better persons could have been chosen for these important places. During a great part of the campaign, Mr. McConville was absent in Chicago, at the head of the National Speakers Bureau, and during his absence, the entire management of the State devolved upon Mr. Durbin, who is known to be a great organizer. The result in the State is a credit to the Democratic State management."

Durbin opens the convention hall door, and we pass through the tree door to Bryan's resting place. The ringing of the convention hall fills my ears as we commence our farewells to Bryan and walk into the sunlight across Arlington's grassy ocean and waves of white crosses to climb the ladder back to the car.

Bryan stands next to the tree. He looks up at us and recites a passage from an immensely popular speech that he gave on the Chautauqua circuit, "The Prince of Peace":

If the Father deigns to touch with divine power the cold and pulseless heart of the buried acorn and to make it burst forth from its prison walls, will He leave neglected in the earth the soul of man, made in the image of the Creator? . . . No, I am sure that He who, notwithstanding His apparent prodigality, created nothing without a purpose, and wasted not a single atom in all His creation, has made provision for a future life in which man's universal longing for immortality will find its realization. I am as sure that we will live again as I am sure that we live today.[26]

"After all," Delbert says to no one in particular, "the plain truth always beats fancy lying."

Bryan nods his agreement and says, cupping his hand to his mouth so we can clearly hear him, "An unbroken chain of life connects the earliest grains of wheat with the wheat that we now sow and reap. There is in the grain of wheat an invisible something which has the power to discard the body that we see, and from the earth and air fashion a new body so much like the old one that we can not tell the one from the other. If this invisible germ of life in the grain of wheat can thus pass unimpaired through three thousand resurrections, I shall not doubt that my soul has the power to clothe itself with a body suited to its new existence when this earthly frame has crumbled into dust."

As we climb back toward the car, I see in the distance, atop of a mausoleum, a marble cross.

Strangely it transforms into smoke and bursts into flames. As I stare, the smoke clears slightly, and I see a gold cross emerging from amid the flames, reflecting the glory and agony of mankind.

➤ 8 ⭠

THE LEVITATION OF PRINCESS KARNAC AND HARRY KELLAR

May 16, 1908

When L. Frank Baum wrote *The Wonderful Wizard of Oz* in 1900, he had in mind a political allegory telling the story of Bryan, McKinley, the Populist movement, and the gold and silver cyclone of 1896.[1]

Oz was the abbreviation for an ounce; the measure used for gold and the sixteen-to-one ratio set with silver. The Wizard of Oz was McKinley, the great and powerful president who ruled by deceiving the people, causing them to believe they lived in an emerald city (with plenty of money) by making them wear green glasses. The Scarecrow was the beleaguered farmer, who for a time, formed an alliance with the Tin Woodman, the urban industrial worker.

Bryan was the Cowardly Lion, full of bluster but ultimately powerless. The group was led to Oz on the yellow brick road, a symbol that represented the gold standard. The Wicked Witch of the East was the power interests of Wall Street and the bankers. She kept the Munchkin people in bondage, "making them slave for her night and day," and cast a spell on the Tin Woodman, causing him to work so hard that he chopped off his arms, legs, and head, which had to be replaced with tin, leaving him a heartless automaton. Dorothy was Everyman, an innocent who was able to see and uncover the truth. She wore silver slippers, not ruby as in the movie, emblematic of the great silver debate.

In the book, the Wizard is unmasked and dethroned, Dorothy returns to Kansas, the Scarecrow rules the City of Emeralds, the Tin Woodman takes control of the East, and the Lion is left to protect all the small animals in the forest. In reality, though, McKinley was reelected in 1900 and Bryan, for a

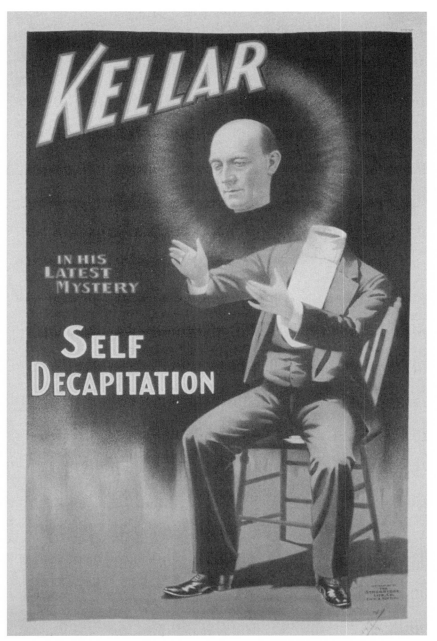

Harry Kellar theater poster. Kellar was the model for the Wizard of Oz. Courtesy CORBIS.

second time the Democrat's nominee, lost, this time by a greater margin than in 1896. In fact the 1896 election was the closest Bryan would ever come to being elected president. McKinley was gunned down a year later by an anarchist assassin in Buffalo, allowing forty-two-year-old Theodore Roosevelt to succeed to the presidency.

Many believe that Frank Baum modeled his wizard on Harry Kellar, a well-known magician in 1900.[2] Bald-headed and with a wrinkled face, Kellar's image was a familiar sight on posters that were plastered on walls and fences around the country in advance of his arrival for a show. Kellar was the first great American-born illusionist who challenged Herrmann for the title of the greatest magician of his time.

"An invisible germ of life in the grain of wheat," Delbert repeats, "now you're talking." The engine huffs as we ascend Laurel Hill.

"What?" Durbin responds.

"Like Mr. Bryan says, there is an invisible germ of life in everything. That's why they love magic. You can't see it, but it's there. Invisible. Can't see nothing. Here one minute, gone the next."

"Hold your enthusiasm, please," Durbin chides Delbert, raising his eyebrows.

"No, sir, I think there's nothing like these here mystery fellows. How do they do it? Like that levitating stuff?"

"I'll levitate you," Durbin replies sharply, "and you won't come back."

"Really," I interject, "levitation? . . . how is it done?"

"Durbin, just wait a year or two and you will see the finest levitation ever put on any stage," a disembodied voice crackles.

I peer over the front seat to see if the Doctor is back. A saddle bag is in the seat, but he is not there. So where is this new voice coming from?

"I remember that Kellar worked on his wonderful levitation for a number of years," Durbin says, in reaction to the voice, apparently unperturbed that the source of the voice cannot be located. "Because when I saw Kellar in Kenton in 1895 he performed what I thought was a very crude form of levitation with a board and wires."

"Ladies and gentlemen, I now introduce to you a mystery of India, the cradle of magic," the spirit voice says. I look again and see a teakettle in the front seat next to the Doctor's saddlebags, and I swear that the voice emanates from it: "During my visit to India six years ago, I had the pleasure to see Koomra Sami. There I saw him cast a spell over a small Hindu boy, possibly some seven or eight years of age. The boy was then placed on some sand and, after certain Hindu incantations, the boy quivered and shook, much after the manner of having convulsions. After a short time the body left the sand and floated up-

ward to a height of, I might say, four or five feet in the air without any visible means of support, defying all known laws of gravitation."[3]

The road signs say we are a few miles from Uniontown, Pennsylvania, but we clearly are in some exotic land.

"Kellar!" Delbert squeals.

Harry Kellar was born in Erie, Pennsylvania, in 1849. His mother died when he was young, and his strict German father apprenticed him to a druggist. There the boy experimented with a concoction of sulfuric acid and soda, causing an explosion that ripped a hole in the drugstore floor. Unable to face his father and stepmother, the ten-year-old Kellar ran away from home.[4]

After a short stay in Cleveland he went to New York City, where he sold newspapers on the street and huddled in a hotel lobby office at night in return for helping the night porter with his sweeping chores. A minister named Hargrove found him in the city and adopted him off the street. Kellar was taken to upstate New York, where it was Hargrove's hope that his new charge would study for the ministry.

Kellar had other ideas.

"He then passed a hoop over the body not once but twice," the voice utters about the Indian levitation, "proving to our entire satisfaction that the boy was in suspension contrary to all known laws of science and mechanics. He then uttered some words of Hindu which, of course, were not understood by me or my assistants. The child then began to slowly descend until he was again upon the sand at the magician's feet."

"Holy cow," Delbert murmurs.

"After a short clapping of hands and slapping the boy's cheeks, which by the way verged on cruelty, the boy slowly opened his eyes and was helped to his feet upon which he seemed scarcely able to stand, but after a short time he walked away apparently none the worse."

Durbin first saw Kellar in Chicago in May 1886.[5] Durbin's boss, Judge Johnson, represented the Chicago and Atlantic Railroad, and Durbin and his pal Phil Crow asked the railroad's general counsel, whom Durbin described as a "big fat fellow," for free passes to Chicago. The railroad counsel wrote down their names, and within a few days the passes arrived in the mail. With eight dollars in their pockets, a fee that Durbin and Crow had earned in one of their first representations, the aspiring lawyers jumped the train for Chicago.

"On the way up," Durbin wrote, "when we had almost reached Chicago, I found a Chicago paper in a seat which gave me the good news that Kellar, the Peerless Magician, was showing at the Grand Opera House, and I said to my pal Crow that that's the place we were going that night." After a supper costing fifteen cents, the two went to the Grand Opera House and, finding most seats priced at two dollars, they purchased twenty-five cent seats in the upper gallery. "This was called the peanut gallery, but in after years, I used to amuse Kellar by reciting to him his whole program he performed, because no one person who paid $2.00 saw more of the show than I did. I can still shut my eyes and detail the performance from beginning to end."

Durbin remembered the Kellar of 1886 as very different looking from his later appearance.[6] "I had read much about him in the newspapers and I was anxious to see what kind of a looking man he was. At that time, Kellar was rather a slim fellow and wore a mustache and had a pretty good head of hair," Durbin wrote in 1927. "I mention this, because in his latter days he was smooth faced and baldheaded and much stouter than he was when I first saw him." Durbin followed Kellar's career. "When I came to Washington in 1886, I saw Kellar in January, 1887, and also in 1888, 1889 and 1890," Durbin wrote in *The Linking Ring*, "but I never got acquainted with him until I moved back to Kenton and when he came there in 1895–1896."[7]

Durbin spent a day with Kellar in 1895 in Durbin's backyard, where they drank beer and talked magic all afternoon. He would always remember Kellar as a great illusionist who had a phenomenal memory, a quick mathematical mind, and a sharp temper.[8]

"I then asked my Hindu friend if he would part with this secret for a sum, which if accepted at the time, I would have been unable to pay," the mysterious voice continues. *"He being a Hindu by birth refused to part with the secret at any price, claiming that should he do so, the cycle within which he was permitted would be broken and he doomed to eternal punishment and much vexation, shame, failures, and accidents during his remaining days upon earth."*

"Sounds a little extreme to me," Delbert quietly blurts out.

"I and my entire company then left this scene, the greatest of all magical mysteries it had ever been my good fortune to witness. My company was mystified, and I was much disappointed at my failure to secure the secret involved in the miracle I had just witnessed."

"A shame," Delbert responds.

"Some three weeks later business called me to Wraitaba, and there again I saw our Hindu friend and his wonderful performance upon the banks of the Ganges, which is the river of mystery, and there I was able to penetrate the much coveted secret after much experimentation, failures and at much cost,

success crowned my efforts, and I now present to you the greatest mystery of all time—the Levitation of Princess Karnac for your approval!"

The car goes quiet. Delbert and I are looking around expecting something miraculous to transpire.

Durbin concentrates on the coin he is walking up and down one of his hands.

After a few minutes, Delbert finally asks, "So, will we see Mr. Kellar tonight or not?"

"Perhaps," Durbin replies and the coin disappears with a turn, "but first we need to stop up here."

We have been on a fast and steep descent into Uniontown. As we enter the town there is a gas station and a nearby hotel. The hotel has a dining room inside that appears to be open.

We pull in to the gas station, and Delbert turns off the engine, shuts down the headlights, gets out, and hands the key to the attendant, saying, "Fill it up."

Durbin opens his door and exits, headed for the hotel dining room. "You can take the country out of the boy . . . hey, come on, son," he calls.

Harry Kellar's introduction to magic came through a magician who billed himself as the "Fakir of Ava." The Fakir was not really from Ava, the old capital of Burma, but was an Englishman named Isaiah Harris Hughes. Kellar saw Hughes perform in a small town near Canandaigua, New York, and would describe the same kind of transcendent moment that Durbin experienced when he saw the circus magician run a dagger through his arm. Kellar told Harry Houdini that when he first saw Hughes he wanted immediately to go on the stage. He became "very restless," buying magic books, practicing, and obsessing about everything to do with magic. He decided then and there that he would leave his benefactor and become a magician.

Kellar could hardly believe his luck when, a few years after first seeing the Fakir of Ava, he read in the newspaper that the Fakir was looking for a boy assistant. Terrified that he would not be chosen, Kellar arrived in an agitated state at the Fakir's home near Buffalo and absentmindedly greeted a black-and-tan dog as he strode up the front stoop to introduce himself to the plump, mustachioed magi. What Kellar did not know was that Hughes considered the dog to be "an excellent judge of character," and he had noticed that the dog wagged his tail in response to Kellar's pat on the head. Dozens of other applicants had come by, but the dog had barked or growled at them all. Kellar, alone happily greeted, got the job.

For six years Kellar traveled with Hughes around New York, Ohio, Illinois, and Michigan, learning the magic art and at times attempting his own shows. He eventually left the Fakir and joined two brothers who performed as successful stage mediums in a time when spiritualism was sweeping the country. The Davenport Brothers developed a program in which they would allow themselves to be bound to seats in a large wooden cabinet called a "spirit cabinet." Once bound, the doors to the cabinet were shut, and instantly queer sounds would start, guitars were strummed, horns blown, bells hurled, and tambourines jingled in the cabinet. The brothers claimed they were in communication with the dead.

Audiences were both alarmed and disgusted. In many instances, riots ensued as spectators cried fraud and attacked the stage. Kellar was hired as an advance agent but soon found the brothers intolerable. "You will do as I tell you," one of them said to Kellar, "and you might as well know you are my servant."[9] Kellar quit and began his own show with another magician from the Davenport troupe, initially featuring a cabinet séance. The two took their show to Cuba in 1873, and then to Mexico. It was the start of Kellar's world travels.

Kellar made his way through South America in 1874 and 1875 and then sailed for England. He was shipwrecked in the Bay of Biscay and lost the money he made in South America and all of his magical apparatus. He played in the Egyptian Hall in London and then took off for the West Indies. He performed in Australia, Capetown, Java, Calcutta, and Shanghai.

By the mid-1880s, Kellar had twice toured the world. In 1884, the year before Durbin first saw him in Chicago, Kellar played before Mark Twain and Edwin Booth in Philadelphia. During the same run in Philadelphia, heavyweight boxer John L. Sullivan was invited from the audience to step inside a spirit cabinet with Kellar, whose hands were bound by Sullivan.

"The next thing I knew," Sullivan told the *Philadelphia Times,* "my overcoat was gone and then I was chucked out of the cabinet onto the stage, as if I had been shot from a cannon. My inside coat was turned inside out, and I lay sprawling on the stage as if someone had tucked me in the jugular." Sullivan said Kellar was "the strongest little man I ever saw."[10]

On Saturday, May 25, 1895, the year Durbin built his little magic theater in his backyard, Kellar came to Kenton to play at the opera house. "He got in early," Durbin wrote, "and I took him all over town. When the curtain rose, Kellar came forward and he looked the part of the magician he was. That bald head was shining and as he began to talk you knew that here was a fellow who knew his business."

The next day, Kellar stayed in town and ended up spending the entire Sunday with Durbin. "Our town had elected a reform mayor just the month before," Durbin would write about the day, "and he locked the whole town up on Sundays, so that when I went to the hotel in the morning, Kellar was cussing around about what a hell of a town we had where a man couldn't even get a glass of beer."

Durbin told Kellar not to worry and invited him to walk to his house. At the time Durbin represented a Columbus brewery, and he was well stocked with beer. "So we went out there about ten o'clock in the morning and I remember that my wife was in Washington and the girl at the house prepared a wonderful dinner for us. During that whole day he related incident after incident in his life and it seemed that there was no place on the globe that he had not visited."

Durbin claimed he had hundreds of letters from Kellar, which were written in "a mighty fine hand" and in which he "used many expressions that only a fellow like Kellar would." Although I saw a similar collection of letters between Harry Houdini and Kellar in David Copperfield's home in Las Vegas, I have never been able to locate the Durbin-Kellar correspondence.

Durbin said Kellar always misspelled his name as "Durban." "He had a fellow with him," Durbin wrote, "when he visited South Africa who stayed down there and became immensely wealthy in the diamond fields, and Kellar always regretted that he had not stayed down there. He always remembered my name because he associated it with 'Durban' which is the capital of Natal in South Africa."[11]

In 1896 Kellar returned to Kenton. "Kellar would have come to Kenton many more times than he did," Durbin wrote, "but he had some mix-up with our opera house manager, and whenever Kellar got mad at a fellow, he quit him for good."

So in 1897, at the height of his fame, Kellar passed up Kenton and entertained instead in nearby Marion, Ohio. "I remember," Durbin wrote, "that I sat right next to Warren G. Harding, who at the time ran the *Marion Star,* but he had no political position of any kind. In 1899, he was elected state senator and then reelected in 1901, and then elected lieutenant governor in 1903, and finally senator in 1914 and president in 1920. Harding liked a magical performance as well as any man I ever knew and always used to come to my performances at Marion, where I played six or eight times."[12]

After the performance, Durbin took Kellar to Harding's office "and they had a long talk together." It was during the show in Marion that Durbin first witnessed Kellar's improved version of his levitation act, which was called "The Levitation of Princess Karnac." Kellar's patter included a story of uncovering the levitation secret in India. "Here is where Kellar shone in his

Egyptian Hall, Kenton, Ohio
Wednesday, January 26, 1921
SPECIAL BENEFIT FOR
The Girl Scouts, Kenton, Ohio

Yours truly
W. W. Durbin

An Evening with

⟨ Durbin ⟩

*...aster of the Black Art in his weird and
...ous exhibition, baffling human belief*

PROGRAM
PART I
...ne's Goldfish
...Dry Problem
...Bonds of Love
...se Checkers
...Mysterious
...ntures of a Handkerchief
...erful Sequence of Colors
...us Fugit
...an Sleighbells
...ry from the Trenches
...isto's Spheres
...Flowers of Simla

PART II
...Dove of Peace
... Lamp
...Enchanted Coins
...nalistic Rings and Rod
...flight of the Rodents
...kull of Ibicus
...Voice from Beyond
8. Crystal Gazing Extraordinary
9. The Fairy Crystal Casket and Balls
The Whole to conclude with
10. The Wonderful Rabbits---a most
marvelous creation

Durbin 1921 magic
program. Note the
devil on his shoulder.
Author's collection.

presentation of these oriental illusions and marvels," Durbin wrote about Kellar's introduction to the levitation act. "Distance lends enchantment to the view and this is very well shown in the great interest people take in feats performed in far off lands, particularly where few have been."

Harding wrote in his *Marion Star* that Durbin's performances in Marion rivaled Kellar's.[13] "About the only time the late President Warren G. Harding occupied the chair of a dramatic critic," a Washington newspaper noted, "he wrote, in the *Marion Star*, of 1896: 'Durbin is not only a friend of the eminent Kellar, but is considered by critics to be greater and he gave a performance that would have graced any temple of amusement in the land.'"

I follow Durbin into the hotel restaurant fully expecting to find Kellar standing there.

No such luck.

The place is filled with ordinary travelers. No one is levitating; there are no flashes of light, just folks drinking coffee and eating homemade pies.

Durbin and Delbert sit in a bench booth and order some food and coffee. I am too revved up to eat, but Delbert offers me some of his dessert when it comes. Delbert pays the check. Pulling his cloth napkin from the front of his shirt, Durbin announces that it's time to get back on our way.

To say that I am disappointed is to put it mildly. We walk out toward the car, and I am stung by the cold. The attendant approaches to give Delbert the keys.

I feel the electricity just as the attendant stops in front of me; he grandly pulls off his cap and makes a slight bow. By his bald head and twinkling blue eyes, I know it is Kellar. Delbert comes over and helps him take off his overcoat, and underneath he is in black tails.

"This way," Kellar says.

We are directed to walk around the road house. In back is a one-story, long structure that is too big to be a garage and not big enough to be a house. The building is covered with white clapboard, and there is a chimney out of which white puffs of smoke gently emerge.

"Ah, yes," Durbin says, picking up the pace and outdistancing the others, "this is my little theater."

Durbin turns and points for us to move up the steps and to enter the hall through matched doors in the front. Our party moves up the stairs into the little magic theater. As I enter behind Durbin and Kellar, I see the audience waiting.

They are all the farmers and townspeople of Kenton of 1895. They have been brought forth for a wonderful evening of "music, mirth and mystery." They are dressed in their Sunday best, in simple black suits, white shirts with starched paper shirt collars. Some of the men are decked out in sartorial splendor with

Outside Egyptian Hall in Durbin's backyard in Kenton. Courtesy Mike Caveney's Egyptian Hall.

detachable collars and cuff links and pocket watches, and there are even a few silk hats and silver-tipped canes.

Cuspidors squat along the aisle walls like solid-brass road markers. The women wear dresses or white shirtwaists with skirts, and most have adorned themselves with elaborate hats, liberally garnished with poufs of lace, ribbons, bouquets of flowers, or foreign bird plumage.

As Kellar and Durbin walk down the center aisle, they are transformed. Both now have full moustaches, and they are in fine evening clothes. The crowd begins to applaud.

The stage is about twenty-four feet across with three stairs up. The curtain evokes the Egyptian theme, with camels and nomads, the pyramids and the Sphinx.

"And the night shall be full of music," Delbert chants from behind me, "and the cares that infest the day shall fold their tents like the Arabs and silently steal away."[14]

The walls down to the wainscot and the ceiling are wallpapered in tan colors with patterned borders. These walls and parts of the slanted ceilings will one day be filled with hundreds of photographs, most autographed, of the masters of magic.

Durbin solicited the pictures in a form letter he mailed to magicians around the country in the 1920s." The theater proper is very prettily decorated," he

Inside Egyptian Hall. Author's collection.

wrote, "and it has been suggested to me that it would be a very nice place to have the pictures of all the celebrities in the magic world. This is the reason I am writing you and I will greatly appreciate an autographed photo from you which I will place in my theater."[15]

The folks in the audience look familiar to me, with hearty, happy faces, their skin brown and creased from the sun. The women all have their hair pulled back. If this is a typical Durbin performance, the audience would have driven their hacks to the Durbin residence to enjoy a supper, costing fifteen cents, on the side lawn. Admission to the show was another twenty-five cents.[16]

Durbin and Kellar take to the stage.

The Doctor, last seen with his head popping behind a curtain in the car, sits expectant in the front row. Delbert and I take the seats on either side of him.

"Hello, boy," the Doctor says to me.

Onstage, Kellar and Durbin face the crowd. The lights drastically dim. The hall is darkened so quickly that an involuntary hush falls over the crowd, and not a whisper is heard as all eyes turn expectantly toward the stage where the footlights are dimmed to a half glow. Gruesome shadows play on the curtain. Kellar and Durbin are gone.

"What mockery can this be?" Delbert says impishly, knowing full well the program to follow.[17]

The tones of a pipe organ begin to play the uplifting music of Tannhaüser. *Slowly, but with increasing volume, an orchestra takes up the theme, and the audience sits entranced in the semidarkness as the stage now gives way to increasing brightness. The curtain arises, the footlights give forth their most brilliant light, and the music changes to "Auld Lang Syne." From out of smoke, Durbin, the master magician, and then Kellar appear, both of them with strong faces and smiles. They simultaneously bow to the crowd and transport them from out of the maze and undefined shadows of the unreal into the cheerful, comfortable brightness of reality.*

Kellar speaks first.

"The art of magic, as recognized by the master minds, which have been given over to years of ingenious invention and daring research in the occult, is not child's play, nor is it a toy for the charlatan or the amateur. It has deeper significance and a broader scope. Only those who have given their lives to the deep droughts of its mysteries are able to present its real and best marvels and to unfold its most weird and seemingly impenetrable mysteries."

"A little learning is a dangerous thing," Delbert whispers to me. "Drink deep or taste not the Pierian Spring."

"Such a man is Durbin," Kellar says as Durbin bows to Kellar in humble acknowledgment. "A man of wonderfully keen and resourceful mind who loves the art for art's sake and with whom it is a passion. The ordinary or vaudeville magic so lightly employed by so many has no charm for him. It is the stronger, deeper, original, and problematic that attracts him. Thirty-three years of untiring exploration amid that which has been most difficult and unfathomable, together with a brilliancy of execution almost startling, a magnetic and compelling personality and genuine artistic finish, have entitled him unquestionably to the degree of Past Master in all that the name implies."

Durbin and Kellar then exchange tricks, much to the delight of all.

On this night, there are no signs of Kellar's legendary temper.[18]

"Kellar had a violent temper," Durbin once wrote, "and if a gimmick didn't work right, he was just as liable to throw it off into the wings, and if anybody was there, they would get it on the head or wherever it hit. Fritz

Bucha, who was one of Kellar's assistants, was hit many times by Kellar in his rage when things didn't go right. Then, of course, Kellar felt sorry about it, and as he knew how Fritz loved shoes, so he would always go and buy him a new pair of shoes. When the season was over, Fritz had about a trunk full of shoes so that he never had to buy any more for years."

Kellar and Durbin finally proceed to climax: the Levitation of Princess Karnac.

A young woman in Hindu costume comes from stage left. Kellar holds out his hands as if he is going to blast her with rays from his fingers. She stops in midstep, hypnotized. She is placed on a couch in the center of a now fully lighted stage.

Wondrously, she begins to rise, slowly upward. I am at the foot of the stage, and I can see no wires. She is suspended six feet in the air.

Two assistants take the couch away and bring Kellar a stepladder. He ascends with a solid hoop, which he passes completely about the floating woman.

Durbin often performed a floating illusion in his shows. One such illusion was called "The Escape from Sing Sing."

A man dressed as a convict was placed in a cage. A curtain on the outside front of the cage was pulled down; instantly the curtain flew back up, and the convict was gone.

The curtain was again pulled down, and the cage was lifted and suspended in midair. Within seconds, the convict would come running down the center aisle through the audience, with all wondering how he got to the back of the building so fast.

The convict was arrested and placed this time in a second cage on the stage. The curtain on this second cage was pulled down, a pistol was fired, the curtain flew up, and the convict was gone again.

Another pistol shot and the curtain on the suspended cage would roll up, and there, suspended in the cage, was the convict.

"A funny thing happened to me in Bellefontaine, Ohio, where we performed this illusion," Durbin wrote.[19] "At the time, I was a member of the Ohio Penitentiary Board and I had real penitentiary clothes for my assistants. Of course, all know that two persons are required for this illusion, and the person who comes running in from the front is not the one who is vanished from the first cage which is afterward suspended in the air.

"So when I first began to perform this illusion, the second person fixed up in the penitentiary suit quickly slipped out the side door to come running in through the audience. But this assistant liked his beer pretty well and he thought he could go into the saloon, which was right next to the Opera House.

"So he went in there and drank the glass of beer and when he came out, he thought he might be a little late, so he began to run. A policeman saw him, a man dressed in penitentiary clothes and running, and so began to chase him. Now, but for the fact there was a crowd in the street, he might have shot at him and killed him.

"The assistant ran up to the Opera House and the policeman chased him right inside. Believe me, this made a most realistic effect. The policeman took in the situation when he saw that this fellow was a part of the show. It was a mighty lucky thing that there were people in the street which caused the policeman not to shoot."

Princess Karnac now begins to return to earth, and the couch is replaced to assure a soft landing. In his same mysterious fashion, Kellar awakens her from the trance. The crowd is buzzing about the illusion. Kellar has crossed the line from mere mortal to some being who touches the mystical.

He walks down from the stage, takes my hand, and says, "Let's go."

Delbert and I get up and walk out with Kellar and Durbin, leaving the Doctor in his seat while the rest of the crowd watches the now empty stage in stiff, stonelike silence. I look around the hall and see that the pictures of the past masters of magic have now found their way to the walls.

Over the exit is a broad, brightly printed multicolored sign that simply says "OTHERS."

Durbin stops at the door, waiting for us to catch up.

We find ourselves back in front of the road house. Kellar stays behind. People walk into and out of the hotel restaurant, taking no notice of us.

Years into the future, after Kellar retired, Durbin had the opportunity to visit him in Los Angeles in the summer of 1920. Durbin was in California along with his family to attend the Democratic National Convention in San Francisco. He could not resist visiting his old friend.[20]

Kellar lived in a richly decorated home located, as Durbin would say, "in the fashionable part of the city," on South Ardmore Road.

"Everything was immaculate," Durbin would later recall, "and that was always the way with Kellar—everything had to be fine to the highest degree."

At the conclusion of the house tour, Durbin and his party were taken into Kellar's living room for a surprise. Kellar showed them a mysterious teakettle and told them that an old uncle who lived with him had asked to be cremated when he died and that his remains be placed in the teakettle.

An obedient Kellar complied with his uncle's request, but, as Kellar warned his visitors, he and his wife had ever since heard noises in the room where the teakettle stood. When they removed the kettle's top, they heard the uncle's voice. "With that," Durbin wrote, "he gave the teakettle to another guest and immediately it recognized him, called his name and told him many things in his life; and then it told me the same and Mrs. Durbin likewise." Durbin remembered: "Of course, I didn't tell Mr. Kellar that I had the same thing in my Egyptian Hall because I didn't want to displease him, and I left him with the belief that he had the only one in America."

"A most beautiful residence in a fine city," Delbert says as we pull away from the hotel and get back on the National Road. The meeting in Los Angeles was the last between Durbin and Kellar. Kellar died a few years later.

Durbin told reporters when he became the register of the Treasury that Kellar had once asked him to become his successor.[21] "The chances are that but few of Mr. Durbin's associates here in Washington even know that he could have been as famous as Kellar, Thurston and Herrmann if he had wished such prominence as a public entertainer," the *Washington Sunday Star* reported. "Kellar, who trained Thurston, asked Mr. Durbin to become his associate and successor long before he broached the subject to Thurston. When the lawyer from Ohio turned 'thumbs down' on the proposition, Kellar interrogated Thurston who, forthwith, accepted the offer. And now Thurston rates in the top flight of magicians."[22]

Historians of magic have long considered the passing of Kellar's mantle to Thurston as one of the art's most important milestones. "The bestowal of Kellar's mantle onto Thurston's shoulders is one of the great events in the history of magic," David Price wrote.[23]

Howard Thurston was born in Columbus, Ohio, in 1870. He was a troubled youth, once being arrested and convicted for picking pockets. Thurston said his interest in magic was traced to a visit by Alexander Herrmann to Columbus. In 1907 Thurston was touring in Australia and the Far East when he heard that Kellar was looking for a successor.

Kellar sold his contracts and his goodwill to Thurston, demanding receipts from shows for ten years and continuing recognition and credit in advertising and printed programs. The two went on tour together for Kellar's farewell performances in the season of 1907–1908. The tour culminated in a grand show in Ford's Opera House in Baltimore on May 16, 1908, when Kellar placed his magical cloak around Thurston's shoulders and bade farewell. Thurston and Durbin became lifelong friends; Thurston even served as a vice president of the International Brotherhood of Magicians during the time Durbin was president.

Although Kellar gave his show to Thurston, his closest friend in magic was Harry Houdini.

In 1917, nine years after Kellar retired, Houdini persuaded him to return to the New York Hippodrome from private life for one last show, a benefit

Howard Thurston and Durbin at the 1930 IBM convention in Ft. Wayne, Indiana.
Courtesy Mike Caveney's Egyptian Hall.

given for families of the first American casualties in the Great War, the men
who died when their ship, the *Antilles,* was torpedoed and sunk by a German U-boat.[24] At the end of the night, an emotional Houdini insisted Kellar
be carried around onstage in a chair and borne off in triumph in his final
public performance. The band struck up "Auld Lang Syne," and six thousand spectators stood on their feet.

As we pull out of Uniontown, our thoughts now turn back to Lima, Ohio,
our destination.

Without speaking, I know Durbin is thinking of his son Francis and Agnes.
We are sobered by the knowledge that time is running out for my grandmother.
Sensing the urgency, Delbert speeds up, and the only sound we hear is the roar
of the engine.

9

WOODROW WILSON: "DESPICABLE, LOUSY, AND CONTEMPTIBLE"

July 2, 1912

Compared to the rather steep descent into Uniontown, we are now on fairly flat ground, yet still in the mountains. The moon illuminates the lightly rolling hills as we make our way toward Brownsville. We are in the Monongahela River Valley. We will cross the great river on the other side of Brownsville.

"I am sorry that it was impossible to have a word with you last Wednesday, but I could not expect it under the circumstances."

Durbin looks at me, but he is clearly having a conversation with someone else. His vacant look worries me. He is an automaton. Maybe he is having digestion problems from our stop in Uniontown.

"Just to give you an idea of where the people stand," he recites, "I will give you the straw vote that was taken on three different trains last Thursday and Friday and on Monday of this week. I printed up several thousand ballots like this one," he says, pulling a ballot from his suit coat, "so that every person who received one could make his own choice for president. These I gave to a friend of mine who is a reliable man and I instructed him to be very careful in taking the poll to allow every person to mark his own ballot and to see that they were accurately counted."

"How did it come out?" Delbert responds, smiling at what he obviously considers tomfoolery, and this reassures me.

"On the train from Columbus to Springfield," Durbin continues in serious-ness, "train number 33, the vote was, Wilson, twenty-four; Taft, six; Roosevelt, nine; and Debs, six."

"Sounds good," I say glancing back at Delbert in the mirror, hoping to join the game.

"On the Big Four train from Cleveland to Columbus, the vote was as fol-lows, Wilson, thirty-one; Taft, six; Roosevelt, nine; Debs, two."

"I detect a trend," says Delbert.

"On Monday I went to Columbus on the Ohio Central from Kenton and helped to count the vote. It was, Wilson, twenty-one; Taft, eleven; Roosevelt, seven; Chafin, one; Debs, three. This last poll was in a Republican community because the district through which we passed is strongly Republican."

"It's going to be our year, all right," Delbert pipes up.

"I wrote you before," Durbin says, now looking directly at me, "that Taft would run third in Ohio, and I am still of that opinion. The only elements we have to look after are the foreign vote and the Catholic vote."

"I am impressed," I say, and Durbin looks at me above his glasses, eyebrows raised.

"Governor," Durbin implores me, "I think it imperative you come and speak in Ohio. In the pre-convention fight I tried to impress upon you and also upon Mr. McCombs that if you could come to Ohio for a few speeches, we would have no difficulty whatever in carrying the state for you. If you make half a dozen speeches, one of them should be made in Ohio."[1]

This monkey business obviously has taken a strange turn; Durbin thinks I am Woodrow Wilson.

"All along I had the notion that Governor Wilson here would not swap horses while crossing the stream, and he will do well not to mix in any of the reaction-aries in his administration," Durbin says leaning forward to Delbert.

"If we are to remain a progressive party, it must be by putting progressives on guard," Delbert responds by rote.

"That's right, that's right," Durbin says, sitting back in his seat.

"Putting progressives on guard" was the battle cry of Durbin in early 1913 after Wilson won the presidency and was organizing his administra-tion. Durbin's letters, still maintained in the Woodrow Wilson Papers in the Library of Congress, speak urgently of patronage and of the imperative to reward the party faithful.

"Frankly," he wrote to Joseph Tumulty, Wilson's private secretary, "this matter of patronage has no charm for me but at the same time if we are to remain a progressive party it must be by putting Progressives on guard and not by appointing those over whose dead political bodies we had to win our victory."[2]

"Remember," Durbin reminded Tumulty, "this is not the last battle and we will need all our good friends to fight for the cause. Many of them, in fact most of them, are not seeking positions but they do not want the reac-

Durbin in 1912. Author's collection.

tionary element of the party recognized when it comes to the distribution of the loaves and fishes."

A battle-hardened veteran of several national political campaigns by 1912, Durbin's letters to Wilson and Tumulty took on an almost desperate tone, pleading for the spoils of victory to go to the true believers. Durbin understood that nothing killed a politician's chance for future success in office quicker than the abandonment of his base.

"Just now," Durbin wrote, "the fellows who fought Wilson the hardest and who were the most pronounced reactionaries are the most persistent in their application for office."

Durbin had reason to be uncertain of Wilson's course when it came to patronage. Wilson was not an easy man to figure out. Even he recognized his own spare, remote, and authoritative personality. Born in Staunton, Virginia, in 1856, the son of a Presbyterian minister and a sickly mother, the baby "Tommy" Wilson and his family moved to Augusta, Georgia, in 1857, and his earliest memory was standing in the gateway to his father's church when he was four years old hearing about the coming Civil War.[3]

"I heard someone pass and say that Mr. Lincoln was elected and there was to be war," Wilson remembered. "Catching the intense tone of his excited voice, I remember running to ask my father what it meant."

Wilson saw firsthand in his formative years the horrors of the war. His father used his church as a hospital for wounded soldiers and the churchyard as a stockade for Union prisoners. A fiery proponent of the Southern cause, Wilson grew up under his strict and scholarly direction. His father had caustic wit and his mother a stubborn Southern reserve. He became a meditative adult, subject to frequent bouts of nervous illnesses. But he was rigorous in his thinking and judgments, as a student, a professor of government, and later president of Princeton.[4]

"The old kink in me is still there," Wilson wrote a fortnight after his inauguration. "Everything is persistently *impersonal*. I am administering a great office,—no doubt the greatest in the world,—but I do not seem to be identified with it: it is not me, and I am not it. I am only a commissioner, in charge of its apparatus, living in its offices, and taking upon myself its functions. This impersonality of my life is a very odd thing, and perhaps it robs it of intensity, as it certainly does of pride and self-consciousness (and, maybe, of enjoyment) but at least it prevents me from becoming a fool, and thinking myself *It!*"[5]

While not thinking himself "it," Wilson's biggest problem was his unbending personality. He was obstinate and uncompromising. These qualities would one day sink the fight for the Versailles Treaty and the covenant for the League of Nations. His battles with Henry Cabot Lodge, his intractable view of his mission, led to his defeat in the Senate and probably caused a stroke as he traveled across the Great Plains in a train in 1919 as he took his case on the treaty directly to the people. Wilson's personality caused his enemies to hate him. Lodge called him "shifty." Theodore Roosevelt referred to Wilson as "that old lady in the White House" and "the schoolmaster."[6]

When a delegation of senators came to visit him in the White House after his stroke (to see if he was fit for office), Republican Senator Albert Fall of New Mexico (who would be one of the lead figures in the Teapot Dome scandal) said: "We have all been praying for you, Mr. President."[7]

"Which way, Senator?" Wilson asked dryly.

As he embarked on his first term in the spring of 1913, however, little was known about him, and it was only beginning to become clear that he was intent on being his own man and keeping his own counsel. He canceled the traditional inaugural ball, much to the dismay of commercial Washington. No president had objected to the ball since Franklin Pierce. He even declined honorary membership in the Chevy Chase Country Club.[8]

And the day after his swearing-in, his secretary, Tumulty, declared, horror of horrors, that Wilson would decline to see applicants for office in person "except when he himself invites the interview." Tumulty announced that it was Wilson's intention to seek only the "best men" for appointments to office. Durbin and other party regulars were alarmed. Albert Sidney Burleson was one such Democrat. A Texas congressman who had served eight terms, Burleson was given the job of postmaster general. With 56,000 local postmaster appointments to be made, his office was most closely associated with the dispensation of patronage. But when Wilson told Burleson that he would only appoint forward-looking men, after satisfying himself they were honest and capable, Burleson became despondent.[9]

"When I heard that it nearly paralyzed me," Burleson said. "I never felt more depressed in my life. I knew it meant ruination for him. These little offices don't amount to anything. They are inconsequential. It doesn't amount to a damn who is postmaster in Paducah, Kentucky. But these little offices mean a great deal to senators and representatives in Congress."

And they meant something to politicos like Durbin.

Durbin obtained his prominence in Ohio politics by carefully tending to his Democratic flock. He and his friends turned Ohio away from the powerful Republican machine, starting in 1905 with the election of John M. Pattison over the Republican governor Myron T. Herrick (who later became the ambassador to France and met Lindbergh at the conclusion of his historic transatlantic flight to Paris).

The rise of the Democrats in Ohio was chronicled by Durbin's friend, Harvey Garber, in a letter that I found in the FDR library in which Garber wrote to Roosevelt recommending Durbin for appointment in the administration.

"Durbin has given many years to the Democratic cause in Ohio," Garber wrote. "He and I together organized this State against Mark Hanna, Herrick and other wealthy Republicans when it was a foregone conclusion that an Ohio Republican majority would be 100,00 and up." Democrats, Garber pointed out, went on to win the governor's seat in Ohio in 1905, 1908, 1910, 1912, 1916, 1918, 1922, 1924, 1926, 1930, and 1932. "Thus," Garber proudly declared, "only three Republican Governors were elected in a period of twenty-seven years."

During this time Durbin would run for state office, his only attempt at winning a state job. He lost a bid to become auditor of the state in 1908, the year Ohioan William Howard Taft crushed Bryan's last attempt at the presidency. But the Democrats were back in the White House in 1913 for the first time in sixteen years and only the second time since the Buchanan administration. The news that Wilson would hold himself above it all created panic.

So just ten days after the inauguration, Durbin went to Washington to see Wilson, who agreed to meet him in the White House. "To reinforce [Ohio's] Senator Pomerene's demand for Ohio's proportion of the good places at the disposal of the Wilson administration, W. W. Durbin of Kenton came to Washington today," a newspaper reported on March 15, 1913. "As one of the recognized Wilson leaders, it is thought he will be able to materially assist the senator in placing some of the Ohio Democratic leaders."[10]

Before meeting with Wilson, Durbin called on his old friend William Jennings Bryan, Wilson's newly nominated secretary of state. The papers reported that Bryan offered Durbin a top job in the State Department, and Durbin turned it down. "Durbin thanked his old friend, but declared that Ohio was good enough for him, and that he had no ambition to come to Washington in any capacity."[11]

The papers also reported that Burleson had offered Durbin the post of first assistant postmaster general, which he also declined.[12] Durbin in fact was overwhelmed with work at the Scioto Sign Company in Kenton, where he was the general manager. In 1902 he had given up his law practice to become manager of the sign company. Scioto Sign became a major manufacturing concern in Kenton, making signs and automobile license plates that were distributed across the United States and Canada. Durbin and his partner, Bill Finley, used their political contacts around the country to help build up the license plate business.

Durbin wrote Tumulty that he had spent so much time in 1912 in both the preconvention and general election campaigns for Wilson that it was time for him to return his focus to business. "I have been so busy in my business that I have not had time to give much time to political affairs." Besides, his partner Finley was taking his turn as the chairman of the Democratic State

Executive Committee in Ohio. Finley, according to Durbin, was "busy at Columbus helping Gov. Cox carry out his progressive program and when they get through Ohio is going to lead all states in progressive legislation."[13]

Durbin therefore was left to run the growing sign company. "Business has started out so well this year that I am simply swamped with orders and have nothing to do but work," Durbin wrote.

On March 15, however, Durbin met Wilson in the White House. "'Put no one on guard excepting progressives,' was the substance of the suggestions W. W. Durbin of Kenton, O., made to the President and Senator Pomerene today in discussing political appointments for Ohio," the *Cleveland Plain Dealer* reported. "Durbin called at the White House this forenoon and held a conference with Senator Pomerene this afternoon."[14]

How did it come to be that Wilson invited Durbin to the White House when Wilson had so recently declared his hostility to meeting with office seekers?

Answers to this and other questions about Durbin's relationship with Wilson are found in a series of letters between Durbin and Ray Stannard Baker. Baker, the well-known "muckraking" journalist from *McClure's* magazine and Wilson's press spokesman during the Paris peace talks, was hand-picked by Wilson and his wife, Edith, to write the story of Wilson's life as his official biographer. After Wilson's death, Baker, with the help of Edith Wilson, began collecting stories and personal recollections of politicians from around the country to assist in compiling his volumes on Wilson. When Durbin wrote to Edith Wilson in March 1926 that he had letters from Wilson and further information about the campaigns of 1912 and 1916, she sent Durbin's letter along to Baker for response.[15]

Baker wrote back immediately, saying he had received Durbin's letter from Mrs. Wilson. "I am much interested, and would be glad if you could give me further impressions of Mr. Wilson, either as a result of personal contact, or concerning the campaign of 1912. I am anxious to make as clear a picture as possible of those important years."

This began a marvelous correspondence between Durbin and Baker, which I found in the Library of Congress's collection of the Ray Stannard Baker Papers, an adjunct to the Woodrow Wilson Papers. None of the original letters, or any copies, survive in my meager family records, including the original Wilson letters.[16]

"I just finished reading your last two volumes on the *Life of Woodrow Wilson* and it reminds me that I let you have a number of letters from Mr. Wilson to me which I would be very much glad to have you return to me because I would not want to lose them for anything," Durbin wrote in 1931, after Baker published his first few volumes on Wilson. "Since my letters related only to matters which appear in these volumes will you kindly return them to me for which accept my thanks in advance."[17]

Baker penned a note to the bottom of the letter to his secretary: "Will you please write Mr. Durbin that I am in Ariz.[ona] and return his letters. Thank him! RSB." Although there is a transmittal letter written in January 1932 purporting to return the original Wilson letters to Durbin from Baker's secretary, the package evidently never made it to Durbin.[18] In 1935 Durbin again wrote Baker asking for the return of his Wilson letters. "I am anxious to get these back," Durbin wrote. "I was promised that they would be returned and while I know it is some trouble to run through your papers yet you can understand that I place much value on these papers and since they are of no value to you, I hope you will send them back to me."[19]

Baker responded that his secretary had returned the letters in 1932. Unfortunately the letters have been lost to history.[20]

"Governor," Durbin says to me, "you remember, don't you, that it was in December 1911 that we first met? I came to Trenton to meet you, and Mr. Alexander introduced us, and we went to your executive office and had a long talk. Mr. Tumulty joined us for lunch together. Do you recall?"[21]

"Delbert? . . . what do I say? . . ."

"Say, sure, you remember."

"Will," a new voice interjects. A small display of fireworks in the front seat next to Delbert results in a woman with a dark complexion and wiry hair sitting next to Delbert. She smoothes her voluminous hair and puts out an errant spark from the fireworks. She is compact and diminutive but looks like Lady Liberty to me, with a full angular face, a small bulb nose, and intense eyes.

"Tell him about how it all started," she says.

"Eliza?" Durbin says a little startled.

"Miss Durbin," Delbert declares, "good to see you."

"Mr. Delbert," the woman responds politely.

This must be Eliza Durbin, the younger sister of Durbin and my great-aunt. She was a schoolteacher in Kenton, never married, but was recognized as the town laureate, a published poet who provided verse for major civic celebrations. She was deeply involved in Democratic politics and her brother's career.

"We had been followers of Mr. Bryan," Eliza starts, not really intending to give her brother the chance to tell the story, "and although we no longer accept his leadership, we still honor him for his stand along progressive lines."[22]

"Here we go," Delbert blurts out.

"My brother had been his ardent supporter, so when he asked Mr. Bryan his views on a candidate in 1911, Mr. Bryan said he favored any progressive man, refusing to become a candidate in Ohio as Democrats asked him to do, giving as one reason the fact that he thought the party had honored him enough."

"After three losses, it starts to sink in," Delbert cracks, which causes both Durbin and Eliza to stop and look at him. He shrugs his shoulders and continues driving.

"Bryan had a leaning toward Governor Wilson, but someone told him there were certain statements in his writings that were not in accord with our Ohio ideas of a progressive."

"No offense," Delbert says to me with a wink.

"So Mr. Bryan asked my brother to get a copy of Mr. Wilson's books and look into the matter."

Durbin nods. It is all coming back.

"You will smile to learn that, there being no copy of Mr. Wilson's works in our little burg, I, being a schoolteacher, sent off to New York and had a friend send me some of his books. I went through and picked out all the statements that seemed to go across the progressive grain, and my brother took it to Mr. Bryan, who was going through the state on a lecture tour. The list of statements made up two typewritten pages. Mr. Bryan read them and said they did not argue well for you as a candidate."

"Right," Durbin remembers it just so.

"But at the end of our talk Mr. Bryan said, 'With all that against him as a progressive, I still believe he is a progressive Democrat.'"

"I am giving you a little political history of the fight which took place in Ohio in 1912," Durbin wrote to Ray Stannard Baker in 1926 at the start of their correspondence, "which resulted in taking away nineteen delegates from Governor Harmon and giving them to Governor Wilson, and which, in my opinion, was the thing that turned the tide in the State Conventions at Primaries which followed Ohio, and which was the key to the situation at Baltimore."[23]

Judson Harmon was Ohio's Democratic governor in 1911. He was a balding, white-mustachioed former Cincinnati attorney and judge; Grover Cleveland had picked him as his attorney general. Harmon won renown for his prosecution of antitrust suits and as the receiver for several railroads. He was a Democrat of high morals, claiming that individuals should be indicted and prosecuted for corporate wrongs. "The evils with which we are now confronted," he declared in a famous letter, "are corporate in name but individual in fact. Guilt is always personal."[24]

Harmon was first elected governor in 1908, the year Durbin barely lost the state auditor's race. He then beat the Republican Lieutenant Governor

Warren G. Harding in 1910 by over 100,000 votes, setting up his second term. He built an admirable record of efficient government and by 1912 was a leading contender for the Democratic nomination for president.

Although Harmon appointed Durbin to the penitentiary board, Durbin became disenchanted with him.[25] Harmon was conservative in temperament, and he violated the fundamental political principle of survival: he did not think it appropriate to show favoritism in his appointments. He also opposed many of the popular progressive reforms, such as the initiative and referendum, which he foolishly derided in an address to the Ohio Constitutional Convention in February 1912 (where Teddy Roosevelt and William Jennings Bryan also spoke).

Durbin and his friend Garber decided to undercut Harmon in his quest for the presidency. Not surprisingly, the heart of the dispute came down to patronage. "So strictly did [Harmon] apply the merit principle in making appointments that he incurred the wrath of Harvey Garber, who broke with the Governor over control of party patronage," one Ohio historian wrote.[26] Garber and Durbin formed the Ohio Progressive League and threw their support to Wilson. "Even though their hostility to the Governor arose over narrow, selfish points of patronage, and their progressivism was suspect, they proved an important force in shifting party control from conservatives to sincere reformers," the scholar concluded.[27]

"Along in 1911," Durbin says to Delbert, "a number of the progressive Democrats of Ohio realized that Judson Harmon was the candidate of the interests in Wall Street, and we determined to make a fight in Ohio to take away the delegation from him if possible.[28]

"With that end in view, Mr. Harvey C. Garber, and myself conferred, and we got in touch with Mr. Harry Alexander, who then ran the Trenton True American, *and also with Mr. McCombs, who was in charge of Mr. Wilson's Bureau in New York City. I went to Washington, where I had an interview with Champ Clark, after which I was firmly convinced that he and Harmon were in a compact to work with each other."*

Champ Clark was a Missouri congressman who, like Wilson and Harmon, emerged in 1911 as one of the "new Democratic" leaders who were said to be remaking the party. Clark became Speaker of the House of Representatives and rose as unexpectedly as Wilson did to the status of presidential candidate. Missouri was the first state in the Democratic primaries, so Clark declared his candidacy early. Charges flew that Clark was in fact a "stalking horse" for Harmon and that Clark's delegates would vote for Harmon at the Democratic convention in Baltimore in 1912. Durbin came to this conclusion.

"When events shaped themselves that Clark was found to be in collusion with the Harmon forces in Ohio," Eliza adds, keeping her gaze on me, "thus removing the obligation to keep from taking sides against a progressive, Mr. Bryan wrote my brother, 'We must win with Wilson,' and the entire strength in Ohio was thrown to Wilson."[29]

The wild card for the Democratic Party, as it had been since 1896, was Bryan.

"At the time, the Progressive Democrats of Ohio had not yet determined upon whom they would center as against Harmon,"[30] Durbin wrote to Ray Baker. "Garber and I had been the old Bryan leaders in the state, and I having been Chairman of the State Committee in 1896 when Bryan made his first campaign, and a follower of his ever since, and Garber, who was Democratic National Committeeman at that time, were opposed to Governor Harmon, and we had an interview with Mr. Bryan who came to Columbus in the summer of 1911 to address the picnic of the Jefferson Club. Mr. Garber and I went with Mr. Bryan out to Mr. Garber's house and had a long talk with him, and at that time Mr. Bryan had not decided who he would support, but we were all agreed that Harmon would not do, and Bryan agreed to come into the state and fight Harmon if Harmon filed in Bryan's state of Nebraska."

"Thus are political alliances made," Eliza says, "thus are the greatest political questions determined. It always begins with a bad feeling about somebody."

"Mr. Durbin, this is most interesting to me," Delbert says, taking on the personage of Ray Stannard Baker, "do you mind if I take notes?"

"Not while you're driving," I mutter under my breath.

"Oh, my," Eliza exclaims. With that, she vanishes. Something clearly frightened her.

"Not at all," Durbin replies to Delbert. He is in focus; it is as if he were reliving those innocent years of 1911 and 1912. Wilson could not have seen in 1911 what was coming—the war, the meltdown of the civilized Western world. Wilson was hardly even wet in politics, having served just two years as governor of New Jersey by 1912. Nor could he foresee that his wife, Ellen, the love of his life, would die in the White House just as the war broke out in Europe.

"After leaving Mr. Clark, I got in touch with Harry Alexander and then went over to New York and saw Mr. McCombs on Sunday, and arranged to meet Governor Wilson at Trenton on Monday," Durbin wrote Ray Baker. "I went down to Trenton and Governor Wilson got on the train at Princeton and I did not see him and did not meet him until I got off the train and was introduced to him by Mr. Alexander who met me. We went up to the executive offices and had a long talk, at which time I met Mr. Tumulty, his private secretary, and at noon we all had lunch together—Governor Wilson, Tumulty, Alexander and myself."[31]

I wonder if Durbin brought some pocket tricks with him; a little magic to break the ice. Durbin liked what he saw of Wilson in their first meeting: "At that meeting I detailed to Governor Wilson what our plan was in Ohio. Garber and I arranged to form the Progressive Democratic League, which should endorse him for President and make the fight for him in Ohio. Without being boastful, I think I impressed Mr. Wilson more that day than anyone had who had been to see him for sometime because Mr. Alexander told me afterwards that Mr. Wilson said I had given him more encouragement than he had received in a long while."

"Is that true, Governor?" Delbert asks me, playing the game.

Durbin looks at me.

"Ah, yes, Mr. Baker," I respond to Delbert. Durbin is satisfied with my response, and Delbert nods his head in agreement.

"Following this I came back to Ohio and on January 2, 1912," Durbin wrote, "we organized the Progressive Democratic League, and we proceeded to distribute over this country no less than one hundred and fifty thousand of the circular which I wrote—'Why a Progressive Democrat should be Nominated for President.' We not only circulated this in Ohio, but through Mr. Garber's large acquaintance in the United States, we helped much in many states in the Union."

Delbert throws some newspaper clippings to me.

"Special to the Plain Dealer," *the top article reads, "Marysville, O., Jan. 3— At a special meeting of the Union County Democratic executive committee held in Marysville tonight, the action taken in Columbus by progressive Democrats to injure Gov. Harmon's candidacy for the presidency was condemned by strong resolutions unanimously adopted. The resolutions condemn William W. Durbin of the eighth congressional district as one of the instigators of the movement. The committee declares Durbin does not represent the party in any way and his action at Columbus is repugnant."[32]*

Another newspaper article attached to the first has underlining, highlighting a quote from a Durbin opponent: "To strike Harmon down because he will not promise everybody everything is a damnable outrage."[33]

Durbin encouraged Wilson to come to Ohio in February to attend Ohio's state constitutional convention. Wilson declined. "I asked him to come to Ohio to address the Convention in favor of the Initiative and Referendum, and while Wilson was strongly in favor of it, yet he was a little chary about coming into the State of Harmon to make a speech of this kind."[34] Durbin felt it was a missed opportunity. "Had Wilson come to Ohio to make a speech before the Constitutional Convention, he would have captured them all because he had that faculty despite the fact that he was accounted as an impersonal man."[35]

Meanwhile, Champ Clark turned out to be much more than a "stalking horse" for Harmon. In the spring of 1912 Clark racked up one primary win after another. Wilson's campaign seemed to be collapsing. Durbin and his Progressive League received a scant $3,500 from Wilson's national campaign.

"I don't know where they got the money," Durbin wrote Baker about the money he received from the Wilson forces. "In fact, I didn't ask them. Except, I remember McCombs told me that there were a lot of old Princeton boys who were glad to put up some money to help Mr. Wilson out."[36]

Then in March, Bryan, seeing the Clark bandwagon and recognizing he had no chance at a fourth run, formally endorsed Wilson in the Ohio primaries, which were to be held in May, this being the first election in which delegates to the national convention were selected by direct vote in a primary. Bryan's support for Wilson had been lukewarm at best, and their relationship had been severely tested in January when Wilson's enemies published a 1907 letter Wilson wrote to a Kansas railroad executive criticizing Bryan. "Would that we could do something at once dignified and effective to knock Mr. Bryan into a cocked hat!" Wilson wrote. His campaign blamed Wall Street for the publication of the letter, and Bryan held his fire.[37]

Wilson began to breathe life back into his campaign in the Ohio primary. While Harmon won the primary and took the majority of the delegates, Wilson won nineteen out of the forty-two district delegates and Harmon's popular plurality was less than ten thousand.[38] Durbin and Garber's plan had worked. Harmon's prospects were gone since it was demonstrated that he could not even hold his own state. More importantly, Wilson was able to continue his campaign.

"We missed out by a very few votes of having a majority of the delegates," Durbin wrote Baker, "but this minority was such a virile force in the convention that it spelled defeat for Harmon, and he has never forgotten it since, and has been a deadly enemy of mine ever since."[39] Harmon's enmity to Durbin showed itself in 1924: "It manifested itself in New York in 1924 when he was a delegate at large and took an active part in my defeat for National Committeeman. However, I am mighty glad to trade him the National Committeemanship for the presidency, and I am sure that the Democratic Party, the country and the world are well satisfied with the job we did at Baltimore in 1912."[40]

Wilson and Clark entered Baltimore at the end of June with Clark in the lead of instructed delegates. Wilson's only chance was to garner enough votes to block Clark in early balloting and then hope for a breakthrough.

The convention opened on June 25, knowing that Theodore Roosevelt and his followers had angrily stormed out of the Republican Convention in Chicago and had vowed to start a new third party, later named the "Bull Moose" Party. The split made it apparent that the Democrats' hour had arrived, and fighting at Baltimore was sure to be fierce.

It was. The first major battle formed over Ohio and the so-called unit rule, requiring a delegation to vote as a unit, all their votes, in favor of the candidate who had won the primary. "The fight developed when the convention committee on rules decreed that the nineteen Wilson delegates from Ohio had to vote for Harmon because the state Democratic convention had thus instructed," Wilson biographer Arthur Link wrote in his book, *Wilson: The Road to the White House.* Durbin argued the unit rule did not apply when a state law provided for presidential primary elections.[41]

"Mr. Baker," Durbin says to Delbert, "I collected all the authorities on the unit rule and wrote a brief on this subject and printed five thousand of them and sent one to each delegate and alternate to the convention and took about three thousand copies with me to Baltimore, where they were distributed to all the leading Democrats over there. Garber and I organized our forces for the fight and practically took charge of the fight to break the unit rule. We enlisted the support of Mitchell Palmer of Pennsylvania, Burleson of Texas, Josephus Daniels and many others, including Bryan. Hon. Robert L. Henry of Texas, who made the minority report of the Committee on Rules and Order of Business, practically copied my whole brief into his report."[42]

The minority report went to the entire convention for a vote. During the debate, a wild demonstration for Wilson was set off, with a dozen pictures of Wilson parading around the hall. Banners were unfurled, and the chants went up, "We want Wilson!" and a band struck up the "Star Spangled Banner."

The convention voted for the minority report by a vote of 565 to 492. "This important Wilson victory," Link wrote, "served as an effective antidote to the growing belief that Clark was certain to be nominated; more important, it added nineteen precious votes to the feeble Wilson numbers."[43]

The battle between the two top contenders was thus joined. Over the next seven grueling days, Clark and Wilson forces struggled to gain the uncommitted votes. Clark actually captured a majority vote but was unable to make any headway toward the required two-thirds. The stubborn Wilson fighters would not relinquish. The delegates rioted in the hot and sultry auditorium. Fist fights, always a rare attraction at a national convention, became common. Most nights, voting went on until almost daybreak.

At one point Wilson thought his cause hopeless and actually instructed his floor manager to release his delegates. The message was never communicated to the delegates. Slowly, monotonously, Wilson gained strength. Finally, on the forty-sixth ballot at 3:30 in the afternoon on July 2, Woodrow Wilson was nominated. William Jennings Bryan spoke to the Ohio delegation about the importance that the Ohio primary played in Wilson's march to the nomination.[44] "There is no doubt in my mind, "Bryan said, "that Wilson and the progressive cause was in a fair way to meet defeat in the Democratic primaries when the victory in Ohio came. You and the rest of the progressives in Ohio contributed as much as any other supporters of Mr. Wilson when you succeeded in splitting the Ohio delegation. Progressives the country over were becoming discouraged and some of them had given up when the news was flashed from Ohio that a reactionary with all the state patronage could not control his state. You remember that victories for the progressive cause followed rapidly on the Ohio primaries." After the convention Wilson came to Ohio, as Durbin suggested, to open the Democratic campaign in September. He spoke in Columbus on September 20, sharing the platform with the still-embittered Governor Harmon and the Democratic nominee for governor, James M. Cox.[45]

The 1912 campaign was one of the most dramatic in U.S. history. "We stand at Armageddon, and we battle for the Lord," Teddy Roosevelt proclaimed at the Progressive Party's national convention.[46] T. R.'s passion was contrasted with Wilson's cool reserve. Taft all but counted himself out of the race as early as July. "There are so many people in the country who don't like me," he complained.[47]

As the campaign came to its climax, Roosevelt was shot by a fanatic who thought no one should have a third term as president. The attack occurred in Milwaukee on October 14, as Roosevelt was giving a speech. The would-be assassin shot point blank into Roosevelt's chest, but a folded manuscript speech and a spectacles case in Roosevelt's coat pocket slowed the bullet and saved his life.[48]

Roosevelt checked to see that he was not mortally wounded before completing his speech. "Friends," he told the crowd, "I should ask that you be as quiet as possible. I don't know if you fully understand that I have been shot, but it takes more than that to kill a Bull Moose."[49]

Roosevelt quickly recovered and rejoined the campaign in late October. Wilson, however, had an insurmountable lead in the three-way race.

William Jennings Bryan, Josephus Daniels, Woodrow Wilson, Henry Breckenridge, and FDR (June 14, 1913). Courtesy CORBIS.

Wilson won Ohio, confirming Durbin's straw polls on the trains. Durbin almost had it right about Taft—he very nearly came in third in his own state. The vote in Ohio was Wilson, 424,834; Taft, 278,168; and Roosevelt, 229,807. Taft did run a poor third in the country as a whole. It was the first time since the birth of the Republican Party in 1854 that Ohio did not cast its vote for the Republican nominee for president.[50]

William Jennings Bryan became Wilson's secretary of state. True to his commitment to nonviolence (based in part on his fundamental Christian beliefs), Bryan insisted that Wilson establish a foreign policy that would require nations to arbitrate disputes before going to war. Each signatory nation would agree that after diplomacy had failed, all disputes would be submitted for investigation and report to a standing commission of five members. War could not be declared until the investigation and report were completed. The newspapers called it the "peace-drag-out idea," and most saw how naïve it was.

Bryan said, "We have now reached a point in civilization's progress when nations cannot afford to wage war." He had army swords melted and made into souvenir paperweight plowshares, inscribing at their base, "They shall beat their swords into plowshares."

A cynic predicted, "When it comes to a crisis someday, Bryan would desert Wilson and do it in the name of God."[51]

Clouds in fact were forming: Clouds for Wilson, clouds for the world, clouds for Durbin.

On March 1, 1914, Ellen Wilson fell in her room, a painful accident from which she did not immediately bounce back. Her condition worsened, and she became confined to her room. "I am very, very blue and out of heart today," Wilson wrote at the end of May. "My dear one absolutely wore herself out last winter and this spring and has not even started to come up hill yet."[52]

On June 28 in Sarajevo, Bosnia, an assassin shot twice into the automobile of the Archduke Frantz Ferdinand, heir to the Austro-Hungarian throne. The first shot hit the Archduke's wife low on her right side; the second struck the Archduke in the neck near the throat, piercing the jugular. Both were dead by the time their panic-stricken driver delivered them to a garrison hospital.

Dr. Cary Grayson, Wilson's personal physician, moved into the White House at the end of July, to attend to Ellen Wilson. In Europe, ultimatums flew and armies mobilized. War broke out on July 28, and Wilson, consumed with his wife's demise, stood paralyzed. He tendered lukewarm offers of mediation. As unknowingly foretold by Theodore Roosevelt two years earlier, the world was indeed on the eve of Armageddon.

On August 6, forty-eight hours after German troops crossed the Belgian border, Ellen Wilson died. Unable to bear the thought of her in a casket, Wilson had his wife's body placed on a sofa in her room, where he and his daughters sat with her remains for the next three days and nights. "God has stricken me almost beyond what I can bear," he wrote a friend. He told his family that it was his ambition and career that had killed her.[53]

Bryan, his peace treaties, his mediation attempts—all had failed. Wilson fell into a deep depression. He asked Americans to be and remain impartial "in thought as well as deed." Neutrality was tested and then literally blown away by German submarine warfare on the high seas. In May 1915 the Germans sank the *Lusitania,* killing 1,200 people, including 128 Americans.

Bryan cautioned restraint, fearing above all the larger horror of war and suspecting that England had been using passenger ships to transport munitions. He advised Wilson to issue a protest to England for violations of American neutrality in addition to the German note. Wilson gave a speech in which he declared, "There is such a thing as a man being too proud to fight."[54]

Eventually Wilson overrode Bryan's objections and insisted that the state department issue a vigorous protest note to Germany alone. When Wilson insisted on a second note to Germany charging that attacks on passenger ships violated the "principals of humanity," Bryan, deeply committed to neutrality, decided to resign. "I think this will destroy me," he told his wife, "but whether it does or not, I must do my duty according to my conscience."[55]

Durbin, a keen observer of Bryan, would write to Ray Stannard Baker about the relationship between Wilson and Bryan: "As bearing upon the relations between Bryan and Wilson, I remember that when I met Wilson in December 1911 at Trenton, New Jersey, he was speaking of what great good Bryan had done in holding the party together for sixteen years—that under his leadership we had a program. 'Program' was one of the words Wilson was particularly partial to, and I remember him saying: 'Durbin, the reason more men are not successful in this world is that they have no program,' and he gloried in the fact that our Party had a program, and he gave Bryan the credit for it, and he said that the pity of it all was that now that Bryan had brought the party to the promised land, that he could not enter in."[56]

Bryan stumped the country speaking out against America's entry into the European conflict. Wilson knew he faced a skilled adversary. "He is absolutely sincere," Wilson told his brother-in-law. "That's what makes him so dangerous."

In Bryan's view, the eastern press and "predatory wealth" advocated war, while his constituency—the farmers, laborers, and those who produced the wealth of the country—the ones who would die in the war machines in Europe, opposed war. Bryan identified this fight with the struggle he waged in 1896. People, Bryan said, "uncorrupted by that fierce struggle for wealth which makes men forget God and the duty which they owe their fellow man" would rise and never yield to war. They would not give their children "to gratify someone's military ambition or to purchase markets."[57]

Durbin's immediate reaction to Bryan's resignation is not recorded; however, after the war, when Wilson was out of office, Durbin's sister, Eliza, wrote a six-page letter to the ill ex-president, setting forth what appears to be her view and her brother's view of Bryan's actions: "It may interest you as a statesman and historian to know that here in Ohio, called a hotbed of Bryanism, we regretted his stand during the trying days of German aggression, and while grieved that he had made a mistake from which he could not come back, we believed in his sincerity."[58]

Durbin faced his own storms during these years. His first son, Francis, was prospering at Notre Dame in his law studies. His second son, Andy, was failing, and not just in his academics. Whether the result of his temperament or perhaps a genetic predisposition, Andy was beginning a lifelong struggle with alcoholism. If Durbin's father, the Doctor, had been overcome by the alcohol demon as is suggested by local histories, clearly Andy followed in his footsteps.

Maybe Andy suffered from comparison to his older brother, the one who was billed as "Master Francis," the world's youngest magician when he was seven. I have found no similar mention of Andy joining his father on the magical stage. Francis was also clearly his father's confidante in politics; Andy became an embarrassment. Francis graduated in 1913 from Notre Dame, and his commencement speaker was Durbin's friend, James Cox, Ohio's governor. Andy was kicked out of Notre Dame, and he gravitated toward everything sleazy and ugly about politics, playing on his father's name and reputation.

Wilson cautiously moved the nation toward a military preparedness program, but he continued to hold the country out of the war. Bryan and Wilson came to an understanding in the summer of 1916 and Bryan, at the Democratic convention in St. Louis, praised Wilson for enacting the greatest domestic reform programs in American history. He then added, "I join the people in thanking God that we have a President who does not want the nation to fight."[59]

"He kept us out of war," became Wilson's campaign slogan.

Writing to Ray Stannard Baker, Durbin relayed what he believed was Ohio's key role in the election of 1916:

Along toward the end of 1915 I went down to New York and I met an old friend of mine, Tommy Cassidy, of Union Hill, New Jersey, just across the river from New York, and who knew all the Democratic politicians in New York City. He asked me, 'Bill, do you think Wilson will be re-elected next year?' I said, 'Yes, I do.' Then he asked me whether I was counting on New York and New Jersey and I told him no. He then said that he didn't believe Wilson would come anywhere near carrying either state and he knew what he was talking about because he talked to Democratic politicians every day.[60]

The East was against Wilson. Winning Ohio became critical:

> When I came back to Ohio, I told my partner that if we expected to
> elect Wilson, Ohio would have to do it. I then outlined the following
> plan to him. We would get a list of fair-minded Republicans whose
> record for voting was such that they had not always voted the straight
> Republican ticket and who would read and consider anything we sent
> to them. Carrying this out, we secured a quarter of a million names of
> the Republicans who were considered independent and began to send
> them the literature in November, December, and January. By April
> [1916] we knew as well as anyone can know a thing of this kind that
> Wilson would carry Ohio, because we heard of Republicans every-
> where openly declaring themselves in favor of him.[61]

Wilson, too, recognized Ohio's importance to his re-election. "Along about
July of 1916, President Wilson sent for me as he wanted to see me," Durbin
wrote Baker. "He was interested in the election of Senator Pomerene who
didn't stand so well, and he wanted to be assured of my support for him.
My son Francis and I went down to Baltimore for the convention of the
Grand Lodge of Elks, to which I was a delegate, and then went over to Washington and had an interview with the President."[62]

Durbin told Wilson to start a direct mail campaign in Maine, where the
election was held two months early, and thus was always seen as an important
bellwether of the November election in the rest of the country. Durbin suggested that state Democratic chairmen across the country divide up the list of
the 75,000 Democrats in Maine and see to it that every Democrat received a
personal letter just before the September election. Wilson thought it a "splendid idea" and sent Durbin to New York to meet with his national campaign
chairman, Vance McCormick, to make the arrangements. "To make a long
story short," Durbin wrote, "this was carried out and Maine made the best
showing for a Presidential year in a long time and it foreshadowed what was
going to happen in November."[63]

Wilson ran against the bearded Charles Evans Hughes of New York, but in
this election he did not enjoy the benefit of a split Republican ticket as in 1912.
Wilson won the election by the closest of margins: 277 electoral votes to 254.
The contest was so close that it took days for the result to become clear.

Ohio was the only state in the Midwest to fall in the Wilson column; the
entire East went for Hughes, except New Hampshire. Wilson's victory in

Ohio, with its twenty-four electoral votes, was pivotal; had Ohio gone for Hughes, the result would have been Wilson's defeat.

"When November came, Ohio went for Wilson by 90,000 majority with only the men voting," Durbin wrote to Baker (women would not get the vote until 1920). "And it was Ohio that saved the day for him and I think one of his letters which you will have will show this." This, of course, is one of the letters lost to history.[64]

"The election this year," Durbin wrote Baker in 1935, when FDR was running for his second term, "has many of the elements that we had in 1916 for Wilson. The leaders of big interests in the East hated Wilson like the devil hates holy water and my friend Cassidy told me right when he told me that Wilson would not carry New York and New Jersey."[65]

Durbin looks at me: "I had been an admirer of Bryan for many years, and I am free to confess that I was not much taken up with the Wilson candidacy, but when I met him and talked to him for an hour, I was completely won over to him, and from that time on I was a Wilson man first, last and all the time, and I am devilish glad of it now."[66]

Although Durbin acknowledged Wilson "was accounted for as an impersonal man," he found him entirely engaging in person and even humorous at times. He told Ray Baker of an amusing reply of Wilson to Durbin's suggestion to get the polling lists of Maine for the direct mail campaign:

President Wilson listened very attentively and said: "That's fine, fine. I suppose we can easily get the polling lists." I replied, "I don't think there will be any trouble about that." Then the President said: "That reminds me of a story of a County Clerk in Maine who received a letter from one of the State Institutions asking him to send the names of all the imbeciles of the County." And, the President, in a drawling tone, said: "The Clerk said to his deputy, 'Better send the entire polling list.'" We all laughed over this much. The President was a droll fellow and he told some wonderful stories and always illustrated his point.[67]

Wilson tried to stop the war in Europe. He called on the warring nations to state the terms upon which the war could be ended and offered to serve as mediator. He told Congress that the war must end without victory by either side. "Only peace between equals can last." This was unacceptable to the combatants; each believed the other had caused the war and that their enemy must be defeated. Germany finally broke all hope of American neutrality

Woodrow Wilson and Georges Clemanceau on a Paris street in 1919. Ray Stannard
Baker stands behind Clemanceau with boater hat, and Rear Adm. Cary Grayson's face
can be seen between Wilson and Clemanceau. Courtesy CORBIS.

when it declared, in February 1917, that its submarine campaign would be
reopened on all ships, including neutral ships, hoping to knock Britain out
before America entered the war.

Wilson broke off diplomatic relations and war was declared in April.
"God helping her, she can do no other," he told Congress.[68]

After horrific casualties and with all combatants except the United States
exhausted and reeling, the war ended with an armistice in November 1918, in
large part because the Germans accepted Wilson's Fourteen Points and believed that he would negotiate a peace without victors. Wilson sailed for Europe to work out the final peace treaty and to form the League of Nations.

HAIL THE CHAMPION OF THE RIGHTS OF MAN, the signs and banners read
in Paris. HONOR TO THE APOSTLE OF INTERNATIONAL JUSTICE. HONOR AND
WELCOME TO THE FOUNDER OF THE SOCIETY OF NATIONS.

One journalist wrote: "No one ever heard such cheers. I, who heard them
in the streets of Paris, can never forget them in my life. I saw Foch pass,

Clemenceau pass, Lloyd George, generals, returning troops, banners, but Wilson heard from his carriage something different, inhuman—or super-human. Oh, the immovably shining, smiling man."[69]

VIVE WILSON! VIVE WILSON!

But after these golden moments, nothing went right. The excruciating negotiations bogged down into petty fighting and grabbing for territory. Huge reparations were demanded. Wilson had been right, there would be no lasting peace unless among equals. He returned to America after almost three months to find hot opposition to the Treaty and the League of Nations. No amendments by the Senate would be acceptable to Wilson.

Traveling the nation in September 1919, in his blue President's train car, the *Mayflower,* he began to lose words in midsentence; he cried, sometimes unable to speak. He suffered a stroke on his way to Wichita, Kansas, and had to cancel the last part of his trip and return to Washington. There he suffered another stroke, leaving him partially paralyzed.[70]

For a time, Wilson's cabinet wondered if he was so disabled that the vice president (the man who said "what the country needs is a good 10-cent cigar") should be sworn in to take his place. Although Wilson lost the fight in the United States for the Treaty and the League of Nations, he did win the Nobel Peace Prizes for 1919 and 1920 in recognition of his work as founder of the League.[71]

Andy Durbin, running from his alcoholic demons, found himself in South America during the war. Writing to his aunt from Santiago, Chile, in May 1918, he told of a perilous voyage and a chance to start over: "At last I have reached where I never intended going but I am just as glad and perhaps more so for this position pays more and Santiago is about as big as Washington only the climate is much better."[72] Francis, by contrast, had married my grandmother, Agnes Kelly, in May 1917 and was busy establishing his law practice in Lima, Ohio. With Andy nothing lasted long, and so by 1919 he was back in Kenton working at the sign company for his father. With the war over, Andy began writing White House secretaries about a position in the Army "to see service in Russia or France."[73]

"Would it be asking too much of you to see if you will take it up with your friends in the War Department and see if they won't commission me on that old application that got almost through the A. G. office when the war was declared off," he wrote in April 1919.

Within two weeks he gave up the idea of a commission but continued to seek appointments in Washington. Tumulty found him a job with the department of commerce in July, but he was fired within six weeks because he

Andy Durbin and the Studebaker (1935). Author's collection.

was absent without leave after the first two weeks. Tumulty then helped Andy get a position in the Army as part of the Graves Registration Service, "in connection with the removal of the dead from Europe."[74]

Andy was placed under investigation almost immediately when an officer uncovered that he was duping other Army recruits by promising to get them jobs in the Graves Registration Service in order to get money for drinking. One victim described his encounter with Andy in an affidavit that for some reason is preserved in the Woodrow Wilson Papers: "I then asked Mr. Durbin if he cared to indulge in a drink of port wine. During the course of the early afternoon between the two of us we finished the pint bottle of wine and Mr. Durbin then through some friend of his secured a bottle of whiskey. There was also registered at the Willard Hotel at this time a personal friend of Durbin's father, from whom Durbin borrowed $50.00. Soon after doing so he left the hotel in anything but a fit condition."[75]

Returning later to the hotel, the recruit was surprised to find that Andy had come back earlier and convinced a maid to open the recruit's room: "He had also put on quite a party having several bell hops as his guests. He made several long distance phone calls and thru the aid of a bell boy he purchased candy at the hotel newsstand under my name to the extent of $5.85."

Another victim described a similar scene: "When I bought my ticket at the Penn. Station the agent handed me five dollars change and Mr. Durbin snatched it. When I asked him to give it to me, he said 'No, surely you would not ask me to give this back after I have done so much for you here.'"

Andy made it to Belgium with the Graves Registration Service in January 1920 only to be sent back and discharged because of the secret investigation. Puzzled, Andy appealed to Tumulty, who immediately agreed to "do all I can to help you." Meanwhile Andy violated regulations by turning in his transportation ticket back to Ohio for $19.83 cash. When Tumulty received the War Department report, Andy told Tumulty he had been "framed." The documents collected in the Woodrow Wilson Papers do not tell of how this episode ended for Andy.[76]

The Durbins did not forget Tumulty's loyalty. Years later they stuck up for him when Edith Wilson publicly attacked him after Wilson was dead. In February 1939 she published an article in the *Saturday Evening Post*, "As I Saw It," in which she was critical of Joseph Tumulty over an insignificant slight. According to Edith, Tumulty had authored, without permission, a message purporting to be from Wilson, which was read at a Democratic dinner in 1924.[77]

Her remarks about Tumulty were so condescending and harsh that Francis Durbin, after reading the article, dashed off his own scathing letter to Edith

Woodrow and Edith Wilson in Bismark, North Dakota (August 16, 1919), a month before Wilson's stroke. Courtesy of Bettmann/CORBIS.

Wilson: "I have just read the copy of the *Saturday Evening Post* in which you wind up your article with the most contemptible story in regard to Joseph P. Tumulty, who was secretary to your husband for eight years when he was President and two years when he was Governor of New Jersey. In this article I think your remarks in regard to Mr. Tumulty are despicable, lousy and contemptible." Francis said Tumulty was "one of the truest, loyal men that ever assisted a President of the United States," and that he could not stand by and see Tumulty's truthfulness questioned. "I do not want to see a spot on that fine man's splendid escutcheon."

"P. S.," he wrote, "You were present when Dean Acheson, Acting Secretary of the Treasury, swore in my father, William W. Durbin, as Register of the Treasury, August 1, 1933."[78]

Delbert notices that I am getting sleepy. "What did you say about contemptible?" he asks me.

"What? . . . I'm sorry, . . . what was that?"

"Lousy and contemptible, you were mumbling."

Several months before Wilson died, in October 1923, Durbin exchanged correspondence with him. Durbin wrote, sending "a little booklet that I got out to be distributed among our Democratic women to acquaint them with the history of the Democratic Party and its principles."[79]

He was pleased, he wrote, to read in the papers that Wilson was recovering his health. He said he could still shut his eyes and see Wilson in Trenton when they first met in 1911: "You had a vision which gave us a program, only broken up by the partisan action of those who thought more of their party than of the country and humanity in general, but in the end good can never be destroyed and in the end truth must prevail."

Durbin predicted victory in 1924. "I feel confident that 1924 will vindicate you and the policies of the Democratic Party during your administration."

Wilson responded, "I have very little doubt that the work you are doing will bear fruit of the sort we desire, and I am happy to learn that you are still 'on the job' with your customary energy." He too agreed with Durbin's view of the future. "I share your confident expectation of the result of the election next year and feel that the country and the world were never more in need of such a result,—for do what they will even the Republicans cannot entirely destroy the leadership of the United States."[80]

"I hope you keep well," Wilson concluded, "and that the common cause in which we are both enlisted will throw us often together."

Wilson died three months later on February 3, 1924.

"The boy is talking in his sleep, Mr. Durbin," Delbert says.

"*I think it was despicable, lousy, and contemptible, too,*" *Durbin says.*

With that, I can no longer hold my eyes open, and I give in to a luxurious sleep, the kind of sleep that is brought on by the hypnotic effect of a long car drive on a straight flat road.

It is the type of sleep that Durbin, looking at his two infant sons dozing, would have called the "sleep of the just."

THE RIVER LETHE
AND WARREN G. HARDING

October 9, 1920

I awake briefly as we are crossing the giant steel span bridge high above the Monongahela on the other side of Brownsville. I am drowsy, slipping in and out of consciousness. The drone of the car sends me back under.

I begin to dream about the rivers of the underworld in Greek mythology: Styx, Cocytus, Pyriphlegethon, Acheron, and Lethe.

Lethe, the River of Oblivion, was the river of forgetfulness. Those souls in the underworld who had been punished for a thousand years for their sins were made to drink of the waters of the River Lethe as a way of releasing all memory and anxiety from the past, permitting them to reenter the stream of life.[1]

Forgetful of the past, they would begin to desire reincarnation. In politics, magic, and family history, it is necessary to drink deeply of the River Lethe.

This sleep into which I have fallen seems to have taken me into the underworld. I swirl and turn downward, sideways, and up, all at once. Figures that threaten me fly past, sounds and colors wash over me like great crashing waves, and I am equally at peace and terror-stricken. Demons guide my subterranean tour of the infernal regions. While I know that ancestral memories have been cleansed from my soul by the waters of Lethe, I suspect that the purification has gone awry, someone has intervened, and I was given a dose of insufficient strength.

With enough prompting, the memories are there, encamped in a multitude of high conical tents near the edge of the River of Oblivion, unwanted squatters in the outer reaches of my consciousness. I fly to the frontier alone, devoid of defenses and helpless to look away.

"I believe in equality before the law," Warren Harding once said in an address delivered in Oklahoma City during the campaign of 1920. "You can't give

rights to the white man and deny them to the black man. But while I stand for that great, great principle, I do not mean that the white man and the black man must be forced to associate together in the acceptance of their rights."[2]

My mind is unsettled. "The greatest indignity suffered by Harding in his career was the allegation made during the campaign of 1920 that he had Negro forebears," a professor of history from the University of Toledo wrote in 1966 in an Ohio history journal.[3]

*A man I see stands with a placard, shaking it hatefully: "No matter how anxious they might be to vote for you they positively would not do so," the sign screams, "*BECAUSE YOU HAVE NIGGER BLOOD IN YOU!*"[4]*

Black soldiers march by the man with the sign; they are returning from the Great War, 400,000 of them, to the searing summer of 1919. There were race riots then, in the cities, all over the country. Lynchings were commonplace. "Lynching" as that term was used in 1919 was more often than not code for burning a man to death.

In my research I came across a story in the Louisville Courier-Journal *in 1920 reporting on the "pluck" of two young female journalists who heard of a lynching in progress and who set out to scoop the story. "Without even stopping to powder our noses we got the only vehicle available," the girls wrote. "We thought we would never get there. Everyone had an eye peeled for a bonfire and his nose primed for the odor of roast Negro."[5]*

All this plays on my tortured mind. Was my own family involved in this madness?

"Ohio has a race problem," the *New York Times* announced on October 22, 1920, during the last few weeks of the presidential contest between James Cox, Ohio's progressive governor, and Warren Harding, one of Ohio's senators.[6] Two Ohioans, both friends of Durbin, faced off, sixty years after the end of the Civil War.

One would not have expected race to be an issue that would infest an election contest between candidates of a northern state. But it was. World War I had stirred up the national question of race, a national shame that would not go away:

> The situation is due directly to the great influx of negroes from the South during the war, when they were "imported" to take the place of white unskilled labor which, under war conditions, had taken advantage of opportunities that opened for employment at higher wages in the war industries and had graduated from the pick and shovel or other branches of less well paid work. Railroad and large industrial

Warren Harding, Florence Harding ("the "Duchess") to his right, and the neighbors from Blooming Grove on Harding's front porch (1920). Courtesy Ohio Historical Society.

plants brought the black workers by the carload and many thousands of them landed in Ohio and apparently are going to stay.[7]

The race card was played in the election of 1920 because Democrats were desperate. Americans were sickened by the war in Europe and Wilson's proposals to entangle the United States in world affairs through the League of Nations. Recognizing that defeat was imminent, Democrats tried to find an issue that would turn the tide rising against them.

Fundamentally, Americans were in 1920 as they had always been—isolationist, inward-looking, and opposed to involvement with the European powers that again showed their pettiness at the Paris Peace Conference. After the war, prices skyrocketed in the United States and in Europe; the Bolsheviks were winning in Russia and threatening international revolution;

and Wilson was incapacitated in the White House. Rumors circulated that he had become a lunatic. People were demanding a change in leadership, and Republican Party bosses picked Harding, a dark-horse candidate, at their convention in the famous "smoke-filled room." Harding seemed by comparison to Wilson quite human, even warm, a latter-day McKinley, the last of the beloved Ohio presidents.

Even Bryan fell out of the ranks in the 1920 campaign.[8] He made no speeches, and some worried that he might actually take the nomination of the Prohibitionist Party, whose cause Bryan had taken up with the same vigor he applied to the silver issue in 1896. The Durbins were not happy with his political abandonment. "Since his insincerity in the last campaign," Eliza Durbin wrote in 1921 to Woodrow Wilson, "no Democrat I know would follow him. Insincerity betrays itself sooner or later, just as Republican insincerity is already betraying itself."[9]

Durbin had good reason to be miffed by Bryan's failure to support the Democratic ticket in 1920. Durbin held a position of some importance that year. He was the chairman of the Democratic State Executive Committee in Ohio, a role he took back in 1917 when his partner Bill Finley became sick. With the presidential contest between two Ohioans, the battle for Ohio had both real and symbolic importance.[10]

Durbin had helped James Cox, the Dayton newspaperman, become governor of Ohio in 1912, and Cox won reelection twice (1916 and 1918). Durbin personally ran Cox's 1918 reelection campaign, when he was the only Democrat elected on the state ticket.[11]

At the same time, Durbin considered Harding his friend and probably had more personally in common with him than he did with Cox.[12] Harding and Durbin grew up in adjoining counties in towns twenty-six miles apart. Both had dominant mothers. Both were sons of physicians (George Tryon Harding was a homeopathic doctor). Harding and Durbin both grew up in relative poverty; they lived in a time when doctors made little money, receiving much of their compensation in uncollectible IOUs, farm animals, or produce. Both would spend their lives worrying about their own health, fearing disease, and taking cures at local sanitariums.

They came from the same milieu: the small, pastoral town in central Ohio, composed of mostly Yankee and German citizens, tough patriotic people whose families migrated from New England, Pennsylvania, Maryland, and Virginia. The families in their towns were the pioneer families in their communities. Harding and Durbin were raised Protestants, and they would spent countless hours in Sunday school and services. They whiled away their summers running barefoot from spring until the first frost; swimming in streams, creeks, and rivers; and playing scrub baseball with friends.

They knew the upkeep of horses and milked and tended to family cows. They were taught the same moralistic worldview from their *McGuffey Readers*. Harding was born in November 1865; Durbin ten months later in September 1866.

Perhaps Durbin knew the pain of a whispering campaign about his father's drinking. In a similar vein, Harding grew up amid hurtful rumors that his ancestors included African Americans. In Blooming Grove, the small village outside Marion where Harding spent his very early childhood, somehow the talk started that the Harding family had "negro blood" in it. The rumor became known as the "shadow of Blooming Grove," a term that was taken by Francis Russell as the title for his 1968 biography of Harding. Schoolmates taunted Harding and according to Russell believed that he was "part nigger."

When Harding married Florence Kling, a divorcee five years his senior, her father, Amos Kling, allegedly confronted Harding in the Marion courthouse after the engagement was announced, and according to Russell, "called him a nigger, and threatened to blow his head off." Russell writes: "The shadow of Blooming Grove was something that in later years he could hardly bring himself to talk about. Once he managed to discuss the matter briefly with his old friend James Miller Faulkner, a political reporter on the *Cincinnati Enquirer*. 'How do I know, Jim?' he remarked finally. 'One of my ancestors may have jumped the fence.'"[13]

But if Durbin and Harding had a common background and might have even been close friends, politics was politics, and in 1920 Durbin became Harding's bitter opponent.

When the Cox special train left from Dayton for San Francisco, where Democrats were holding their national convention, Durbin was one of the high-ranking party members on board. In his autobiography Cox wrote, "Ohio had never sent a delegation surpassing in quality that which was chosen in 1920."[14]

Francis Durbin, as was now customary, went with his father to the convention. With Wilson out of the picture (although he entertained delusions from his home on S Street in Washington that he would be selected for a third term), the convention was another lengthy affair, much like the 1912 Baltimore convention, convening on June 28 and adjourning on July 6. There were forty-four ballots before Cox was nominated.

By tradition, a candidate did not attend the convention in person in those days, so Cox waited for news back in Ohio in his office at the *Dayton Daily News*. "There was no radio in those days," Cox wrote later, "and I received the returns at the *News* office in Dayton over the telegraph. The nomination was made at 1:50 A.M., Tuesday, July 6. That was 4:50 A.M. in Dayton."[15]

The question quickly turned to the selection of a candidate for vice president.

In letters written to FDR in the 1930s Francis and his father claimed that, along with friend Tim Ansberry, they were the first to suggest FDR to Cox. "In 1920 at San Francisco I met you there in the New York delegation," Durbin wrote to Roosevelt in a lengthy letter in August 1934. "My son, Francis, was with me and also Tim Ansberry who now lives in Washington."

Ansberry came from a town in northwest Ohio not far from Kenton, had been a congressman, and in 1920 was a judge. Like Francis he was a graduate in law from the University of Notre Dame, and he was a close political friend of the Durbins.

Durbin wrote FDR: "Tim and my son Francis, after Cox's nomination, phoned to him and suggested you for vice president and he was much taken with it saying that the name Roosevelt meant a million voters in the country for the Democrats."[16]

FDR was then thirty-eight and the assistant secretary of the Navy. He was not favored in his own home state (Tammany Hall disliked him), and he was therefore a highly unlikely choice for vice president. Cox, who slept not at all that night, returned to his home at dawn and spoke by telephone with his floor manager, Ohioan Edmund H. Moore, who asked Cox for his preference for vice president. "I told him," Cox wrote, "I had given the matter some thought and that my choice would be Franklin D. Roosevelt of New York." Cox said Moore was surprised by the choice. "Moore inquired, 'Do you know him?'" Cox wrote. "I did not. In fact, as far as I knew, I had never seen him; but I explained to Mr. Moore that he met the geographical requirement, that he was recognized as an Independent and that Roosevelt was a well-known name."[17]

Ansberry was given the job of nominating Roosevelt. Geoffrey C. Ward, a Roosevelt biographer, tells the story: "At the last moment it occurred to him [Ansberry] that his candidate might be too young: the Constitution required him to be at least thirty-five." Ward says Ansberry found Roosevelt near the speaker's platform:

"How old are you," he asked.
"Thirty-eight. Why do you want to know?"
"I'm going to nominate you."
"Do you think I ought to be around when you do?" Franklin asked.
"No," Ansberry said, "I'd leave the hall."

Ward writes:

> The judge made his way to the podium as Franklin hurried out a side entrance. "The young man whose name I'm going to suggest," Ansberry said, "is but three years over the age of thirty-five prescribed by the Constitution . . . but he has crowded into that short period of time a very large experience as a public official. . . . His is a name to be conjured with in American politics . . . Franklin D. *Roosevelt!*"[18]

Conjured with, yes, Durbin must have thought, a nice description, a magical term for a magical name. Roosevelt campaigned across the country that year with Cox and on his own, Eleanor always at his side. He towered over Cox, making him look short.

FDR took his formal leave of the Navy Department in early August, where he had served for eight years under the secretary of the navy, Josephus Daniels. Daniels was, as FDR once described him, "the funniest looking hillbilly I ever saw." Yet a genuine respect and affection developed between the two over the years. The short and paunchy North Carolinian, who had been the editor of the *Raleigh News and Observer,* was a Bryan man, devoted to democracy, a children's rights advocate, a renowned pacifist, and like the Southern president he served, a racist.[19]

Racism was the slimy underbelly of the Democratic Party. For all of Bryan's radical agitation for the common man, for all of Wilson's lofty pleas for the international rights of man, the common man was never black, and the international rights of man did not extend to African Americans or anyone else of color. Wilson in fact blocked blacks from entry to Princeton while he was president of the university. He removed most black officeholders when he became president of the United States.[20]

Similarly, a Bryan biographer has written that there was "a glaring exception to Bryan's democratic sentiments. It was on the issue of race, especially regarding blacks. The Jeffersonian phrase that he so fondly quoted—'Equal rights to all and special privileges to none'—was in fact something that he applied primarily to Caucasians. He did so with little intellectual discomfort. Beliefs in white supremacy suffused his culture."[21] When Theodore Roosevelt invited Booker T. Washington to the White House in 1901, for example, Bryan protested. "When Mr. Roosevelt sits down with a negro," Bryan said, "he declares that the negro is the social equal of the white man."

Daniels supported the disenfranchisement of blacks in his state. In 1912 during the election and just before Wilson selected him as his secretary of the navy, Daniels wrote editorials that breathed the fire of prejudice. "The attitude of the South regarding the Negro in politics is unalterable and uncompromising," Daniels wrote in 1912. "The South is solidly Democratic because of the realization that the subjection of the negro, politically, and the separation of the negro, socially, are paramount to all other considerations in the South short of preservation of the Republic itself. And we shall recognize no emancipation, nor shall we proclaim any deliverer, that falls short of these essentials to the peace and the welfare of our part of the country."[22]

I have come to rest in my flight to this squalid battlefield, and now I am face-to-face with the reality of our national shame, the Democratic Party's shame, and my own family's shame.

Durbin sits in an office in Columbus, Ohio, the headquarters of the State Democratic Committee. He drafts a circular entitled "A timely warning to the white men and women of Ohio." His work is intense. He writes: "An ominous cloud has risen on the political horizon which should have the attention and consideration of all men and women before casting their ballots. That cloud is the threat of Negro domination in Ohio."[23]

The clock in the room ticks quietly, beating out second after second the sad, slow, everyday moments of intolerance.

"It is a well-known fact," Durbin scrawls, "that the influx of Negroes from the South into the industrial centres of Ohio during the past years has been of such proportions as to give rise to a real race problem. Herded together like cattle and brought here by selfish employers to work in our industrial establishments, their presence has brought about serious consequences in many of our cities."

He stops writing when a lieutenant interrupts to tell him that a reporter is on the phone. He gets up and leaves to take the call.

The *New York Times* did run two lead stories in October 1920 about the Negro vote in Ohio and the Democratic warning that disaster was in the offing. "These black immigrants from south of the Mason and Dixon Line do not begin to compare in intelligence to the Northern negroes," the *Times* wrote. "Many are illiterate, but they are being coddled by the Republicans, who have had them and their women folk herded to the registration places to qualify for the right to vote the 'straight' Republican ticket."[24]

There is no reference point for me in all of this. These revelations, these writings hit me in the stomach, knocking away my breath. When I grew up, Lyndon Johnson, a southern Democrat, brought about the Civil Rights Act of 1964. Seared in my memory is the image of Bobby Kennedy, on television, speaking to a black crowd in Indianapolis, reliving the pain of his own brother's assassination, in an effort to try to calm the storm on the night that Martin Luther King Jr. was killed.

My mother told me that the Ku Klux Klan burned a cross in her front yard when she was a girl because her father, Francis, represented a black man in our hometown.

I spent my summers in college working in city parks among mostly young African American kids. I still remember twin girls, maybe five or six years old, staring at me for the longest time, without comment, and later confessing that they could not understand how I breathed through my thin straight nose.

In my world, the Democratic Party was the party of equality, diversity, affirmative action, Jesse Jackson, the keepers of faith in civil rights, the rightful home of minorities and all oppressed people. The New York Times *was the liberal newspaper, a champion of civil rights.*

My world—these pillars of the Democratic Party and of my family—all were destroyed by my discovery in an Ohio history magazine of the so-called "Durbin circular" written about the threat of "Negro domination" in the 1920 campaign.

"There were approximately 80,000 Negro votes in [Ohio] before women were enfranchised," the *New York Times* declared. "This year, as a result of the Nineteenth Amendment, this vote if not doubled will be very largely in excess of what it has been. The Democratic State Committee has taken such a grave view of the situation that in a circular letter recently sent out it warns the white voters against the menace of 'negro domination.'"[25]

Durbin returns to the room and sits back down to continue his circular.

"We see negro newspapers in the State," he writes, "boasting loudly of the increased balance of power held by their race through the enfranchisement of their women. We find them openly predicting that full social equality will be insured them by the election of the Republican candidates.

"White workingmen in many communities owning or paying for homes in factory districts can testify to the effect which the importation of these negroes into the community has had upon the values of their properties. In many of our cities it is well known that the best residential districts have not been free from invasion of negroes. It naturally follows that the efforts upon the part of the Republican candidates and leaders to further intensify negro ambitions can only result in greatly magnifying the evils we are already facing."[26]

To Durbin and some Ohio Democrats, the chaotic days of Reconstruction in the South were in danger of being visited on the North: "Ohioans should remember that the time has come when we must handle this problem in somewhat the same way as the South is handling it, and in such a way bring greater contentment to both whites and Negroes. We should remember what history tells us of the dark days when negroes controlled the government in the South, the enormous expenditures and debts incurred, the indignities heaped upon the white women and children, the vicious attempt of the South Carolina Negro legislature to give every negro forty acres of land and a mule."[27]

"DEMS IN DESPERATION RAISE COWARDLY CRY OF 'NEGRO DOMINATION,'" read the headline of the *Cleveland Advocate,* one of the black newspapers that Durbin had charged with predicting full social equality. "The forbearing public is holding its nose and reaching for its gas masks, because the Democratic burrowing carnivore, conforming to the predisposition of its counterpart in natural history, is driven to desperation and is beginning to emit noxious odors. One of the unfailing signs of Democratic desperation is when the cry goes up of 'Negro domination.' The whipped Hun cried 'Kamerad,' but the cornered Democrat and the skunk, alike in many things, perfume the air with the noxious gases and filth from nether sources."[28]

"The fight in the last week of the campaign," a *New York Times* article read on October 23, as the election drew near, "is likely to be marked by bitterness, owing to the use that is being made by the Democrats of the 'negro social equality' issue and the scurrilous attacks from anonymous sources on Harding, in which the Democrats say they have taken no part. As yet there has been no rejoinder by the Republicans, but leaders are beginning to realize that the attacks must be met and are preparing to do so. The crisis is likely to come next week with an answer from Harding himself."[29]

An uninformed reader would have found it difficult to discern just exactly what was meant by "scurrilous attacks from anonymous sources on Harding."

Something unmentionable was going on: "The Democrats are making much of the fact that the Republicans have nominated six negroes for the State House of Representatives. Posters bearing the pictures of the negro candidates with that of Harding and the candidates for United States Senator and Governor are being nailed up by the Democrats all over the State and are being torn down in many localities as soon as they have been displayed."[30]

The scurrilous attacks in fact referred to a circular, not the "Durbin circular," but one that was being distributed door-to-door under the heading "Harding Family Tree." This circular was written by William Estabrook Chancellor, a college professor of economics and social sciences at the College of Wooster (Ohio). The pamphlet charged, "Warren Gamaliel Harding is not a white man; he is not a creole; he is not a mulatto; he is a mestizo, as his physical features show. . . . I might cite the names of scores of persons who have always considered Warren Gamaliel Harding a colored man and who resent his present masquerade as a white candidate upon the ticket of a hitherto honorable and dignified party."[31]

Ohioans were ripe for such racist talk. Even as late as 1912, when Ohio held a constitutional convention to modernize its constitution, a statewide proposal to eliminate existing language that permitted "male whites" only to vote was defeated. It was only because the state had ratified the Fifteenth Amendment to the United States Constitution that blacks were given the right to vote in Ohio. Indeed, when the Fifteenth Amendment was first submitted in Ohio to a popular referendum ratification, it was defeated only to be ratified by a subsequent Ohio Legislature that ignored the popular verdict.[32]

The *New York Times* reported that Durbin thought the "negro domination" issue was changing voters' allegiances: "W. W. Durbin, Chairman of the Democratic State Committee, said that this issue was beginning to cut a considerable figure in the campaign and was driving voters away from the Republican candidate by the thousands."[33]

But was Durbin behind the Chancellor circular?

He denied any connection in the *New York Times*. "Chairman Durbin said that the personal attacks on Harding which are being embodied in circular letters sent out to voters, not through the mails but through other agencies, are not new to the campaign, but were in general circulation during the primaries, when [General Leonard] Wood and [Illinois Governor Frank] Lowden contended with Harding for the delegates to the National convention. The same rumors have figured more or less in other campaigns when Harding has been a candidate, but the clandestine attacks were never carried on as intensively as they have been in this campaign."[34]

Even the *New York Times* would not publish the subject of the "scurrilous attacks," leaving most readers to guess what they were about: "Some of the matter that is being circulated is of unprintable character. The Republicans say they are prepared to meet the attacks, if it should be deemed advisable to dignify them with a reply, in a fashion that will take the perpetrators off their feet. They hold the Democratic State Committee responsible, but Chairman Durbin said today with great emphasis that the committee had nothing to do with them and did not know the source. 'We are too busy expounding the issues to the people to bother with any of these dirty reports,' he said. 'If they are untrue, why don't the Republicans nail them?'"[35]

In truth, it is hard to determine whether Durbin and the Democratic State Committee were behind the Chancellor publication and its distribution. When the chairman of the Ohio Republican committee, George Clark, issued a statement accusing the Ohio Democratic State Committee of "the foulest campaign in Ohio's history," he charged, "Paid emissaries are now employed to go from house to house, spreading vile slander relative to the

Republican candidate." "From vest pockets," Clark wrote, "are drawn statements which dare not be printed in the open."[36]

Durbin responded with his own statement, denying the charges but in the process slyly agitating for a response that would give further publicity to the slander:

> Mr. Clark further says that paid emissaries are going about from house to house spreading propaganda calculated to injure the reactionary candidate for President. This statement is an absolute unqualified lie.
>
> In the first place, this committee has no paid emissaries to travel about the State or nation; neither has any other Democratic organization.
>
> Now as to Mr. Clark's statement of underhanded scandal, I deny it absolutely. Furthermore, I challenge him to come out in the open and frankly tell the people of Ohio and the United States what reports he means, which he charges the Democratic State Committee with circulating.
>
> When Mr. Clark does this we will then know what he means and will be prepared to give full answer.[37]

Although Durbin suggested the Republicans "nail" the allegations if untruthful, nailed is what happened to Professor Chancellor. Under intense pressure, the trustees of his college summoned Chancellor to a hastily organized special meeting. A Harding biographer described the meeting:

> Chancellor, nervous, voluble, and highly excited, denied having written or printed the broadside but admitted that he had made a study of the Harding family and had supplied the genealogical "proofs" in the pamphlet material. He told the trustees in a trembling voice that Harding's nomination was a plot to achieve Negro domination in the United States. Wishart [the college president] said that he did not wish to know the truth as to whether Harding was colored or white. All he and the trustees wanted was a written denial by Chancellor that Harding was colored. When Chancellor refused to give this, the trustees unanimously requested his resignation and voted him four months' salary.[38]

On the next day, October 31, the *New York Times* reported of Professor Chancellor's forced resignation on its front page, quoting extensively from a Dayton newspaper, the *Dayton Journal*.[39] The *Journal* refuted the "whispering campaign" against Harding and recited an "authoritative" genealogy of the Harding family. The point of the *Journal* article was clear: "The answer to this conspiracy, this plot, is that its base allegations ARE A LIE. Warren G. Harding has the blood of but one race in his veins—that of the white race—the pure inheritance of a fine line of ancestors, of good men and woman. That is sufficient!"

Harding, according to Russell, was "wild with rage" when the *Journal* article appeared because previously the charges had only shown up in generalities in the newspapers. Now the claim that Harding had "negro blood in his veins" was out in a general circulation newspaper, even if refuted. Harding blamed his campaign manager and future attorney general, Harry Daugherty, for the press slip up. "Wild with rage," Russell wrote, "Harding stormed through the train to Daugherty's car with a copy of the *Journal* in his hand, accusing his manager of being responsible for the headlines. Daugherty had never seen him so angry but finally managed to convince him that he had nothing to do with it, that his instructions had always been never to mention the subject."[40]

Attacks such as those waged in 1920 have a long aftereffect. In the 1960s when Andrew Sinclair was researching his biography of Harding, he asked an Ohio farmer about politics, and the farmer replied that he had not been much interested in politics since the 1920 election. According to Sinclair, the farmer said: "*That* was an election. Of course Cox was up to his elbows in filth, and Harding was a nigger."[41]

"Not heroism but healing," Harding said in his campaign, "not nostrums but normalcy." In the end, the League of Nations was the dominant issue on the mind of most voters. The hope that playing the race card would miraculously turn the tide at the last minute was a bankrupt strategy.

On election day, November 2, Harding awoke on his fifty-fifth birthday to a gray and cold day. He enjoyed his favorite breakfast of waffles with chipped beef and gravy, went off to vote, and then drove to Columbus to play golf at the Scioto Country Club. By evening the returns showed a Republican landslide for the national ticket and in Ohio. Harding's newspaper, the *Marion Star,* carried headlines proclaiming the victory and, not coincidentally, prominently displayed in the middle of its front page a copy of the newspaper's creed: "Remember there are always two sides to every question. Get both. Be truthful . . . and, above all, be clean. Never let a dirty word or suggestive story get into type."[42]

Cox and Roosevelt were soundly defeated, Wilson was repudiated, and the League of Nations was dead.

The loss was not for lack of effort by Durbin. Indeed, in a letter to FDR written in 1932, Durbin claimed he put up $40,000 of his own money for the campaign. "You were on the ticket in 1920," Durbin wrote FDR, "and realize how long it took to get things going in our National Committee, and out here in Ohio had it not been for the fact that I went ahead and obligated myself for $40,000 to get literature, lithographs, etc., we would have been beaten twice what we were, which was bad enough God knows (400,000)."[43]

Even then, Durbin wrote, it was too little, too late. The literature did not come out until late in September, "when it was a case of sending for the doctor when it was time for the undertaker."

Durbin's prediction of "negro domination" did not come true; indeed, African Americans had little to cheer about in the America of 1920. Harding courageously tried to change some things, such as asking Congress to pass a federal anti-lynching law. He also delivered a remarkable speech on civil rights to a carefully segregated crowd in, of all places, Birmingham, Alabama. He asserted that blacks had to be given political and economic equality or else democracy in the United States was a lie:

> Just as I do not wish the South to be politically entirely of one party, just as I believe that it is bad for the South, and for the rest of the country as well, so I do not want the colored people to be entirely of one party. I wish that both the tradition of a solidly Democratic South and the tradition of a solidly Republican black race might be broken up.[44]

The white segment of the crowd stood in stunned silence throughout the speech while the blacks, equally stunned, cheered heartily for Harding:

> I want to see the time come when black men will regard themselves as full participants in the benefits and duties of American citizenship. . . . We cannot go on, as we have gone on for more than a half century, with one great section of our population, numbering as many people as the entire population of some significant countries of Europe, set off from real contribution to solving national issues, because of a division on race lines.

The Democratic reaction was predictable. Said Senator Tom Heflin of Alabama, "God Almighty has fixed limits and boundary lines between the races, and no Republican living can improve on His handiwork." Senator Harrison of Mississippi said: "If the President's theory is carried to its ultimate conclusion, namely, that the black person, either man or woman, should have full economic and political rights with the white man and the white woman, then that means that the black man can strive to become the President of the United States, hold a Cabinet position and occupy the highest place of public trust in the nation. It means white women should work under black men in public places, as well as in all the trades and professions."[45]

But courageous as Harding was that day in Birmingham, little of substance was accomplished in his administration. In the same speech, he spoke of the natural segregation of the races and said there could never be racial amalgamation. "Men of both races," Harding asserted in Birmingham, "may well stand uncompromising against every suggestion of social equality. Indeed, it would be helpful to have the word 'equality' eliminated from this consideration; to have it accepted by both sides that this is not a question of social equality, but a question of recognizing a fundamental, eternal and inescapable difference."

The remarks were eerily reminiscent of another Republican's comments on the issue sixty-three years earlier: "I am not, nor ever have been, in favor of bringing about in any way the social and political equality of the white and black races," this early Republican said to a crowd in Charleston, Illinois, in 1858. "I am not nor ever have been in favor of making voters or jurors of negroes, nor of qualifying them to hold office, nor to intermarry with white people," Abraham Lincoln told his audience in the southern part of his state as he ran against Stephen Douglas for the senate. "There is a physical difference between the white and black races," he said that day in 1858, "which I believe will forever forbid the two races living together on terms of social and political equality."[46]

The mixed theme Harding expressed in Birmingham—political and economic equality but social and racial segregation—was the same mixed message he delivered during the campaign. African American delegations who visited Harding at his house in Marion on "Colored Voters Day" during the campaign found Jim Crow alive and well at Marion's hotels and restaurants. In a speech in Oklahoma City on October 9, Harding spoke against a law that would authorize the federal government, by force if necessary, to supervise elections in the southern states and said, "I do not mean that white people and black people shall be forced to associate together in accepting their equal rights at the hands of the nation."[47]

Harding's administration got bogged down in scandal. The sleazy Daugherty did not forget about Professor Chancellor. After Chancellor was fired by the College of Wooster, he set about to complete a book, *The Illustrated Life of President Warren G. Harding*. Daugherty learned of the project and sent government agents to investigate. In the presence of a Post Office inspector and two secret service agents, Chancellor was forced to burn his manuscript in his backyard. He fled to Canada with an extra copy he had not burned and returned in 1922, published it, but again Daugherty, the nation's top law enforcement officer, suppressed the book, causing FBI agents to buy up or seize copies distributed in Ohio. Russell wrote, "Chancellor's book became one of the rarest bibliographical items in twentieth-century American history."[48]

Harding would die under suspicious circumstances in San Francisco on August 2, 1923. Some claimed his wife poisoned him after learning of his marital infidelities. She did spend weeks after Harding's funeral in the White House and elsewhere "gathering up and destroying every bit of her husband's correspondence, official and unofficial, that she could lay her hands on," Russell writes. "Her last year of life—she died on November 21, 1924—was a busy one, but her motives were incendiary rather than sentimental."[49]

Did FDR know of or participate in the spread of rumors about Harding's ancestry? Geoffrey Ward wrote that twenty years after the election of 1920 (during the presidential campaign of 1940) Roosevelt offered an "eccentric theory" to explain the election's outcome. Roosevelt claimed that Harding's own campaign manager, Harry Daugherty, planted the story that Harding had a black ancestor by purposely telling a Methodist minister in Marion of the rumor. "The Methodist minister, who was a Democrat, got all upset and he started the story all over the place," according to Roosevelt. "The press took it up, and it was the most terrific boomerang against *us*. . . . He [Daugherty] planted it on *us*."[50]

Ward also noted, "The rumors of Harding's black ancestry continued to fascinate Franklin. Even after he and Cox were defeated he eagerly shared the latest allegations with Josephus Daniels, who noted them in his journal on December 10, 1920: 'FDR here. He said that in 1854 a man named Butler killed a man named Smith for calling his wife a negro. Later Gov. of Ohio at the request of Harding's grandfather pardoned the murderer.'"[51]

But a strange and almost undetectable transformation began in the 1920 campaign. While it represented the low point in Democratic racist attacks, and Harding was courageous in his fight for equal rights, the Democratic defeat was followed by one of those strange magical paradoxes of history, especially American history—the type that turn matters on their head—in this case, changing everything in the politics of race in the United States.

James Cox and FDR in Dayton, Ohio (August 7, 1920). One of the last photos of FDR walking. Courtesy Franklin D. Roosevelt Library, Hyde Park.

The summer after the election a tiny virus invaded Franklin D. Roosevelt and took the use of his legs. Roosevelt went to a Boy Scout summer camp—a last public appearance before returning to private life—where it is believed that he contracted infantile paralysis. This agent of personal disaster became the spark for national change and healing. Felled by polio, FDR spent the next eight years desperately trying to teach himself to walk again. It was a frustrating, agonizing, and ultimately fruitless exercise.

During this time, Eleanor Roosevelt ascended. She was propelled into the spotlight, speaking on her husband's behalf, and becoming his legs. In her effort to keep his political career alive, she became a political force in her own right. Her rise in power and influence, coupled with FDR's own awakening brought on by his struggles, would ultimately lead to the great migration of African Americans from the Republican Party to the Democratic Party, a movement that began during the Roosevelt years.

Meanwhile, Durbin and Cox would break in 1924, and this split would play a role in Durbin's stance at the 1932 convention, where he would become the first Ohio delegate in the 1932 convention to bolt for Roosevelt.

Light above begins to break and fall into this dismal place I have been inhabiting. There will be redemption, and it will come in spite of my great grandfather's and the Democratic Party's bigotry; indeed, it sometimes seems that the forces that eventually push through to enlightenment and freedom are forces that originally appear to be going in just the opposite direction.

A strange-looking man, resembling Louis Howe, the gnome who managed FDR through his long struggle to overcome paralysis, the man Eleanor could not abide at first but who would become one of her closest friends, descends toward me, bringing a glass filled with water from the River Lethe.

"Here, drink, you must," he says, coughing, as he pulls on a cigarette and hands over the glass.

I take the glass but hesitate. I do not want to forget. The man-gnome encourages me, "I made the boss drink the same glass, trust me."

I take a big, long drink.

The gnome smiles and turns to walk away, floating upward.

As he fades out of sight, I spit most of the water on the ground. I hear the Doctor laughing and start my flight back, like Satan escaping from hell, to the upper world.

A car horn rouses me.

⇒ 11 ⇐

KENTON, MAGIC CAPITAL
OF THE WORLD!

June 9 and 10, 1926

"Those had been desperate days, the natives informed me, days fraught with unknown dangers."[1]

Another car horn blasts.

I hear the words, waking from my sleep, or at least I think I am awakening. I have cut through my fogginess and disorientation, but the sounds around me take precedence over everything else. I stand for a moment and stretch, eyes closed, just listening to the voices.

"But I say to you," someone says, "love your enemies, and pray for those who persecute you, that you may be children to your heavenly Father, for he makes his sun rise on the bad and the good, and causes rain to fall on the just and unjust."[2]

"It was nothing, I'm told," another voice says to my left, "for a good housewife to wend her way down Kenton's principal thoroughfare only to be stopped by some bearded stranger who immediately took three chickens and a head of cabbage out of the market basket that she believed to be empty."

"Yes," another says, "sleek-faced old gentlemen, of the most benign appearance, stood beneficently in hotel lobbies and in the midst of fatherly conversations with little boys, suddenly burst into flames. The moral is obvious. Young men, who seemed in the best of health, sat themselves at luncheon tables only to become suddenly pale and tortured looking. Then they extracted daggers from their throats."

"Hey, young fellow, you best open your eyes if you're going to walk down the street!"

Durbin with dove outside his house in Kenton (ca. 1920). Author's collection.

I slowly open my eyes, expecting to be safely back in the car, awakened from my trip to the netherworld. We should be well on the way to Washington, Pennsylvania, with Wheeling and the Ohio River not far beyond.

Delbert will be there, a welcome face. I wonder how I will react to Durbin; what will I say after what I have learned?

But I am standing; there is no car. I must still be dreaming, taken to a deeper dimension.

As I open my eyes, I am rocked back on my heels by the sight: a beautiful, breezy day, clouds floating like great cotton balls, pale blue sky, and all around me is Kenton, Ohio.

Old Fords, Studebakers, and other sedans, roadsters, and coupes motor around the streets of the city's quaint public square. People walk briskly, and big streetbanners and large posters in redbrick storefronts welcome magicians to this, the first annual convention of the International Brotherhood of Magicians.

And damned if I am not in Kenton, and it is June 1926!

Kenton, the Jerusalem of the magic world during the first days of June, was alive with mystery in the summer of 1926. The city would host the first two conventions of the International Brotherhood of Magicians, and journalists came from all over to write with delight of the convocations of the magi in what would be the very first conventions of the IBM.[3]

"Wizards and warlocks, necromancers and magicians, may they long live and prosper, may they thrive in the land of the free and the home of a race which, by the grace of providence, does not lose its love of wonder or its craving for mystification," a reporter from the *Cleveland Plain Dealer* wrote about one of the conventions. "At Kenton the wizards of the United States gathered in mock-solemn convention are showing their tricks to each other and presenting some of the best for the bewilderment and edification of the citizenry. We think Kenton is a lucky city. It is not a big city, and doubtless does not hope for many national conventions. If we were choosing a convention for sheer downright joy we would select this gathering of light-fingered adepts to make us forget how wise and sophisticated and blasé the world has become."[4]

These were the "bunny snatchers" conventions. "For the remainder of the week the bunny snatchers—journeyman and apprentice—will borrow tall hats from unsuspecting residents of this community and produce anything from a Belgian hare to an Asiatic elephant," one paper wrote.[5]

One journalist for the *St. Louis Post-Dispatch*, Julius Kleimann, found the atmosphere in Kenton during one of these IBM gatherings there nothing short of astounding. "I had not been off the train two minutes," wrote Kleimann, "and had walked into the dining room of the nearest hotel, when I apprehended a stoutish gentleman with a flowing mustache shaking fifteen silver dollars out of a banker's nose. It was reported to me that this was the first time an Ohio banker had fifteen dollars of any kind or denomination shaken from him in the history of that commonwealth."[6]

"Now, in the Empire of Magic, Kenton, Ohio, is its capital," Kleimann wrote. He was particularly interested in meeting the man who was behind such a convention. "I asked for [Durbin] and he was pointed out to me, there in that very dining room, engaged in vociferously applauding the mustachioed creature who was extracting 15 silver dollars from an Ohio banker's nose. This didn't mean that Mr. Durbin was anticapitalist, for he is, as I have before noted, the head of a large sign-making plant.

"I found him a tall, slender man of about 60. He was very neatly dressed. He stooped a bit. He seemed kindly, a bit nervous in his actions; he seemed pleasant and gentle. But I remembered the benign old gentlemen who, in the midst of fatherly conversations with little boys, suddenly burst into flames, and as I walked toward this Durbin I kept on my guard."[7]

I look around and see the faces of the magicians mixing with townspeople in this square. Harry Blackstone, with his signature wavy, dark, full head of hair and trim mustache, is here somewhere in this town. Harlan Tarbell, the author of a seven-volume work, The Tarbell Course in Magic, *is here too. His work will become a classic in magic.*

In fact over one hundred magicians from all over the country and the world converged on Kenton in the summer of 1926. They included such notables as El Barto, Sarvias LeRoy, and Dean Powell.

El Barto was Jim Barton, the "dean of Philadelphia magicians." Barton was old enough to remember as a child being lifted up by his foster mother to get a glimpse of Lincoln in his casket in New York's City Hall. "We waited in line five hours," he wrote, "and when we finally filed past that huge coffin she lifted me up to peer into that calm and rugged face. It made an indelible impression."[8]

The magicians walking the streets are well dressed, many with double-breasted wool suits and almost everyone has their hair slicked straight back. They have IBM *convention badges attached to their lapels. They stop and greet one another and mingle with regular townsfolk. Backslapping and laughter abound.*

The convention ran for two days, Wednesday and Thursday, June 9 and 10. Early in the week the weather threatened to be disruptive. High winds and gales swept across the country and cold weather made the first days of June feel like March. The newspaper reported that the cold spell "sent the thermometer this week about 30 degrees lower than it was at the same time last year."[9]

Fortunately the weather cooperated, and things warmed up. The town was abuzz with anticipation. "Elaborate preparations for the entertainment of the notable guests have been completed under the direction of W. W. Durbin, manager of the Scioto Sign Co., and host," the newspaper announced on June 5. "Judging from the acceptances that have been received, Mr. Durbin stated that the convention here promises to mark the greatest gathering of magi ever brought together at one time."[10]

Durbin convinced magicians to come to Kenton before he was the president of the IBM or the editor of *The Linking Ring*. The draw was Durbin's magic theater, which he called Egyptian Hall.

"The two-day session will be held in Durbin's Egyptian Hall, which has become familiarly known as the 'Mecca of Magicians,'" the Kenton newspaper reported. "It was constructed by Mr. Durbin in 1895 for the performance and study of the magic art as a hobby. Through his research, study, and extensive work in this field, the Kenton man has become prominently known in the profession.

"One of the features of the convention will be the inspection of the notable gallery of more than 3,000 photographs of the great and near-great magicians, illusionists, mind-readers, spirit mediums and ventriloquists from the time of Castiostro down to the present day. The gallery was completed by Durbin and installed in his Egyptian Hall. During these thirty-one years there have sat within these walls most all the magicians in America, and many of the lesser lights."[11]

David Price of Tennessee bought what was left of the innards of Egyptian Hall, including the picture gallery in 1953, almost thirty years after the first IBM convention was held in it. He moved everything he bought to his home in Nashville, where he built a museum dedicated to Durbin.[12]

When I went to visit Price and his wife, Virginia, in October 1993, he was eighty-three and all but completely wheelchair-bound from foot injuries he suffered during WWII. He had broken both of his arches during the war, and when we met he could only pad his way across the room in his wheelchair, stand for a moment, and then take a few precarious steps to get something to show me. And then he would sit back down. He was a Southern gentleman, a gracious host with thinning, stringy white hair and a gray goatee. He spoke with such a deep Southern accent that I think I missed half of what he said. Price joined the IBM in 1929. He told me that it was a source of great pride that W. W. Durbin signed his membership card. He met Durbin in person at the 1930 convention held in Fort Wayne, Indiana. Price bought the Egyptian Hall relics from Tom Dowd.

Dowd and his brother Bob acquired Egyptian Hall from Durbin's widow a few years after Durbin died. "When the Durbin estate was settled," Bob Dowd wrote in an article that appeared in *The Linking Ring* in 1994, "I was living on my own in Cincinnati. His apparatus, books and whatever paraphernalia existed [had been] sold." The structure and some of its contents, however, were still extant. "At any rate," Dowd continued, "the building, with its vestibule, walls and ceiling covered with a plethora of photos mounted under glass, as well as the large book-like folio of 8 x 10's which stood head-high, to the right of the stage, remained." Also unsold were the "distinctive front curtain with its Egyptian painting" and the large glass cabinets in which Durbin stored his tricks behind the stage.[13]

Dowd had been fascinated by the magic hall while growing up. He was drawn to it, reveling in its mystique and its history. "As a kid, often on my two mile walk from school, I would go a bit out of my way to walk through an alley behind the Hall and stare at the doves [in a wire cage hung outside], remembering how they magically appeared during Uncle Bill's performance at the Grand Opera House."

The Dowds moved the theater from Durbin's backyard to their farm just outside town. A mover "placed beams under the building carefully and, once raised, Egyptian Hall moved slowly off its lot, down a wide alley, and onto the National Highway which led to our farm home," Dowd wrote, "its destination."

The move was risky. "It was a curious show for small-town people to see a rather large, ungainly building moving slowly down the highway like a ship on a country canal," Dowd remembered. "But, then came the tricky part. Coming to a stop, the building had to be moved sideways, over a ditch, and about sixty feet away from the road, to match up with its foundations—hopefully to be set in place without event."

Durbin might have been disturbed at the sight of his wondrous hall being spirited away. But, as recounted by Dowd, Durbin still had one last trick to perform in the little theater.

"Now," Dowd wrote in *The Linking Ring*, "I'm going to tell you about a strange coincidence which can never be written for the general public because it would be scoffed at and called hype or a public relations put-on. But, I can assure you that this little quirk happened in exactly the following manner." Everything was left in place during the move, including the photos on the wall. The final maneuvering involved carefully setting the building onto its newly constructed foundations. "The moving crew and all of us involved were standing outside the building watching as the last jack was removed and the Hall settled perfectly on its foundations."

For a split second, it seemed that all was well, then everyone heard the crash.

"Hurrying inside," Dowd recalled, "we stopped in surprise and with a feeling of uncertain wonderment. After all the wear and tear and displacement of moving, no glass was broken over any of the mounted photos. But, lying on the walk across the center foots, its glass shattered into bits and pieces, face up, was the photo of 'Uncle Bill.'"

Dowd and his friends were sure the crash of Durbin's photo was no accident. "Dramatic in its timing, it left us all with more than just a touch of strangeness," he wrote. "It was, indeed, a theater of mystery."[14]

Egyptian Hall became the center of activity at the 1926 convention. On the opening day, magicians all registered there and inspected the photo gallery. A luncheon was served downtown at noon as part of a joint session of the Chamber of Commerce and the Kiwanis Club, but the opening session commenced at two in the afternoon back in Egyptian Hall. A group photo was shot in Durbin's backyard near the theater, and there then followed a program of old and new magic presented by magicians for magicians only.[15]

"You can always get the boys to come if there is going to be a show," Durbin said, "but if you are going to sit around and talk there will not be the same attraction."[16]

Fred Hurd of Fort Wayne, an old-timer, came out dressed in knee breeches, a stiff bosomed shirt, and swallow-tailed coat. "This is the get-up I wore thirty years ago," he said, "except I can't buy any detachable cuffs anymore."[17]

The members then paraded to the square, establishing a tradition of parades that would become more elaborate, with floats and bands, each following year.

Wednesday evening featured a grand banquet with entertainment at the Elks' Home. A local orchestra provided music, and the master of ceremonies was the inimitable "Dorny" from Chicago.

"Dorny" was Werner Dornfield, IBM member number ten, the author of a magic book, *Trix and Chatter*. He was a comedic magician. His stage name might as well have been "the inimitable Dorny" because that adjective always appeared before his name in any story about him. His "funny antics and droll manner of delivery had them falling out of their seats," one reporter wrote. His performance in 1926 was so compelling that he set himself up to return as the master of ceremonies for the IBM conventions in the next four years.[18]

"The IBM convention without Dorny would be like the play Hamlet with Hamlet left out," Durbin wrote in 1928. "The many funny skits he puts on, particularly the one where he shot dead the medium who had vanished his wife and who told him that no one else could bring her back, is something we shall never forget."[19]

But fame is a fleeting thing. Dorny eventually fell out of favor, burning out like a moth in a flame. Something happened to cause a rift with Durbin, and Dorny became disgruntled and resigned. "By the way," Durbin wrote his lieutenant Al Saal in November 1930, "I received a letter from Dorny resigning from the IBM. I mention it to you because I want it kept quiet because I think he would like to have it broadcast that he is resigning from the IBM, and that is exactly what we don't want to give him, any more publicity."[20]

Although there is no record of the genesis of the dispute, Durbin seemed to think that Dorny was not pulling his weight and that he was ungrateful for the attention and honors he had received from the IBM.

"You know as well as I do that reduced to his lowest terms, Dorny is nothing more than a baby," an angry Durbin wrote Saal. "He has never been a success at anything and possesses some little cheap wit which has secured him a little notoriety and then we of the IBM got back of him by making him Master of Ceremony for four years and he got more acquaintances and publicity than he ever got in his life. . . . [H]e has never had the manhood and the gratitude that comes from manhood to stand up and say a good word for us."[21]

Whatever it was, Durbin was at peace with his handling of Dorny. "Dorny," he concluded his letter to Saal, "has never put anything into the IBM but on the contrary he has drawn out much. If he is satisfied, I am because I know we have done our full duty by him and we leave it to time—the time that cures all things."

But on the opening night at the Elks' Home, there were no signs of trouble, and Dorny was a hit, the toast of Kenton.

Inez Blackstone, Harry Blackstone's wife, played piano accompaniments for the evening program at the Elks, as over three hundred people—magicians, guests, and lucky townsfolk—ate lavish dinners and settled in for a night of mystery and intrigue. One after another, magicians popped up to perform, each trying to outdo the other. They performed card tricks, coin tricks, the Indian rope trick, and other acts of legerdemain. Harry Blackstone unveiled a new illusion called "The Man Who Walks Away from His Shadow."

Durbin, Harry Blackstone (cap), and friends outside Egyptian Hall. Courtesy Mike Caveney's Egyptian Hall.

"In this latest illusion," the Kenton newspaper reported, "Blackstone permits his shadow to be thrown on an ordinary window shade behind which is located an arc lamp. The shadow is clearly seen and as Blackstone steps out of the range of the light, the stage is darkened and the silhouette continues to stand clearly on the shade."[22]

Harry and Inez Blackstone were a formidable team in 1926. Harry was originally from Chicago, born there in 1885, and christened Harry Boughton. His early act included his brother Pete, a cabinetmaker and mechanic. Harry was the real showman of the brothers. "The Two Franciscos" or "Harry Bouton and Company" toured in the Midwest before Harry began starring on his own as "Fredrik the Great" in 1915.

Inez met Harry in 1917. Inez was a vaudeville performer from Wisconsin who was quite musical. She was billed as the "Little Banjophiend" because of her proficiency on the banjo. She was also a talent on the piano. She became Harry's musical director and led his orchestra, sometimes playing banjo during interludes.[23]

The two were married in 1919; he changed his name to "The Great Blackstone," and his stock rose. By the time of the first convention in Kenton, he was one of the established names in magic. "One of the most noted of the famous magicians of all time," the Kenton newspapers declared when he came to town.[24]

In a group picture taken in the backyard near Egyptian Hall, Inez stands right next to Durbin and Harry stands some distance away. Inez thought that this convention was "one of the high-lights of my life."

"As I recall it now," she wrote years later, "it stands out like a single constellation in the sky." There were "those clubby little shows in our president's own Egyptian Hall," and "the lawn fete tendered us by our president and his charming wife." The gathering was like that of "a lot of kids on a picnic, playing pranks on each other, kidding, joking, fun!" Everywhere, mystery sparkled. "Like a school child with many little secrets to whisper among friends, we see little groups here and there with their heads together, greatly mystified or laughing heartily over some newly discovered twist of the wrist."

"Oh! them were the happy days!" she wrote. "But we were very young then and gay and carefree as all young things are. A beautiful memory!"[25]

There was no time for sleeping at this first convention. One participant wrote: "Everyone had a good time, even Magical McGuirk, and magic was discussed and cussed until three and four o'clock every A.M. by mutual consent, for no other reason at all other than, 'Didja ever see this one?' or 'I remember when. . . .'"

Durbin shows Blackstone a trick. Courtesy Mike Caveney's Egyptian Hall.

"The Necromantic Cards." Durbin in earlier times (ca. 1900). Author's collection.

"When several hundred good fellows get together and have nothing else to do but talk and perform magic for two days, well, take a pencil and draw your own conclusions."[26]

Despite the late night on the first day, things got started early the next morning with an automobile tour of Kenton that included a stop at the Scioto Sign Company.

Freelance performances sprouted up everywhere, "At noon Robert H. Gysel, of Toledo, O., surprised the citizens of Kenton by walking and running through heavy traffic while blindfolded."

Later Gysel held a private performance at Durbin's sign company. "This afternoon at one o'clock, while one hundred or more employees and officials of the Scioto Sign Company, a handful of newspapermen and a few other invited guests watched with mouths agape, Mr. Gysel jammed six large darning needles through his left arm. The young ladies in the audience saw fit to emit a few exclamations, while the men contented themselves with trembling. Gysel continued to smile and talk as if it were merely the day's business, which with him it is."[27]

This was no ordinary trick. "The needles were real needles and he really pushed them through his arm. This morning a representative of the *Daily Democrat* was permitted to draw taut the skin of his upper arm for the demonstration. No blood flowed from the wound. Gysel claims that the secret of the trick is that he stopped his heartbeat."

The town also delighted in the antics of George G. Polley, "The Original Human Fly." "Mr. Polley will give a thrilling performance on the Hardin County courthouse Thursday," the newspaper predicted. "Using only his hands and feet, he will ascend from the ground to the top of the flag pole on that building. He will use neither hooks or ropes nor rely on the assistance of anyone in getting over the most difficult projections on the sides and corners of the courthouse."[28]

At two in the afternoon, the magicians returned to Egyptian Hall, this time to conduct their business session and to elect their officers. Len Vintus, the young Canadian who started the IBM with two Americans, had named himself president of the order, although never elected, and he was there to preside.[29] Durbin later claimed that he did not seek the presidency and had no beef with Vintus, but I suspect the experienced politician left nothing to chance. In his own town, on his own turf, it is no coincidence that when the ballots were counted, Durbin was elected president. Harry Blackstone was elected the first vice president and Dean Frederick Powell the second vice president. Vintus was caught off guard. To soothe the wound, Durbin appointed Vintus secretary, presented him with a medal for his service as past president, and encouraged him to retain his title as editor of *The Linking Ring*. Within a year, the editor's job also passed to Durbin, leaving no doubt as to who was in control.

Durbin was important to the growth of the order. He applied his political and organizational skills to its membership. The IBM was just 600 members

Len Vintus, one of the founders of the IBM, Durbin, and Percy Abbott in Durbin's yard.
Courtesy Mike Caveney's Egyptian Hall.

in 1926. In the next year, through Durbin's constant prodding, membership
rose to 1,800. It passed the 2,500 marker in 1928 and continued to accelerate.

Durbin asked members to "cudgel their brains" about how to get new
initiates and he said the motto should be "do it now."[30]

"Don't wait for George to do it," was his constant refrain.[31]

He worried about expenses and was constantly looking for money. "I presume," he wrote, "that many of you will imagine in my life I have been a minister because I always speak of money."[32] When he took charge of moving the printing of *The Linking Ring* from Winnipeg to Kenton at the Scioto Sign Company, he improved the quality of paper stock and produced the monthly at a fraction of the cost it took to make it in Canada.

By 1935, the roles of the IBM had swelled to over five thousand. In *The Linking Ring,* Durbin kept careful track of the lives and doings of his members, reprinting complimentary newspaper stories, profiling professional and the amateur magicians alike, posting performance and route schedules, and asking for help when someone fell on hard times.

"Peace to his ashes," he would write when someone died. There was a steady stream of sentimental memorials and obituaries. He reminded members of significant birthdays of older magicians, suggesting, for example, when Dean Powell turned eighty, "In honor of this wonderful old man who has done so much for magic," the order should "give him a letter or postcard shower so as to reach him" on his birthday.[33]

Magicians referred to Durbin affectionately as "Uncle Bill" or "Colonel Durbin" and named the local IBM club in Rochester, New York, the "W. W. Durbin Ring."

Strong as his personality was, though, Durbin was not without his detractors. He was attacked outside the IBM for increasing membership by accepting people of limited or questionable experience as magicians. For Durbin, such matters were treated like any other political fight. When an article critical of Durbin, "IBM or Friends of Magic," appeared in *Billboard* in 1928, he took the fight to the membership: "It is time for every member to stand up and be counted. Those who are not with us are against us." To Durbin, you were either a booster or a knocker. "I realize," he wrote, "that when one is successful in this world he always excites envy, jealousy and malice, but that should never deter any honest man from going ahead and doing his full duty as God gives him the light to see and do it. Whenever the IBM wants a new president the members know how to get one, and I will always be found working in the ranks with the other loyal members to uphold and support him."[34]

He also had opponents within the order. Len Vintus, the founder of the IBM, resigned in 1927.

"Len is only a boy," Durbin wrote Al Saal in May 1927. "He started this order but he never was elected president of it. He elected himself and kept himself in office for four years. Then unfortunately for him, without any knowledge of mine, he put my name on the ticket for president, and God knows I didn't want the office, but the boys elected me and insisted that I could serve, and I think my record will compare favorably with his."[35]

The final straw for Vintus came when Durbin insisted that *The Linking Ring* be printed in Kenton rather than Winnipeg. Durbin claimed that the cost to print in Canada was double the cost of printing in Kenton. "I argued this to him and pleaded with him, but he is only a boy and he plead the baby act and is still pleading it, but he finally resigned and I can't help it. I babied him all I am going to, and this order is too big to be run by fellows who can't be criticized in their actions. I am glad to accept any criticism that is coming to me at any time, and I will always take my medicine. The great trouble with Vintus is he thought he 'owned' the order. He forgot that some of you fellows had something to do with it."[36]

Much to my surprise, I found Vintus still alive in 1994. I tracked down his telephone number and called him on a cold Sunday afternoon in January. His real name was Vincent McMullen, and he was ninety years old when we spoke, but he was still sharp as a tack and very friendly. He had an exact memory of the events of 1926 and 1927. "Mr. Durbin was a very able businessman who could talk by the hour without taking a breath," he said. He characterized Durbin as "a very kindly man," who could be "abrupt at times."

Durbin was described by Vintus as a "wealthy man and an able, top politician." Vintus had especially fond memories of the 1926 convention. "People came from so far away. New Zealand and England. It was like a country picnic with a fete on the side lawn. Dorny ran around dressed as a cop arresting anyone who did a card trick."

I did not ask him if he harbored hard feelings toward Durbin, but he did tell me that he had kept a picture of Durbin's grave.

After I hung up, it occurred to me he may not have kept the photo out of respect for my great grandfather.

Since no one has come to meet me, I have decided to leave the town square and to walk out to the Durbin house.

I suppose by now Delbert and Durbin are nearing the Ohio River at Wheeling in the car on the National Road. I am beginning to wonder how I will get back to the car or if my absence has been noticed. When will I wake from this disconnected series of dreams?

Pondering these things, I start walking toward Resch Street. Then of all the strange things I see a man who looks remarkably like Delbert, jogging down a side alley. Just as he turns the corner out of sight, he releases two doves from nowhere, and they fly right past me and swoop up, turning in the direction of the Durbin house and Egyptian Hall.

I use them as guides and finally come to the home.

There, I find groups of magicians are gathered on the side lawn, mingling and eating outdoors in the bright but dappled fading sun of a long June day.

A string of flags runs from the house to Egyptian Hall and then out into the back lawn. There are people sitting on the wicker chairs on the porch that wraps around the front of this white clapboard house.

The name Durbin is engraved in the cement steps leading up to the porch. Everyone looks relaxed, some whisper secrets while others are boisterous and loud. They are so involved in the festivities that no one takes notice of my approach.

On the side of the house, there are a few men in dark suits who appear to be secretly drinking from silver flasks, a reminder to me that this is still the heart of Prohibition.

Most of the people on the side lawn are pointing to a couple of magicians who have managed to climb onto the roof of Egyptian Hall.

Len Vintus described this scene in a piece he wrote about the first convention, during which several magicians appointed themselves "card trick cops": "I will always take my hat off to Joseph Schreck, of Cincinnati, and Carl S. Lohrey, of Dayton, Ohio, who handed me the biggest laugh of my life, when to evade the persistent 'Dorny,' the official cop, and feeling a new card trick coming over them, they ascended to the roof of the Egyptian Hall and started exhibiting same in view of all the boys who were eating on Mr. Durbin's lawn."[37]

I circle around to the area just below the two exhibitionists and stop to take in the group, leaning against a tree. I want to pick out my grandparents, Francis and Agnes, because I know they must be here. I see the Blackstones sitting at a table, and I find Durbin in the middle of an engrossing conversation with two men whom I don't recognize. I can't find my grandparents.

Durbin stands and tings his glass with his fork and announces it is time to move inside. The magicians all begin to file into Egyptian Hall for the closing program. There are not enough seats inside, so many take up positions outside the windows looking in to hear the speeches and to watch the short magic program.

Occasionally someone outside will make a remark through the windows, and the group inside will yell back.

I walk a little closer across the matted lawn and see Durbin inside the hall giving a speech.[38]

"We desire to cultivate a spirit of harmony and brotherhood among all magicians," he says, "wherever they may be. We deprecate the idea of copying of acts and programs of magicians, and we would inculcate the idea of a magician

being original." There is a smattering of applause. "We are unalterably opposed to the exposing of the principles of this wonderful art, believing it is undermining the foundations which underlie our art and which cannot but result disastrously to all concerned." This brings much applause.

Exposé, of course, is death to magic. Secrets must be carefully guarded or the wonder of it all would be lost. Durbin felt so strongly about this that he set up an Exposé Committee within the IBM. Even Blackstone was almost thrown out of the IBM in 1930 when he allegedly wrote an article in the *Billboard* advocating the exposition of old tricks. "This has raised particular hell," Durbin wrote to Saal, "and you ought to see the letters I am getting about this."[39]

Durbin heard through Howard Thurston, the other well-known magician of the day, that Blackstone said the article was written as a joke by his advance agent. "But you know this is a mighty serious joke," Durbin wrote, "and it is like putting a tripping rope across the sidewalk after dark and allowing someone to fall and fracturing his skull. It may be a joke for the foolish boy who did it but it is mighty serious to the one whose skull is fractured."

A few days later, Durbin wrote again to Saal: "This is all I am going to say about this matter and don't bother yourself about him and let the boys keep on pelting him. Of all the fool things anybody ever had, this is the worst. It almost looks like a man hanging himself to get on the front page of the newspaper."

Blackstone eventually sent a telegram to Durbin claiming innocence. "Just a wild press story of my advance agent," he wired. "I am against all that class of exposing, nevertheless it woke up the magicians. Long live good magic."

Durbin was placated, saying, "Since Blackstone repudiates this," it would be counterproductive to further reprimand him. This, Durbin wrote, would only provide "our enemies a chance if we fight among ourselves."

So intent was Durbin on keeping secrets that he routinely warned magicians not to leave copies of *The Linking Ring* lying around the house.[40] "We have had several complaints from members of the order who have gone into places where the Linking Ring has been lying around so that any person could pick it up and read it," Durbin wrote in 1928. "Just remember that the Linking Ring is not a magazine that circulates outside of our own membership. Naturally it should be kept within the membership, and we want to suggest to all members that when you get your copy that after you read it you put it away so that outsiders can't see it and read it."

When Durbin finishes his speech in Egyptian Hall, the boys give him a standing ovation, including Harry Blackstone.

Durbin drinks it in, standing with a wide smile as he acknowledges their cheers.

For the next twelve years, Durbin would guide this group, solidifying his leadership with the deft moves of the savvy politician. He wrote endless "confidential" letters, started a fight when necessary, and kept his counsel when he sensed it was the best course.

In one of his disputes with Doc Wilson, the editor of the rival magic magazine *Sphinx,* Durbin showed he could walk away from a fight. "I am too smart for that," he wrote Saal. "I know he lives and thrives on personal quarrels. Look at his picture and you can see it in his face. . . . The boys are on to him. Let him go and we will saw wood and say nothing."[41]

Like any good politician, Durbin took care of patronage, promoting his friends within the IBM. To the loyal Saal, he wrote a letter encouraging him to run for two offices at once. That way Saal would have a good chance of winning at least one of them. "I think you get the idea," Durbin wrote of the scheme and then illustrated his point. "A fellow took his mother-in-law out to Colorado and she died there. He telegraphed his brother-in-law, 'Shall we embalm, bury or cremate?' To which the brother-in-law promptly replied: 'Take no chances, do all three.'"[42]

The centerpiece of Durbin's IBM was the annual convention. In 1927 the IBM brought the convention back to Kenton. It was moved to Lima, Ohio, in 1928 and 1929, and then to Fort Wayne, Indiana, in 1930. In addition to conventions, a core group would organize a series of "Back to Kenton" weekends over the years to recall the earliest conventions.[43]

The convention of 1927 was five times the size of the 1926 gathering. Fox and Paramount came to film the parades and showed newsreels of the event in ten thousand movie houses around the country. The *New York Times* began to cover the festivals. Magicians came from England, Scotland, Germany, France, Australia, and Canada.[44]

Blackstone and Thurston, despite their competition, appeared together and were wildly applauded by the magicians when they held private performances. In 1928 Asa Chandler, the chairman of Coca-Cola, came to the Lima convention, bringing his fourteen-year-old son and a Filipino retainer, hired to act as the boy's magic assistant.[45]

There was little to compare to these invasions of magicians. The group staged outdoor entertainments, grand matinees for the "kiddies," and nightly programs for adults. Strong men burst blood vessels while struggling to lift diminutive magicians who seemed to be nailed to the ground. Daredevils would allow themselves to be suspended, upside down in straitjackets, from a local bank or office building, and would escape in minutes. Others were bound, handcuffed, tied in a sacks and locked in trunks, but they too would liberate themselves in seconds. Lester Lake was always buried alive or burned alive, until his unfortunate accident. Someone was always driving blind-folded through traffic. In hotel lobbies and on street corners, magicians of every shape and size plied their trade. There was the amateur's contest and prizes were given for the best card trick, the best trick with coins or money, the best trick with livestock, the best trick with balls, the best trick utilizing flowers, the best escape or self liberation, the best anti-spiritualistic or mind-reading effect, the best trick by a lady magician, and the best impromptu trick without apparatus.

Humor suffused everything and came out in the news media's reports of the affairs. "In some respects, all these sorcerers are like ordinary citizens, Lima residents have already learned," one journalist wrote. "They forget magic while at their meals, it was demonstrated at the opening night ban-quet. A portion of them go about in fear of their wives, it must also be recorded. One wonder worker stopped at the office of the Lima Star late Thursday and pleaded with the editorial staff to use his name in at least one story. He wanted to take home a clipping proving that he actually had at-tended the convention."[46]

In the end, I wanted to be here not because of the zaniness or the magic or the hilarity of it all. I wanted to be here because this was my family.

In 1928 the convention ended with a major performance in a crowded theater in Lima that was outfitted with radio transmitters so that "everyone in the remotest corners could distinctly hear every word."

"The atmosphere sparkled with mystery as the great show began," a writer for *The Linking Ring* reported. "Again the lid of the magic cauldron was removed and magic, mirth and mystery came forth to the delight of the mystified eyes of the assembly."

Durbin would close this night. "As a crowning feature, Colonel Durbin closed the entertainment with a flow of his best illusions. He received many floral gifts as a token of high esteem from his hundreds of admirers and friends. The applause rang to the roof of the theatre and the show had to be stopped until the great demonstration ceased."

And here is where it becomes magic for me:

Then he performed the doll house illusion and much to the delight of the awe-stricken spectators, out jumped little Miss Durbin, the at-tractive five-year-old daughter of Mr. and Mrs. Francis Durbin. The audience was deeply touched as the sweet little child threw her arms

Durbin and his granddaughter, Margaret Morgan Durbin, at the 1926 IBM Convention
in Durbin's backyard. Courtesy Mike Caveney's Egyptian Hall.

around her grandfather's neck and kissed him. Some were respectfully silent, many were moved to tears, and many cheered wildly with
delight.[47]

*The door to Egyptian Hall flies open and an older woman steps out. She
looks at me and smiles, says a polite, "Hello." She walks right past me to go into
the house. After a moment, I realize that this is Mary Durbin, my great-grandmother. She had no idea who I was.*

*Others begin to trundle out of the hall and, eventually, Durbin himself
emerges. He glances at me, but says nothing. There is no hint of recognition.*

*I stand among all these characters, and I wonder what happened to all of
their lives. Where did they go?*

*Then it hits me: I am stranded here in Kenton. Durbin does not seem to know
me, and Delbert is running loose in town. There is no sign of the Studebaker.*

*My guess is that Durbin and Delbert now have entered Ohio and are headed
for Cambridge and Zanesville. I hope they know I am already here in Kenton.*

It is getting dark, and I think it is best to head back downtown to find a place for the night. I may try dinner at Abe Martin's; perhaps I can get a room at the Weaver Hotel.

I bump into the group that has been secretly drinking on the other side of the house, and I recognize Andy Durbin. He is beginning to stagger.

In my slow stroll back downtown, I think about how quickly it all goes. Even the great disappear, leaving behind various degrees of proof of their existence, most of which washes away under the unceasing waves of the tides of time.

Houdini did not come to Kenton in 1926. He was a leader in a rival organization known as the Society of American Magicians. That fall Houdini died in Detroit on Halloween night after his appendix burst. Durbin knew Houdini, having met him in 1909 when he played at the Keith Theater in Columbus. "I went around to the stage door," Durbin wrote, "and just as I got there, out came Mr. and Mrs. Houdini and I walked with them back to their hotel and had quite a nice talk with them." Later, Durbin met with Houdini several times when he came to Ohio. "A number of years ago during the World War, I remember I was trying to get an Italian flag and I wrote down to Houdini," Durbin remembered, "and didn't he go way over to Brooklyn to an Italian magician to get a flag, which he sent along with his compliments."[48]

Durbin also wrote that he had handcuffs that belonged to Houdini that were given to him by Bess Houdini, Harry's widow. These were the handcuffs, Durbin wrote, that were "made by a Birmingham blacksmith and who took five years in making the same, which [Houdini] got out of in the London Hippodrome after he worked for almost seventy minutes to release himself."

"I have never been able to find any magician or other person who can open and close these handcuffs," Durbin wrote.

I have no idea what happened to the handcuffs.

"It was a pity," Durbin penned in 1934, "that Houdini had to be carried off so early in his lifetime because he was just at the height of his career when he died at Detroit."

I check into the Weaver Hotel, deciding against a visit to Abe Martin's restaurant, which is overcrowded with magicians who are getting a meal before they hit the road or take a train back home.

I trudge upstairs to my room. I am exhausted, feeling like it is the middle of the night my time. I am too tired to take off my clothes.

This day has ended. I find my mind wandering back to politics, with my thoughts centered on FDR. In 1926 he was still battling to learn to walk, mostly in Warm Springs, Georgia, and had not yet started his political comeback.

Thinking of the warm Georgia sun and the cool pool where FDR and others recovering from polio exercised their wasted limbs, I fall into a deep sleep.

Before I know it, it is morning.

I get up and look out the window and see I am still in Kenton.

The town is shut down, and evidence of arrangements for a funeral are all around, with black crepe draped on buildings and the flag at half-mast at the courthouse.

A great flock of doves circle the square and then disappear behind the courthouse.

I wonder if Durbin knows of the funeral.

≫ 12 ≪

THE MAN WITH THE LIGHTS

February 11, 1927

The construction of the National Road into Ohio started in 1825 when Congress finally appropriated $150,000 after years of delay. At Wheeling, a river and a creek on each side of the Ohio cut channels that were used as the path of the road. From there, the road follows the beginning of Zane's Trace, which had been blazed by Ebenezer Zane in accordance with a 1796 federal grant of property in Ohio. Zane's Trace was built to link Wheeling with Maysville, Kentucky.

Once in Ohio, the road follows low ridges across St. Clairsville to Zanesville. It is hilly country up to this point and then it levels out between Zanesville and Columbus.

"Come out!"

I hear a voice on the other side of the door. It sounds like Delbert.

A knock confirms that someone is at the door. I open the door, and there is a smiling Delbert.

"Come on, come on," he blurts out, "time's a-wasting."

He turns and starts down the steps, bounding two at a time, waving for me to follow.

Rushed, I grab my coat and throw it on in such a hurry that it gets caught in the door when I slam it shut. I have to fool for my room key in my pocket to get free, all the while Delbert yelling, "Come on, time's a wasting."

Outside the hotel, Delbert continues to press, walking so fast he almost appears to break into a trot.

"What's the hurry?" I ask.

"I want to show you his office before it's too late," he responds.

Al Saal, "The Man with the Lights" (ca. 1925). Courtesy
Mike Caveney's Egyptian Hall.

"Durbin's office?"

*"Yep. It's up in this building," he says, pointing to one of the redbrick structures.
"It's the same office the Doctor used as his medical office when he was alive."*

*We climb some stairs and enter the office, which has "W. W. Durbin" stenciled on the glass of the door. There is no receptionist, no lights; everything is
dark and shadowy.*

*Delbert flips a light switch and we walk into Durbin's inner sanctum. He
has photos on the wall and a copy of the multicolor sign that reads, "*OTHERS*"
and other slogans mounted in wooden frames.*

*Delbert pulls a bundle of papers from a file cabinet. It is a collection of
correspondence between Durbin and Al Saal.*

"Listen to the voice," Delbert says, giving me the Saal correspondence file.

Al Saal was a magician from Toledo, Ohio, who made his living as an
undertaker. In the magic world of the 1920s, he was known as "The Man
with the Lights," a wizard with cigarette tricks. Saal became one of Durbin's
lieutenants in the early days of the International Brotherhood of Magicians.
It was my good fortune to discover, early on in my search for anything

Durbin, a collection of correspondence between Durbin and Saal in a run-down magic store in Toledo. Ted Carrothers, the owner, had carefully preserved the letters in protective plastic sheet covers kept in three-ring bingers. The letters had been given to him by Al Saal's widow.[1]

I drove over to Toledo one Saturday in 1992 to meet Carrothers and found him to be a thoughtful but mysterious and strange-looking man. He had a magician's goatee and one eye that wandered. He was best known in Toledo for once levitating Miss Toledo over the Anthony Wayne Bridge, which spans the Maumee River near the downtown.

Carrothers allowed me to review and make copies of the Durbin and Saal letters. We met several more times to discuss magic, Durbin, and the early IBM. He was a knowledgeable historian of magic, but he died suddenly in 1996, falling from a ladder that he was using to install a ceiling fan in his home.

The Carrothers' collection of correspondence begins with a letter from Durbin to Saal, dated February 11, 1927, eight months after Durbin became president of the IBM. The correspondence ends in 1935 with a letter written from Washington, D.C., where Durbin was serving as register of the Treasury.

The letters provide a rich record of Durbin's efforts to build the IBM. They document the petty fights, the attacks, and the trials and tribulations of the wacko characters who made up this magic brotherhood.

Many of the letters are marked "Personal" or "Confidential," and some of Saal's indicate in handwriting at the bottom that he immediately answered with a return letter or a phone call.

The regularity of the communication reflected in these letters harkens to a time when correspondence was part of daily life. Trains would regularly deliver letters on the same day they were mailed. Sometimes a letter would be delivered and responded to on the same day.

Between politics and magic, Durbin was a busy correspondent. "I shall be glad to see and talk to you sometime when I can talk to you about some things that I can't put on paper," Durbin wrote Saal in the summer of 1929. "I have so many letters to write that I can't write you at great length, but I hope to see you before long because there must be a radical change about some things on our programs. I think you understand."[2]

"Read," Delbert says in a soft voice, "you will find his voice."

I flip through the letters, turning page after page, walking through a silhouetted golden past. The room becomes hushed, noiseless, as even the sound of the traffic outside fades away. Delbert himself becomes monklike, almost prayerful. It is as if he has opened sacred scrolls for me.

The topics in the letters run from everyday business to chitchat and major decisions for the growing organization. The great magicians of the time are figures in the correspondence. In one letter from 1927 Durbin handwrote, "Busier than H—l. Blackstone just left here for Wapakoneta. We'll go over tonight to see show."[3]

Other letters discuss Howard Thurston, perhaps even better known in his time than Blackstone. "You will look in vain in the magic column of Blei," Durbin wrote Saal of a dispute Thurston had with the magic editor of *Billboard*, "for any mention of Thurston's show which has been playing in Cincinnati the past two weeks." Durbin thought he understood Blei's snub of Thurston. "The reason is very plain to me and to Thurston also. It is because Blei runs the magic page as he pleases, to the detriment of the Billboard."[4]

Durbin suggested Saal write a letter of complaint to the *Billboard* editorial staff because Durbin recognized that he was considered by Blei to be a troublemaker. When Saal begged off, based on some disagreement with the way Thurston was conducting himself, Durbin didn't push. "So let it go," he wrote. But Durbin was mad on Thurston's behalf, and he unleashed his feelings about Blei to Saal:

> Whatever else may be said of Thurston, he gets the crowds and I believe he is trying to do what he can now to boost magic, and while I have been against the things you speak of, it is these things we want to stop, and I believe Thurston has learned a lesson that will serve us pretty well. However, all I want to do is set myself right with you, and to let you see that the fellow I am after is Blei who has been nothing but a mean lowdown enemy of the IBM, doing everything he can against us, publishing everything detrimental, and nothing commendatory, and I think the Billboard people ought to know about it. A drop of water dripping on a stone makes a hole in it, and if enough of our boys write to Miss McHenry in care of the Billboard at New York, or to Don Gilette, the Editor in Cincinnati, we would soon dislodge this enemy of our order.[5]

Celebrity magicians were not the only subjects of the letters. Practitioners whose names would not go down in the annals of magic history found their way into the correspondence.

One person in particular dominated much of the correspondence. His name was Robert Gysel, the Toledo magician who ran darning needles through his arm at the Scioto Sign Company in Kenton in 1926. Gysel, it turned out, became a giant thorn in Durbin's side. The Gysel saga began with a series of disparaging letters that Gysel wrote about Durbin to Dr. A. M. ("Doc") Wilson, the editor of another magic magazine called the *Sphinx*. Wilson reprinted some of Gysel's letters, and Durbin initially held his fire. Emboldened, Gysel then began to harass Durbin directly with letters expressing his unhappiness with Durbin's leadership.

"Don't bother about the Wilson and Gysel matter," Durbin wrote Saal in March 1927. "Gysel wrote me about seven letters in three days, and that was too much and I simply wrote him that whenever he could write like other people, I would answer his letters, but I wouldn't pay any attention to such letters as he was writing."[6]

Durbin was equally disturbed with Doc Wilson, an IBM member but a competitor of sorts with his magic magazine. "[Gysel] wrote some terrible letters to Wilson, and I wrote Wilson and told him that he was foolish to publish such letters, and advised him against publishing them anymore," Durbin wrote. "We don't want to get mixed up in a personal quarrel because it will hurt the IBM to have members think we are engaging in little personal quarrels. I don't care what anybody thinks of the IBM, we will have to show for ourselves."[7]

Gysel did not give up easily. A week later, Durbin wrote Saal, "I simply quit writing to Gysel, and I told Doc Wilson that he was foolish to print Gysel's letters, and if he will persist in doing it after that, then I will put him in the same class with Gysel. Doc is coming on to the convention. I have not heard from Gysel for a long while until this morning when I received some little tablets to put on a cigar to make a snowstorm. I wouldn't try anything of the kind, and the devil only knows what they are. They will go in the sewer so far as I am concerned."[8]

Durbin counseled Saal that it was best simply to ignore Gysel: "Don't bother about Gysel. He will subside by and by. I returned his letter with the little tablets, and if he says anything to you, you tell him Durbin is damn mad and thinks you have treated him shamefully. I want him to appreciate he can't write such letters as he has been writing and get away with it."[9]

"Don't bother about Gysel," Delbert chants.

I notice he has lit candles around the office, giving the place a feeling of a chapel.

"What's next," I ask, "incense?"

"Don't bother about Gysel," Delbert repeats, grinning like a schoolboy, and then returning to a more serene look.

As the second annual convention of the International Brotherhood of Magicians approached, the tiff between Durbin and Gysel intensified. Durbin wrote Saal advising that Gysel had resigned, but that he still expected to attend the 1927 convention in Kenton:

> I don't hear from Gysel anymore, and I may tell you that I am devilish glad of it. He now is bothering Dorny to death about putting on some act down here, but really Saal we don't want him bothering around down here. He sent in his card, and said he didn't want to be a member, so let it go at that. Really, I never was so disgusted with a fellow as I am with him because you don't know how disgusting he is with his letters, six or seven a day, and abusive as the devil, and we don't have to put up with such things as this and we won't put up with it. If he does come down here, he will have to run around by himself. Of course, I don't want to get you into the thing, but you be diplomatic about it and let him know that he has greatly offended me if he asks you anything about it.[10]

Letters concerning Gysel abounded in April 1927. "Gysel sent in his card," Durbin wrote, "and really is not a member, and he has no business getting up in the convention and will not be recognized if he does. This fellow has to be set down upon good and hard."[11]

On April 28, Durbin wrote: "I note what you say about Bob [Gysel], and I'm sorry for him too. Any fellow in his condition is to be pitied. He don't bother me anymore, and I don't presume he is coming to the convention. If he comes and behaves himself, all right, if not, we will have to look after him."[12]

Durbin seemed finally to relent, perhaps responding to some peacemaking overtures by Saal on Gysel's behalf. "Your letter of May 23 received, and also the other letter you sent to me about Bob, and we will have to work this out the best way we can. This fellow makes a fool of himself, and I think we can work it out all right."[13]

Gysel may have attended the convention in Kenton in 1927, but Durbin apparently did not come down "good and hard" on him, because a year later the old squabble started back up.

"This fellow Gysel has gone on the rampage again," Durbin wrote in March 1928, "and I keep getting letters and telegrams from him."[14] Based on one of Gysel's letters, Durbin concluded that he "must be nuttier than ever." Durbin was particularly upset when one of his officers, Arthur Gans, appointed Gysel to the Outdoor Amusements Committee of the IBM for the upcoming convention in Lima:

I do think that Gans certainly wished an awful thing on me when he had him appointed for the Outdoor Amusements at the convention. I didn't want to do this, but Gans recommended it, and then to find out whether the Executive Committee would approve it, I wrote to the other members and a number of them put on it that it would be all right but he would have to act under my directions. I think it is time to talk out plainly to this fellow.

Once again, Durbin called on Saal to play the middleman:

I wish you would call him down and simply say to him that unless he ceases this kind of business I am going to have him put out of the IBM and I'm going to do it mighty quick too, and I don't propose to have any fooling. Last year about this time he got on the rampage and sent in his card and then complained because we didn't print his picture in the program. Well he wasn't a member anymore, and I can see now it was a great mistake to do anything for him because he hasn't any mentality to appreciate it. I shall not answer any of his letters and you can tell him this. If I lived in Toledo I would hie myself to Judge O'Donnell's court and have him put where he belongs. Any fellow who writes a letter of this kind shows exactly that there is something the matter with his upper story.

Now Saal, I don't want to bother you too much, and don't let him know you have these letters, but simply say: "Gysel, you can't fool with Durbin the way you have done." . . . If you want to, you can call me up by telephone at my expense so that you can talk with me about this. I appreciate your position with him and know that he is a bad customer to deal with, and if you don't want to do anything about it, it will be all right, but I want to get word to him someway without writing him because I don't propose to have him bandying any of my letters around.[15]

"There was something wrong with his upper story," Delbert says. "Don't you think?"
"To whom do you refer?"
Delbert does not respond. He takes off his hat and scratches his head.
The matter would not go away and it bedeviled Durbin. Again with a convention to put on, he wrote Saal:

I'm in receipt of your letter enclosing the various letters and telegrams, and I just want to tell you what has happened since I wrote you. I called up Gysel's sister at the Fel Shop in Secor, [Michigan], and she was very sorry about it and she told Gysel just what I said. She wrote me a letter special delivery, which I got yesterday afternoon, in which she said she was so glad that I called her yesterday and she could not say how deeply ashamed of Bob she felt because of the manner in which he acted toward me and she said she told him all I said to her and that she told him he ought to be man enough to see his error and acknowledge it.[16]

On the same day, Gysel wrote a letter to Durbin, claiming to be his sister, Marguerite. Using her stationery, Gysel gave Durbin "particular fits" for the telephone call. "I could see right away that it was Gysel who did it himself because the signatures did not correspond," Durbin wrote Saal. "My secretary and I compared them and agreed that this was nothing more or less than Bob's doing; so I wrote a letter to Ms. Gysel and sent it to her at Secor and it is going on the same mail as this, in which I enclose the letter so that she might see some of his underhanded tricks. He may think he is fooling some of the people but he is not fooling me."[17]

Durbin finally proposed that Gysel be permanently expelled from the IBM because, he wrote, there was "no use in fooling with a fellow of this kind any longer." With every delivery of the mail, the case against Gysel mounted: "Now in this morning's mail, I got a letter from Toledo, supposed to be from Leonard Fern, and I have compared the signature with that of Fern's signature to his [IBM] application, and they are not one in the same. This letter has been written by Gysel also, and I want you to call Fern in and tell him for me that he must tell Mr. Gysel that he has to stop this kind of business."[18]

Other magicians also brought to Durbin's attention letters Gysel was writing to them about Durbin. They were, according to Durbin, threatening "in such a way that it would put him in the penitentiary if I turned them over to the postal authorities." As Durbin noted: "He not only wrote one letter, but he wrote another of the same character to another fellow in Montreal."

Durbin stood fast in his conclusion that Gysel had a screw loose. "This fellow is bughouse right, and if he comes within the jurisdiction I will have him locked up quicker than you can say Jack Robbins."[19]

Durbin assured Saal that he did not need to worry excessively about Gysel: "Now don't worry about taking care of him at the convention because Francis and I will look after that. We will not be bothered with this fellow around, and I'm not concerning myself about that."

"This fellow is bughouse right," Delbert intones. "I'm telling you, bughouse right."

I am beginning to understand why I have been brought here.

At long last, Durbin convinced his executive committee to expel Gysel from the IBM at the end of March 1928. He made it very clear that Gysel would not be well treated if he attempted to come to the Lima convention in June.

> I have your letter of 19th and was sorry that I couldn't get up to your Wednesday meeting but I think it was best that I didn't come, even if I had time, because it probably would have resulted in a personal row between Gysel and myself, but let me tell you he won't come to Lima and start anything because if he does we will finish it. He mustn't imagine that he can come down there and start a roughhouse because we will be on our own dunghill and take care of him properly. To start any proceedings against him outside of one for lunacy would be foolish. What you boys ought to do if this fellow don't behave himself is simply go in and explain to Judge O'Donnell and I will be willing to come up there and go into court and swear he is crazy, and I will bring along Dr. Snodgrass who will testify to this as he is an expert on mental diseases.[20]

I look up from Durbin's desk where I have been perusing the Saal letters and see that Delbert is gone. His hat sits on the chair he once occupied.

Strangely, it is night outside. Could the entire day have already passed? I hear a rustling in the next room, and then Delbert screams out, "Christ!"

I could tell from the Saal letters that Durbin was dictating to a secretary off the top of his head, filling the letters with his voice. They are breezy, free flowing, and uncensored. In a very real way, they constitute a bridge across time, allowing me to sit in his office while he spoke his mind. It is as if I could approach him from one side of the bridge, and he from the other, meeting halfway, with him alive, across the divide of space and time. His voice reaches me sixty years later.

His style was rambling, funny, and sarcastic. Sentences could run on for miles:

> I am making a broad appeal for members to contribute to the Christmas number [of *The Linking Ring*]—sort'o an Easter offering. They never contribute a penny to help the magazine. This is the way it is in

all churches, lodges, parties, etc. There are fellows in the church who soak up all the heat and if there is anything free going on they are always there and there are fellows in the party who never do anything but when the election is won always want the best office and usually get it and so it is in our order and we've got to try to arouse the members to their sense of duty.[21]

He saw things in black and white. If someone was ungrateful or against him, they were "nothing more or less than a baby."[22] To him, those in the wrong knew it but usually were not man enough to admit it. "Bennett sent it to me," he wrote of one magician who complained of something in a letter to Durbin, "and of course he knows he is a dirty skunk and yet he don't want you to mention him in connection with it."[23] He referred to Doc Wilson's magic magazine, the *Sphinx,* as the "Stinx" when he became irate over adverse publicity.[24]

His proposal for action was always swift and certain: "When these fellows in Detroit do what they say they are going to do, then you and I will get a hold of Harry Cecil and we will show these fellows a trick."[25] He encouraged Saal to be aggressive. "You might as well come out in the open and fight this fellow because he is a bitter enemy of yours, and this crops up in the letters which he writes around. The only way to whip him is to go after him with hammer and tongs just as I have done."[26]

There seemed to be a sharp division in his world. When speaking of friends he might refer to them as "my old pal" or "our good brother" or "he is a mighty good boy." With Saal he was always solicitous, complimenting him, for example, on his new son or on a magic program: "I have your letter enclosing the picture of little Alfred P. Saal, Jr., and shall use this later on in the Linking Ring. It is a splendid picture."[27]

On the other hand, if someone crossed him, like Gysel, they were likely to be labeled a "nut" or worse. "This fellow," Durbin wrote of another magician, "knows so little that he ought to be denominated a nit on the nut of a knat, which is somewhat smaller than a pin head."[28]

And anyone fraternizing with a Durbin enemy was thrown in the same pot: "Of course I can understand what is the matter with Bauersmith. He talks to Gysel and anybody who talks to him better talk to a rabbit, they would get more sense out of it."[29]

A similar result came about for a magician who sided with Felix Blei of the *Billboard:* "I am going to write Birch and he's got to get off his perch one way or the other. It is written in the Bible that you can't serve both God and mammon and Birch can't serve both the IBM and Blei. He's got to get off of one or the other."[30]

His phrases could be old-fashioned and then, just as quickly, turn remarkably modern.

Using 1920s' lingo, for example, he spoke often of providing Saal with the "straight dope," and he was always "mighty glad" to get a letter or hear good news.[31] Yet in another 1928 letter, after telling Saal he was happy to hear he had so many performance engagements, he concluded with what sounds to me like a 1960s expression, "and more power to you."[32]

The letters revealed a personal side too. They were not all just business. In one, Durbin complained about his health: "I have your letter of September 23rd, and note that you are going to have your meeting on Wednesday evening at 8 o'clock and I should be glad to be there but really Al I have been bothered with rheumatism so much in my shoulder that I don't dare move about much, and I am going down to Magnetic Springs to get this boiled out."[33]

Hard times, of course, raise their head following the crash in 1929.[34]

"You know, Al," Durbin wrote on October 19, 1931, "that with the hard times you have an awful time to keep fellows paid up on their dues. Some of the very best fellows that we have and that you would think would never fail to send in their dues are in arrears and letter after letter sent them only brings back the answer that while they would like to continue, they can't spare the money. It isn't a question of being made, it's simply they haven't the money. I know this, that when fellows get the magic bug they will almost go without their meals to get a magic magazine, but when it gets down to it that he doesn't have enough money to take care of the kiddies, then I can see why he would drop out so that he will have money to buy something to exist on."

After Roosevelt's election, Durbin wrote Saal in 1933: "I think things are going to get better and we are finding it so here in our business because we are employing more people now than we have for two years and business is coming better. God knows we needed a change."[35]

I have listened deeply to the voice in the letters. I read and reread them until I felt like I got the cadence. I could speak his words and understand his constructions. I even reached a point where I could even get worked up over Doc Wilson and the "Stinx."

"Christ!" Delbert cries again, this time rushing back into the room out of breath.

"What's going on?" I ask.

"We are surrounded."

"Surrounded? What are you talking about?"

Just then, I notice flashing lights outside, and I hear the wail of an old-fashioned police siren.

"Remus," Delbert says in disgust, "Goddamn Remus."

He surveys the room, pacing like a wild animal trapped in a corner, and then something comes to him.

"We'll go out the back way," he whispers. "Come on," he says, and he quickly blows out the candles.

In the dark we steal away down the back staircase, scurrying like mice. Heavy feet pound up the front stairs. I hear shouts.

"Oh shit," is all I can think. I am hoping I wake up in Zanesville or Columbus, safe in the car.

→ 13 ←

MASTER FRANCIS AND
THE KING OF THE BOOTLEGGERS

March 1928

"Oh crap!" Delbert spurts out as we try to sneak around the corner of the back of the building. "The place is crawling with cops."

I peek over his shoulder, the outline of his protruding ears blocking some of the view, and behold an army of police officers gathering in front of the building, some pouring out of a paddy wagon. Delbert and I are pressed with our backs against the wall. This is beginning to feel like some James Cagney film.

"It's a raid," he says.

Some flashlights streak beams in our direction.

"Now what?" I ask.

"I told you time was a-wasting," he chastises me.

"This is no time for recriminations." It occurs to me how much I have always wanted to use that line. "You got an idea?"

"Well, let's see," he says, and I notice he has pulled out a fake mustache and is sealing it to his upper lip.

"Come on," I implore him, "get serious. What are we going to do?"

"Oh, follow me," he responds, unhappy with my tone.

We trot across an alley, undetected, although the activity of the police has increased.

"It's getting hot," Delbert says.

A couple of blocks away, we emerge from the side of one of the downtown buildings and start walking on the sidewalk of the town square as if ordinary pedestrians out for an evening stroll. The Durbin office building is now engulfed with police, and no one seems to take notice of us.

Delbert leads me across the street, away from the action, toward the court-house. He climbs the stairs to the courthouse with me in tow and takes a key from his coat pocket and begins to work on the lock in the door. His counterfeit mustache flaps half off his face, and he smoothes it back down.

The door pops open, and we go inside, quickly but quietly closing it behind us. Our steps in the marble halls echo with a "click, click, click."

Past the darkened County Recorder's Office and the Clerk of Courts, Delbert takes me to the great swinging doors of a courtroom. He pushes the doors open and a strong swoosh of air blows out.

Suddenly, lights blind me from inside, there is the clatter of a busy court-room, and I am confounded by flashbulbs of cameras exploding like lightning strikes in a farmer's field in the dead of a stormy country night.

Courtrooms were the bailiwick of Durbin's first son and my grandfather, Francis. Durbin only practiced law for a dozen years or so before becoming the general manager of the Scioto Sign Company. Francis made his living as a lawyer, and he became known nationally for one representation that set up his career. The case involved a man named George Remus, who was known in his time as the "King of the Bootleggers."[1]

Durbin tried his best to encourage Francis to take up magic, but Francis gave up performing after a promising start. "About this time [in 1898]," Durbin wrote about Francis, "I added a little act to my program for Francis when he was seven years old; and I advertised him as the world's youngest magician." He was billed as "Master Francis":

I had a regular dress suit made for him and he opened his perfor-mance by putting a silk flag inside a water bottle and then called at-tention to another stand on the other side of the stage which had an empty bottle on it. Clapping his hands, the flag disappeared out of the one bottle and appeared in the other one from which he took it. Then he came down in the audience and had someone draw a card from a pack of cards and he performed the torn card trick.

A precocious performer, the young Francis delighted the ladies. "Francis had to run up and down the steps to the stage several times and the ladies always wanted to take him and kiss him, which he didn't want because he thought he was a big man."[2]

"Then," Durbin wrote, "he did the Inexhaustible Box trick of showing a box empty and turning it over and then from it he produced a glass of

Master Francis Durbin (1898). Author's collection.

water, many handkerchiefs, and a live guinea pig (and I may mention he was always afraid of it), and then he produced flags of various nations, and as they were produced, he put them in a high hat and then he held the hat and my assistant came forward and fastened a hook from both sides of the stage, and to the music of the Star Spangled Banner, the U.S. flag would appear from the hat and all the other flags disappeared."

The patriotic theme always worked well with these Ohio crowds. "This is how he closed his act," Durbin wrote, "and it is unnecessary to say that a little fellow like that got much applause and more publicity than his dad. I had him on the stage with me in my show for about two or three years, but, while he is much interested in magic and likes it ever so much, yet he never gives any performances."

Francis would become the legal adviser to the International Brotherhood of Magicians, which is about as close as he would come to professional magic. He did carry pocket tricks and would privately entertain a friend or acquaintance on occasion, but he never took part in any of the IBM shows. His passions were law and politics. The Remus case was the case that catapulted Francis to national attention. Durbin, as usual, was not far from the action; his fingerprints were all over the case.

"Order!" Slam, slam, slam, a gavel raps. "Order or I'll clear this court!"

The courtroom Delbert and I have entered is a beehive. A black-robed judge presides on the bench. Leaning over, he is red-faced with anger, brandishing his gavel.

Standing in the court dock, two men exchange pugilistic jabs with their fingers in each other's face.

"I would wreck you physically if I had you in the corridor," a beefy, ham-fisted man blares at a distinguished young man in a wool suit with a vest.

The place is in an uproar. The beefy man is in a rage.

"Mr. Remus, sit down!" the judge yells.

Delbert and I slide into the room, blinking from the light, and we take two seats next to several members of the press.

A man sitting next to me has a stenographer's pad and is furiously taking notes. He chuckles at the scene and leans over to fill me in on what's going on.

"That lawyer," he points with his pencil, "that's Charles P. Taft, the son of William Howard Taft and the county prosecutor for Hamilton County here in Cincinnati. A former Yale football player and captain of the basketball team. Today he takes on the King of the Bootleggers. Can you beat this?"

Now Remus shakes his fist at one of Taft's assistants.

"When you were on the eastern trip taking depositions, you, sir, drank whiskey by the pint—you did so!"

"Judge," the assistant implores dropping his hands to his side, "stop this vilification."

"The charge is murder. My life is at stake. I will show by proper evidence, Mr. Basler, that you drank liquor by the pint, not by the ounce!"

"Mr. Remus that is enough, more than enough," the judge reprimands. "You will lose the right to act as your own counsel if you make such a demonstration again."

Remus shakes but backs off.

"How'd this start?" I whisper to the newspaper reporter.

"Taft argued that there were other reasons besides his conviction on a liquor violation charge that caused his disbarment in Illinois."[3]

Remus, a stocky, bald businessman and lawyer, with crystal blue eyes, was on trial in November 1927 in Cincinnati for the murder of his wife. He was born in Germany to Jewish parents, but his family immigrated to the United States, and he grew up on the northwest side of Chicago. All his life he spoke with a trace of a German accent, which made him all the more intimidating and sinister in his demeanor.[4]

He began working when he was fourteen at an uncle's drugstore. With characteristic gumption, Remus bought the drugstore from his uncle before he was twenty. He purchased a second drugstore, attended night law school, and became an astute criminal lawyer. Clarence Darrow, a fellow Chicago lawyer, became a friend and would testify as a character witness on behalf of Remus at the murder trial in Cincinnati.

Remus was clever, incisive, brilliant, volatile, and had a gift for personal persuasiveness. He acted boldly in the face of opportunities. He understood the drugstore business and the law. His opening came on January 16, 1920, the night prohibition went into effect, thanks in large part to the efforts of William Jennings Bryan. Knowing of a legislative loophole that allowed the purchase and sale of liquor for medicinal purposes, Remus began to amass his empire, using his drugstores as fronts. Remus acquired distilleries and drugstores, greased the hands of officials in the Harding administration, and bought up government permits to buy and sell liquor—legally, of course. At the time Cincinnati was the hub of a three-hundred-mile wheel that included most of the major distilleries and government-controlled liquor warehouses in the country, so Remus moved there. Before leaving Chicago for the Queen City, Remus divorced his first wife and married his mistress and secretary, Imogene Holmes.[5]

Imogene herself was a divorcee and the mother of a thirteen-year-old daughter. Remus and Imogene moved to a ten-acre estate in Cincinnati's Price Hill district, and he set up his office in a downtown building he purchased and renamed the "Remus Building," located at the corner of Race and Pearl Streets.

The money he made was well spent on politicians, on prohibition officers, and on anyone else who would advance his business. The difficulty was meeting the demand for "medicinal" whiskey. Remus found he could not purchase sufficient permits to release whiskey fast enough from his warehouses. Government prosecution was a constant worry, so as he bought more permits; he also purchased what he thought would be immunity from arrest from a sleazy operator named Jess Smith, an Ohio man connected to Harding's attorney general, Harry Daugherty. Daugherty and Smith lived together in a house in Washington. In congressional investigations that followed Harding's death, there was testimony that Remus paid over $300,000 in protection money to Smith.[6]

Remus had not anticipated Mabel Walker Willebrandt, an assistant attorney general in charge of prohibition enforcement at the Department of Justice. On October 21, 1921, she ordered federal agents to raid one of Remus's bottling works outside Cincinnati. Remus was indicted for violations of the prohibition laws. He paid Jess Smith more money and was assured the fix was in, that even if a jury convicted him, a court of appeals would be paid off, and Remus would never see the inside of a jail cell.

All the money Remus spent did him no good. The jury convicted him in May 1922, and he was sentenced to two years in prison in the Atlanta federal penitentiary.

"We will, of course, file our appeal," Remus confidently told reporters.

Out on bail waiting appeal, Remus again met with Jess Smith. Smith once more took a bribe and told Remus he had nothing to worry about. Encouraged, Remus resumed his business and waited for the case to slowly wind its way through the appeal process. His revenues had grown to a staggering $50 million. On New Year's Eve 1923 George and Imogene invited fifty couples to their estate for a party that was much publicized in the newspapers. Guests gathered around a huge indoor swimming pool surrounded by exotic plants and flowers, and professional swimmers performed a water ballet.[7]

Imogene, to the applause of her husband, appeared in a one-piece suit and dove off the board into the pool. An orchestra played while everyone sipped champagne, bourbon, and gin. Remus, a lifelong teetotaler, slipped off to his study to eat ice cream and read a new book on Lincoln. Rumors abounded that Remus planned some grand climax to the party, and so no one left until Remus emerged from his study as dawn approached to announce the time had come for him to show his appreciation for his guests. Waitresses brought the men diamond cuff links and diamond pins as party favors.

Then, as the guests lined up to leave, the front doors were opened to a stupendous sight: fifty brand new 1923 Pontiacs, one for each of the couples. Remus, the King of the Bootleggers, and Imogene, his confidante and adviser, were on top of the world.

Eight months later, on August 2, 1923, Harding died unexpectedly in San Francisco. Scandal had engulfed his administration, and the president died under mysterious circumstances after a long trip across the country and up into Alaska. Before Harding's death, Jess Smith, paranoid about being one of the scapegoats for the spiraling mess of the Harding administration, committed suicide.[8]

Toward the end of January 1924 Remus's appeals ran out, and he was finally sent to serve his term.[9] Several hundred well-wishers appeared at the Cincinnati depot to see him off. He was gracious, dressed in a silk shirt and a pearl-gray suit with spats. Imogene was on his arm as they boarded a private railway car bound for Atlanta. She was given power of attorney to run the businesses while Remus was gone. The Jack Daniels Distillery had been added to the Remus empire the previous summer.

In Atlanta Remus joked with reporters that he would miss his personal valet: "I shall have to apologize for being forced to appear unshaven before the warden." Despite the creature comforts Remus purchased for himself in prison, he grew restless when none of his political friends could secure his early release after over a year. He learned that a man at the Justice Department, who along with Mabel Willebrandt had directed the original investigation against Remus, might be "approachable." Remus asked Imogene to meet with this man to argue his case.[10]

The man's name was Franklin Dodge; he was a tall, handsome agent. Remus had some vague hope that Dodge would intervene with Mabel Willebrandt. Nothing promising seemed to come from the original meeting between Imogene and Dodge, and Remus continued to push for further meetings.

Had he known of the electric spark that flew between Dodge and Imogene, he would have given second thought to his insistence on continuing contacts.

Two days before Remus was to be released from prison, Imogene filed suit for divorce in Cincinnati. Remus refused to believe the reports. It was true, however, and a long property battle followed. Dodge seemed to be in conspiracy with Imogene, and Remus believed that together they misappropriated his vast fortune.[11]

Remus was a tortured soul. He became convinced that Dodge and Imogene were conspiring to kill him or have him deported. On October 6, 1927, Imogene was scheduled to appear in court in Cincinnati to finalize the divorce. Remus would not have it, even though he had declared to the press that his wife had become "repulsive" to him.

Imogene emerged from the Alms Hotel with her now twenty-year-old daughter around eight in the morning to grab a taxi. It was bright and sunny, an Indian summer fall day. Remus in his chauffeur-driven limousine waited outside. Imogene and her daughter got into a taxi.[12]

"Catch the cab," Remus calmly told his driver.

Driving through downtown and into Eden Park in rush-hour traffic, Remus's car pulled alongside the taxi, and Remus gestured for the driver to pull over. Imogene told the driver to stop, but her daughter sensed the danger and yelled for the taxi to go faster. The taxi sped away and Remus's car gave chase, eventually catching and cutting it off. Imogene's daughter tried to open her door to run, but Imogene pulled her back into the car. Remus jumped out of his car and walked quickly to the taxi, reaching it just as Imogene was opening her door. Remus grabbed her and began to shout, "I'll fix you, I'll fix you." Imogene then saw the pearl-handled revolver she bought Remus years earlier for his protection.

"Oh, Daddy, you know I love you! You know I love you. Don't do it! Don't do it!"

Remus put the revolver in Imogene's stomach, pointed it upward, and fired one shot. She fell to the ground but pulled herself up and crawled back through the backseat of the taxi and began running up the sidewalk before collapsing.

Her daughter jumped on Remus and screamed, "Do you know what you are doing!"

Remus shook her off and said, "She can't get away with that."

Meanwhile a passing motorist stopped to help Imogene. Stumbling into the car, Imogene told her daughter, "I'm dying. I know I'm dying." A few hours later, following emergency surgery, she was pronounced dead in Cincinnati's Bethesda Hospital. Remus went directly to the First District police station and turned himself in. When he was told of Imogene's death, he said, "She who dances down the primrose path must die on the primrose path. I'm happy. This is the first peace of mind I've had in two years."[13]

On November 14, 1927, the newspapers carried two lead stories. One was a report on Lindbergh's return to Roosevelt Field in New York, following a victory tour around the United States in celebration of his transatlantic flight. The other was the commencement of the Remus murder trial. Remus sat as the defendant and as his own counsel. Early on he had openly scoffed at the suggestion of newspapermen that he might plead innocence by reason of insanity.

"Anyone who thinks I am insane needs a mental examination," he told reporters.[14]

Fortunately for Remus he hired co-counsel Charles Elston, a former district attorney who was one of Cincinnati's most distinguished lawyers. A slender, middle-aged man with prematurely white hair, Elston convinced Remus to put the dead Imogene and Franklin Dodge on trial and to contend that their actions left him temporarily insane at the time he killed Imogene.

This must be the start of that trial. Delbert looks ridiculous with the mustache, but he is greatly enjoying the scene.

A team of three attorneys for the State of Ohio stand at a small table to the left of the jury box, led by Charles P. Taft. Judge Chester Shook presides. The jury is composed of two women and ten men. The courtroom is packed with reporters, most of whom would meet with Remus in his jail cell and sip his whiskey during interviews that he frequently granted throughout the trial.

The witness stand would produce some dramatic testimony. Eyewitnesses, including Imogene's daughter and Remus's driver, all gave their version of the murder. Scores of additional witnesses would take the stand to describe the illicit love affair between Imogene and Franklin Dodge, the plans to steal and hide Remus's property, and the conspiracy to deport him or to have him killed. A small-time criminal testified that Imogene had hired him for $10,000 to kill her husband.

Remus was said by witnesses to have had "brainstorms" in which he would fly into fits of rage whenever Dodge's name was mentioned.[15]

Taft, in his rebuttal case, introduced the one-page report of three state-appointed alienists who sat through the entire trial and who had the right to stop the proceedings at any time if they believed Remus was insane. The alienists unanimously opined that Remus was sane at the time of the murder and at the time of trial. Judge Shook allowed Elston and Remus to divide the closing statement. When it came Remus's turn, he delivered a long, rambling indictment of prohibition, the Volstead Act, and the kind of cynical public servants it produced. He referred to Franklin Dodge as a "deuce of society that Volsteadism made."

Remus contrasted his humble origins with those of Taft: "This defendant started in life at five dollars a month, and he may have contaminated his neighbors, but ladies and gentlemen of the jury, we could not all be born with a golden spoon in our mouths like Charles P. Taft."

Finally, after two hours of speaking, Remus put his fate in the hands of the jurors: "The defendant does not desire any sympathy or compassion. If you, who have a higher power than the President of the United States in this case, feel that the defendant should go to the electric chair, do not flinch. The defendant will not flinch."[16]

Leaning on the jury box, Remus reminded the jury of his major theme: "The defendant stands before you in defense of his honor and the sanctity of his home. The defendant is on trial for that. If that is a crime, punish him. As you ponder your duty bear in mind that that which is most sacred is your home and family."

He then thanked the jurors and, as the trial had run to December 20, he wished them "Merry Christmas."

An ominous sign for the prosecution was visible on some of the jurors' lapels: six of them wore sprigs of Christmas holly.[17] After a mere nineteen minutes of deliberations, the jury returned with a verdict of not guilty by reason of insanity. The foreman of the jury told reporters that the jury would have acquitted Remus outright had they been allowed: "We decided that the man had been persecuted long enough."[18]

As three state alienists had declared Remus sane, Elston and Remus were confident that Remus's sanity hearing before the Probate Court would be nothing more than a perfunctory ratification of the jury's partial acquittal. If found sane in the present tense, Remus would go free.

Things did not go as expected. Outraged by the verdict, the Cincinnati probate judge found Remus "a dangerous person to be at large" and, contrary to the opinion of the state-hired alienists, declared Remus was still insane. Remus was remanded to the Lima State Hospital for the Criminally Insane.[19] If he were to go free from this "hospital," a novel legal precedent would be needed.

Remus and Elston sought out Francis Durbin, my grandfather, who at the time was a lawyer with fourteen years of experience in Lima. His principal credential probably was that his father was the former law partner of a judge on the court of appeals, Phil Crow.

Elston and Remus had calculated that a writ of habeas corpus, that is, a directive to the jailor to "produce the body" of the inmate before a judicial officer, could be filed in the lower court or directly in the court of appeals. On January 31, 1928, George Remus met with Francis Durbin at the Lima State Hospital, and both signed the writ for filing in the court of appeals, stating that Remus was "being unlawfully restrained of his liberty by detention and imprisonment in the Lima State Hospital."[20]

The writ asked that the superintendent of the state hospital be commanded to discharge Remus. This was a case of first impression in Ohio. A state law provided that the superintendent of the hospital was given the authority to determine if an inmate had, in his judgment, "recovered," or if not recovered, was in such condition that his release would not pose a detriment to the public welfare.

A defiant George Remus (bald) in the center, with Francis Durbin to his right. Charles Elston is second from left. (1928) Author's collection.

The state would argue that to allow a court to intervene and second-guess this determination would subvert the legislature's intent to leave this decision solely to the expert judgment of the medically trained superintendent.[21]

The writ of habeas corpus is, of course, one of the prime safeguards in Anglo-American law. The United States Constitution provides that the writ cannot be suspended except in cases of rebellion or invasion. Even Lincoln was severely criticized when he suspended the writ during the Civil War. The Remus case would present the legal question of whether the writ of habeas corpus applied to a criminally insane patient incarcerated in a state mental institution.

The strategy that evolved was to rely on the very same state alienists who had sat through the murder trial. If they thought he was sane then, they would be hard pressed to reverse their position. In addition, the legal team hired five local Lima physicians to observe Remus and to have them testify before the court. Remus continued his public relations battle, of sorts, by granting interviews to reporters while in the hospital. "The king of the bootleggers is brilliant," wrote one female reporter for the *Lima News*. "His more than surface knowledge of an extraordinary wide range of conversational topics is an indication."[22] When asked to compare his situation with other notorious murder cases at the time, including the Hickman trial in California, Remus said, for publication, "Womanhood besmirched is an awful thing and adultery something not to be tolerated. Slaying under those circumstances is justified—the natural end. The other cases were perverts.'"

The hearing started on February 20, 1928. Remus entered the courtroom dapper as ever, wearing a neat blue suit, a four-in-hand black tie with a pearl stick pin, and a white handkerchief protruding from his breast pocket. My mother would remember having the police escort her to and from school during these days of the hearing, so violent was the emotion over the prospect of an admitted murderer being set free.[23]

The hearing went well for Remus. The Lima physicians all agreed Remus was sane. One testified that he believed Remus posed no further threat to society or even to Franklin Dodge. "He told me he desired to let bygones be bygones," the physician testified.

The state attorneys, recognizing the case was in jeopardy, called Remus as a witness, hoping to trip him up. Their strategy was to question Remus at length about his bootlegging past and about the murder of Imogene:

Q: You are a better businessman than a lawyer, are you?
A: As a businessman I think I am a colossal fizzle. A man who has made as many millions as I have made and cannot put his hands on only a few thousand dollars should have his head examined.
Q: Then you are in the right place here?
A: Yes, before the honorable jurists, I am. [Laughter].
Q: Why did you kill your wife?
A: Because of an irresistible impulse.
Q: When did you find you were in the throes of an irresistible impulse?
A: At the time of the shooting.
Q: Oh?
A: Don't smile at the matter.
Q: I didn't smile.

A: Yes you did. Your sarcasm will get you nowhere.

Q: Do you think the first Mrs. Remus would have been justified in killing you when you took up with the other woman?

A: Yes, I think she would have been justified.

In the end, Judge Crow and one of his fellow jurists on the court found that Remus was sane. The third judge dissented. Remus was set free. An appeal to the Ohio Supreme Court resulted in an opinion that still stands as one of the seminal opinions on the rights of patients in state hospitals to have their cases reviewed by courts. "The proposition that the Legislature has clothed the superintendent of the asylum at Lima with the sole and exclusive right to determine when an insane patient under his care shall have been restored to reason, and that, no matter how arbitrary or wrong his decision may be, it cannot be reviewed by a court, impresses me as untenable," wrote one of the concurring justices on the Ohio Supreme Court.

Remus turns to take his seat after his shouting match with Charles Taft and his assistant.

Suddenly, he looks directly at me and stares for a long moment before sitting down.

Delbert shifts nervously. Remus has cold eyes, but for the second that we exchange stares he reacts as though he has seen a ghost. So intense is the stare that it makes me turn around to see if there is someone behind me who caught his sight.

At first, I see no one as I pass over the faces. Then I see the Doctor sitting in the back bench, reclining casually, legs crossed, watching me, and smiling. His look seems to say, "I know about insanity."

"He's back," Delbert whispers to me.

The Remus case made Francis famous. When Francis died, his obituary spoke of the importance of the case to his career: "The Remus case established a legal precedent on which [Francis] Durbin, during the following 20 years, secured the release of a hundred other persons from such institutions."

One of his few letters to my mom that still exists shows the commonplace of his involvement with these habeas cases. "Dear Margie," he wrote while she was in the Navy, "we received all of your letters and you certainly did a fine job as a typist." After discussing local politics, he reported, "Julius Callahan died this morning. It's too bad but he is really better off. And LeRoy Beard died last night at 8:10 at the Lima State Hospital. You remember the Beard case don't you? LeRoy had convulsions all the time. It happened at the Hospital while he was watching a picture show. When he saw Betty Grable on the screen, he jumped up and hollered 'Come here, baby,' and then fell flat, and the convulsions started. He never came completely out of it, and they notified his parents right away. They were here yesterday."[24]

Durbin of course was never far away from the limelight. When the Remus writ was filed, a South Carolina newspaper took notice. Predicting a magical outcome of the hearing should legal resources fail, an editor wrote, "The attorney and his father might approach the hospital grounds as the moon rises some evening. 'Hokus Pokus!' the younger Durbin might command. Silence. 'You try one, dad.' 'Abracadabra!' the elder Durbin might say in his best Aladdin's lamp voice. More silence. 'Out!' the two voices might blend in the command. And presently three figures might walk away in the deepening twilight; the two Durbins and—Remus!"[25]

A couple of policemen nudge their way into the courtroom and begin to scan the gallery. This makes Delbert especially nervous, and he pokes me in the ribs and motions for us to leave. Pulling up the collar of his coat, Delbert puts his hand on my shoulder, and we both get up and walk out, keeping our heads down and not making eye contact with the policemen, who look past us at some commotion the Doctor is making as a diversion. Outside the padded courtroom doors, we move down the now darkened halls and exit through the front doors.

"Whatever happened to Remus?"

"He died penniless in Covington, Kentucky," Delbert says, ripping off his mustache with a wince.[26]

"Where to now?"

"Looks like they didn't find what they were looking for," Delbert says, pointing to the police who are dispersing from around the Durbin office building. "Let's get to the car."

The Studebaker is parked in front of the courthouse, but Durbin is not in it. We jump in, and Delbert says, "To Egyptian Hall we go."

This voyage of mystery is not over yet, not by a long shot.

⇒ 14 ⇐

"I AM MIGHTY GLAD YOU
WERE ELECTED"

November 1928

Somewhere out there Durbin and Delbert hit Columbus and turned off the National Road, probably heading northwest on Route No. 21, which is a straight line through Marysville to Kenton. Durbin sometimes took Route No. 4 to Marion and then drove across Route 10, the Harding Highway, west to Kenton. I guess I will never know which way they took.

Right now, I am trying to figure out what is happening here in Kenton.

We drive through dark streets. Black crepe is still draped around the town.

Parking in front of the Durbin house on Resch Street, Delbert shuts off the car and jumps out. He checks for something in his pocket and pulls out a gold watch.

"I think the governor is here," he says, checking the watch.

I get out and follow Delbert to Egyptian Hall in the rear of the house, which has a light on inside. We enter, and there is an odd-looking, empty wheelchair in the center aisle. It looks homemade, like an ordinary armless wooden kitchen chair, with its legs cut off and wheels attached in their place.

Delbert runs up the aisle and disappears behind the distinctive Egyptian-theme curtain. I am left in the middle of the photo gallery with all the magicians staring at me.

Time began to accelerate for Durbin in 1928. Different vectors of activity began to intersect. The March decision of the court of appeals in Remus habeas corpus hearing was followed by the appeal to the Ohio Supreme Court. A ruling was expected in the first days of June. That same month, the IBM was holding its third annual convention in Lima, and the Democrats were scheduled to meet in Houston for their national convention. Everything was merging together.

The International Brotherhood of Magicians convened on June 7. Two thousand "visiting mystics" converged on the railroad town of approximately fifty thousand people.[1]

The mammoth street parade in Lima was attended by a United States senator, Cyrus Locher; state officials; boy scouts; police; ten bands; and necromancers from around the country and the world. As usual, news cameras from Fox and Paramount whirled, capturing the grand spectacle.

The group photo on Lima's high school steps following the parade captures a precious instant in time for my family. It is a last moment of unfettered happiness.

Durbin sits dead center, with Harry Blackstone and T. Nelson Downs, the great coin manipulator, to his right. Senator Locher from Cleveland is on Durbin's immediate left. Francis Durbin squints in the sun and sits on the concrete sidewalk at the base of the steps, almost directly in the middle of the group in front of his dad. His stubborn, thick hair is greased back yet still falling in his face, and he has removed his boater and placed it upside down between his legs. It looks like a beggar's collection plate. The hole in his shoe completes the effect. There is a man completely covered by oversized playing cards holding the hand of a young girl, an Indian chief who looks hostile and glares at the camera, a professor with a bad toupee and half glasses, projecting a quirky smile, and another guy with a flower growing from his hat. Agnes Durbin, who had given birth to my aunt three months earlier, during the height of the Remus hearing, sits in the front row next to people I do not recognize. Her eyes closed at the moment the camera shutter clicked, an ominous sign. And on Durbin's lap is my four-year-old mother, dressed like an Indian.

Eleven days after the magic convention, on June 20, the Ohio Supreme Court in a four-to-three vote released its opinion, affirming the ruling of the court of appeals and ordering the release of Remus from the asylum.[2] Francis rushed to meet Remus the same day at the state hospital. The two men, dressed in summer white suits, posed in front of the administration building and shook hands for the press. "Francis Durbin," the *New York Times* reported the next day, "Remus's attorney, was summoned to the hospital and Remus, refusing to await for a train, left in Durbin's car for Cincinnati, the attorney remaining at the wheel." When Francis returned, he met his dad in Kenton, and they loaded up a car and drove to Houston for the Democratic National Convention.[3] Durbin was a delegate-at-large and would be appointed the chairman of the powerful Committee on Permanent Organization.[4]

1928 IBM convention group photo. Author's collection.

Al Smith, the Irish-Catholic Democratic governor of New York, asked Franklin Roosevelt to make his nominating speech. Four years earlier in New York's Madison Square Garden, Roosevelt had given a rousing speech for Smith, subsequently known as the "Happy Warrior" speech ("Victory is his habit—the Happy Warrior—Alfred E. Smith!").[5] Smith was not nominated in 1924. The Democrats in 1924 deadlocked between Smith and Woodrow Wilson's son-in-law, William McAdoo. A weak compromise candidate, Ambassador John W. Davis, was nominated, and he picked William Jennings Bryan's lackluster younger brother, Charles, as his running mate. Coolidge won going away.

While Roosevelt gave a courageous performance in 1924, he did so on crutches, visible reminders to the country that he had not overcome the paralysis brought on by the 1921 attack of polio. He knew, as did his handlers, that he would never be accepted as a national candidate if he were required to ambulate on crutches. Crutches were the sign of a cripple.

The wheelchair starts to move on its own up the center aisle. Delbert sticks his head through the curtain, wearing pince-nez glasses and chewing on a cigarette holder.

"Almost ready," he says and disappears.

The wheelchair starts to turn circles, slowly rotating. "Happy Days Are Here Again" swells up, music comes from behind the curtain. I hear a crash, and someone yells, "Dang it!"

As the 1928 convention approached, FDR began to practice a "new way of walking" at his institute in Warm Springs, Georgia. His goal was to convince a national audience that he was "back on his feet." It was an illusion as fine as any Blackstone, Houdini, or Durbin could have conjured; Roosevelt remained paralyzed from his waist down from 1921 until his death.

His "walking" was accomplished by locking into position heavy steel braces on his legs and then allowing strong men to drag him to his feet. He would then push and pull his six-foot two-inch frame forward, with a cane in his right hand and with his left hand squeezing the arm of an assistant, usually one of his strongly built sons.

"In this posture," Hugh Gallagher wrote in his book, *FDR's Splendid Deception,* "he could 'walk,' although in a curious toddling manner, hitching up first one leg with the aid of the muscles along the side of his trunk, then placing his weight on that leg, then using the muscles along his other side, and hitching the other leg forward—first one side and then the other, and so on and so on. He was able to do this because his arms served him in precisely the same manner as crutches."[6]

It was a precarious mode of locomotion. At any moment, if he lost his delicate balance or slipped with his cane, he was liable to crash hard to the floor, destroying the very illusion he so intensely desired to create. It was also a slow, awkward, and physically exhausting method of movement. Even short "walks" would leave him breathless and sweating profusely. But through it all, he would turn his head from side to side, greeting and smiling at the crowd, and appearing to be relaxed and in control.

On the last night of the 1936 Democratic National Convention in Philadelphia, FDR did fall on his way to the speaker's platform in front of a crowd of one hundred thousand in Franklin Field and with an estimated one hundred million listening in on the radio. The fall happened just before he accepted the nomination and delivered what some think was his greatest political speech, in which he attacked "economic royalists," the people Durbin would have called the "moneyed interests."

But as he crossed the stage to give the speech, Roosevelt stopped to shake hands with the poet Edwin Markham, shifted his cane from his right hand to his left, lost his balance, and began to twist slowly out of control. The forces generated were so great that one of his locked leg braces snapped open, and he began to fall, throwing his copy of his speech across the stage.

Before he could hit the ground, his aides grabbed him under his armpits and raised him up. "There I was hanging in the air," he later told reporters in an off-the-record interview, "like a goose about to be plucked, but I kept on waving and smiling, smiling and waving. I called to Jimmy [his son] out of the corner of my mouth to fix the pin. 'Dad,' Jimmy called up, 'I'm trying to pick up the speech.' 'To hell with the speech,' I said . . . 'Fix the Goddamned brace. If it can't be fixed there won't be any speech.' But I didn't lose a smile or a wave."[7]

Al Smith won the nomination in Houston but lost the general election to Hoover. The first Catholic to run for the presidency, he knew little about the country outside of New York, and he was seen as "wringing wet" at a time the nation still was deeply divided over Prohibition. Smith even lost in his home state of New York.[8]

Worse for the Democrats, Smith left the party in the dubious hands of leaders who were philosophically aligned with big business. Smith appointed John J. Raskob, president of E. I. du Pont de Nemours, a major contributor and a lifelong Republican, as the chairman of the Democratic Party in 1928. Democrats smelled a sellout. Even the national headquarters was located in the General Motors Building on Broadway in New York City.

There was a saving grace from the campaign of 1928. Smith asked FDR to run for governor of New York as his replacement in 1928. After the Houston convention, Roosevelt retreated to Hyde Park to rest and then went back to Warm Springs, Georgia, to continue his rehabilitation. He believed that with another two years of hard work, he could regain the use of his legs, and he had no intention of running for any office in 1928.

Smith, however, thought Roosevelt would be a formidable candidate, an upstate Protestant with a famous name who could help him carry New York. He was also someone that Smith thought he could control once in office. Smith pestered Roosevelt, and it was only in October, a month before the election, that Roosevelt finally relented and agreed to accept the nomination.

Louis Howe, Roosevelt's political manager, openly wept when he was told the news, thinking defeat was certain and that his boss needed to regain his health before running in the 1932 elections.

FDR barely won, carrying the state by a slim 25,000 votes out of 4.2 million cast. He jokingly called himself the "one-half of one percent Governor."[9]

Delbert again pokes his head through the curtain. "There will be a slight delay," he says. "Some technical difficulties."

Franklin Roosevelt sent letters to Democratic leaders around the country immediately following the 1928 election, seeking opinions on what went wrong and how things could be straightened out.[10] One of those letters was sent to Durbin.

Durbin wrote back on December 13, 1928: "I have your letter from Warm Springs, Ga., and I am of the opinion that we lost the election because we didn't keep up our organization between elections." Durbin then took on the Raskob issue. "If we now opened a modest headquarters in Washington and put in charge some real politician and by this I mean one big enough to know the issues and to take in the whole country, we would get somewhere. I am not disposed to be criticizing but there were many mistakes made in the organization of the National Committee. Mr. Raskob may be a good business man and all that but what he don't know about politics would fill a good many volumes."

In the FDR library in Hyde Park, Durbin's letter has marks on it placed by Roosevelt with a pencil, with stars in the margin and underlining. The word "real" before politician in his letter was underlined with multiple swipes of the pencil. "I am not discouraged in the least," Durbin wrote. "The same issues will be with us again and they will be most acute by 1930 and 1932. We ought to begin now to prepare the ground for the campaign then. I shall be glad to cooperate with you."[11]

"I was mighty glad you were elected," he concluded, "and this takes some of the sting out of our defeat."

The curtain begins to rise. Delbert stands in the center of the stage directly under Durbin's portrait. "It's all my fault," Delbert says abjectly, "all my Goddamn fault."

He steps down from the stage and sits in the wheelchair. He glides past me and stops at the back of the hall to look at some photos on the wall of Harry Kellar. "It's all my damn fault."

Durbin accurately forecasted that conditions would become more "acute" by 1930. In 1929, within a month of the stock market crash, he wrote to FDR about warning signs that signaled the major difficulties to come.

"I think it must be admitted," Durbin wrote FDR on November 22, 1929, "that the times are not what they should be and our farmers are more depressed than ever." The stock market crash alone did not worry Durbin; he saw more endemic problems in the economy. "The building program has been off from 25 to 40 per cent of 1928. Collections are mighty slow and all these facts can readily be ascertained by reading Dun's Review each week as I do. As a business man doing business in every State in this Union I have occasion to get in touch with salesmen everywhere and this is a mighty bad year."[12]

Durbin blamed Hoover, a Stanford mining engineer, for the country's predicament: "Evidently our 'engineer' at Washington realizes that his engine is slipping on the track and he has called the big wigs to Washington to see if he can't get some 'sand' to put on the track to make it go." Using a medical analogy that would have made his father happy, Durbin concluded: "The trouble is that he is not getting to the real seat of the trouble and he is like a doctor who uses shin plasters to bind up a sore or a blood disease; or an opiate to allay the pain of a deep seated trouble that needs an operation."

FDR heavily underlined these sentences.

"I am going to die insane," Delbert says, speaking out to no one in particular. "John Brown, Remus, Gysel, and now me."

I am not sure how to respond to this turn of events. Delbert is not himself. He is preoccupied and heavyhearted.

"The way to end the war," he says in a low voice, "is to kill the Germans, kill more Germans, then kill more Germans."

Durbin's sound instincts for national politics and the economy did not extend to his one major attempt to seek election to national office for himself. In 1930, he declared his candidacy for the Democratic nomination for the United States Senate. He was the early favorite because he was "by far the best known [candidate] to the party workers," declared the *Cleveland Plain Dealer,* "and most frequently only party workers take the trouble to vote in the primaries."[13]

But Durbin missed the groundswell of public reaction against prohibition. Although he straddled the fence on the issue, declaring himself a "dry," he nevertheless advocated the initiative and referendum—letting the people vote directly on the issue—as the solution. "I still favor that principle, not only in the state but in the nation, as the best means of enabling the people to rule themselves," he said.

"This is as far as Durbin went on the prohibition issue," the *Plain Dealer* wrote.[14]

Durbin lost to Cleveland congressman Robert Buckley, who jumped into the race as an unflinching wet, calling for the repeal of the Eighteenth Amendment. In *The Linking Ring* Durbin licked his wounds and moved on. "Durbin took second money," he wrote, "and but for the massing of the wet vote in the cities, would have received the nomination beyond question. He carried his own precinct 175 to 1."[15]

"I admit it," Delbert shrieks. "I was the one who voted against Durbin in 1930."

Durbin continued to lead the International Brotherhood of Magicians, and he suffered the occasional jabs of dissenters. In 1931 a lawyer in Detroit, W. H. Domzalski, who was active in the IBM, wrote a letter to one of the editors of *The Linking Ring,* asking that he publish what appeared to be an innocuous poem ostensibly in praise of a fellow magician. Read as an acrostic, however, the first letters of each line spelled out "DURBIN IS A NUT."[16]

Domzalski's letter stated: "I am enclosing you a little tribute that I penned to Ade Duval. Ade hasn't played Detroit in quite some time and you, of course[,] know that he and I have been friends for many years, in fact most of my silk act comes from him. I understand that he has played Toledo some few weeks ago. I want to ask you a favor. Would you include the little verse in your next Toledo write-up for the *Linking Ring[?]* I don't need to tell you that none of my things would be published as you probably have noticed for some time past. Many thanks for your courtesy." The attached "tribute" is as follows:

AN ODE TO ADE.

Don't often see a magic man
Untie a silk-like Duval can,
Runs his hand, a silk to produce
Brings out so many, it just beats the deuce.
I've often wondered just how it's done
Now that I've seen, I'm not the only one
In magic who has been amazed,
Startled and Perplexed and even dazed.
A clever chap is Duval, as magi and man
No other quite as neat in the magic clan,
Unless your vision is blurred, without ado
Take off your hat to Ade Duval and True.

The editor who caught the wordplay was incensed by it. He wrote to Durbin:

As you can see from the letter and also the envelope, it was sent to me last fall. If you will examine the poem closely, and read down the first letter of each line, in the manner of an acrostic, you will see that this is an insult to you such as only a man of that type would stoop so low as to compose. I was "burned up" for several weeks after receiving it, but finally I cooled down and decided to let it ride and say no more about it. The letter itself is a masterpiece of hypocrisy, and the whole thing reveals pretty clearly the character of the man. I saved the envelope, for I found that the envelope is of equal importance with the letter in the case of any complaint.

I do not know if this letter will have any practical value to you. If you are unable to use it I will appreciate its return.

Despite his loss in the Senate race, Durbin played an important role in Ohio politics, though increasingly as a gadfly. His break with Cox was complete as 1932 approached. He was also at odds with Newton Baker of Cleveland, former mayor and secretary of war, because Durbin thought he sold out to big business when he started a corporate law firm.[17]

Durbin moved entirely into the Roosevelt camp and became his leading spokesman in Ohio. In 1931 he wrote to FDR excoriating Baker and Cox, who were considered the most serious Ohio contenders for the Democratic presidential nomination in 1932: "In the old days of Tom Johnson [Cleveland populist mayor at the turn of the century] when Baker followed him, he stood for the people but when Tom Johnson died the big interests lured Baker off and he has never been the same kind of Democrat."[18]

To compound his sins in Durbin's eyes, Baker had made harsh anti-German statements as the secretary of war for Wilson, and Durbin thought that the Germans and German descendants in Ohio would not forget. Baker was quoted as saying, "The way to end the war was to kill Germans, kill more Germans and then kill more Germans."[19]

Durbin wrote FDR: "I know what I am talking about when I tell you, to use your own expression, 'He won't click.'"[20]

Cox was little better in Durbin's book: "Cox became obsessed with the idea that we must destroy German influence and had a bill passed by the Legislature to take all teaching of German out of the public schools and in some places they took the German books and burned them up and only the other day before I came to New York I was in a barber shop where a German who loafs a great deal was still talking about that, and he is a Democrat and he didn't vote for Cox just because of it."[21]

"Interesting fellow, Durbin," a friendly editor of the *Columbus Dispatch* wrote in 1931. "He is one of the old Jeffersonian–Grover Cleveland type of politicians, and a man who believes in the old-fashioned Democracy, straight dealing, low tariff, and the common people. He has held high posts in the Democratic Party and his hand has been at the helm in almost every voyage to victory the party in Ohio has sailed during the last thirty-five years. He is known by almost every Democrat in the country, but he has asked little, nor wanted much from the party, although once a candidate for the United States Senate. He might have had that [seat] had he been willing to do a little prestidigitation to get the votes and backing, and he might have been chairman of the National Democratic committee had he used sleight of hand instead of dealing straight."[22]

Durbin moved more and more outside the party circles and began making his reputation as the voice of insurgency in Ohio. As it had been in Baltimore in 1912, so it would be in Chicago in 1936: Durbin would buck Ohio's Democratic leadership. "Like a Mohawk chieftain, he can be a devoted friend, but when he is on the warpath he is implacable," a Dayton paper wrote about him.[23]

With the 1932 election on the horizon, Durbin stepped up his efforts on behalf of Roosevelt. A critical planning meeting took place in November 1931. Durbin and both his sons, Francis and Andy, drove to Albany to discuss the Ohio situation with FDR. They met on November 15 in the governor's office. There were echoes of the 1911 meeting between Durbin and Governor Wilson in his Trenton, New Jersey, office almost twenty years earlier to the date.[24] The Durbins carried with them a message from Ohio Democrats. Democratic governor George White, they told Roosevelt, would run in the Ohio primary only as a favorite son, but he would support Roosevelt at the convention. Roosevelt therefore would not have to file in Ohio or run in the Ohio primaries. Durbin had received this assurance from White personally before traveling to Albany. It was an important message from a state that had traditionally played such a large role in the making of presidents.

"After leaving you on Monday afternoon we motored to Kingston, Port Jervis, Stroudsburg, Pa., where we stayed all night and then cut across to York, Pa., down into Washington," Durbin wrote FDR a week later. "We talked to quite a number of Senators and Members including Cordell Hull who is mighty friendly to you. Many members were absent and probably will not be in for a week or ten days. We talked with Jack Garner [the newly elected Speaker of the House] who received us very kindly and I just wondered if you had telephoned him about my son, Andy."[25]

At the time of Durbin's trip, both Hull of Tennessee and Garner of Texas were undeclared candidates for the Democratic nomination. Garner would eventually become FDR's vice president and Hull his secretary of state. Durbin argued that his interest in finding Andy a job was to provide a watchman for FDR in Washington during the campaign season: "He can be of more service finding out things for you down there because he won't be there very long until he knows every Democrat and will get in touch with them. I'll guarantee that."[26]

"Everywhere we went we inquired about two people," Durbin wrote, "Hoover and Roosevelt. We found nothing but opposition to Hoover and enthusiasm for Roosevelt."

"It is good to get your letter," FDR replied on November 27 to Durbin, "and I appreciate all that you say. I did send a line to the next Speaker and I hope everything will be all right for your boy."[27]

Andy joined the correspondence to FDR. In December 1931 he wrote a letter to Roosevelt warning that the anti-Roosevelt people in Ohio, including Baker, were a genuine threat: "We want to put the skids under this fellow Baker and we will need some help to do this." Andy recommended a visit from Jim Farley, a Hudson Valley native who was named by FDR as his national campaign manager.[28]

Farley was as affable as Roosevelt, had a phenomenal memory for names, and a genius for organization. He always signed his letters in green ink, emphasizing his Irish roots. Loyalty was his middle name. "I have never held a card in the Disloyal Brotherhood of Political Switchmen," Farley was fond of saying.[29]

"I don't want to bother you with a lot of things," Andy wrote, "but I think [Farley] better stay away from Cincinnati, for the Gang down there will double deal you if they get a chance."

Double-dealing has always been a political art form, especially in Ohio. Appearing as a friend while working behind the scenes with a foe is all in a day's work in politics, and the Durbins knew it better than most. The election of 1932 brought the double deal to new heights because every hopeful Democrat, especially favorite sons, thought there might be an opportunity for them at the convention. Hoover and the Republicans were beatable, and this caused Democratic contenders to dream of the possibility of a convention stalemate and a wild stampede to their banner.

Deadlocks were not uncommon, given the two-thirds voting requirement still followed by the Democratic Party. Any combination of interests that could muster one-third of the delegates could block a candidate, even one who walked into the convention with a convincing majority.

The contenders who lusted for the opportunity in 1932 included Roosevelt's erstwhile patron Al Smith, who began to rethink his reentry into the presidential sweepstakes. Ohio, Durbin would find out, was rife with double dealers. Newton Baker and James Cox had both organized secret ententes in the hope of a convention opportunity and a nomination for themselves. The knives came out, duplicity reigned, and Roosevelt was in grave danger. Meanwhile, however, there was the business of getting Roosevelt delegates in the primaries.

"Congratulations on your victory in New Hampshire," Durbin wrote in a telegram to Roosevelt on March 9, 1932. "Keep up the fight and don't concede any state in New England. The Middle West, South and West are with you. Get plenty of your literature into all states. Let your slogan be 'We must nominate a Progressive candidate' if we are to command the support of the people who are tired of Hoover prosperity."[30]

"I never was so anxious to hear from an election as I was to hear from New Hampshire and when I found out you carried the election two to one

I felt that we had broken the Hindenberg line," Durbin wrote on March 10. "That is why I wired you as I did not to give up a single State in New England or any place else."

Durbin thought Roosevelt's strength was particularly evident in the rural states. In Minnesota the country folks were with him. "That is the way they will be in Iowa too and Indiana and way down in Egypt," Durbin wrote, referring to southern Illinois (the nickname comes from comparisons between the Mississippi and Nile rivers).[31]

By March, Durbin was confident enough of convention success to write to FDR that he should start thinking about the party platform. He warned him to "guard against" promising too much. "You will have much to say about the making of the platform and we ought to be very careful not to get our foot into it as the Republicans did. When we come into power we are getting a sick child from the hospital and it is going to take some time to nurse it back to health and strength."[32]

Roosevelt had to be the one to set the agenda. "I only ask that you turn these things over in your mind because you want to begin to get ready because you are going to have to boss the job and don't make the mistake Hoover made [in letting others set the agenda]."

Almost as an afterthought Durbin wrote, "There is no opposition here in Ohio. I am on the ticket for Delegate-at-Large without opposition. I have been in touch with Chairman Farley and am helping all I know how in other places." Durbin later would concede that he had never been so badly taken as he was by the Ohio Democrats who pledged their preconvention support of Roosevelt. "I am sorry to acknowledge," Durbin wrote Roosevelt after the convention, "this is the first time I ever was fooled so badly."[33]

But it was not until the opening of the convention in late June that the secret Ohio scheme to stop Roosevelt came to light. When Al Smith turned on Roosevelt, Durbin reassured Roosevelt to stay his course. "Whom the gods would destroy they first make mad," Durbin wrote about Smith on April 14, 1932, "and they are certainly getting their work in on Al."[34] He encouraged FDR to "keep right at it, no matter what the *New York Times* or Al Smith say." Durbin embraced the charge that FDR was instigating class conflict:

> You are on the right track. . . . You have the Democrats with you, and you are right in your contention that Hoover has started at the top instead of starting at the bottom. That's the doctrine of monarchy and it's the doctrine of Republicanism and always has been. . . . We

have to get the farmer and the laboring men some purchasing power and we are not going to get it by lending the money to the railroads so they may pay off J. Pierpont Morgan and the other big international bankers. The people of this country are beginning to realize that the wealth of the nation has concentrated in the hands of a few until a few percent own more than half the wealth of the nation, and now that you have spoken out for the great common people, it comes as bad grace for Al Smith, who always claimed to represent the common people, to find fault and charge you with arraying the poor against the rich and class against class.

FDR responded on April 18, "I have several letters and telegrams to thank you for, but I think you realize my failure to answer sooner does not mean that your correspondence has gone unread, and I am always delighted to hear from you and pass on your comments to others who find them most enlightening. I particularly liked your statement that when the Democrats return to Federal control they must remember that the country will be like a sick child, to be nursed back to health. I am afraid that too many will expect an immediate return to health instead of a slow up-building."[35]

The door in the back of Egyptian Hall bangs opens, and the Doctor walks in. He is wearing a black armband, and as he removes his hat, he reaches over to shake the hand of Delbert, who continues to sit in the wheelchair. The two exchange some warm words, and the Doctor pats Delbert on the shoulder, seeming to comfort him.

The hall seems to rumble as if in a slight earthquake. As the rattling subsides, it is replaced by the sound of a loud crash. Delbert looks up, and the Doctor raises his head.

Durbin's portrait, which had hung directly above center stage, has fallen to the floor and its glass has splintered across the floor.

Just then, Tim Kelly arrives; then Kellar, Herrmann, William Jennings Bryan, and Billy Robinson enter behind the Doctor. They all are wearing the same black armbands, and they each take a turn greeting Delbert.

Durbin's mother, Margaret Born, and Jacob Born, he in Civil War uniform, come through the door. They take seats next to others who are filling this little theater, faces I don't recognize, but all in period costumes.

When I think this cannot get any weirder, Delbert spins around in the wheelchair, and there instead of Delbert is FDR himself.

He smiles and starts to wheel himself to the stage.

"*My friends,*" *he says and waves to everyone who has turned to watch him.*

Delbert, transported as if in a magic illusion, now stands at the base of the stage. He prepares a way for Roosevelt by sweeping up the shards of glass scattered on the floor and picking up the broken Durbin portrait.

"*There is no unsolvable problem if we face it wisely and courageously,*" *FDR says.*

Delbert bows and mumbles something about killing more Germans and backs away.

I long for the National Road.

⇒ 15 ⇐

"TAKING UP THE CUDGELS
IN MY BEHALF"

July 1932

The Democratic National Convention in Chicago opened on Monday, June 27, 1932. Durbin attended as a delegate with a one-half vote. My grandparents, Francis and Agnes, traveled with him to Chicago, and they all took rooms in the Palmer House.

In two letters, one written just after the convention and another, an eleven-page, single-spaced missive written a year later, Durbin detailed for Roosevelt the entire saga of the Ohio delegation's actions at the convention. "I want you to have the full story of the plot that was hatched in Ohio to keep you from getting the nomination at Chicago in 1932," he wrote. "You will agree that there was some treacherous work that went on."[1]

The story of deceit began in the summer of 1931. Ohio's Democratic governor, George White, invited Durbin to the governor's house in Columbus in June to meet with FDR, who was returning to New York through Ohio from a governors' conference in French Lick, Indiana.[2]

White knew of Durbin's friendship with Roosevelt and said to Durbin, "You know, he is going to be our candidate for President." It so happened that the IBM was holding its sixth annual convention in Columbus at exactly the same time Roosevelt was scheduled to stop through. Durbin agreed to put aside magic for a night, and he showed up early for dinner, finding that he was alone with FDR. "You remember we had quite a long talk before the other guests arrived," he reminded Roosevelt.[3]

Governor White arrived and during the dinner told Roosevelt directly that he had his full support.

Five months later, in November 1931, before Durbin's visit to Albany, he stopped in Columbus to visit Governor White to confirm his intentions. As Durbin remembered it, "I looked him squarely in the eye and Governor White said, 'Well, Bill, you can explain to him that I am not a candidate for president in the sense of being a real candidate but the only reason I file is because it is necessary to do this to comply with our laws in the election of delegates. But you can say to Governor Roosevelt that we are all for him and want a progressive nominated for President.'"[4]

White promised Durbin that the Ohio delegation would vote for FDR on the second ballot. White expected nothing more than a "complimentary vote" from the delegation on the first ballot. "Had I not believed him," Durbin wrote FDR, "I would have been the first to tell you that you ought to file yourself and you would have received every delegate in Ohio and they would not have made asses of themselves as they did at Chicago."

The chairman of the Ohio Democratic State Executive Committee, Henry Brunner, however, had his own plans. He organized a "stop Roosevelt" movement and was in cahoots with Newton Baker, James Cox, and the public utilities, which were deathly afraid of Roosevelt because of his record of attempting to regulate utility companies in New York.

"I don't want to indulge in recrimination," Durbin later wrote, "but I say upon the honor of a man, that Governor White and Chairman Brunner deceived me in every way, because when I came to Albany on November 15, 1931, I did it with their knowledge and consent and the understanding that they were for you as the best possible choice of the Democrats for President. The most that Chairman Brunner hoped for, was that Governor White might go on the ticket for Vice President."[5]

On the Friday evening before Durbin traveled to Chicago, Governor White came to Durbin's house in Kenton to reiterate a previous commitment that Durbin would be Ohio's delegate to the Committee on Permanent Organization, the committee that picks the convention's permanent chairman. Jim Farley had asked Durbin to make sure he was on this committee to represent the Roosevelt campaign. The plan was to keep Raskob's choice away from the permanent chairmanship. Perhaps in a diversionary maneuver, White told Durbin before leaving Kenton that he was concerned that "Cox was trying to take over the Ohio delegation and he was not in favor of it."[6]

George White now comes into Egyptian Hall. He looks somber but is dressed oddly enough in old-fashioned golf knickers. Everyone stares at him with looks of anger and disgust.

He sits in the back, away from everyone.

Meanwhile two uniformed army officers have straightened FDR's heavy steel leg braces, and they have lifted him to an upright position. He is carried by his massive shoulders to the stage and takes up a position behind a podium. He steadies himself by holding on to the sides of the rostrum and looks out over the group with a characteristic flip of the head.

Delbert, clearly out of it, walks around aimlessly until settling again into the wheelchair. He rolls away from the stage.

"I went with my son and his wife to Chicago on Saturday before the convention and arrived at 3 o'clock in the afternoon," Durbin wrote. He found out right away that he would not be the Ohio delegate on the Committee on Permanent Organization. Instead, Henry Brunner proposed to nominate Frank Dore, an attorney who worked for the biggest utility company in Ohio, the Ohio Power Company. Durbin immediately knew he and Roosevelt had been double-crossed. "I didn't need any further demonstration to show me where Brunner and the Ohio delegation were going," Durbin wrote. He confronted Brunner who "jumped on me with both feet and we had a quarrel." Durbin said, "We got the same reception from Brunner at Chicago that one gets when he sticks his finger into a hornet's nest."[7]

On the warpath, Durbin immediately tried to call White, who was golfing back in Ohio. Through some friends White was tracked down, and Durbin asked him to stop at his house in Kenton on his way back to Columbus so that Durbin could talk to him privately by phone. When White could only "hem and haw" on the phone, Durbin wrote, "I knew then that I had been betrayed."

Still hoping White was not part of the conspiracy and that Cox was behind it all, Durbin fired off a telegram to White from the Palmer House:

IT IS ALL THAT I SUSPECTED AND WHAT YOU TOLD ME AT MY HOUSE FRIDAY EVENING. STOP. COX HAS BEEN WORKING TO TAKE OVER THE OHIO DELEGATION FOR HIMSELF AND HENRY [BRUNNER] HAS GONE OVER BODY AND BREECHES AND ALLIED HIMSELF WITH THE STOP ROOSEVELT MOVEMENT.

It was not the personal loss of the position on the Permanent Organization that angered Durbin:

FAR FROM THAT. IT ONLY MEANS THAT A FRIEND LIKE ME WHO WENT TO YOUR ASSISTANCE WHEN YOU NEEDED HELP THE MOST IS CRUCI-FIED BECAUSE HE WILL NOT ALLY HIMSELF WITH THE ELEMENT THAT DEFEATED THE PARTY IN TWENTY-FOUR AND TWENTY-EIGHT AND WHO

WOULD PREFER HOOVER TO ROOSEVELT BECAUSE HE WILL NOT LEND
HIMSELF TO THE INTERNATIONAL BANKER AND THE PUBLIC UTILITY
INTERESTS.

Henry Brunner, Durbin wrote White, "IS NOT THE SMARTEST POLITICIAN
BY ANY MEANS AND HE NEEDS GUIDANCE AND ADVICE DIFFERENT THAN HE
IS ACTING UNDER. IN THE LANGUAGE OF JOHN ALDEN, WHY DON'T YOU SPEAK
FOR YOURSELF, GEORGE?"[8]

George White was in it up to his neck. He was summoned by Brunner to
come to Chicago to help Brunner control the delegation, with Durbin agitating to break for Roosevelt after the first ballot. Delegates were threatened
with loss of their state jobs if they didn't hold the line, according to Durbin:

> The next thing I knew, [White] was in Chicago and brought with him
> his Highway Commissioner and between them they threatened every
> man on the delegation who held a [state] position that he must stand
> by them or they would lose their jobs or the jobs of their friends.

It was an uncomfortable position for Durbin: "Governor White came and
sat in the delegation and importuned the delegates like a candidate for con-
stable."[9]

Roosevelt experienced some surprising weakness in the first ballot. New
York, for example, split its vote between Roosevelt and Al Smith. Cox, Baker,
Al Smith, and William McAdoo all were working feverishly to block a Roosevelt
nomination. Smith and McAdoo, bitter rivals since the 1924 convention, met
in the Blackstone Hotel to join forces against Roosevelt. Smith predicted that
if the convention went to a fifth ballot, "We've got him licked."[10]

"Baker was the man of choice to break through the Roosevelt lines,"
Durbin wrote. "[Cox] knew that if Baker would do this that Baker would
never get anywhere with the large Roosevelt majority in the convention and
possibly they might compromise on Cox. Soon we heard of $50 bills that
were being distributed in the Mississippi delegation but you can depend on
it they were not Cox's bills because he doesn't spend his own money that
way. They came within one vote of having enough to turn [the Mississippi
delegation] over to Baker but [Senator] Pat Harrison got back in time to
thwart the whole scheme."[11]

Because some of the preliminaries went on too long, the voting on the first
ballot did not happen until four o'clock on the morning on Friday, July 1.
Farley was convinced Roosevelt would take the nomination on the first bal-

lot—he made the mistake of predicting this in a press conference—and so he pushed for the vote.[12]

While Roosevelt had a clear majority when the ballots were counted, he was still 104 votes shy of the required two-thirds. Farley started to regret his press conference, and he became concerned that his candidate would stall and eventually lose steam. He was desperate for a delegation to break on the second ballot to put it away on the morning of July 1. Roosevelt in his shirt-sleeves listened anxiously to the entire proceeding on his radio as he sat chain smoking in his office in Albany.

Word spread at the convention that there was not a single vote in the Ohio delegation for Roosevelt. "Representative Joe Shannon of Missouri, whom I have known for many years," Durbin recalled, "sat across the aisle from me and he was afraid they would get the Mississippi delegation and he told me, 'Well, Bill, they are telling around that there isn't a single vote in the Ohio delegation for Roosevelt.'"[13]

Durbin decided that it was time to show the convention differently: "When the second ballot came I felt that the other States should know that Ohio was about to break for you. On the second ballot I challenged the vote and cast my lone vote for you simply to appraise the other State delegations of what was coming."

Durbin's challenge was carried on national radio; he demanded a roll call:

THE PERMANENT CHAIRMAN: Who is the gentleman addressing the chair?

HON. W. W. DURBIN (OHIO): W. W. Durbin of Ohio. I challenge the vote on our last roll call.

THE PERMANENT CHAIRMAN: The Ohio vote will be polled. Will the Chairman of the Ohio delegation give his attention to the Chair?

HON. W. W. DURBIN (OHIO): Yes, sir.[14]

When the poll was taken, every Ohio delegate voted for Governor White, save one. Durbin cast his one-half vote for Roosevelt. He had bolted, and the convention, FDR, and the nation knew it.

The second and third ballots showed gains for Roosevelt, but Farley finally decided to call for a rest, and the yawning convention was adjourned at nine in the morning, set to reconvene at eight-thirty that Friday evening.

Francis and Durbin resolved before going to breakfast that they would send fifty to seventy-five telegrams from their hotel to influential Democrats back home so they could "get busy with the delegation in Ohio." It was a "trick" Durbin said he learned from William Jennings Bryan at the 1912 convention in Baltimore.

The return flood of telegrams to the Ohio delegates kept the bell boys at the Palmer House busy all day. "I learned from the bell boys at the Palmer House where we stayed that they never delivered so many telegrams in all their lives," said Durbin.

A bellhop enters crying that he has a telegram from the White House.

Delbert rolls over to him and says, "I'll take that!" He snatches the telegram and opens it and reads.

FDR looks as if he is about to start speaking.

"Then we went to bed," Durbin recalled, "and at 4 o'clock I was awakened by my son who shook me and said, 'Dad, get up. Governor Roosevelt wants to talk to you.' I still remember that conversation which you opened by saying, 'Is that you, Bill?' and I said 'Yes, Governor.' Then you said, 'Well, your voice sounded mighty good this morning.' Then you told me to get in touch with Jim Farley and you repeated to me what I knew—they were trying to get Maine and Mississippi from us but they couldn't do it, and then you asked me the question, 'How many can we get from Ohio?' and to be very conservative, I told you 15 for sure. You said, 'Fine.' We got 29 but I think that at least 9 or 10 of these were band wagon delegates including Brunner, Pomerene, and Buckley."[15]

That night when the convention resumed, Roosevelt was nominated on the next ballot, the fourth. The Ohio delegation stubbornly refused to vote until the last state, district, and territory had voted, including the Virgin Islands, and even then with Roosevelt holding 166 votes more than required, Ohio split its vote among Roosevelt, Smith, White, Ritchie, and Cox. "Democrats from Ohio were disgusted and I received no less than 500 telegrams commending me for having stood out for you," wrote Durbin.[16]

"IT HAS ALL PANNED OUT AS WE THOUGHT IT WOULD," Durbin wired FDR from Chicago late that night. "MY HEARTIEST CONGRATULATIONS AND BEST WISHES."[17]

"Your early morning telegram gave me a great deal of pleasure," Roosevelt wrote Durbin on July 22, "and should have been acknowledged before this. You may be sure that I am counting on you and your friends for the loyal support you have given in the past. Our campaign must be an aggressive one if we are to roll up the landslide victory which we hope to achieve next November."[18]

When Durbin wrote his first letter describing the Ohio "treachery" at the convention, a Roosevelt secretary attached a cover memo to it and sent it to

Louis Howe: "MR HOWE! Please note this choice little package of dynamite. Will you answer?"

Howe sent the letter along to Jim Farley: "Dear Jim: Here is a communication from your friend Durbin. How shall I answer? L. H."

Farley responded on August 29, "I am returning the long letter Governor Roosevelt received from Bill Durbin, a copy of which was also forwarded to me at the same time. There isn't to do about it now. It is a sleeping dog. Why not let it lie?"

"OK," Howe initialed.[19]

The Durbins campaigned hard for Roosevelt that fall. In a preconvention letter to Francis Durbin, FDR sent a letter thanking him for his help, saying, "I very much appreciate your taking up the cudgels in my behalf." Taking up the cudgels was an understatement. A cudgel is a short heavy club; the Durbins brought out the heavy artillery for Roosevelt. Most of the return fire, however, was from Ohio Democrats angered over Durbin's bolt in the convention.[20]

"I've got a cudgel for you!" Delbert yells and produces from nowhere a big stick, which he uses to whack the unsuspecting bellhop on the head.

The blow knocks him out cold, but no one takes any notice.

"That'll start things off with a bang!"

"Senator Wagner, Governor Lehman, ladies, and gentlemen," FDR begins.[21]

Eliza Durbin wrote her congratulatory letter to FDR after the convention, enclosing her poem "The Radical," which she had originally composed for William Jennings Bryan. She wrote Roosevelt, "In every age there have been valiant souls that found the cause of democracy swell within them until it crowded out selfish consideration of personal welfare . . . and we are sure you, such a leader, are come at the happy time of ultimate victory."[22]

Durbin asked Roosevelt to convince vice-presidential candidate Garner to come to Kenton in August to start off the campaign: "THE DEMOCRACY OF NORTHWESTERN OHIO WHICH IS THE GIBRALTER OF DEMOCRACY IS GOING TO HAVE A MONSTER BARBECUE AT KENTON TO START THINGS OFF WITH A BANG. WE WANT JOHN GARNER HERE AS THE MAIN SPEAKER."[23]

"Have not answered your telegram of August 14 for two reasons," FDR replied, "one being that I have literally been swamped, as you can well realize, and the other, because I have been waiting to hear something a little more definite about the plans that are being made for my running mate's itinerary."

To Francis on October 5 Roosevelt cautioned against the danger "of over confidence" and admonished, "We must in no way slacken our pace until November 8." Realizing he was preaching to the choir, FDR wrote, "I know that I

Double-dealers and the candidate. "Big" Jim Farley, Newton Baker, James Cox, FDR, George White, and Robert Bulkley in Columbus (August 1932). Courtesy Ohio Historical Society.

have no need to urge you to keep up the good work." FDR let it be known that the Durbins would be remembered: "Your firm stand by me in the Chicago convention and your fine efforts in this campaign, make me realize that I have no more loyal and devoted workers than yourself and your father."[24]

But loyalty came with a stiff price tag in Ohio. Durbin predicted his lone stance for Roosevelt at Chicago would bring down the wrath of the regular Democratic Party of Ohio on him after the election, especially if White were reelected governor. Writing Jim Farley on July 7 when he returned to Kenton from Chicago, he foretold the story: "These fellows know that I always was for Roosevelt and they seek now to belittle me and my influence and they use this fellow Mengert, who is a tool of Cox, and it is unnecessary to tell you what Cox did against Roosevelt. Mengert was mean in his opposition and he would say to fellows that would say they were for Roosevelt:

'So you're for the paralytic?' This gives you an idea of the lowdown, dirty tactics I am being subjected to and all I ask, Jim, is that I get a square deal."[25]

"So you're for the paralytic?" Delbert echoes from the back of the hall.

Roosevelt won, of course, promising a new deal: "I pledge you, I pledge myself, to a new deal for the American people." Unfortunately for the Durbins, George White also won reelection as governor of Ohio. Suspiciously, Roosevelt's majority in Ohio was much smaller than had been predicted and not consistent with his numbers in the rest of the country. Newspapers forecast Roosevelt would carry Ohio by 300,000 or 400,000 votes, whereas he only received a 74,000 majority. By contrast White, "a weak candidate" according to *Plain Talk* magazine, won his race with a 200,000 majority. Unmistakable proof, Durbin would say, "That there was some treacherous work that went on" in Ohio. Durbin contended that Brunner and White were joining Republicans in an anti-Roosevelt campaign. They were "linking up with Republicans," *Plain Talk* magazine agreed. "There can be no reasonable explanation that will convince the Democracy of Ohio that there was an honest effort to carry the state for Roosevelt and elect the state ticket."[26]

"But the election was barely over," Durbin wrote FDR, "until the slaughter of the innocents began. All over the state those who had not been for George White had their heads cut off. Democrats were mighty sore because they realized that you had been sold out by Brunner, White and the State Committee."[27]

"Tonight I call the roll," FDR starts, "the roll of honor of those who stood with us in 1932 and still stand with us today."

Bright applause from the group.

"Written on it are the names of millions who never had a chance—men at starvation wages, women in sweatshops, children at looms."

"Hurrah for the paralytic!" Delbert mumbles like a lost street person.

"Written on it are the names of those who despaired, young men and young women for whom opportunity had become a will-o'-the-wisp," FDR continues, oblivious to the ravings of Delbert.[28]

Ohio Democrats were not the only people Durbin had to worry about in the summer of 1932. Republicans were after him too. In Bucyrus, a town in the middle of Ohio, a group of Republicans decided to indict him for alleged electioneering violations in connection with the May congressional primary race in his home district. He was also charged with attempted bribery and blackmail.

As if that weren't enough, Walter Domzalski, the author of the "DURBIN IS A NUT" acrostic and a Detroit lawyer, filed a one million dollar libel suit in Detroit federal court against Durbin for an article that appeared in the December 1931 edition of *The Linking Ring*.

The problem started when Domzalski apparently had a friend send out a questionnaire to IBM members that, according to Durbin, "was full of insults not only to the President of this order but to other officers and members who are entitled to better treatment."

Durbin responded with a broadside in *The Linking Ring*, which never mentioned "Dom" by name but noted that the questionnaire was "sent out by a party in Detroit, Mich." Durbin wrote that while the offending mailing "bears the name of the person who sends it out, it is well known that he is only the tool of the real person who dictated the letter but who is so cowardly that he remains in the background and has someone else do his dirty work for him."[29]

The questionnaire, Durbin contended, was "actuated by envy, jealousy and malice of the coward who stays in the background and nurses his wrath because he could not be elected to [an IBM] office."

He invited the true author and his backers to come to the next IBM convention to have it out: "There will be a convention in Kenton next June, let them come if they dare, and then we will see what there is to all their contentions."

Meanwhile Durbin had to contend with the criminal indictment. The charge was that he had sent out a campaign circular without signing it, a violation of the "anti-dodger" law in Ohio, which required all campaign literature to identify the proponent of the publication. The dodger in question was a simple reprint of an editorial from an Ohio newspaper, the *Ohio Examiner*, which was critical of the two opponents of a candidate that Durbin favored.

The grand jury in Bucyrus, under the guidance of a Republican prosecutor, J. D. Sears, returned its indictment on May 31, 1932, and an arrest warrant was issued on the day before the IBM's convention was to begin. One of Durbin's friends described meeting him on the street in Kenton just after the indictment and Domzalski's lawsuit had been announced in the newspapers: "Here comes Mr. Durbin. First thing he says to me, 'Well, sue me.'"[30]

"Well, sue me!" Delbert repeats, now whirling around in the wheelchair.

"Written there in large letters," Roosevelt croons, "are the names of countless other Americans of all parties and all faiths, Americans who had eyes to see and hearts to understand, whose consciences were burdened because too many of their fellows were burdened, who looked on these four years ago and said, 'This can be changed. We will change it.'"

Durbin appeared in court in Bucyrus on June 6, bond was set at one thousand dollars, and he was ordered to plead to the indictment by June 13.[31] Initial motions by Durbin's lawyers to quash the indictments were denied.

Durbin's defense was that the circular was nothing more than a reprint of a newspaper article, which does identify the owner of the newspaper and therefore was not an anonymous publication.[32]

"Never before in all our history," FDR continues, "have these forces been so united against one candidate as they stand today. They are unanimous in their hate for me—and I welcome their hatred." The group livens up and starts spanking their legs and lightly applauding. "I should like to have it said of my first administration that in it the forces of selfishness and of lust for power met their match." Loud noise greets this line. "I should like it said—wait a minute!—I should like it said of my second administration that in it, these forces met their master." Roars.

Durbin was next in court on July 7, just after returning from the Chicago convention. He pled not guilty, and trial was set for August 1. The blackmail and bribery charges were deferred until a jury made a decision on the electioneering charge.

Durbin had had some good news the day before. "The morning papers of July 6th carried news from Detroit, Michigan, that in the case of W. H. Domzalski versus the International Brotherhood of Magicians and W. W. Durbin, the service of summons was quashed, so the whole matter is the same as if no suit had been filed," Durbin wrote in *The Linking Ring*. "It is unnecessary to say that there never was anything to this, but some people like to get a lot of publicity out of nothing."[33]

On Monday, August 1, a jury of eleven men and one woman were selected in Bucyrus. Prosecutor Sears called witnesses from the Scioto Sign Company, but they testified that Andy Durbin, not his father, tendered the $19.50 paid for the reprinting of the circular. They testified that they did not think W. W. Durbin had anything to do with the distribution of the circular, but under lengthy cross-examination by Sears, one of the women who helped to fold and address the envelopes for the circular admitted that Durbin "had come into the work room and asked them to 'hurry a little.'"

Sears sarcastically referred to Andy as "Handy Andy" in his closing remarks to the jury and charged that Durbin was attempting to "save his own hide" by blaming his son.

The defense called sixteen witnesses. They were mostly character witnesses who told of Durbin's accomplishments and public service. Sears, who had little notice of the names of the witnesses, cried foul, calling it a "typical Durbin trick." The character witnesses were allowed over the objection. They included the mayor of Kenton and superintendent of its schools, a few bankers, a minister, a professor, a champion corn grower, and some friends and

Durbin plucks handkerchiefs in his U.S. Treasury office (1934). Author's collection.

neighbors. Sears asked only one question of all: had they ever heard it said that Durbin "was a crooked or tricky politician?" The defense rested after two hours and fifteen minutes. Durbin did not take the stand.

The jury deliberated for four hours and returned with a guilty verdict. "Durbin, who was in the courtroom when the verdict was read showed no signs of emotion," the *Telegraph-Forum* read. "His counsel announced at once that the error would be prosecuted to the court of appeals in Lima. A motion for a new trial will be probably be filed within a few days."[34]

The motion for a new trial was filed and, perhaps not so coincidently, the court granted it on November 9, the day after FDR was elected president: "Under the evidence received there is no question but that a crime had been committed, and under this evidence there is no question but that the person referred to as Andy Durbin committed it."[35]

Sears continued to keep the matter alive for almost two years, seeking a rehearing.

The criminal conviction and its uncertainty caused Durbin trouble with an appointment to a job in the Roosevelt administration. But FDR and Farley would not forget their friend. Durbin was recommended for the post of commissioner of internal revenue, then commissioner of customs, and finally Farley settled on the register of the Treasury. The press had a field day with the idea of a magician as treasury official.[36]

"Presto! Magician Durbin Pulls a Treasury Job Out of Political Pie," one of the New York papers read. The *Philadelphia Public Ledger* headline was: "An Honest-to-Goodness Magician Holds Office in Washington." "Durbin (Rabbits From Hats) Turns Magic Art to Politics, Lands U S. Treasury Job," read another.[37]

"Hereafter when problems arise to baffle the 'Brain Trust,' the Administration may find it advisable to turn them over to Bill the Wizard for solution,"

Cartoon of Durbin as register of the Treasury that appeared in newspapers in 1934. Author's collection.

the *New York Evening Post* noted on August 2, 1933. "If he can pull rabbits out of hats, which he can, perhaps he can be helpful in making the Treasury deficit look like a surplus."[38]

"When he took over the office of Register of the Treasury yesterday, it was remarked by those who know that Mr. Durbin will have need for his magic," the *Marion Star* editorialized. "For one thing, there are some $60,000,000 in canceled bonds down there that should be made to disappear. They have been hanging round since the Harding administration."[39]

On Tuesday, August 1, 1933, exactly a year after the start of the Bucyrus trial, Edith Wilson and others came to see Durbin sworn in.[40] Taking his desk in the Bureau of Printing and Engraving, Durbin had fun sparring with the press. "'What I'd like to do most of all,' he said, with solemn mien, sitting afterward in his office down at the old Bureau building, Fourteenth and B streets northwest, 'is fool a lot of newspapermen.'"

Revenge for the Durbins came in the summer of 1934. George White ran for the Senate. The score would be settled. Durbin told FDR the fall before, "We are going to beat the devil out of him with Vic Donehey."[41] In the Democratic primary, Donehey carried seventy-six counties, while White and another candidate carried just twelve. Donehey won the general election, and White was out of politics.[42]

The result was justice of sorts. Durbin ending up concluding that White was so low-down that he was "one of those fellows who when he dies will have to take a stepladder along with him to get into his eternal home."[43]

"'Peace on earth, good will toward men'—democracy must cling to that message," FDR says, winding up his speech. "For it is my deep conviction that democracy cannot live without that true religion which gives a nation a sense of justice and of moral purpose. Above all our political forums, above all our market places stand the altars of our faith—altars on which burn the fires of devotion that maintain all that is best in our Nation."

"Walk humbly with thy God," Delbert adds.

Then the door to Egyptian Hall opens again, and everyone freezes in place. A thin-faced man dressed in a black suit and heavy wool overcoat, wearing tortoiseshell glasses, walks in and stares at me.

After a moment he approaches me and holds out his hand.

"I'm Andy Durbin," he says.

≫ 16 ≪

UNDAUNTED BY THE DEEP
MENACING DIRGE

February 4, 1937

Andy has melting snow on his overcoat. We consider each other for a moment, and I can see a resemblance to one of my brothers, but there is something off.

Andy lived long enough that I could have met him as a young boy, but my mother and her sisters shielded us from him. He was the alcoholic uncle, the family scoundrel they kept in the background.

It did not help that Andy brought a lawsuit against my mother and her sisters when his mother died in 1955. Andy challenged the will, which divided a small estate among Andy, my mother, and her sisters. He took exception to everything and lost all of the legal battles. In one of the papers he is even referred to as the "Exceptor," and I guess that about sums him up.

Andy walks over to Delbert, who is still seated in the wheelchair, and takes the crumpled telegram the bellhop had delivered. Delbert puts up no fight. I can see "The White House" printed on the telegram.[1]

"The thought came to me," Andy says in a formal way, "and I don't know if I'm being presumptuous or not, but . . ."

"Yes?"

"Well, I feel I might owe you something and, anyway, well, I wanted you to see this," he says and hands me the telegram.

The White House telegram is directed to Francis Durbin and is dated February 5, 1937, "I WAS DEEPLY SHOCKED TO HEAR OF THE SUDDEN DEATH OF YOUR FATHER, MY OLD FRIEND, AND HAVE JUST LEARNED OF YOUR DOUBLE LOSS. STOP. MRS. ROOSEVELT JOINS IN DEEPEST SYMPATHY TO YOU AND THE FAMILY. FRANKLIN D. ROOSEVELT"

Attached to a copy of this telegram in the Franklin D. Roosevelt Library in Hyde Park is a White House memo, stating, "Mary Kelly [Durbin's secretary in Washington] reports that W. W. Durbin passed away last night. Has two sons—older son is Francis W. Durbin—Kenton, O. Francis' wife died night before last—Mr. Durbin was very fond of her and the shock must have affected him."[2]

"So it is over? Agnes is gone? He's gone?" I ask Andy.

"Yes."

We both stand in silence for a moment.

"I thought you might want to come to the funeral," Andy says. "I'll be out front waiting in my car. Why don't you come out when you're ready?"

He turns around and walks to the door of Egyptian Hall, just below the "OTHERS" *sign.*

I go over and sit among the now-frozen figures in the hall. I am stunned, even though this is a story I heard throughout my whole growing-up. My mother was thirteen when her mother died of cancer on one day in February, and her grandfather, the great magician, died the next day. How could they both be gone so quickly, so completely, within one day?

"You must be strong," Francis told my mom.

There were signs in 1937 that time might be limited for Durbin. Andy wrote to FDR after Durbin's funeral that the family had been worried about his health: "Many months ago he wanted to resign his position in Washington, and the family all advised that he do so, but the answer was that people would think he was running out on the President when he needs all the help he can get from his friends!"[3]

Durbin in fact had been down sick in the winter of 1935, just as he had been sick for over a month in the winter of 1934.[4] His age, the political fights, and the intensity of his life seemed to be catching up with him. "From my sick bed here I send my hearty congratulations on your 53rd birthday," Durbin wrote on January 30, 1935, in a telegram to FDR from the Lee House in Washington, where he stayed: "God spare you and bless you for our great country and the noble ideals you have so ably championed."[5]

At the bottom of Durbin's birthday telegram in the Franklin D. Roosevelt Library, there is typed a "MEMO FOR MAC," referring to Marvin McIntyre, the diminutive appointment secretary to Roosevelt. Mac, as he was known to FDR, was described as "happy-go-lucky and fond of people," but he was a sufferer from "long sieges of illness," and a man who "never weighed more than one hundred twenty pounds with his shoes on."[6]

"Find out if he is still ill," FDR asked Mac, "and how he is getting on."

In handwriting on the birthday telegram someone, probably Mac after a call to Durbin, wrote, "bronchial cough."

On February 15, 1935, Mac typed a memorandum to Missy LeHand, Roosevelt's personal secretary since 1920 and the woman who was constantly at his side. "Mr. Durbin was delighted to hear from the President and to have his expression of sympathy," Mac wrote. "He has been confined to bed with a very bad bronchial cough since January twenty-first and is now able to sit up for a few hours each day."[7]

A few days later, on February 18, another "MEMO FOR MAC" issued from the president. "Will you send him a little line saying I hope he is all right again and thanking him for his telegram? F.D.R."[8]

"My dear Mr. Durbin," Mac wrote on February 19, "The President was glad to hear that you are now able to sit up for a few hours each day, and he is asking me to convey his hope, in which I join, that you will have a very speedy recovery."[9]

"I thank you very much for your kind note of February 19 from the President," Durbin replied, "and I appreciate this ever so much." Apparently Mac's mother had recently passed away, and so Durbin wrote: "I regretted to learn of the death of your good mother, and I tender my sincere sympathy in your great loss."[10]

Of course being for mothers, as Durbin knew well, was good for politics. Presidential secretary Grace Tully, in her book about FDR, wrote, "Ed Flynn, one of the Boss' oldest and closest political friends, was not often called upon for assistance in speech preparation but Ed always was convinced that the most sure-fire appeal in an address to the electorate was to say something nice about mothers." As Tully recalled, Flynn had reduced it to an irrefutable axiom. "'Everyone has them, Mr. President,' Ed often grinned, 'and you ought to be for them.'"[11]

Durbin got back to work sometime that spring of 1935, and by May 6 he asked Mac for a few minutes with the president.[12] FDR agreed to meet and wrote to Mac that he wanted "to see W. W. Durbin someday."[13]

On June 24, 1935, FDR returned to Washington from Hyde Park, and he met with Durbin at 12:45 in the afternoon. The meeting lasted for fifteen minutes. There is no record of what they talked about, but a month later FDR wrote to Henry Morgenthau, the secretary of the Treasury, about a raise for Durbin.[14]

"In compliance with your request, I have been glad to arrange for an increase in Mr. Durbin's salary as Register of the Treasury from $5,600 to $6,000 per annum," Morgenthau responded. "This will be effective September 1, 1935."[15]

Durbin's frequent illnesses may have been a sign of congestive heart failure or hardening of the arteries. His heredity certainly suggested that his biological clock likely was winding down. His father, the Doctor, had died when he was just shy of seventy, and Durbin turned sixty-nine on September 29, 1935.

Early in September Andy Durbin, using his father's register of the Treasury official stationery, wrote to Irene McKenna, an old Albany secretary of FDR's who stayed on in the governor's office in New York, about his father's upcoming birthday: "The thought came to me, and I don't know whether I am presumptuous or not, but my father's birthday is the 29th day of September, and he will be sixty-nine years old. Will you be so kind as to pass along the information as to his birthday to your friend, Grace Tully, and see if she can't have the President write him a letter on this day? I will appreciate it more than I can tell you if you will do this."[16]

Andy wrote a postscript: "P. S.—I think perhaps the President might be going west, so you better get this information to him immediately."

"Dearest Grace," Irene wrote when she forwarded the letter to Grace Tully, "This *pest* is on your trail again. If it is not the thing to do, don't ask the President. I don't care at all."[17]

On September 16, 1935, a letter signed by FDR went out to Durbin: "I have just learned that on September twenty-ninth you will celebrate your sixty-ninth birthday anniversary. I am happy to join your friends in extending congratulations and the very best wishes on this occasion."[18]

As if he sensed what was happening to his health, Durbin began to spend considerable time working on two autobiographical projects. On April 30, 1935, the *Washington Court House (Ohio) News* reported that Durbin was writing a book about his years in politics: "The announcement that Hon. W. W. Durbin, Register of the treasury of the United States, is to write a book—Fifty Years in Ohio Politics—has aroused the interest of thousands of Ohioans."[19]

About the same time Durbin also began his series in *The Linking Ring,* "My Life in Magic," which chronicled his interest in magic from his early youth to the heyday of the IBM. In fact, the series would run once a month from September 1935 to June 1937, concluding four months after his death. "In my boyhood days," Durbin started the first of these articles, "the street fakirs, who sold patent medicine and various other things, engaged much of my time, particularly if they performed sleight-of-hand tricks, which they usually did."[20]

As he sat writing or dictating these stories from his life, Durbin called on a prodigious memory. No detail seemed too remote to pull up. "He could

Durbin at register's desk in Washington (ca. 1935). Author's collection.

recite passages of the finest poetry and prose at great length; relate conversations that had taken place decades ago in his experience; accurately recall
family connections for all of the oldest and most of the more recently established families both in Kenton and in the county," the *Kenton News-Republican* reported in the days after his death. "His memory for details, dates
and places was almost miraculous, and he lost none of the chronological
facts of his numerous and varied experiences."[21]

"My pal, Stevenson, myself, and another fellow who went with us carried
all our traps, including curtains, Punch and Judy stand, etc., out to the school
house," Durbin could write in 1935 of an event that took place half a century

earlier. "None of us had any supper except Stevenson, who went into the butcher shop and got a ring of bologna and went into the baker shop next door and got a few crackers; and like the Lord, who fed the multitudes on five loaves of bread and two fishes, Stevenson fed all four of us on a ring of bologna and eight or ten crackers—while a farmer boy who wanted to come to the show, brought us an apple apiece for which we let him in the show."[22]

Unlike the *Linking Ring* series on magic, nothing apparently has survived of Durbin's efforts at writing his political autobiography. There are stories of a manuscript that was carefully guarded and perhaps destroyed by my great-grandmother after Durbin died.

There are only hints of what Durbin had in mind for this political history. "'Bill' Durbin has been one of the most colorful figures in Ohio politics for fifty years," the *Washington Court House News* reported. "There has never been a campaign nor a factional party fight in all that time in which Durbin has not been a participant. He has made fast political friends by his loyalty and fearlessness. The odds that he had against him never in the least deterred him from pursuing the course he had charted for himself. Bitter political opponents became his friends and allies, once the battle was over. Friends of one campaign became the enemies of the next campaign, and vice versa, as the changes occurred during those eventful fifty years. And now he is to write a book, recounting the friendships of yesteryears, the wars in which he has fought and the great men of Ohio and the nation with whom and against whom he waged battle."[23]

But what of Durbin's legacy? There is little doubt that the insurgency he helped to lead in Ohio had world-changing impacts. It made a difference in history—as it still does today—that Woodrow Wilson served two terms as president and that FDR was not stopped at the 1932 convention. Wars in the Balkans and continuing tensions in the Middle East prove the point. Efforts by the United Nations to control violence and to work toward world peace prove the point. But did Durbin's participation in certain precise moments provide the spark to move things in just the right direction at just the right time? Or perhaps did his actions defeat a counterforce that would have taken the nation or the world on a different course? Was he instrumental in the flow of things, without which matters would have been radically changed? As with all of history, these questions of contingency are intriguing but ultimately unanswerable. But still the questions must be asked.

Just as important is the question that a magician would love: Can someone rise up from history, act at a critical time, and then recede into obscurity, as if in some great illusion? Do people in a democracy have the ability to help create and define the world even though, in the end, they fall below the historical radar screen? Obscurity aside, that this happens, even with some degree of frequency, is a hopeful thing for our democratic form of government. Everyone counts.

So in looking at Durbin, there are some things that are clear. He was on the wrong side of the issue of race in America. However, to paraphrase the Doctor, perhaps no more so than many in those benighted times. Still I had hoped to find evidence that Durbin had had some breakthrough, some moment of lucidity where he overcame his time and his party on the question of race. No such luck. A memorandum from FDR to Morgenthau in 1935 suggests that Durbin's views on race probably never changed. The memo asks: "Will you look into this which comes to me in a very roundabout way?"[24]

Attached was an anonymous statement from an African American who worked for the register's office:

> The colored section in the office of the Register of the Treasury has been located in one comfortable room on the third floor for nearly eight years, separated as it is from all other clerks in the office. This arrangement has proven popular and satisfactory if there must be a separation.
>
> It is now proposed to divide this one room of their's by a partition which if done will create a crowded condition. If this partition is put up and the few colored clerks are forced to give up their room, it will bring criticism against Secretary Morgenthau.
>
> We respectfully urge you, Mr. President, to stop this thing now before it actually happens. The contemplated partition will be erected in the next day or so, maybe on Wednesday or Thursday of this week.

The next day Morgenthau reported back to the president that the matter had been looked into and that the partition idea had been abandoned. "The present arrangement will not be disturbed," Morgenthau wrote.[25]

While Durbin was not mentioned as the originator of the idea for the partition, the disturbance in his office was either at his direction or at least one about which he apparently showed little concern. Indeed a year later a second memo from FDR to Morgenthau dated June 5, 1936, advised of complaints concerning the Treasury Department's apparent practice of filling of vacancies with "white help" in the place of "colored persons." Two cases were cited by FDR: one in the Treasury building and the other in the office of the register of the Treasury. The president asked Morgenthau to make an effort to correct the situation by "taking on some colored people at the bottom."[26] An attached memo reminded FDR to take this matter up at the next cabinet meeting.

The position of the register had been traditionally set aside for an African American. "The position, a Presidential appointment carrying a salary of $6,000 a year and requiring Senate confirmation, is actually under the Commissioner of Public Debt, an office responsible neither to the Senate nor the President," one newspaper wrote. "This ambiguous arrangement is said to have been conceived years ago, with the understanding that a colored man would occupy the post."[27]

When Durbin died, Roosevelt received a flurry of applications from African Americans. One wrote, "Negroes throughout the length and breadth of the U.S. expect and hope that this office will be restored to the race; quite naturally my hope is, that as the ranking career man of my race both in the Register's Office and the Treasury Department, I will be promoted to fill the job."[28]

Two weeks after Durbin died, FDR penciled an inquiry to Henry Morgenthau: "Sully Jaymes of Springfield, Ohio—Colored man for Reg. of Treasury?"[29]

There was an effort to have Francis Durbin appointed to his father's job. Jim Farley, as chairman of the Democratic National Committee, was peppered with letters from congressmen and party leaders endorsing Francis. "The Durbins have always been militant democratic workers whether the party was in season or out of season," a commissioner of the civil service of Ohio wrote to Farley. "You always found them on the firing line and I was pleased to have worked, as state committeeman, with the Durbins through these many years and know of their worth to the party. . . . I would be very pleased if you would lend your valuable influence toward [Francis's] appointment and feel that if you do the position will be secured."[30]

Farley sent along the endorsements to Morgenthau with an unenthusiastic note: "This is for whatever consideration you feel the case merits."[31]

Andy Durbin decided to again pester Irene McKenna, this time to ask her to intervene on Francis's behalf with Grace Tully at the White House. He sent along a clipping from a Lima newspaper with a picture of Francis handing over a check of some six hundred dollars to a committee member of the Allen County Children's Home. Francis had been the chairman of the local FDR birthday ball, an affair celebrated every year and used as an occasion to raise money for the March of Dimes and other children's causes.

FDR's birthday was January 30. This was a week before Francis's wife and father would die. Francis looks like he has been through the ringer. He is overweight and bloated, his eyes dark and partially closed. When I found this faded photocopy of the newspaper photo in the Franklin D. Roosevelt Library in 1998, I realized that this is the only photographic evidence that exists from that horrible time in the beginning of February 1937, and it gives me some dim view into Francis's pain during his nightmare time. Irene McKenna wrote a short note on Andy's letter to Grace Tully: "Dearest Grace— Just to satisfy this individual who has been writing me about daily asking me to write you about his brother am sending this evidence. I can now write and tell him that I have at least sent this. Much love and will write soon."

Her postscript tells of Andy's persistence: "P. S. He has called me from Columbus and asked me to call you about his brother. I told him I would do no such thing. Now he comes along with this. He's crazy. I guess you know he doesn't mean a thing to me."[32]

I do not know who was selected eventually as register of the Treasury, but it was not Francis Durbin.

In many ways, Francis was a natural choice to take his father's place. He was schooled in politics, having trotted along with his dad to every Democratic convention since he was a child. He filled in for his father in important political matters, when his dad was sick, for example. In the 1936 Democratic National Convention in Philadelphia, Francis was required to stand in when Durbin fell ill. Francis took his place on the Subcommittee on Rules at the crucial moment when that subcommittee took up the highly charged debate over whether to keep or discard the rule that the nomination required a vote of two-thirds of the delegates. The time-honored rule was bitterly opposed by many, especially in the north, as undemocratic, because minority groups could band together and conspire to block the wishes of the majority.

For this very reason Southern states with smaller delegations opposed the abolition of the rule, recognizing they would have less say in the nomination. The issue had always been sharply divisive, and it was a dangerous matter to take on. Durbin's role on the subcommittee, therefore, was of some significance in 1936. When he got sick, he turned it over to Francis, who had his proxy and complete trust. Remarkably, the rule was thrown out, but not before there was a vigorous convention fight and an important compromise. The trick turned out to be a suggestion that small state delegations could be strengthened through a reapportionment plan.

At least one reporter for the *Philadelphia Record* thought Francis played the pivotal role in the compromise:

The inside solution of the two-thirds rule compromise came not from the top of the convention but from an alternate with half a vote on the rules committee.

As insiders tell it, one Francis Durbin, of Ohio (Lima), was sitting in as an alternate for his father, a treasury official who is an amateur magician by avocation. The appointment of the prestidigitator to the treasury was considered particularly significant in view of the money magic going on at that time. The younger Durbin is said to be something of a trouble-maker within the Ohio organization, but apparently he knows how to settle it as well as to make it. He sat around listening to the bigwigs argue until he wearied and suggested that the national committee study reapportionment of state delegation strength to cool off the hot-blooded southerners. The idea was taken up immediately by the committee and adopted.

As usual, Boss Farley is getting credit for having instituted it.[33]

Thus died the rule that made Woodrow Wilson possible (Champ Clark came to the convention with a decided majority), the rule that allowed James Cox to become the nominee in 1920 (on the forty-fourth ballot), the rule that ruined Al Smith's first attempt at the nomination, and the rule that threatened Franklin D. Roosevelt in the 1932 convention, where he held a clear preconvention majority.

Although Francis continued in his father's political footsteps, without him he never again held a major position of power. He did continue in the Durbin tradition of being a gadfly at conventions. In 1940, when FDR made his controversial decision to run for a third term, Francis and other conservatives violently opposed his choice of Henry Wallace for vice president in place of Garner from Texas. Wallace from Iowa had been a Republican before converting and becoming one of the more liberal of the New Dealers. FDR appointed him secretary of agriculture in his first term in return for Wallace's farming newspaper's endorsement. By 1940 FDR was breaking with Farley, who thought the president should not run for a third term and that he, Farley, should be the party's nominee.

FDR therefore turned to Wallace, believing him to be a sincere liberal who would carry forward the New Deal if need be. It was a controversial choice. Many of the delegates thought Wallace quirky, a mystic of sorts, a farmer who was an expert in plant genetics but not a natural politician. One newspaperman wrote, "Henry's the sort that keeps you guessing as to whether he's going to deliver a sermon or wet the bed."[34] But even more galling was that Wallace was a defector from the Republican Party, an apostate who renounced his allegiance and converted to the Democracy, and this was a real affront to the true believers.

Francis would have none of it. "In 1940," a Lima newspaper wrote about Francis, "Mr. Durbin created a sensation by fighting his way to the microphone on the chairman's stand at the Democratic convention to nominate Bascom Timmons, a Washington newspaper correspondent, and Charles Sawyer, Cincinnati, for vice president. Franklin D. Roosevelt's forces were pushing Henry A. Wallace, who, subsequently got the nomination."[35]

My mother was seventeen in 1940 and was taken by her father to the convention in Chicago. She knew of her father's plans to make a stir, and so she sent a telegram to her sisters back in Ohio alerting them to be sure to listen to the radio on the night of Wednesday, July 17. "Listen to WSAI tonight at 6:30," she wired, "Daddy will be interviewed."[36]

Roosevelt was not happy that his pick for vice president caused such a ruckus. He even said he considered withdrawing from the race if the convention voted against his wishes. According to Grace Tully, he sat in the Oval Study playing solitaire on the night of July 18, listening to the convention, and wrote out a statement declining the nomination if Wallace was rejected. "It never left the White House," Tully wrote.[37]

Francis, though, would have a grand time at the convention that evening. As the *New York Times* reported it:

This was Francis W. Durbin's night to howl, and neither man, gavel, [Chicago] Mayor Kelly's gendarmes nor the convention's sergeant's at arms could prevent it. Mr. Durbin, before 25,000 damp Democrats assembled, fought for the wine of true democracy and found it sweet on his lips. Mr. Durbin is a portly gentleman and a delegate at large from Ohio. Mr. Durbin, to the joy and amusement of a rebellious convention, turned out to be a man who knows his rights.

He showed up on the speakers' platform struggling with Colonel Halsey, sergeant at arms, then with Leslie Biffle, the Colonel's assistant. He surged forward toward his goal—the microphone.

At this point three of Mayor Kelly's bluecoats discarded the courtesy-to-guests rules.

Back on the floor, Mr. Durbin, full-throated and hoarse, addressed the chair from the Ohio State microphone.

"I have the right to a voice in this Democratic convention," he thundered. "I insist on that right. I want to make a speech."

Chairman Barkley conceded the delegate's right but would the gentleman say what he had to say from the floor?

Not Mr. Durbin. Mr. Barkley hesitated only a second. He invited the sturdy member from Lima, Ohio, to come to the stand.

A cheer rolled up when Mr. Durbin got to the rostrum. He pumped Mr. Barkley's hand. He peeled off his jacket, picked up the speaker's glass and drank, a long and deliberate drink. He wiped his lips. He braced himself at the rostrum. [The *Cleveland Plain Dealer* account here describes Francis passing his coat to Senator Barkley to hold. "The disrobing revealed a green-striped shirt as wet with sweat as if it had just been dunked in the lake. Rivulets of perspiration trickled down his neck."]

"I want to thank Mayor Kelly of Chicago," Mr. Durbin yelled hoarsely, "for the swell job he has done with this convention." Cheers and boos.

" . . . but," he roared, "the only thing I don't like in Chicago is the Tribune and the Hearst newspapers."

Cheers and boos. [The *Plain Dealer* noted that at this point "the organ played, 'Chicago Chicago' and several Ohioans attempted to wave Durbin down."]

Just because the Republicans, Mr. Durbin thundered, nominated an "apostate Democrat" [Wendell Wilkie] was no reason for this convention to make the same mistake.

Cheers, groans, boos.

" . . . but I have a candidate. I nominate Mr. Bascom Timmons of Texas!"

Tumult, screams, stamping. The delegates didn't know Mr. Bascom Timmons. Only the press rows knew him. He is the Washington correspondent from Mr. Jesse Jones's paper and other papers.

[The *Plain Dealer* reported that at this point "Timmons bashfully stood up in his place in the gallery, saluting Durbin. Durbin grinned again."]

Mr. Barkley moved slightly forward, but Mr. Durbin imperiously waved him back. His face was a rich tomato shade and he put it right in the microphone.

["I was an original Roosevelt man in 1932 and 1936 and I voted for him last night," cried Durbin, the *Plain Dealer* account noted.]

"For God's sake, Mr. President," he shouted emotionally, "if you are listening in let's have some one like Jim Farley or Charlie Sawyer (of Ohio)."

Francis Durbin at the 1940 Democratic Convention (Alben Barkley stands to his right).

Mr. Durbin was through. He straightened. A grin spread over his full, honest face. The floor and galleries shrieked and pounded in tribute.

This was Frank Durbin's night to howl—and he howled.[38]

The *Plain Dealer* explained why Francis picked Timmons: "Timmons is the veteran Washington correspondent of southern newspapers. He is also delegate from Texas and holds the personal proxy on the Democratic national committee of Vice President John N. Garner. His candidacy was the cocktail hour inspiration of fellow correspondents several days ago when boredom at a dull convention was at its height."

No doubt, Francis's father would have been proud of his son's performance. Francis's mother, however, listening to the convention on the radio with my two aunts, was mortified. When Francis screamed, "For God's sake, Mr. President," she nearly passed out. "Oh my," she said to my aunts, "he just took the Lord's name in vain on national radio."

Eleanor Roosevelt delivers her "no ordinary time" speech just after Francis Durbin addressed the 1940 Democratic National Convention. Courtesy Bettmann/CORBIS.

Eleanor Roosevelt, who had come to the convention at FDR's request to soothe the rancorous situation, sat quietly on the crowded platform as the debate over Wallace raged. She spoke to the convention just after Francis's fiery address. She quickly reversed the insurgency and chaos his speech had generated by reminding delegates of the precarious and dangerous world situation and of the need for continuation of the Roosevelt leadership.

"This is no ordinary time," she squealed in her high pitch voice, "no time for weighing anything except what we can best do for the country as a whole."

As if addressing Francis directly, she said, "You will have to rise above considerations which are narrow and partisan. This is a time when it is the United States we fight for." Wallace secured the nomination.

A few weeks after the convention, Francis wrote FDR a lengthy letter on Democratic prospects in Ohio. He took the opportunity to explain his actions at the convention: "In the evening that the vice-president was nominated I made a speech in which I called for a Democrat for vice-president. However, before the ballot was over we in Ohio found that Wallace had a majority of the votes and like good Democrats we cast our unanimous vote for him. More than half the delegation was against Wallace if he had not been nominated on the first ballot. I think Mr. Sawyer will tell you this. As a good Democrat I am out hitting the ball for Wallace and feel that he will grow on the people as vice-presidential material."[39]

FDR read the letter and on August 2 asked Pa Watson, his aide, to "Send him a nice letter of thanks." At least while an election was on, FDR apparently showed no hard feelings.[40]

Again in 1944 Francis led the charge against Wallace. "In 1944, Mr. Durbin again opposed Wallace for the vice presidential nomination," the *Lima News* reported. "This time he backed Harry Truman, who was successful."[41]

By 1944, however, Francis was already a sick man. In 1941, at just fifty years old, he suffered a cerebral hemorrhage while driving from Marion to Kenton. He survived but had difficulty talking and struggled for a couple of years to learn to regain full command of his ability to speak. He would lose words in midsentence and, more often than not, he would blurt out "damn" or "Goddammit" when words escaped him.

His mother, Mary Durbin, wrote to my mom in 1948 when she was attending Ohio State that Francis had stayed up all night on election night, worrying over Truman's election. "Well, the election went over swell," Mary Durbin wrote on November 6, "so very much better than anybody expected. But my, oh my, what a job our President has facing him." She wrote my mother how glad Francis had been "over the great sweep the old Democrats made," but that "it was 8 [A.M.] when your Daddy lay down."[42]

Francis, spent by age fifty-eight, died on December 1, 1949, from heart failure. I missed knowing him by seven years. The first days of February 1937 had taken their toll and reaped their harvest.

Durbin did drive over the National Road to Ohio with his chauffeur, Delbert Krock, the night of Monday, February 1, 1937. Durbin's papers contain an invitation to attend a reception for departmental heads at the White House on Thursday, February 4. The rush and sadness of the journey to return to Ohio because of the swift decline of Agnes Durbin must have been a traumatic time for both Durbin and Delbert. Given his age and health, Durbin had to have wondered about his own mortality.

Something went wrong on the trip home to Kenton. The newspapers reported Durbin had a bad cold and had had a heart attack or a heart disturbance when he arrived home.[43] I remember hearing my mother say that her grandfather had had a stroke during the car ride home. Judge Thomas Dowd of Kenton wrote me in 1995 that in fact something bad did happen during the

car ride from Washington, "You (or someone close to you) must have interviewed the late Delbert Krock. Deb told me many incidents of that sad journey. He felt a grave responsibility and related his regret for not taking charge
and driving to a Hospital in Washington, Pa. or Wheeling, W. Va."[44]

Some older residents of Kenton who knew Delbert told me that he died
insane. They speculated that he never got over his guilt from the last journey with Durbin. Whatever happened during the car ride, Durbin had a
heart attack on Wednesday, February 3, when he was told of Agnes's death.
"Apparently recovered from his first illness, Durbin suffered a second heart
attack Wednesday afternoon from which he failed to rally. News of the death
of his daughter-in-law is believed to have hastened his death," the *Lima
News* reported.[45]

Durbin died Thursday, February 4, at ten after ten in the evening. He
suffered, earlier in the day, a cerebral hemorrhage. Francis did not make it
in time: "Grief-stricken over the death of his wife, Durbin's son, Francis,
was summoned to his father's bedside when it became known the end was
near. A hurried motor trip to [Kenton] failed by only a few minutes to bring
the son to the father's side before death came."[46]

Andy Durbin, according to the newspapers, was "en route home Friday
from Florida by plane" the day after his dad died.

So FDR'S telegram went out from the White House on February 5 to Francis
Durbin,[47] and a letter followed to Mary Durbin. "I am shocked and saddened
by the news of the passing of your devoted husband," Roosevelt wrote to
Mary, "and offer you and the family an assurance of sympathy. The country
loses an able public servant and I mourn the loss of a faithful friend."[48]

"My brother Francis has shown me your wonderful telegram expressing
your sorrow at the passing of my Father to him," Andy wrote FDR on the
day after Durbin's funeral. "My mother has shown me your deep sympa-
thetic letter. To think that the President of the United States, as busy as he is,
could find the time to write a letter of condolence to our family in the time
of our great sorrow! I could not let the day pass without expressing my
gratitude for this wonderful act.

"I am standing right now in the office in which my Father sat for thirty-
five years, I am looking at one of his mottoes—'He loves God most who
serves Man best.'"[49]

Typical of Andy and probably without anyone's permission, he took it on
himself to order that a ship model Durbin had in his office in Washington be
delivered to FDR, knowing full well of Roosevelt's fondness for anything nau-
tical, especially models and paintings of ships. Andy wrote, "There is a very

beautiful ship model in his office at the Register of the Treasury that he intended to present to you, and I am directing that they take it from the office to the White House." Next to this paragraph, someone—I suspect FDR himself—slashed three lines to emphasize its importance.

On February 28 FDR responded to Andy: "Many thanks for your very kind letter. I have been deeply interested in what you say about your father and, of course, I am most appreciative of your kind thought in regard to his desire to present the ship model to me. It had been delivered to me here, and I am delighted to have it."[50]

When I visited the FDR library in 1998, no one was able to identify this particular model among the enormous collection they keep. Nor could I find the motto "OTHERS" that Durbin gave FDR. Durbin claimed that he first took this simple word as his personal motto after Bryan told him of the quaint story of a man who placed the word on a plaque on his fireplace mantle to remind his family of the need to think always of others.

Durbin had the word framed and placed on the wall of his office in Kenton and in Egyptian Hall. When he moved to Washington, he took a copy with him. "Upon the wall of his Washington office," one of *The Linking Ring* writers noted in June 1936, "as upon the wall of his famous Egyptian Hall in Kenton hangs the motto which reads 'OTHERS.' Mr. Durbin's lifetime has been spent in aiding OTHERS in Magic, Politics, and Business. So Democratic is the thought that upon the desk of Franklin D. Roosevelt, President of the United States, stands framed in an easel the motto 'OTHERS' and you will see upon it where it was presented by W. W. Durbin."[51]

"It occurred to me," Durbin wrote Inez Blackstone not long before he died, "that here in one word was the essence of the Christian religion—the thing that stood out in the life of Christ more than anything else. If you think of those who are gone and that you admired much when here, and then think of them now that they are gone, you think in terms of what they did for others rather than what they did for themselves."[52]

David Price in Nashville still had the multicolored sign "OTHERS" in his American Egyptian Hall when I visited him in 1994.

Durbin's fondness for simple slogans reflected his direct approach to life. He was not one to sit around and brood. He was an actor, a person who clearly felt a sense of mission. "Because after all is said and done," he would write to Inez Blackstone, "the sum total of this life is human happiness and in doing for others."

Written about FDR in the 1936 campaign, Eliza Durbin's poem could very well have been about her brother:

But even from the first there sometimes stood
A soul made strong by inner vision's urge
To cry the righteous right of common good,
Undaunted by the deep menacing dirge
Greed's minions chanted over worldly hopes.
And though it seemed his voice was ever vain
The place he stood grew ever hold ground,
And always he was born to cause again
In newer voice with richer, stronger sound.[53]

The dirge that followed Francis that week in February 1937 was a song of sadness so profound that I truly wonder how he survived. Agnes's funeral was sung at a Catholic High Mass at St. Rose's Church on Saturday, February 6. On Monday afternoon, February 8, Francis traveled the thirty miles to Kenton to bury his father.

On March 3 Francis finally responded to FDR's telegram of February 5, "My wife was a wonderful wife and mother, leaving three beautiful daughters, one thirteen, the other nine, and the youngest two and one half, but they are a great inspiration and we will carry on."[54]

It is time for me to leave Egyptian Hall to head out to meet Andy in his car.

The characters in the room are all still frozen in place, like some strange wax museum. Only Delbert retains his vitality, but he now is passive, lost in thought.

The weather outside is cold, and a light rain mixes with the falling snow. Andy sits in his sedan, with the engine running. Cars line the street as far as I can see around the Durbin home. I run out, jump in, and close the door.

"I'm ready," I say, "let's go."

⇒ 17 ⇐

CROSSING THE BAR

February 8, 1937

To members of the International Brotherhood of Magicians in 1926, Durbin wrote about his fund-raising for the order: "I presume that many of you will imagine in my life I have been a minister because I always speak of money."[1] He was not a minister, nor was he an active member of any organized church. He married a Catholic and his sons were raised Catholics, but he never converted.

Nevertheless, the pastor of the Church of the Immaculate Conception and Father John Kelly, Agnes's brother, officiated at the funeral services of Durbin, which were held in his home. "The many rooms of the Durbin home were filled with friends gathered to pay final tribute to the prominent leader, while many others remained outside during the funeral rites," the Kenton newspaper reported. "City police and state highway patrolmen directed traffic in the vicinity of the home."

His pallbearers were selected from some of his longtime friends at the Scioto Sign Company. The music was inspirational. As reported in the paper: "Beautiful were the vocal selections given by Guy Laubis during the final rites." Out of respect, local banks were closed at noon along with most of the public offices.[2]

Andy and I join the caravan that is headed to Grove Cemetery, located about a mile outside of town. By the time we arrive the casket has been placed over the freshly dug hole, and the family has gathered around under a tent. The priests are sprinkling the casket with holy water and reciting prayers. Francis stands next to his mother with his two oldest daughters, my mom and her

*sister Diane. Mary Durbin and her sister Sara Danaher quietly weep. Francis
and Eliza Durbin stand stoically while my mother fights back her tears.*

*Then a man I do not know stands at the head of the casket and holds out a
white magic wand. He begins to read from a sheet of paper: "The symbol of the
mystifier has ever been the magic wand, while white, emblem of all that is
good, has been the mark of purity. May this wand, then, emblematic of the art,
rest with our brother's earthly frame, which we have known best. And may the
soul, now that the mystery of life and death has been solved, stand before the
Creator who knew him best, ready for whatever supreme mystery our God
may have programmed for him." Oddly enough, everyone, including Al Saal,
says, "Amen."*

*The man takes the wand in both hands and holds it out, saying, "As the
silver thread of life of our brother has been broken, and the spirit has been
mysteriously and invisibly drawn upward, let us sadly learn the lesson of our
mortality." He then breaks the wand and places it on the casket. "We know that
the life of our brother is not ended, but only that the spirit is levitated and
transported through the dark curtains of death, to a brighter world, where
there is eternal peace and joy forever-more."*

The International Brotherhood of Magicians prescribed a ritual "to be
used by officers or delegated persons of the local rings, as a service for a
departed brother or sister; for use either in the home or at the grave of the
deceased. The President stands at the head of the casket or grave, and Chaplain at the foot." The breaking of the magic wand was performed at Durbin's
grave site: "The I.B.M. Wand Ritual was very impressively carried out at the
grave by the above members [including Al Saal], with Mr. John H. Davidson
as our new President and Dr. Kenneth Sheelor, taking the active parts prescribed therein of President and Chaplain."[3]

In the late 1920s Durbin had been presented with a magic wand made
from wood that was recovered from the original flooring of Independence
Hall in Philadelphia when it was renovated. There were only three such
wands made. They were ornately carved and had gold tips. One went to
Harry Blackstone; one to Jim Barton (El Barto), a Philadelphia magician;
and one to Durbin. Durbin said that he would take it to his grave with him,
and I wonder if he did.[4]

*Andy has joined the family near the grave. I peel away from the crowd and
start to wander through the cemetery, and soon I come to the graves of Durbin's
father and mother. "William W. Durbin, M. D., July 3, 1803–Feb. 13, 1873,"
reads one headstone. "Margaret M. Durbin, Jan. 4, 1833–Nov. 28, 1919," reads
the other. They are buried right next to Margaret's parents, the Leibolds, who*

came to the United States from Germany in the 1850s. The Leibold grave marker is made of a stone that is so badly weathered that I cannot read dates and what appear to be some poetic inscriptions.

Tennyson's poem, "Crossing the Bar," was reprinted in part in Durbin's funeral card:

> Sunset and evening star,
> And one clear call for me!
> And may there be
> No moaning of the bar
> When I put out to sea,
>
> . . . .
>
> For tho from out our borne
> Of Time and Place
> The flood may bear me far,
> I hope to see my Pilot—
> Face to face,
> When I have crost the bar.[5]

On immortality, Harry Blackstone once said, "What's that?" in an interview with *Billboard* about spiritualism, palmistry, mind reading, and mediums: "What do I think of immortality? Ah, that is a belief, something about which I have no more right to speak than any other man. What I've been telling you [concerning the "unadulterated bunk" of spiritualists] I know. I can prove it. But immortality—come on, let's go have a pot of tea."[6]

I turn and, for a flash, see four figures, dressed in turn-of-the-century garb, standing around the Durbin and Leibold graves. Just as quickly they are gone. I want to imagine that Durbin's parents and grandparents and ancestors, ad infinitum, are there waiting to greet him. It is a pleasant thought.

Looking down at these graves, I really wonder what these people gave me. What of their earthly stuff do I carry with me? They are now like John Brown, a-moldering in the grave, with little, if any, of their physical existence remaining. Ashes to ashes, the Doctor might say, dust to dust.

"Magicians—Notice!" read an advertisement placed by Mary Durbin in the June 1937 edition of *The Linking Ring*. "All tricks and magic paraphernalia formerly owned by the late W. W. Durbin, including illusions and card tricks, and all trunks, curtains, and stage equipment, can now be sold pursuant to an order of the Probate court of Hardin County, Ohio, for cash."[7]

Was it all just sold or thrown away? Is it lost forever?

I have some of the physical characteristics and mental constructs of the people buried in this cemetery. My eyes, my nose, my hair, my height, my weight, my claustrophobia—all of these things come from these people and my other ancestors.

But has the essence of these people been handed down? The experiences and memories, where did these things go?

Henry Ridgely Evans, a friend of Durbin and a scholar of magic, asked this question in October 1929 in an article about Harry Houdini:

Mr. Houdini, who possessed inventive genius of a high order, enriched the stage with some of its finest tricks and illusions. In his studies of the occult, he was very much impressed with the Hindoo doctrine of reincarnation. Plato believed in the pre-existence of the soul, and declared that knowledge was largely reminiscence. If reincarnation be true, and we have lived other lives than our present ones, then light is thrown on the extraordinary talents possessed by some that the doctrine of heredity fails to account for. In an interview with a Philadelphia journalist Houdini once remarked: "I must have had other incarnations on this earth-plane, the memories of which are stored up in my subliminal self and bubble up to the surface at times in my waking consciousness, else how could I have gone into an ancient prison in Moscow, Russia, every step along its intricate corridors familiar to me, known at once the great lock I was to open, and opened it as easily as with the proper key? . . . " But many will say that the ingenious Mr. Houdini was romancing; others that he was actuated by ancestral memories. We inherit much from our ancestors, why not their memories? To a certain extent, they live again in us. But we are wading into deep waters here, and better seek dry land again lest we be overwhelmed in mysticism.[8]

I feel a hand on my shoulder. I turn around and see Delbert, my old friend, restored to sanity. He smiles widely.

"The Boss wants to see you."

Durbin's car is waiting in the winding road near the Durbin and Leibold graves. We walk over and Delbert opens the door, and in the backseat are Durbin and Francis, both looking healthy and strong. They greet me with handshakes, and I get in with them.

Delbert turns around and says in imitation of the popular cartoon character, Mr. Dooley, "These ere mistery fellars need some close watchin. First place t'aint right, ner ethical, ter take advantage of their spectaters, ter get em to look where they hadn't ought ter look. This ere is down right shikaneri and scul-dugery."[9]

"It's fun to be fooled," Durbin says to me.

"Never tell your audience beforehand what you're going to do next," Francis says.

"Right you are," Durbin says, "right you are."

With that we pull out of the cemetery, past the gathered crowd, and drive away.

Magic is a powerful thing.

NOTES

Works and persons frequently cited have been identified by the following abbreviations:

Baker Papers Ray Stannard Baker Papers, Library of Congress
FDR Franklin D. Roosevelt
FDRL Franklin D. Roosevelt Library, Hyde Park, New York
LC Library of Congress, Washington, D.C.
LR *The Linking Ring* magazine
NA National Archives, Washington, D.C.
RSB Ray Stannard Baker
Saal Letters Alfred Saal Letters, author's collection
WW Woodrow Wilson
WWD William W. Durbin
Wilson Papers Woodrow Wilson Papers, Library of Congress

PROLOGUE: WASHINGTON, D.C.

1. *New York Evening Post,* August 2, 1933.

2. David Fromkin, *In the Time of the Americans: FDR, Truman, Eisenhower, Marshall, MacArthur—The Generation That Changed America's Role in the World* (New York: Knopf, 1995), 35; 129–30; 266, 318–19; Ted Morgan, *F.D.R.: A Biography* (New York: Simon and Schuster, 1985), 398–99; David M. Kennedy, *Freedom from Fear: The American People in Depression and War, 1929–1945* (New York: Oxford Univ. Press, 1999), 197, 511–12. Dean Acheson, *Present at the Creation: My Years in the State Department* (New York: Norton, 1969), 3.

3. "'Wild Bill,' as he is jocularly known in his native State of Ohio, performed the somewhat eye-deceiving feat of landing the $6,200 Treasury job without the blessing of a single 'regular' Democrat in Ohio." *New York World Telegram,* August 10, 1933.

4. "W. W. [It's-Fun-To-Be-Fooled] Durbin, magician and new Register of the Treasury, smiles when he recalls how, by the magic of politics, he put one over on his Democratic enemies." Ibid.

5. Durbin's fondness for *Tannhaüser* is referenced in a magic program I found when I visited Bob and Elaine Lund in Marshall, Michigan, where they kept a Durbin file at their American Museum of Magic. Durbin also explored music in an article in

The Linking Ring: "Waltzes, marches, weird music, oriental music, etc., can work nicely. For instance, you can fire a pistol which will be the cue for music to start up." "Programs," *LR* 8, no. 2 (Apr. 1928): 90.

6. WWD, "My Life in Magic," *LR* 14, no. 11 (Jan. 1936): 977.

7. WWD to FDR, August 21, 1934, FDRL.

8. "Notables Wait in Vain for Durbin's 'Black Magic,'" *Marion (Ohio) Star*, August 5, 1933; *Columbus Citizen,* August 3, 1933; *Cleveland Plain Dealer,* August 6, 1933.

9. Gene Smith, *When the Cheering Stopped: The Last Days of Woodrow Wilson* (New York: William Morrow, 1964), 80–96, 128; Tom Shachtman, *Edith and Woodrow: A Presidential Romance* (New York: Putnam's, 1981), 203–6.

10. WWD and his son Francis wrote letters to FDR stating that Francis and Judge Timothy Ansberry called Governor James Cox early on the morning that Cox was nominated to recommend FDR for the vice presidency. WWD to FDR, August 21, 1934, FDRL; Francis W. Durbin to FDR, September 8, 1932, FDRL; Francis W. Durbin to FDR, March 3, 1937, FDRL. Ansberry found FDR on the convention floor to tell him he was going to be nominated and then gave FDR's nominating speech. Geoffrey C. Ward, *A First-Class Temperament: The Emergence of Franklin Roosevelt* (New York: HarperPerennial, 1989), 511.

11. *Marion Star,* August 5, 1933.

12. WWD, "The Invention of New Tricks and Illusions," *LR* 14, no. 2 (Apr. 1934): 81.

13. Henry R. Evans, "Flying Leaves from the Journal of an Amateur Magician and Mystic," *LR* 9, no. 8 (Oct. 1929): 779.

14. *New York Evening Post,* August 2, 1933.

15. Henry Ridgely Evans, *History of Conjuring and Magic* (Kenton, Ohio: International Brotherhood of Magicians, 1928), 215.

1. And Things Are Not What They Seem

1. Durbin's car ride is referred to in the *Kenton News Republic,* February 5, 1937: "Mr. Durbin came home from Washington early this week, suffering from a bad cold and a heart disturbance. His condition was not believed serious; he planned to attend funeral services for his daughter-in-law, Mrs. Francis Durbin, scheduled for Saturday morning in Lima."

In a letter dated August 7, 1995, Judge Thomas Dowd, a retired common pleas judge from Kenton, Ohio, wrote to me about an early draft of this book: "To my mind you have chosen an excellent vehicle for relating your chronicle in retrospect. The physical events are so relevant that you (or someone close to you) must have interviewed the late Delbert Krock. Deb told me many incidents of that sad journey." Thomas Dowd, letter to author, August 7, 1995.

2. Hazel M. Krock, "Dear ibm Friends," *LR* 37, no. 3 (May 1957): 24.

3. The Bureau of Engraving and Printing is identified in a 1933 newspaper article as the building where WWD had his office in Washington as the register of the Treasury. "'What I'd like to do most of all,' he said, with solemn mien, sitting afterwards in his office down at the old Bureau building, Fourteenth and B streets northwest, 'is to fool a lot of newspapermen.'" *Marion Star,* August 5, 1933.

4. Harry E. Cecil, "Back to Kenton," *LR* 15, no. 9 (Nov. 1935): 788. In this article Cecil references Durbin's "fine new big super charged magical Studebaker automobile."

5. Albert Douglas, "Auto Trip Over the Old National Road," *Ohio Archaeological and Historical Quarterly* 18, no. 4 (Oct. 1909): 504–12. Douglas is the source for the stories of Andrew Jackson and Henry Clay using the road.

6. Arthur D. Gans, "Kenton—The Convention City," *LR* 6, no. 11 (Apr. 1927): 330. Many of the facts about the National Road are taken from Merritt Ierley, *Traveling the National Road: Across the Centuries on America's First Highway* (Woodstock, N.Y.: Overlook, 1990); and Karl Raitz, ed., *A Guide to the National Road* (Baltimore: Johns Hopkins Univ. Press, 1996).

7. John Gabriel Hunt, ed., *The Essential Franklin Delano Roosevelt* (New York: Gramercy, 1995), 113–19.

8. "'Sub-Delegate' from Ohio, 12, Plans to Be Congresswoman," *Camden (New Jersey) Courier-Post,* June 26, 1936.

9. My source for many of the facts about Durbin's political career, especially the early years, is a 1930 campaign piece put together by the Durbin for U.S. Senate Committee, "The Story of W. W. 'Bill' Durbin" (hereafter, "The Story of Bill Durbin"). I have one in my personal collection, and one is housed in the Democratic National Committee (DNC) collection, box 609, folder Ohio: After the Election–D, folder 2, FDRL. The campaign brochure is sixteen pages long and includes a detailed political biography and "tributes" from Woodrow Wilson, William Jennings Bryan, Newton Baker, James Cox, and newspaper editors. Durbin ran for the Senate in 1930 and lost in the Democratic primary in August.

10. Herbert T. O. Blue, *Centennial History of Hardin County, Ohio* (Canton, Ohio: Rogers Miller, 1933). This book is the source of most of my facts about the founding and history of Kenton. Durbin and his sister Eliza contributed to the book.

11. William Pittenger, *Daring and Suffering: A History of the Great Railroad Adventure* (Philadelphia, Pa.: J. W. Daughaday, 1863); Charles Kendall O'Neill, *Wild Train: The Story of the Andrews Raiders* (New York: Random House, 1956); "The Big Engine That Couldn't," *Cleveland Plain Dealer,* August 11, 1996.

12. Andrew Sinclair, *The Available Man: The Life behind the Masks of Warren Gamaliel Harding* (New York: Macmillan, 1965), 25–32; David Fromkin, *In the Time of the Americans: FDR, Truman, Eisenhower, Marshall, MacArthur—The Generation That Changed America's Role in the World* (New York: Knopf, 1995), 17; Roger Butterfield, *The American Past: A History of the United States from Concord to Hiroshima* (New York: Simon and Schuster, 1947), 274–75.

13. Sinclair, *The Available Man,* 33.

14. Butterfield, *The American Past,* 275.

15. Sinclair, *The Available Man,* 5.

16. WWD, "My Life in Magic," *LR* 15, no. 11 (Jan. 1936): 977; WWD, "My Life in Magic," *LR* 14, no. 12 (Feb. 1936): 1084; WWD, "My Life in Magic," *LR* 16, no. 7 (Sept. 1936): 546.

17. Durbin's "cussing" seemed to have been legendary. Julius Kleimann penned an article about Durbin: "Mr. Durbin also is one of the most distinguished cussers I have ever met. His oaths are always wholesome but never severe, he uses them sparingly but with great gusto, he ever places them perfectly in their context and he lets them spout out of his mouth with spontaneity and precision. But then Mr. Durbin is a magician." The article is peppered with deletions. For example, speaking of his experience seeing his first magician at a circus, Durbin is quoted: "I never forgot that man and the dagger. All summer long I thought about it. I thought about it all winter.

[Deleted.] I couldn't forget about the [deleted] thing." Kleimann, "Manufacturer, Politician—And a Master of Black Magic," *St. Louis Post Dispatch,* July 17, 1927.

18. Walter Gibson, *The Master Magicians: Their Lives and Most Famous Tricks* (New York: Doubleday, 1966), 105–9. Max Auzinger, or "Ben Ali Bey," is profiled in a chapter about Billy Robinson (Chung Ling Soo). I have never found a good explanation about why Durbin chose "Past Master of the Black Art" as his moniker. Perhaps it was because the Black Art was at its height of popularity when he was thinking of becoming a professional magician.

19. Angelo Lewis (1839–1920), a London lawyer, journalist, and amateur magician, published magic books under the pseudonym "Professor Hoffman," including *Modern Magic,* written in 1876. Durbin described this book and others written by Lewis as some of the first he consulted on the art of magic. "In my younger years when I started in magic," WWD wrote, "I had little if any money to put into apparatus, but that did not keep me from trying to make many of the things that were described in Professor Hoffman's book, 'Modern Magic.'" WWD, "My Life in Magic," *LR* 15, no. 8 (Oct. 1935): 703. "Professor Hoffman wrote four books," Durbin wrote, "Modern Magic, More Magic, Later Magic, and Latest Magic. Only three of these books were good. The latter one was written in his later years and, while there was something to be gained from it, yet very little. But the other three brought you right down to date, and any person who has these three books can learn the art of magic without any trouble." Ibid. Professor Hoffman, *Modern Magic: A Practical Treatise on the Art of Conjuring* (ca. 1877), (reprint, Biblo-Moser, n.d.), 3. According to Henry Ridgely Evans, Harry Houdini pronounced Angelo Lewis "the brightest star in the firmament of magical literature." Evans, *History of Conjuring and Magic* (Kenton, Ohio: International Brotherhood of Magicians, 1928), 12.

20. Hoffman, *Modern Magic,* 4.

21. My aunt keeps this framed invitation on a wall in her home, with a car pass to the White House, for Thursday, February 4, 1937.

22. Eliza Durbin to FDR, July 20, 1932, FDRL.

23. FDR to Eliza Durbin, August 27, 1932, FDRL.

24. WWD to FDR, August 14, 1932, FDRL.

25. FDR to WWD, August 24, 1932, FDRL.

2. "Tim Kelly Will Not Soon Be Forgotten"

1. *The History of Marion County, Ohio* (Chicago: Liggett, Conaway, and Co., 1883), 596.

2. WWD, "My Life in Magic," *LR* 16, no. 1 (Mar. 1936): 52–53.

3. National Park Service, U. S. Department of Interior, *John Brown's Raid* (Washington, D.C.: U.S. Government Printing Office, 1973), 28.

4. Ibid., 67.

5. John Anthony Scott and Robert Alan Scott, *John Brown of Harper's Ferry: With Contemporary Prints, Photographs, and Maps* (New York: Facts on File, 1988), 13–18; Stephen B. Oates, *Our Fiery Trial: Abraham Lincoln, John Brown, and the Civil War Era* (Amherst: Univ. of Massachusetts Press, 1979); Paul Finkelman, ed., *His Soul Goes Marching On: Responses to John Brown and the Harpers Ferry Raid* (Charlottesville: Univ. Press of Virginia, 1995).

6. National Park Service, *John Brown's Raid,* 60.

7. On August 6, 1992, I sent in a form request to the National Archives and Records Administration for Tim Kelly's military and pension files. Within the month I received copies of his files including enlistment sheets, affidavits, wounded sheets, and company muster rolls. For information on his regiment I have relied on Whitelaw Reid, *Ohio in the War: Her Statesmen, Her Generals, and Soldiers* (Columbus, Ohio: Eclectic, 1893); Frederick H. Dyer, *A Compendium of the War of the Rebellion* (Des Moines, Iowa: Dyer, 1908); and *Official Roster of the Soldiers of the State of Ohio in the War of Rebellion 1861–1866,* 9 (Akron, Ohio: Werner, 1887).

8. Shelby Foote, *The Civil War, a Narrative: Red River to Appomatox* (New York: Random House, 1974), 319.

9. Walter H. Herbert, *Fighting Joe Hooker* (New York: Bobbs-Merrill, 1970), 272–83. Lincoln's letter to Hooker of January 26, 1863, is reprinted in the foreword.

10. Margaret Mitchell, *Gone with the Wind* (New York: Macmillan, 1936), 300.

11. *Marion Daily Star,* August 20, 1892. I found this on microfilm in the Marion Public Library.

12. Francis Russell, *The Shadow of Blooming Grove: Warren G. Harding in His Times* (New York: McGraw-Hill, 1968), 47; Andrew Sinclair, *The Available Man: The Life Behind the Masks of Warren Gamaliel Harding* (New York: Macmillan, 1965), 7, 85.

3. The Doctor

1. Eugene H. Roseboom and Francis P. Weisenberger, *A History of Ohio* (Columbus: Ohio State Archaeological and Historical Society, 1973); Carl Wittke, *History of the State of Ohio* (Columbus: Ohio State Archaeological and Historical Society, 1942); P. P. Cherry, *The Western Reserve and Early Ohio* (Wooster, Ohio: Fouse, 1920).

2. John Anthony Scott and Robert Alan Scott, *John Brown of Harper's Ferry: With Contemporary Prints, Photographs, and Maps* (New York: Facts on File, 1988), 13–18; Stephen B. Oates, *Our Fiery Trial: Abraham Lincoln, John Brown, and the Civil War Era* (Amherst: Univ. of Massachusetts Press, 1979), 20–42; National Park Service, U. S. Department of Interior, *John Brown's Raid* (Washington, D.C.: U.S. Government Printing Office, 1973), 65–69; Paul Finkelman, ed., *His Soul Goes Marching On: Responses to John Brown and the Harpers Ferry Raid* (Charlottesville: Univ. Press of Virginia, 1995).

3. Garry Wills, *Lincoln at Gettysburg: The Words That Remade America* (New York: Simon and Schuster, 1992), 101.

4. Scott and Scott, *John Brown of Harper's Ferry,* 29.

5. The sources for this mysterious man are few. Two histories of Hardin County, Ohio (where Kenton is located), contain biographical sketches: *The History of Hardin County, Ohio* (1883; rep., Evansville, Ind.: Unigraphic, 1973), 524, and Minnie Ichler Kohler, *The Twentieth Century History of Hardin County, Ohio* (Chicago: Lewis, 1910), 236. A third source is the campaign brochure that Durbin had prepared for his run in 1930 for Democratic nomination for United States senator, "The Story of Bill Durbin." This brochure claims that WWD's father was appointed as agent to the Indians in Ohio by Andrew Jackson in 1833, "and that's how the Durbin family tree was transplanted from Baltimore, Md., to Kenton, O." A search of the Bureau of Indian Affairs in 1993 failed to locate any appointment of Dr. Durbin as an Indian agent. Durbin's obituary in 1937 states that it was his grandfather who was appointed as an Indian instructor by Jefferson "in the Marseilles neighborhood." *Kenton Daily Democrat,*

February 5, 1937. *The History of Hardin County* (both the 1883 and 1910 versions) record that Dr. Durbin came to Hardin County in 1840. They also state that he went back to Columbiana County, Ohio, "where he read medicine," and then returned to Kenton around 1872–73. A fourth source, *The Centennial History of Hardin County,* written in 1933 by Herbert T. O. Blue, recites that Dr. Durbin lived at Marseilles, "having been appointed to the Indian service on the Indian reservation at that place." According to this book (written while WWD was alive and indeed contains reminiscences from WWD and poems by his sister, Eliza) the Doctor "learned to speak the Wyandot language while he lived with them." Blue, *Centennial History of Hardin County, Ohio* (Canton, Ohio: Rogers Miller, 1933), 70. The United States census records show Dr. Durbin in Green Township, Columbiana County, Ohio, in 1830. Extracts from a daybook kept by David Simon in Canfield, Ohio, tell of a son of W. W. Durbin, "who died yesterday [October 23, 1854] of consumption and was 20-odd years old." According to Simon, the son was buried with Masonic rights. Simon's daybooks, as extracted and translated (the originals were in German) by a descendant, Margaret Miller Simon, are found in the Mahoning Valley Historical Society. All of this confusion was cleared somewhat in July 1995 when I found, quite by accident, a letter from Doctor Durbin written in 1859. Even more illuminating were the Doctor's daybooks that I discovered in 1998. I found these daybooks in a building my dad owned in downtown Lima. He asked us to look through the boxes kept there as he was getting ready to sell the building.

6. Several sources claim Dr. Durbin was the first cousin of John Price Durbin. Blue, *Centennial History of Hardin County,* 70; a biographical sketch of Francis Durbin was created by the Citizens Historical Association in Indianapolis in 1948 and can be found in the Lima Public Library that claims, "Dr. William W. Durbin was a first cousin of John Price Durbin, who was chaplain of the U.S. Senate when Andrew Jackson was president of the U.S."; and "The Story of Bill Durbin." In addition to his role as chaplain of the Senate, J. P. Durbin was a Methodist minister, president of Dickinson College, and a world traveler. John Roche, *The Life of John Price Durbin, D.D., L.L.D., with an Analysis of His Homiletic Skills and Sacred Oratory* (New York: Eaton and Mains, 1889). John Price Durbin says his paternal grandfather was from Havre-de-Grace, Maryland.

7. Frederick Waite, "The Professional Education of Pioneer Ohio Physicians," *Ohio State Archaeological and Historical Quarterly* 48, no. 3 (July 1939): 189–97; Howard Dittrick, "The Equipment, Instruments, and Drugs of Pioneer Physicians," *Ohio State Archeological and Historical Quarterly* 48, no. 3 (July 1939): 199–209. According to Waite, "Sometime in the early part of the course [under a preceptor], and in the cold weather, a cadaver was obtained by resurrection in some quiet country churchyard, and in the preceptor's barn loft he and the student dissected it. The student would clean the skeleton and keep it as the first item in the equipment of his office. Later in the course a second cadaver was obtained and a series of surgical operations, mostly amputations at various levels, were carried out" (193).

8. WWD wrote nothing about the Doctor's drinking habits, but two versions of the *History of Hardin County* published almost thirty years apart have notably different accounts of the issue.

9. An exhilarating day. I found nothing in the William Jennings Bryan file after hours of digging. Truly, while waiting for one of the last boxes of Bryan documents,

I glanced through a card index and found the reference to "W. W. Durbin of Ohio stating Brown's insanity on the subject of slavery and asking his reprieve."

10. Scott and Scott, *John Brown of Harper's Ferry,* 153.

11. Ibid., 54.

12. *Cleveland Plain Dealer,* March 22, 1859.

13. National Park Service, *John Brown's Raid,* 51.

14. Ibid.

15. Ibid., 53.

16. Jonathon Metcalf was the only other physician to opine on Brown's insanity. Oates, *Fiery Trial,* 39.

17. Robert E. McGlone, "John Brown, Henry Wise, and the Politics of Insanity," in *His Soul Goes Marching On,* ed. Finkleman, 218.

18. *Cleveland Plain Dealer,* December 3, 1859.

19. Scott and Scott, *John Brown of Harper's Ferry,* 158.

20. National Park Service, *John Brown's Raid,* 57.

21. Ibid., 60.

22. John Fiske, *The Critical Period of American History 1783–1789* (Boston, Mass.: Houghton, Mifflin, 1897), 264.

23. Matt. 7:7.

24. The Doctor's daybooks are in the author's possession. It is remarkable to think these dirty and dusty old books of no apparent significance were kept when so much else, letters from FDR and Wilson, for example, were thrown out. The daybooks are priceless resources.

25. Roche, *The Life of John Price Durbin,* 59–79.

26. *Register of Debates,* 22nd Congress, February 13, 1832, 367–78. John Marshall's letter is reprinted in the debates.

27. The address was published by order of the Pennsylvania Colonization Society in Philadelphia, 1852. I found a copy in the Western Reserve Historical Society Library.

28. Paul Angle and Earl Miers, ed., *The Living Lincoln: The Man, His Mind, His Times, and the War He Fought, Reconstructed from His Own Writings* (New York: Barnes and Noble, 1992), 639–40.

4. My Good Old Mother

1. Her obituary, "Beloved Woman Called," *Kenton Daily Democrat,* November 29, 1919, provided some facts. A death certificate also added facts. She was born on January 4, 1833, in Hintersteinau, Germany. Her father was John Leibold. She died of pneumonia on November 28, 1919, at age eighty-six. She came to Kenton in 1852 and married Jacob Born in 1854. Born died from a wound he suffered during the battle of Chickamauga. She had two children from this marriage: John, who was living in New York in 1919, and Andrew, who still lived in Kenton at the time of her death. She married the Doctor in 1866. She developed pneumonia after falling and breaking her hip in an accident at home.

2. WWD, "My Life in Magic," *LR* 15, no. 7 (Sept. 1935): 602.

3. Ibid., 603.

4. WWD to FDR, November 23, 1931, FDRL. Durbin was trying to explain why Newton Baker would not do well in the Ohio primary in 1932. According to Durbin,

Baker, Wilson's secretary of war, said that the way to win the war was to "kill the Germans, kill more Germans, then kill more Germans." Durbin noted, "When you realize that here in Ohio we have many Congressional Districts filled with Germans and their descendants, you will see what will happen to such a candidate as that." James Cox, another potential candidate, likewise became "obsessed with the idea that we must destroy German influence and had a bill passed by the Legislature to take all teaching of German out of the public schools and in some places they took German books and burned them up."

5. The battle specifics are from Peter Cozzens, *This Terrible Sound: The Battle of Chickamauga* (Chicago: Univ. of Illinois Press, 1992). Jacob Born's military and pension files are from the National Archives and Records Administration obtained in April 1994. Like Tim Kelly's files, Jacob Born's files contained his muster rolls, a casualty sheet, and regimental information. But Born's files also had a detailed extract from the Monthly Reports of the Sick and Wounded at U.S. General Hospital No. 1, Louisville, Kentucky. The report is of A. G. Watson, surgeon in charge, relating to a gunshot fracture of the femur suffered by Jacob Born. The extract follows Born's progress from his admission to his death on November 18, 1863. The enlistment papers describe Born as twenty-nine years old on May 18, 1861, five feet eight and one-half inches tall, with a sandy complexion, hazel eyes, and red hair. He was born in Switzerland, a cooper by trade. He enrolled at Monroeville, Ohio, for a three-year term. From March to May 1862 he was sick in a hospital in Nashville.

6. A friend of mine, Kent Mann, has a copy of his ancestor's Civil War diary and let me read it. Henry Mann wrote about his experience at Chickamauga, which I have quoted.

7. Cozzens, *This Terrible Sound*, 380.

8. Ibid., 247.

9. "Reminiscences of Gettysburg Battle," *Lippincott's Magazine of Popular Literature and Science* 32, no. 6 (1883): 56.

10. James C. Clark, *The Murder of James A. Garfield: The President's Last Days and the Trial and Execution of His Assassin* (Jefferson, N.C.: McFarland, 1994), 70–79.

11. A copy of the letter is in Born's war records. The inventory of Born's effects is there too.

12. *Marion Star*, August 5, 1933.

13. *Columbus Evening Dispatch*, July 24, 1933.

5. Taking Second Money

1. "Ohio Politician Whose Hobby Is Magic," *Cleveland Plain Dealer*, Sunday Magazine, February 22, 1920.

2. A writer from the *St. Louis Post-Dispatch*, Julius Kleimann, went to Kenton to visit with Durbin and to witness the second annual convention of the IBM, and he was told about Durbin's initiation into the magic world. Kleimann, "Manufacturer, Politician—And a Master of Black Magic," *St. Louis Post-Dispatch*, July 17, 1927. Kleimann took his article and sold it to the magazine *Personality*. It appeared in an edited form in the July 1928 edition, along with articles about Teddy Roosevelt, Lord Mansfield, Calvin Coolidge, and Sam Houston. See Julius Hart Klyman, "Black Magic: An Account of One Who Practices It to the Advantage of Himself and Others," *Personality* 2, no. 3 (July 1928): 86. Kleimann changed the spelling of his name for this

article, calling himself "Julius Hart Klyman." WWD also wrote about his beginnings in magic in *The Linking Ring*. WWD, "My Life in Magic," *LR* 15, no. 7 (Sept. 1935): 602–5.

3. *Hardin County Democrat,* May 18, 1876, contains the advertisement for Old John Robinson's circus, coming to Kenton on Monday, May 22, 1876. This is the exact date Durbin identified almost sixty years later when he wrote about it. WWD, "My Life in Magic," *LR* 15, no. 7 (Sept. 1935): 603. On John Robinson's Circus, I found Richard E. Conover, *Give 'Em a John Robinson: A Documentary on the Old John Robinson Circus* (Xenia, Ohio: n.p., 1965).

4. "In Memoriam," *LR* 7, no. 5 (Jan. 1928): 862. His brother Ed Camper is mentioned in "In Memoriam," *LR* 9, no. 9 (Nov. 1929): 920.

5. WWD, "My Life in Magic," *LR* 15, no. 7 (Sept. 1935): 604. On his death, "Stevenson Dead," *LR* 5, no. 6 (Feb. 1927): 199.

6. *Cleveland Plain Dealer,* February 20, 1920.

7. WWD, "My Life in Magic," *LR* 15, no. 7 (Sept. 1935): 605.

8. WWD, "My Life in Magic," *LR* 15, no. 9 (Nov. 1935): 779–80.

9. Ibid., 781.

10. Ibid., 782–84.

11. James C. Clark, *The Murder of James A. Garfield: The President's Last Days and the Trial and Execution of His Assassin* (Jefferson, N.C.: McFarland, 1994); Allan Peskin, *Garfield* (Kent, Ohio: Kent State Univ. Press, 1999).

12. Doctor Durbin's last will and testament, including the codicil, were found in the Hardin County, Ohio, probate court.

6. Our Fiery Trial

1. Lester Lake, "Men of Magic and Me," *LR* 6, no. 2 (Apr. 1927): 328.

2. *New Philadelphia (Ohio) Daily Times,* August 26, 1929.

3. Lake was pictured and written about in several issues of *The Linking Ring*. "Buried Alive," *LR* 9, no. 7 (Sept. 1929): 748, 759; "Lester Lake," *LR* 9, no. 6 (Aug. 1929): 622; "Lester Lake: A Review of his Magical Comedy Revue," *LR* 9, no. 9 (Nov. 1929): 924; and "Howard Thurston Assembly Ring No. 9, Columbus, Ohio," *LR* 10, no. 7 (Sept. 1930): 877.

4. "Lester Lake Injured," *LR* 12, no. 5 (July 1932): 410.

5. Ibid.

6. "Magician Is Stabbed by Excited Spectator," *LR* 16, no. 8 (Oct. 1936): 609.

7. David Price, *Magic: A Pictorial History of Conjurers in the Theater* (New York: Cornwall, 1985), 81–86; Milbourne Christopher, *The Illustrated History of Magic* (New York: Crowell, 1973), 181–97; William Doerflinger, *The Magic Catalogue: A Guide to the Wonderful World of Magic* (New York: Dutton, 1977), 21–24; James Randi, *Conjuring* (New York: St. Martin's Press, 1992), 68–77; Walter Gibson, *The Master Magicians: Their Lives and Most Famous Tricks* (New York: Doubleday, 1966), 66–85.

8. WWD, "With the Old Masters," *LR* 8, no. 7 (Sept. 1933): 451–59; "Alexander Herrmann," *LR* 9, no. 7 (Sept. 1929): 652–53 (Herrmann pictured on cover); WWD, "My Life in Magic," *LR* 15, no. 10 (Dec. 1935): 877; WWD, "My Life in Magic," *LR* 16, no. 2 (Apr. 1936): 151; WWD, "My Life in Magic," *LR* 16, no. 3 (May 1936): 256–57 (the last time WWD saw Herrmann and the Jersey Lily).

9. WWD, "Alexander Herrmann," *LR* 9, no. 7 (Sept. 1929): 652–53; "Bullet Catching Trick One of Few Pitiful Tragedies in Magic History," *LR* 9, no. 12 (Feb. 1930): 1337; Henry R. Evans, "William E. Robinson," *LR* 11, no. 11 (Mar. 1931): 4–5 (Robinson pictured on cover); WWD, "With the Old Masters," *LR* 13, no. 7 (Sept. 1933): 451–59.

10. Price, *Magic,* 502–5; Christopher, *Illustrated History of Magic,* 249–58 (detailed description of the inquest); and Gibson, *The Master Magicians,* 104–30.

11. WWD, "Heart Failed at Last Moment," *LR* 10, no. 9 (Nov. 1930): 1123–24.

12. WWD, "Dangerous Feats and Foolhardy Acts," *LR* 1, no. 9 (Nov. 1930): 1122.

13. *Washington Sunday Star,* September 30, 1934.

14. "The Story of Bill Durbin."

15. WWD, "My Life in Magic," *LR* 15, no. 10 (Dec. 1935): 874.

16. *Washington Sunday Star,* September 30, 1934.

17. "The Story of Bill Durbin."

18. WWD, "With the Old Masters," *LR* 13, no. 7 (Sept. 1933): 451–59; WWD, "My Life in Magic," *LR* 16, no. 3 (May 1936): 256–57.

19. WWD, "With the Old Masters," *LR* 13, no. 7 (Sept. 1933): 451–59.

20. Ibid., 453.

21. WWD, "Alexander Herrmann," *LR* 9, no. 7 (Sept. 1929): 653.

22. *Kenton Democrat,* April 3, 1890.

23. Henry Ridgely Evans, *History of Conjuring and Magic* (Kenton, Ohio: International Brotherhood of Magicians, 1928), 213.

7. A Cross of Gold

1. *New York Herald Tribune,* February 5, 1937; *Cleveland Plain Dealer,* February 5, 1937.

2. Wilson to Bryan, February 23, 1913, Bryan Papers, Library of Congress.

3. Horace Samuel Merrill, *Bourbon Leader: Grover Cleveland and the Democratic Party* (Boston: Little, Brown, and Co., 1957), 61. For information about Cleveland, I relied on Roger Butterfield, *The American Past: A History of the United States from Concord to Hiroshima* (New York: Simon and Schuster, 1947), 236–43.

4. "The Story of Bill Durbin."

5. See Butterfield, *The American Past,* 257.

6. Merrill, *Bourbon Leader,* 129–34; and Butterfield, *The American Past,* 253.

7. Merrill, *Bourbon Leader,* 141–45; and Butterfield, *The American Past,* 254.

8. Merrill, *Bourbon Leader,* 147–67; Butterfield, *The American Past,* 259–65.

9. I have taken material about Durbin in Kenton and his construction of a "little cottage," the American Egyption Hall, and Andy Durbin's suggestion to build it, from "The Story of Bill Durbin" and WWD, "My Life in Magic," *LR* 15, no. 11 (Jan. 1936): 972–73.

10. "The Story of Bill Durbin."

11. Butterfield, *The American Past,* 259–75; Louis W. Koenig, *Bryan: A Political Biography of William Jennings Bryan* (New York: Putnam's, 1971), 115–208; LeRoy Ashby, *William Jennings Bryan: Champion of Democracy* (Boston: Twayne, 1987); Genevieve Herrick and John Herrick, *The Life of William Jennings Bryan* (Chicago: Buxton, 1925); William J. Bryan and Mary Baird Bryan, *The Memoirs of William Jennings Bryan: By Himself and with His Wife May Baird Bryan* (Philadelphia, Pa.: United Publishers of America, 1925).

12. Koenig, *Bryan,* 658. "Broken heart, nothing," Darrow is supposed to have responded, "he died of a busted belly."

13. Koenig, *Bryan,* 658; Herrick and Herrick, *Life of William Jennings Bryan,* 384.

14. 1 Cor. 7:29–31.

15. Koenig, *Bryan,* 182.

16. Herrick and Herrick, *Life of William Jennings Bryan,* 115–27; Butterfield, *The American Past,* 259, 271.

17. Bryan and Bryan, *The Memoirs of William Jennings Bryan,* 101–18.

18. Koenig, *Bryan,* 182.

19. *Kenton Democrat,* July 16, 1896.

20. WWD, "With the Old Masters," *LR* 8, no. 9 (Nov. 1933): 610; WWD, "My Life in Magic," *LR* 16, no. 2 (Apr. 1936): 152; *Kenton Democrat,* August 13 and September 10, 1896.

21. Butterfield, *The American Past,* 272.

22. Ashby, *William Jennings Bryan,* 54.

23. *Kenton Democrat,* September 4, 1896.

24. "The Story of Bill Durbin"; *Kenton Democrat,* November 5 and November 12, 1896; Koenig, *Bryan,* 252–54: Ashby, *William Jennings Bryan,* 67–71; *Cleveland Plain Dealer Sunday Magazine,* May 18, 1996, 8–12.

25. *Kenton Democrat,* November 5, 1896.

26. Bryan and Bryan, *The Memoirs of William Jennings Bryan,* 510–11.

8. The Levitation of Princess Karnac and Harry Kellar

1. Peter Dreier, *Cleveland Plain Dealer,* March 5, 1995; Frank L. Baum, *The Wonderful Wizard of Oz* (New York: Dover, 1900).

2. Walter Gibson, *The Master Magicians: Their Lives and Most Famous Tricks* (New York: Doubleday, 1966), 94.

3. Durbin reproduced Kellar's patter on how he discovered the secret of levitation in a 1936 article in *The Linking Ring.* One of Kellar's assistants repeated the routine verbatim to Durbin. This is the voice coming from the teakettle in the car. WWD, "My Life in Magic," *LR* 16, no. 7 (Sept. 1936): 546–47.

4. David Price, *Magic: A Pictorial History of Conjurers in the Theater* (New York: Cornwall, 1985), 141–49; Milbourne Christopher, *The Illustrated History of Magic* (New York: Crowell, 1973), 198–221; William Doerflinger, *The Magic Catalogue: A Guide to the Wonderful World of Magic* (New York: Dutton, 1977), 25–28; James Randi, *Conjuring* (New York: St. Martin's Press, 1992), 107–13; Gibson, *The Master Magicians,* 86–103.

5. WWD, "My Life in Magic," *LR* 15, no. 10 (Dec. 1935): 874–75.

6. WWD, "Recollections of Kellar," *LR* 7, no. 1 (Sept. 1927): 536–38.

7. WWD, "My Life in Magic," *LR* 15, no. 10 (Dec. 1935): 876.

8. Ibid.; WWD, "My Life in Magic," *LR* 15, no. 12 (Feb. 1936): 1083; WWD, "An Evening with the Great Kellar," *LR* 11, no. 12 (Feb. 1932): 1209.

9. Christopher, *Illustrated History of Magic,* 203.

10. Ibid., 217.

11. WWD, "My Life in Magic," *LR* 15, no. 12 (Feb. 1936): 1083.

12. Ibid., 1083–84. See also WWD, "My Life in Magic," *LR* 16, no. 7 (Sept. 1936): 546; and WWD, "My Life in Magic," *LR* 15, no. 11 (Jan. 1936): 977.

13. *Washington Post Magazine,* December 17, 1933; *Marion Star,* January 19, 1898. An original is pasted in a press book Durbin kept, which ended up in David Price's hands in Nashville, Tennessee.

14. Taken from a Durbin magic brochure, dated sometime after 1922 and before 1926. It references Kellar's death and has the IBM's rival, Society of American Magicians, stamp on the back cover. The brochure is a twenty-two-page book advertising Durbin's feats with photos and descriptions of his shows. The quote is:

Durbin's matchless performance which baffles human belief and rivals the feats of the famous Yogi and Mahatmas of the East is a realization of the poet's words:

> "And the night shall be full of music
> And the cares that infest the day
> Shall fold their tents like the Arabs
> And as silently steal away."

15. WWD to Augustus Rapp (Madison, Wis.), March 16, 1916.

16. The side lawn feat is described in the *Kenton Democrat,* August 20, 1896: "Mr. Durbin has erected a large hall 24 x 44 feet, which is fixed up in an excellent manner with seats, large stage, curtains and all necessary paraphernalia requisite to make it a complete hall for holding entertainments. Besides rendering the above excellent program, supper will be served from 5 to 8 P.M. for 15 cents, during the intermission refreshments will be served. Arrangements have been made to run free hacks to and from Mr. Durbin's residence. All are invited to come and enjoy a good time."

17. Durbin magic program from the Lund collection.

18. WWD, "My Life in Magic," *LR* 15, no. 10 (Dec. 1935): 876–77.

19. WWD, "My Life in Magic," *LR* 15, no. 12 (Feb. 1936): 1082.

20. WWD, "My Life in Magic," *LR* 16, no. 5 (July 1936): 406–7.

21. Durbin claimed to the *Washington Post,* July 5, 1936, that he was asked to be Kellar's successor: "I have known all the great magicians and at one time had an opportunity to take over the work of the great Kellar which was subsequently assumed by Thurston."

22. *Washington Sunday Star,* September 30, 1934.

23. Price, *Magic,* 148: "The reason Kellar chose Thurston over [Paul] Valadon is not known. Some said Kellar chose Thurston because he was such a handsome fellow"; Christopher, *Illustrated History of Magic,* 220; Doerflinger, *The Magic Catalogue,* 26; Gibson, *The Master Magicians,* 147.

24. Price, *Magic,* 148–49.

9. Woodrow Wilson: "Despicable, Lousy, and Contemptible"

1. WWD to WW in Sea Girt, New Jersey (the Governor's Cottage), August 14, 1912, Wilson Papers. Durbin's quotes here are directly from his letter to Wilson in the summer of 1912. Durbin had made a special trip to New Jersey the December before (1911) to meet Wilson to see if he would support his candidacy for president. This August letter was written after Wilson had won the long and uncertain battle at the

Democrat's convention in Baltimore that ended in Wilson's nomination on July 2. Now Durbin and his business partner and political friend, W. L. Finley, who was then the chairman of the Democratic State Executive Committee, wanted to make plans for Wilson's campaign in Ohio. Durbin wrote that he and Mr. Finley were "very anxious to have you present at the opening of the Democratic campaign in Ohio between the 10th and 15th of September."

2. WWD to Joseph Tumulty, Secretary to Governor Wilson, February 6, 1913, Wilson Papers.

3. Arthur Link, *Wilson: The Road to the White House* (Princeton, N.J.: Princeton Univ. Press, 1947), 1–4.

4. Tom Shachtman, *Edith and Woodrow: A Presidential Romance* (New York: Putnam, 1981), 21: "Thomas Woodrow Wilson had grown up surrounded by the stress of war. Born in Virginia in 1856, his earliest times were shadowed by the Civil War and Reconstruction. Once, a small spectator in a large crowd, he saw General Lee pass by on a horse; years later he wrote that Lee was a character too large ever to be contained on a stage, that men could write about Lee but they could never explain his greatness."

5. Ray Stannard Baker, *Woodrow Wilson: Life and Letters,* vol. 4 (New York: Doubleday, 1931), 38–39.

6. Edward J. Renehan Jr., *The Lion's Pride: Theodore Roosevelt and His Family in Peace and War* (New York: Oxford Univ. Press, 1998), 38, 119–24.

7. Shachtman, *Edith and Woodrow,* 236, recorded by Edith Wilson, who attended the meeting to make sure there was no misunderstanding; Gene Smith, *When the Cheering Stopped: The Last Days of Woodrow Wilson* (New York: William Morrow, 1964), 134.

8. Baker, *Woodrow Wilson,* 5, 14. "No President since Franklin Pierce had objected to the ball."

9. Ibid., 23–54.

10. *Cleveland Plain Dealer,* March 15, 1913.

11. Ibid.

12. *Kenton Daily Democrat,* March 5 and 7, 1913.

13. WWD to Tumulty, February 6, 1913, Wilson Papers.

14. *Cleveland Plain Dealer,* March 16, 1913: "W. W. Durbin of Kenton Calls at White House and Afterwards Says Ohio Appointees to Federal Jobs Should Be Chosen from Among Progressive Ranks."

15. WWD to Edith Wilson, March 10, 1926, Baker Papers.

16. Baker to WWD, March 17, 1926, Baker Papers (also referred to in Durbin's letter of March 20, 1926, to Baker); WWD to Baker, March 20, 1926, Baker Papers: "I have your letter of March 17th with reference to the two letters from Woodrow Wilson which Mrs. Wilson forwarded to you, and I thought you would want to know in what connection they were received."

17. WWD to Baker, December 31, 1931, Baker Papers.

18. Secretary to Baker to WWD, January 12, 1931, Baker Papers.

19. WWD to Baker, December 5, 1935, Baker Papers.

20. Baker to WWD, December 10, 1935, Baker Papers.

21. WWD to Baker, March 20, 1926, Baker Papers.

22. Eliza Durbin to WW, May 21, 1921, Wilson Papers:

My dear Mr. Wilson

For a number of years I have been very proud that I had some little part in the political activity in Ohio that led up to your nomination at Baltimore, and I feel that you will be interested in a few details of the pre-convention campaign. Progressive Democrats in Ohio were not satisfied with Gov. Harmon as a candidate. We had been followers of Mr. Bryan, and although we no longer accept his leadership we still honor him for his stand along progressive lines. My brother, W. W. Durbin, whom you may possibly remember, had long been his ardent supporter, so when my brother asked him his views concerning a candidate Mr. Bryan favored any progressive man, refusing to become a candidate in Ohio as the newly formed Democratic Progressive League asked him to do, giving as one reason the fact that the party had honored him enough. He had a leaning toward you but wished to keep an impartial attitude toward all progressive Democrats who might be candidate. Later, however, someone had told him there were certain statements in your writings not in accord with our Ohio ideas of a progressive, and he asked my brother to get a copy and look into the matter. You will pardon this now, I know, as being only political minutes. You will smile to learn that, there being no copy of your works available in this burg, I being called upon—I am a school teacher—sent to New York and had a friend send me one. Then I went through the book and picked out all the statements that seemed to go across progressive grain, and my brother took it to Mr. Bryan who was going through the state on his lecture tour. The list of statements made up two typewritten pages. Mr. Bryan read them, and said they did not argue well for a candidate, but he said at the end of the talk, "With all that against him as a progressive I still believe he is a progressive Democrat. I believe in his sincerity." My brother organized the Democratic League, of which John J. Lentz was president, and when events shaped themselves that Clark was found to be in collusion with Harmon forces in Ohio, thus removing the obligation to keep from taking sides against a progressive candidate, Mr. Bryan wrote my brother "We must win with Wilson," and the entire progressive strength in Ohio was thrown to you. John McLean furnished part of the money for the campaign. One of the funny incidents was that my brother was in McLean's office in Washington when James Ross, a Harmon lieutenant, was announced. My brother retired to an inner room and Mr. McLean told him Ross had solicited his aid for Harmon, and being denied, exclaimed "I hope at any rate you will not support the college professor," and, McLean answered, "Now Jimmy, I won't listen to a word against Wilson. You know I've always been a great friend of education." It was not friendliness toward you, however, that moved him, but hostility toward Gov. Harmon, of which my brother knew and took advantage. It isn't true that McLean's assistance was given because of hope of political reward, as some have said, because the progressive element to which my brother belongs was always at sword's point with the McLean element. You know the result of the League's fight in Ohio, a split delegation, eliminating Harmon.

Until Clark's alignment with the reactionaries, Mr. Bryan wished to have a fair show in the convention. It has been said that Mr. Bryan desired the nomination. That may have been true, but a man has a right to an ambition so long as he is honorable in pursuing it and Mr. Bryan honorably left the field open by refusing to become an avowed candidate. It may interest you as a statesman and historian to know that here in Ohio, called a hotbed of Bryanism, we regretted his stand during the trying days of German aggression, and while grieved that he had made a mistake from which he could not come back, we believed in his sincerity. Since his insincerity in the last campaign, no Democrat I know would follow him. Insincerity betrays itself sooner or later, just as Republican insincerity is already betraying itself. I often think of Mr. Taft's speech in which he asked the man fighting the League because he did not like Pres. Wilson what his grandson would think of him, and I compare what Mr. Taft's grandson will think of his attitude in the late campaign with what your grandson will think of you. May I be pardoned the presumption of congratulating you on the difference?

I sometimes write verse and I enclose a copy of some lines I wrote when to be a progressive was to be considered radical. My brother always refers to you when he reads it, and while I make no pretense to poetic vision I am seer enough to know that "They seek the way you went." Washington, Lincoln, Wilson, and the greatest of these is Wilson, for the efforts of the others were for their people alone, while yours were for all humanity.
Yours sincerely,
(Miss) Eliza W. Durbin

23. WWD to Baker, March 20, 1926. Wilson Papers.

24. Landon Warner, "Judson Harmon," in *The Governors of Ohio* (Columbus: Ohio Historical Society, 1954), 152.

25. "The Story of Bill Durbin"; "Governor Harmon, who recognized Bill's ability as an organizer and as a businessman of sterling honesty, appointed him a member of the Board of Managers of the Ohio Penitentiary, and it was while he was helping to run things there that new cell blocks, dining hall and power house were built. . . . It was Bill, as a penitentiary manager, who brought about the abolition of such inhuman punishments as hanging by the thumbs, whipping, shocking with electricity, and other such practices."

26. Hoyt Landon Warner, *Progressivism in Ohio* (Columbus: Ohio State Univ. Press for the Ohio Historical Society, 1964), 223.

27. Ibid., 362.

28. Durbin's quote to Delbert is taken from WWD to Baker, March 20, 1926, Baker Papers.

29. Eliza Durbin to WW, May 21, 1921, Wilson Papers.

30. WWD to Baker, March 20, 1926, Baker Papers.

31. Ibid.

32. *Cleveland Plain Dealer,* January 4, 1912.

33. From *Cleveland Plain Dealer,* January 3, 1912: "ANTI-HARMON MEN ORGANIZE IN STATE, Form progressive League at Conference in Columbus. Former State Chairman W. W. Durbin of Kenton was in charge of the early arrangements and had the assistance of John J. Lentz and others so that everything was ready for the gathering at 2 o'clock when Durbin called the conference to order"; *Cleveland Plain Dealer,* January 4, 5, 6, 7, and 8, 1912: "Columbus, O., Jan. 5—Headquarters for the progres-

sive Democrats of Ohio were taken today at 510–11 Harrison building and arrangements made to get under way at once. By the 10th of the month, Chairman Lentz says, the campaign will be going. It will do its important work before the election of delegates to the national convention. W. W. Durbin will be in charge."

34. WWD to Baker, March 20, 1926, Baker Papers.

35. WWD to Baker, May 10, 1926, Baker Papers. See also Francis Russell, *The Shadow of Blooming Grove: Warren G. Harding in His Times* (New York: McGraw-Hill, 1968), 223; and Alexander P. Lamis, *Ohio Politics: A Historical Perspective* (Kent, Ohio: Kent State Univ. Press, 1994), 7.

36. WWD to Baker, May 14, 1926, Baker Papers. For collaboration of Princeton support, see Arthur Link, *Wilson: The Road to the White House* (Princeton, N.J.: Princeton Univ. Press, 1947), 403: "Wilson's old Princeton friends and supporters, therefore, contributed $85,000, or almost half the money McCombs spent before the Baltimore convention." See also ibid., 418–19 n99: "McCombs subsequently gave Ohio Wilson men $4,500 with which to finance the state campaign." Durbin wrote Baker that he received $3,500. He also wrote Tumulty in November 1912 that he personally spent over $1,000 during the primary for Wilson. WWD to Tumulty, November 19, 1912, Wilson Papers.

37. Bryan was not out in the open for Wilson in January 1912, hoping against hope to make his own run. Indeed the tenuous support Bryan was showing for Wilson behind the scenes with Durbin and Garber was severely tested in January when a letter Wilson wrote to a railroad executive while Wilson was still president of Princeton criticizing Bryan came to light. *Cleveland Plain Dealer,* January 8, 1912: "BRYAN IS CENTER OF PARTY STORM"; Link, *Wilson,* 352–60. The Wilson camp was "elated" when Bryan refused to comment on the letter. The publication of the letter (known as the "Joline letter" because it was written to Adrian Joline) was characterized by Wilson's campaign manager as "a continuation of the efforts to dynamite Gov. Wilson from Wall Street." *Cleveland Plain Dealer,* January 8, 1912. Bryan's overt support for Wilson did not come until March: "On the advice of William Jennings Bryan the pioneer progressive Democrats of Ohio today voted to endorse Woodrow Wilson as its candidate for President. His name will go on the progressive ticket for the May primaries, and Bryan will come to Ohio in April and again in May to make speeches for the pioneers." *Cleveland Plain Dealer,* March 27, 1912.

38. Link, *Wilson,* 418–19, Durbin is referenced in footnote 99.

39. WWD to Baker, May 10, 1926, Baker Papers.

40. Link, *Wilson,* 431–65.

41. Ibid., 439.

42. WWD to Baker, March 20, 1926, Baker Papers. In this letter, Durbin argues that Newton Baker, Cleveland's reform mayor who became Wilson's secretary of war, actually hurt Wilson's chances to walk into the Baltimore convention with a majority of the Ohio delegates. Durbin pointed out that the new law that allowed delegates to be chosen directly in primaries did not address what happened to delegates-at-large, "of which we were entitled to six, four for the two senators and two for one congressman-at-large." To address the issue, Durbin and other Harmon opponents suggested allowing the delegates-at-large to be chosen also in the primary by declaring their allegiance to a candidate before the primary election. Baker voted against the plan as a member of the Democratic State Central Committee and in favor of Harmon's

plan to allow the winner of the majority of the district delegates (forty-two of them) to take all the delegates-at-large. Had they been directly elected, Durbin believed adding the five or six of these delegates to Wilson's nineteen would have given him the majority (twenty-four out of a total of forty-eight). After all, Harmon had only carried Ohio by nine thousand votes and even lost in his own precinct so it was possible for Wilson to have won these delegates in a direct election. "As it was Baker voted with Harmon at Columbus at the meeting of the State Committee, and then went to Cleveland and filed as a Wilson delegate, and practically locked the stable after the horse was gone," Durbin complained. Baker did deliver a critical speech at Baltimore against the unit rule, which when broken, allowed Wilson's nineteen Ohio delegates to cast their votes for Wilson. Durbin claims he wrote Baker's speech. "However, I got him a fine speech against the adoption of the Majority Report [for the unit rule], and in favor of the Minority Report, and it had much to do with swaying the Convention, although much good work had been done by us who were opposed to it throughout the various delegations," Durbin wrote Ray Stannard Baker. On Baker's speech, see Link, *Wilson,* 439: "In an impassioned appeal to the convention, Baker insisted that the law of Ohio had taken from the state convention the authority to select delegates to national conventions and vested it with the people." Baker's speech at Baltimore propelled him into national prominence. C. H. Cramer, *Newton D. Baker: A Biography* (Cleveland: World, 1961), 64–70.

43. Link, *Wilson,* 439–40.

44. *Cleveland Plain Dealer,* July 3, 1912: "Ohio's gallant band of progressive Democrats are credited by William Jennings Bryan with having turned the tide in the campaign for delegates in favor of Woodrow Wilson."

45. Link, *Wilson,* 505–7. For another letter to Wilson and his campaign managers on the importance of Wilson coming to Ohio to open the campaign, see W. L. Finley to McCombs, August 10, 1912, Wilson Papers. This letter references the meeting in New York with McCombs that Durbin refers to in his letter of August 14 to Wilson. James Cox also wrote a letter to A. Mitchell Palmer (later Wilson's attorney general) on the same subject. James M. Cox to A. Mitchell Palmer, August 12, 1912, Wilson Papers. Cox points out that Durbin's and Finely's trip to New York was ill-timed because it was "overshadowed by the notification [the day when the candidate is officially notified by representatives of the convention of his nomination]." Notification day was August 7. Link, *Wilson,* 472. This explains Durbin's opening sentence to Wilson in his letter of August 14: "I am sorry it was impossible to have a word with you last Wednesday but I could not expect it under the circumstances." Cox and Newton Baker followed up with more urgent letters for Wilson to come to Ohio as Chairman Finely requested. Cox to Palmer, August 17, 1912, and Baker to Wilson, August 19, 1912, Wilson Papers.

46. Link, *Wilson,* 474.

47. Ibid., 475.

48. Ibid., 517–18.

49. Peter Collier with David Horowitz, *The Roosevelts: An American Saga* (New York: Simon and Schuster, 1994), 167–69.

50. Link, *Wilson,* 524–25; Eugene H. Roseboom and Francis P. Weisenberger, *A History of Ohio* (Columbus: Ohio State Archaeological and Historical Society, 1973), 325.

51. Louis W. Koenig, *Bryan: A Political Biography of William Jennings Bryan* (New York: Putnam's, 1971), 502–52.

52. Baker, *Woodrow Wilson*, 475. The best guess is that Ellen Wilson had Bright's disease. Shachtman, *Edith and Woodrow,* 35.

53. Baker, *Woodrow Wilson*, 479–81; Smith, *When the Cheering Stopped,* 9–10.

54. Koenig, *Bryan,* 541–50.

55. Ibid., 548.

56. WWD to Baker, May 14, 1926, Baker Papers. Baker replied, "Thank you very much for your letter of May 14th with its interesting further information. I am glad to have it, especially the reference in regard to the relationship between Bryan and Wilson." RSB to WWD, May 19, 1926, Baker Papers.

57. Koenig, *Bryan,* 552–70; LeRoy Ashby, *William Jennings Bryan: Champion of Democracy* (Boston: Twayne, 1987), 158–69.

58. Eliza Durbin to WW, May 22, 1921, Wilson Papers. WWD to FDR, November 23, 1931, FDRL.

59. Koenig, *Bryan,* 563–65.

60. WWD to RSB, December 12, 1935, Baker Papers (written by Durbin on his register of the Treasury stationery).

61. WWD to RSB, December 12, 1935, Baker Papers.

62. WWD to RSB, December 12, 1935, Baker Papers.

63. WWD to RSB, December 12, 1935, Baker Papers.

64. WWD to RSB, December 12, 1935, Baker Papers.

65. WWD to RSB, December 12, 1935, Baker Papers.

66. WWD to Baker, May 14, 1926, Baker Papers.

67. WWD to Baker, May 14, 1926, Baker Papers. The story is repeated in a 1935 letter. WWD to RSB, December 12, 1935, Baker Papers.

68. Koenig, *Bryan,* 567; Arthur Link, *Campaigns for Progressivism and Peace 1916–1917* (Princeton: Princeton Univ. Press, 1965), 423–27.

69. Smith, *When the Cheering Stopped,* 37–39.

70. Ibid., 80–85; Shachtman, *Edith and Woodrow,* 201–6.

71. Shachtman, *Edith and Woodrow,* 259.

72. Andy Durbin to Sara Danaher, May 2, 1918, Santiago, Chile, author's private collection.

73. Andy Durbin to Thomas Brahany, April 30, 1919, Wilson Papers.

74. Sam Rogers to Tumulty, July 9, 1919, Wilson Papers; Sam Rogers to Tumulty, August 26, 1919, Wilson Papers.

75. Andy Durbin to Tumulty, December 27, 1919, Wilson Papers. Other documents in the Wilson Papers relating to his investigation and discharge are a Ben Bradford affidavit, January 12, 1920; an Alexander Kopp affidavit, January 13, 1920; Port Commander Lieut. Col. W. C. Koenig, Antwerp, to the Chief of the Graves Registration Service, January 29, 1920; Embarkation Orders, January 29, 1920; William F. Riter, Captain, Q. M. Corps, Assignment of Andy J. Durbin in Hoboken, New Jersey, February 24, 1920; Cablegram, West, Acting Military Attache, Paris, to the Adjutant General, February 6, 1920; Andy Durbin to Lt. Col. W. C. Koenig, February 26, 1920; Discharge Notice, War Department, by E. P. Jackson, Lieut. Colonel, Q. M. Corps, March 22, 1920; Travel Orders, War Department, by E. P. Jackson, Lieut. Colonel, Q. M. Corps, March 22, 1920; and a First Class Transportation Order, by Lt. Col. R. E. Shannon, March 22, 1920.

76. Andy Durbin to Tumulty, March 24, 1920, Wilson Papers; Tumulty to Andy Durbin, March 26, 1920, Wilson Papers. See also H. L. Rogers, Quartermaster General,

U. S. A., to Tumulty, April 1, 1920, Wilson Papers. This attaches an additional complaint, dated March 27, 1920, from H. F. Spellinger to Col. C. C. Pierce, Wilson Papers.

77. Wilson, Edith Bolling, "As I Saw It," *Saturday Evening Post* (Feb. 28, 1939). See also Smith, *When the Cheering Stopped,* 205–7, on the incident of Tumulty writing to the Jefferson Day banquet without Wilson's permission. It was the last time Tumulty was allowed to see Wilson.

78. Francis Durbin to Edith Wilson, March 3, 1939, Wilson Papers (marked "Rcvd. Mch. 4, 1939; No reply").

79. WWD to WW, October 11, 1923, Wilson Papers.

80. WW to WWD, October 14, 1923, Wilson Papers.

10. The River Lethe and Warren G. Harding

1. Philip Mayerson, *Classical Mythology in Literature, Art, and Music* (Lexington, Mass.: Xerox College Publishing, 1971), 232–36.

2. *Daily Oklahoman,* October 10, 1920.

3. Randolph C. Downes, "Negro Rights and White Backlash in the Campaign of 1920," *Ohio History* 75, nos. 2 and 3 (Spring–Summer 1966), 85–107nn184–85.

4. Downes, "Negro Rights," 103, 185, qtg. from a letter from Don Cox to Harding, October 18, 1920, Harding Papers. Ohio Historical Society. "For God's sake," Cox wrote, "get busy stamping it out."

5. "Girls View Lynching; Are Dubious Heroines," *Cleveland Advocate,* April 10, 1920. The *Cleveland Advocate* on its masthead states: "This newspaper receives the Services of the Associated Negro Press and is the only paper published in the interest of the race in Ohio carrying this service." In this edition the newspaper reported on an article that appeared in the *Louisville Courier Journal* on the two girls who witnessed a lynching. On the same page the *Advocate* took note of Harding's trip south: "Senator Harding is the first, and the only member of congress from a northern state, Republican or Democrat, to come south and align himself with our oppressors."

6. *New York Times,* October 22, 1920.

7. Ibid.

8. Louis W. Koenig, *Bryan: A Political Biography of William Jennings Bryan* (New York: Putnam's, 1971), 590–91.

9. Eliza W. Durbin to WW, May 22, 1921, Wilson Papers.

10. WWD to FDR, August 21, 1934, FDRL. "My old partner, Bill Finley, became ill in 1917," Durbin wrote to FDR, "and I was called upon to take over the reins of the State Executive Committee which I held up to 1924. I conducted Cox's campaign in 1918 when he was the only candidate on the ticket elected. It will be a long story to go into this but I mention it as a showing of my good faith to him."

11. James M. Cox, *Journey Through My Years* (New York: Simon and Schuster, 1946), 211. Cox barely won the election. The vote was Cox, 488, 403, the Republican Willis, 477, 479. Cox wrote to Durbin on November 1, 1918, before the result of the election was known: "Between the receipt of this letter and the counting of the votes, I shall not see you. I want to express to you my appreciation of the services you have rendered. I recognize that for a time you abandoned your business, and that only one thing has claimed your thought and labor, and that has been the success of our cause. Regardless of what the result may be—whether victory or defeat—I am not only satisfied, but highly pleased with the manner in which you have conducted the cam-

paign. The long hours—the zealous effort and intense loyalty have inspired my deepest gratitude." This letter is reprinted in the brochure, "The Story of Bill Durbin."

12. Francis Russell, *The Shadow of Blooming Grove: Warren G. Harding in His Times* (New York: McGraw-Hill, 1968), 37–48.

13. Russell, *Shadow of Blooming Grove,* 40, 85; Carl Sferrazza Anthony, *Florence Harding: The First Lady, the Jazz Age, and the Death of America's Most Scandalous President* (New York: Quill William Morrow, 1998), 38–39; Andrew Sinclair, *The Available Man* (New York: Macmillan, 1965), 168–72.

14. Cox, *Journey Through My Years,* 226.

15. Ibid., 225–33.

16. WWD and Francis wrote several letters to FDR stating that Francis and Judge Timothy Ansberry called Cox early on the morning Cox was nominated to recommend FDR for the vice presidency. WWD to FDR, August 21, 1934, FDRL; Francis W. Durbin to FDR, September 8, 1932, FDRL; and Francis W. Durbin to FDR, March 3, 1937, FDRL. If the call was made as they claimed, I suspect Cox took the call and was influenced by their recommendation. Cox's autobiography, *Journey Through My Years,* does not reference the Durbin-Ansberry call and makes it seem that Cox came up with the idea all by himself (231–32). One important corroboratory fact of the Durbin-Ansberry call is Ansberry's nomination of FDR. Ansberry found FDR on the convention floor to tell him he was going to be nominated and then gave FDR's nominating speech. Geoffrey C. Ward, *A First-Class Temperament: The Emergence of Franklin Roosevelt* (New York: HarperPerennial, 1989), 511.

17. Cox, *Journey Through My Years,* 231–32.

18. Ward, *A First-Class Temperament,* 511.

19. Ibid., 216–18, 766–67n8.

20. Arthur Link, *Wilson: The Road to the White House* (Princeton, N.J.: Princeton Univ. Press, 1947), 500–505; Link, *Wilson: The New Freedom* (Princeton, N.J.: Princeton Univ. Press, 1956), 243–54.

21. LeRoy Ashby, *William Jennings Bryan: Champion of Democracy* (Boston: Twayne, 1987), 103–4.

22. Link, *Wilson,* 501.

23. Downes, "Negro Rights," 98–99, 185n34 (referred to as the "Durbin circular"). Downes wrote that copies of the Durbin circular were contained in Boxes 606 and 610 of the Harding Papers, but I have been unable to locate a copy. The circular is substantially reprinted in the *New York Times,* October 22, 1920, and the *Cleveland Advocate,* October 23 and 30, 1920.

24. *New York Times,* October 22, 1920.

25. Ibid.

26. Ibid.

27. Ibid.

28. *Cleveland Advocate,* October 30, 1920.

29. *New York Times,* October 23, 1920.

30. Ibid.

31. Russell, *Shadow of Blooming Grove,* 372, 403–4, 412–16, 528–31; Anthony, *Florence Harding,* 229–34. Ward, *A First-Class Temperament,* 547–48.

32. Eugene H. Roseboom and Francis P. Weisenberger, *A History of Ohio* (Columbus: Ohio State Archaeological and Historical Society, 1973), 323.

33. *New York Times,* October 23, 1920.

34. Ibid.

35. Ibid.

36. *New York Times,* October 17, 1920.

37. Ibid.

38. Russell, *Shadow of Blooming Grove,* 415.

39. *New York Times,* October 31, 1920.

40. Russell, *Shadow of Blooming Grove,* 413.

41. Sinclair, *Available Man,* 169.

42. Russell, *Shadow of Blooming Grove,* 416. *Marion Star,* November 3, 1920.

43. WWD to FDR, June 17, 1932, FDRL.

44. Russell, *Shadow of Blooming Grove,* 471–72; Sinclair, *Available Man,* 321–35; *New York Times,* October 27, 1921.

45. *New York Times,* October 28, 1921; Russell, *Shadow of Blooming Grove,* 472.

46. Paul Angle and Earl Miers, ed., *The Living Lincoln, The Man, His Mind, His Times, and the War He Fought, Reconstructed From His Own Writings* (New York: Barnes and Noble, 1992), 265-66.

47. Russell, *Shadow of Blooming Grove,* 411–12; *Daily Oklahoman,* October 10, 1920.

48. Russell, *Shadow of Blooming Grove,* 431, 528–31.

49. Russell, "The Four Mysteries of Warren G. Harding," *American Heritage* (Apr. 1963): 72.

50. Ward, *A First-Class Temperament,* 557–58.

51. Ibid.

11. Kenton, Magic Capital of the World!

1. Julius Kleimann, "Manufacturer, Politician—and a Master of Black Magic," *St. Louis Post-Dispatch,* July 17, 1927.

2. Matt. 5:44–45.

3. Kleimann a year later would call Kenton the "Empire of Magic." Kleimann, "Manufacturer, Politician."

4. *Cleveland Plain Dealer,* June 1927, reprinted in "Plain Dealer Editorial," *LR* 6, no. 4 (June 1927): 424.

5. *Cleveland Plain Dealer,* June 3, 1930.

6. Kleimann, "Manufacturer, Politician."

7. Ibid.

8. Vivian Shirley, "Vivian Shirley Is Guest at Dinner for 'Uncle Jim' Dean of Phila. Magicians," *LR* 9, no. 8 (Oct. 1929): 869.

9. *Kenton Daily Democrat,* June 5–10, 1926.

10. *Kenton Daily Democrat,* June 5, 1926.

11. Ibid.

12. "David Price, Jr.," *LR* 74, no. 8 (Aug. 1994): 57–58. Price is pictured on the cover of this edition.

13. Bob Dowd, "Egyptian Hall, the Reprise," *LR* 74, no. 8 (Aug. 1994): 62–66.

14. Ibid.

15. *Kenton Daily Democrat,* June 10, 1926.

16. WWD, "Notes and Jottings," *LR* 7, no. 5 (Jan. 1928): 865.

17. *Cleveland Plain Dealer,* June 9, 1926, reprinted in the program for the 1927 convention.

18. *Kenton Daily Democrat,* June 10, 1926; "W. F. Dornfield," *LR* 6, no. 1 (Mar. 1927): 246 (Dorny pictured on cover); "I.B.M. Convention," *LR* 4, no. 5 (July 1926): 76.

19. WWD, "Notes and Jottings," *LR* 7, no. 6 (Feb. 1928): 952.

20. WWD to Al Saal, November 24, 1930.

21. Ibid.

22. *Kenton Daily Democrat,* June 10, 1926.

23. The facts on Blackstone have been taken from: Henry Ridgely Evans, *History of Conjuring and Magic* (Kenton, Ohio: International Brotherhood of Magicians, 1928), 290–300; Milbourne Christopher, *The Illustrated History of Magic* (New York: Crowell, 1973), 368–78; William Doerflinger, *The Magic Catalogue: A Guide to the Wonderful World of Magic* (New York: Dutton, 1977), 35–36; James Randi, *Conjuring* (New York: St. Martin's Press, 1992), 139–50.

24. *Kenton Daily Democrat,* June 8, 1926.

25. Inez Blackstone, "Dreams of the I.B.M. Conventions," *LR* 9, no. 10 (Dec. 1929): 1154–56.

26. Ray Vaughn, "Legerdemainiacs," *LR* 6, no. 1 (Mar. 1927): 261.

27. *Kenton Daily Democrat,* June 7, 1926.

28. *Kenton Daily Democrat,* June 9, 1926.

29. "I.B.M. Convention," *LR* 4, no. 5 (July 1926): 76.

30. WWD, "From the President's Chair," *LR* 5, no. 6 (Feb. 1927): 218.

31. WWD, "From the President's Chair," *LR* 7, no. 6 (Feb. 1928): 999; WWD, "From the President's Chair," *LR* 6, no. 5 (July 1927): 449.

32. WWD, "From the President's Chair," *LR* 5, no. 4 (Dec. 1926): 119.

33. "In Memoriam," *LR* 9, no. 9 (Nov. 1929): 920; "In Memoriam," *LR* 8, no. 1 (Mar. 1928): 7; WWD, "Notes and Jottings," *LR* 9, no. 1 (Mar. 1929): 53.

34. WWD, "A Call to Loyal Members of the I.B.M.," *LR* 8, no. 7 (Sept. 1928): 519.

35. WWD to Saal, May 19, 1927.

36. WWD to Saal, May 10, 1927.

37. Len Vintus, "Notes and Jottings," *LR* 4, no. 5 (July 1926): 84.

38. Durbin's speech in Egyptian Hall has been taken from the resolutions passed by the members at the convention. "I.B.M. Convention 1926," *LR* 4, no. 5 (July 1926): 76, 89.

39. WWD to Saal, January 6, 10, and 14, 1930.

40. "Notice!" *LR* 9, no. 8 (Oct. 1929): 837; "Don't Let Your Linking Rings Lay Around," *LR* 8, no. 7 (Sept. 1928): 575.

41. WWD to Saal, August 3, 1927.

42. WWD to Saal, April 17, 1930.

43. Ted Heubec, "Why? When? Where?" *LR* 8, no. 11 (Jan. 1934): 774; Harry E. Cecil, "Back to Kenton," *LR* 15, no. 9 (Nov. 1935): 787.

44. Eliza W. Durbin, "The 1928 I.B.M. Convention," *LR* 7, no. 4 (June 1928): 274, 285.

45. Howard Wolf, "Young Chandler Enters," *LR* 8, no. 5. (July 1928): 366.

46. *Akron Beacon Journal,* June 8, 1928, reprinted in Howard Wolf, "Tribute is Paid Memory," *LR* 8, no. 5 (July 1928): 363–65.

47. S. B. Blodgett, "Vest Pocket Convention News," *LR* 8, no. 4 (June 1928): 352–53.

48. WWD, "With the Old Masters," *LR* 13, no. 12 (Feb. 1934): 839–40.

12. The Man with the Lights

1. Ted Carrother's magic studio was located in 1951 in Sylvania near Toledo. It was a typical magic shop, selling a bizarre combination of magic tricks, costumes, masks, and novelties. I first talked to Ted by phone on September 30, 1992. Looking back, it was a major discovery for me. It was in this call that I first got an inclination that Durbin memorabilia was abundant and retrievable. It was also the first time I began to think there was a big story attached to Durbin. He told me of Bob Lund in Michigan, the Al Saal letters he had in his collection, and that a man named David Price had the insides of Durbin's Egyptian Hall. He also gave me Harry Blackstone Jr.'s home phone number. I met Ted a couple of times in Toledo, one of those times being when I was allowed to copy the Saal letters. Ted had a number of the group photos of the early IBM conventions in the backroom of the studio, just tacked up to the walls. He was always willing to answer my questions and give me leads. When Ted died on January 21, 1996, he was only sixty-five. The Saal letters were sold to a magician in Minnesota. I have no idea what happened to the photos. Ted's obituary in the *Toledo Blade* (January 23, 1996) told of his levitation of Miss Toledo over the Anthony Wayne Bridge. All the Saal letters are from the Carrothers' collection.

2. WWD to Saal, July 26, 1929.

3. WWD to Saal, September 21, 1927.

4. WWD to Saal, February 23, 1929.

5. WWD to Saal, March 6, 1929.

6. WWD to Saal, March 4, 1927.

7. Ibid.

8. WWD to Saal, March 11, 1927.

9. WWD to Saal, March 16, 1927.

10. WWD to Saal, March 28, 1927.

11. WWD to Saal, April 5, 1927.

12. WWD to Saal, April 28, 1927.

13. WWD to Saal, May 25, 1927.

14. WWD to Saal, March 5, 1928.

15. Ibid.

16. WWD to Saal, March 8, 1928.

17. Ibid.

18. Ibid.

19. Ibid.

20. WWD to Saal, March 24, 1928.

21. WWD to Saal, August 21, 1930.

22. WWD to Saal, November 24, 1930.

23. WWD to Saal, January 31, 1931.

24. WWD to Saal, September 28, 1927 and November 3, 1927.

25. WWD to Saal, January 31, 1931.

26. WWD to Saal, March 14, 1928.

27. WWD to Saal, August 14, 1928.

28. WWD to Saal, September 28, 1928.

29. WWD to Saal, September 13, 1928.

30. WWD to Saal, September 25, 1928.

31. WWD to Saal, February 18, 1930.
32. WWD to Saal, December 19, 1928.
33. WWD to Saal, September 24, 1927.
34. WWD to Saal, October 19, 1931.
35. WWD to Saal, March 27, 1933.

13. MASTER FRANCIS AND THE KING OF THE BOOTLEGGERS

1. Charles L. Mee, *The Ohio Gang: The World of Warren G. Harding* (New York: M. Evans, 1981); Thomas Coffey, *The Long Thirst: Prohibition in America, 1920–1933* (New York: Norton, 1975); Francis Russell, *The Shadow of Blooming Grove: Warren G. Harding in His Times* (New York: McGraw-Hill, 1968); Andrew Sinclair, *Available Man: The Life behind the Masks of Warren Gamaliel Harding* (New York: Macmillan, 1965): "George Remus, the so-called King of the Bootleggers who was said to have made $40,000,000 from his trade, was one of the few sent to jail as an example, despite spending huge amounts of bribes in Washington. 'I tried to corner the graft market,' he said sourly, 'only to find that there is not enough money in the world to buy up all the public officials who demand a share in the graft.'"; and Carl Sferrazza Anthony, *Florence Harding: The First Lady, the Jazz Age, and the Death of America's Most Scandalous President* (New York: Quill William Morrow, 1998). I also consulted microfilm copies of *The Lima News* from 1927 to 1928.
2. WWD, "My Life in Magic," *LR* 15, no. 12 (Feb. 1936): 1885; WWD, "My Life in Magic," *LR* 16, no. 1 (Mar. 1936): 50. *Marion Mirror*, March 9, 1898: "Mr. Durbin's son was a whole show in himself. Although but seven years old, he possesses a pleasing stage presence, and loud clear voice and he performed a number of tricks equally as clever as Durbin here. The illusion 'She' which concluded the entertainment was one of the most elaborate and beautiful ever seen in local play houses." A picture of Francis in his formal suit was in the scrapbook found in the Price collection.
3. "Remus to Tear Things Open in Slaying Trial," *Lima News*, November 19, 1927.
4. Coffey, *The Long Thirst*, 29–31, 226.
5. Ibid., 30–32, 44–46, 64–67; Mee, *The Ohio Gang*, 145–47.
6. Coffey, *The Long Thirst*, 66–67, 93–94; Mee, *The Ohio Gang*, 146–47, 199–201.
7. Coffey, *The Long Thirst*, 101–4; Mee, *The Ohio Gang*, 199–201.
8. Coffey, *The Long Thirst*, 129–30; Mee, *The Ohio Gang*, 210–14; Anthony, *Florence Harding*, 404–11.
9. Coffey, *The Long Thirst*, 129–31; Mee, *The Ohio Gang*, 201.
10. Coffey, *The Long Thirst*, 158–60; Mee, *The Ohio Gang*, 230–32.
11. Coffey, *The Long Thirst*, 172–73; Mee, *The Ohio Gang*, 230–32.
12. On Remus killing Imogene and turning himself in: Coffey, *The Long Thirst*, 215–18; Mee, *The Ohio Gang*, 231–32.
13. Coffey, *The Long Thirst*, 218.
14. Ibid., 222–29.
15. *Lima News*, February 27, 1928.
16. Coffey, *The Long Thirst*, 227–29.
17. *Lima News*, December 20, 1927.
18. Coffey, *The Long Thirst*, 228.
19. Ibid., 228–29.

20. The original petition for the writ of habeas corpus, dated January 31, 1928, and signed by Remus and Francis Durbin (as the Notary Public) was in files in boxes I was allowed to look through in 1995 in the Allen County, Ohio, jail. I made a photocopy of the writ, and my guess is the original has since been thrown away. The boxes were of the files of the Allen County Court of Appeals (Third Appellate District), and they were being kept in the old county jail (where John Dillinger once was imprisoned and escaped by killing the sheriff).

21. The Remus case is a reported case of the Supreme Court of Ohio. *Ex parte Remus,* 119 Ohio St. 166, 162 N.E. 740 (1928).

22. *Lima News,* February 21, 1928 (Norma Mitchell reporting).

23. *Lima News,* February 22–25, 1928.

24. Francis Durbin to Margaret Durbin, May 24, 1944, author's private collection.

25. *South Carolina Record,* February 2, 1928: "Francis Durbin, Remus' attorney, has practiced law in Lima for the past fifteen years. He was graduated from Notre Dame University in the class with Knute Rockne. It is not known whether Durbin said any magical phrases over Rockne's famous pigskin at the start of its career." See also Tom Bowyer, "Francis Durbin," *LR* 8, no. 1 (Mar. 1928): 53.

26. Mee, *The Ohio Gang,* 232.

14. "I'm Mighty Glad You Were Elected"

1. *Lima News,* June 7–10, 1928.

2. "Remus Goes Free By Court Decision," *New York Times,* June 21, 1928.

3. "Off to Houston," *LR* 8, no. 4 (June 1928): 282: "On Thursday, June 21st, the Editor will leave for Houston, Texas, to attend a Democratic National Convention, to which he is a delegate at large. We mention this because there may be many things which are missing in this issue which we will naturally have to take up later. This convention took up much time and we do not have enough time between the time of the convention and leaving for Houston to get everything attended to, so we hope you will pardon anything that will be omitted. With the writer will go his son, Francis W. Durbin, brother John C. Robinson, and Mr. Carl W. Smith of Kenton, Ohio. We will drive through and hope we may meet some of the brothers on the way."

4. *New York Herald Tribune,* February 5, 1937.

5. Geoffrey C. Ward, *A First-Class Temperament: The Emergence of Franklin Roosevelt* (New York: HarperPerennial, 1989), 691–99. FDR's speech ended: "He has a personality that carries to every hearer not only the sincerity but the righteousness of what he says. He is the "Happy Warrior" of the political battlefield. . . . Alfred E. Smith!" Hugh Gregory Gallagher, *FDR's Splendid Deception* (Arlington, Va.: Vandamere, 1994), 59–63. Ted Morgan, *F.D.R.: A Biography* (New York: Simon and Schuster, 1985), 269–72.

6. Gallagher, *FDR's Splendid Deception,* 63–67.

7. Ward, *A First-Class Temperament,* 783–84n18; Gallagher, *FDR's Splendid Deception,* 101–5.

8. Morgan, *FDR,* 286–96. Ward, *First-Class Temperament,* 786–88.

9. Ward, *First-Class Temperament,* 787–99. Morgan, *FDR,* 286–96.

10. Morgan, *FDR,* 323. "Roosevelt mailed 5,000 letters to Democratic leaders shortly after his election, asking for suggestions on how to strengthen and unify the party.

Louis Howe tabulated the results. What were the reasons given for Smith's defeat? How many 'Raskob must go' letters were there? How many proposed Roosevelt in 32?"

11. WWD to FDR, December 13, 1928, FDRL.

12. WWD to FDR, November 22, 1929, FDRL.

13. *Cleveland Plain Dealer,* August 12, 1930: "Of the five candidates in the field, he [Durbin] is by far the best known to party workers and most frequently only party workers take the time to vote in primaries. This gives Durbin a big advantage. However, there are two strong candidates in the field who are bound to divide with him the votes that will be cast outside Cuyahoga and Hamilton Counties, where sentiment for prohibition repeal is strongest. . . . If the supporters of Traux and McSweeney are correct in believing that these two candidates have a good chance to defeat Durbin in the less populous counties, then Buckley, by dividing the forces opposed to prohibition repeal, should win."

14. *Cleveland Plain Dealer,* June 6, 1930.

15. "The Senatorship Fight," *LR* 10, no. 6 (Aug. 1930): 714.

16. Robert J. Ungewitter to WWD, undated, enclosing a letter from W. H. Domzalski ("Dom") to Ungewitter, September 10, 1931, author's private collection.

17. WWD to FDR, Aug. 21, 1934, FDRL. Durbin told FDR that Cox and Baker had double-crossed him in the 1930 Senate race by "bringing out Buckley" after pledging support to Durbin.

18. WWD to FDR, Nov. 23, 1931, FDRL.

19. WWD to FDR, Nov. 23, 1931, FDRL.

20. WWD to FDR, Nov. 23, 1931, FDRL.

21. WWD to FDR, Nov. 23, 1931, FDRL.

22. *Columbus Dispatch,* July 1, 1931.

23. *Dayton Daily News,* July 30, 1933.

24. WWD to FDR, November 23, 1931, FDRL. The meeting is also referred to in subsequent letters from Durbin to Roosevelt. WWD to FDR, July 8, 1932, FDRL; and WWD to FDR, August 21, 1934, FDRL.

25. WWD to FDR, November 23, 1931, FDRL.

26. WWD to FDR, November 23, 1931, FDRL.

27. FDR to WWD, November 27, 1931, FDRL.

28. Andy Durbin to FDR, December 21, 1931, FDRL.

29. Morgan, *F.D.R.,* 329; Ward, *A First-Class Temperament,* 138–39.

30. Western Union telegram, WWD to FDR, March 9, 1932, FDRL.

31. WWD to FDR, March 10, 1932, FDRL.

32. WWD to FDR, March 25, 1932, FDRL.

33. WWD to FDR, August 21, 1934, FDRL.

34. WWD to FDR, April 15, 1932, FDRL.

35. FDR to WWD, April 18, 1932, FDRL.

15. "Taking Up the Cudgels in My Behalf"

1. WWD to FDR, August 21, 1934, FDRL.

2. The following is taken from Ted Morgan, *F.D.R.: A Biography* (New York: Simon and Schuster, 1985), 329:

In June, Roosevelt went to French Lick, Indiana, to attend the governors' conference, and heard some favorable noises from the Indiana organization. On his way back through Ohio, he saw Governor George White and his 1920 running mate, James Cox. The meeting with Cox was to have unforeseen consequences, for Cox asked him, now that he had been governor for two years, for an estimate of Al Smith's administration. Roosevelt replied that it had been first rate in many ways, but that in two ways he had been able to improve it— he cut the overhead on state buildings from 7 percent to 4 percent; and as for power legislation, Smith had recommended a program at the start of each legislative session, and sent fiery messages asking why nothing had been done, while in reality he had an understanding with upstate leaders that his fiery messages were for public consumption only. Cox later repeated all of this to Smith (apologizing to Roosevelt afterward), and Smith took it as a wholesale condemnation of his administration and broke off relations. The rumors circulated that Roosevelt had said: "Smith was a rotten Governor. I didn't know it until I got into the governorship myself." This was published in the January 16, 1932 issue of *Collier's,* by someone who signed himself "The Gentleman at the Keyhole," and Roosevelt responded with the anger he reserved when he knew he had been caught out, saying: "Any man who circulates a story of that kind is not only a liar, but a contemptible liar."

In June 1931 the International Brotherhood of Magicians met in Columbus, Ohio, for its annual convention. Because Durbin was in town, Governor George White invited Durbin to dinner with Roosevelt, knowing that Durbin was one of Roosevelt's leading supporters in Ohio.

3. WWD to FDR, August 21, 1934, FDRL.

4. WWD to FDR, August 21, 1934, FDRL. The same meeting with Governor White in November 1931 before Durbin visited FDR in Albany is recounted in a letter from Durbin to James Farley. WWD to James A. Farley, July 7, 1932, FDRL. In addition, the meeting with White is described in a 1931 letter from Durbin to Roosevelt. WWD to FDR, November 23, 1931: "P.S. I saw Gov. White Friday and told him about our conversation and he has agreed that we must nominate a Progressive to be successful. He was much pleased when I told him your position and will co-operate to that end."

5. WWD to FDR, July 8, 1932, FDRL.

6. WWD to James Farley, July 7, 1932, FDRL. The meeting with White on the Friday evening before Durbin traveled to Chicago is also recounted in Durbin's letter of July 8, 1932, to Roosevelt and in his letter of August 21, 1934, to Roosevelt. WWD to FDR, July 8, 1932, FDRL.

7. WWD to FDR, July 8, 1932, FDRL; WWD to FDR, August 21, 1934, FDRL.

8. Western Union telegram, WWD to George White, June 26, 1932, FDRL.

9. WWD to James Farley, July 7, 1932, FDRL.

10. Morgan, *F.D.R.,* 348.

11. WWD to FDR, August 21, 1934, FDRL.

12. Morgan, *F.D.R.,* 348–54.

13. WWD to FDR, August 21, 1934, FDRL.

14. Proceedings of the Democratic National Convention, 1932, 304, FDRL.

15. WWD to FDR, August 21, 1934, FDRL.

16. WWD to FDR, August 21, 1934, FDRL.

17. Western Union Social Message telegram, WWD to FDR, July 1, 1934, FDRL.

18. FDR to WWD, July 22, 1932, FDRL.

19. WWD to FDR, July 8, 1932, FDRL. Howe to Farley, undated, FDRL; Farley to Howe, August 29, 1932, FDRL.

20. FDR to Francis Durbin, June 20, 1932, FDRL.

21. Text for FDR's speech in Egyptian Hall has been taken from his campaign address at Madison Square Garden, October 21, 1936. Richard D. Polenberg, *The Era of Franklin D. Roosevelt, 1933–1945* (Boston: Bedford/St. Martin's, 2000), 53–57.

22. Eliza Durbin to FDR, July 20, 1932, FDRL.

23. Western Union telegram, WWD to FDR, August 14, 1932, FDRL; FDR to WWD, August 24, 1932, FDRL.

24. FDR to Francis Durbin, October 5, 1932:

Upon my recent return from my western trip, I found your letter of September 8th awaiting me.

Your firm stand by me in the Chicago convention and your fine efforts in this campaign, make me realize that I have no more loyal and devoted workers than yourself and your father. It is fine to know that your organization is in such excellent shape and I can see that you have a very progressive campaign program. There is probably no better way to sustain high enthusiasm and keen interest than by holding meetings, especially among the farmers.

Because of the extent of your political experience, I placed great confidence in your prediction that we will carry every township in your county. I know you are, indeed, a competent judge of the situation and you may be sure that I am particularly encouraged in view of the fact that your district is usually so strongly Republican. As a matter of fact, we are securing heartening reports from all sections of Ohio and it is my belief that you loyal workers are destined to see your state in our column on election day.

While we have every reason to be optimistic we must guard against the dangers of over confidence and we must in no way slack in our pace until November 8th. However, I know that I have no need to urge you to keep up the good work.

Assuring you my very deep appreciation for your loyalty and good wishes, I am yours very sincerely.

25. WWD to Farley, July 7, 1932, FDRL.

26. *Plain Talk Magazine*, April 1933, FDRL (attached to Durbin's letter of August 21, 1934, to FDR).

27. WWD to FDR, August 21, 1934, FDRL.

28. Polenberg, *The Era of Franklin D. Roosevelt, 1933-1945*, 53–57.

29. WWD, "To the Members of the I.B.M.," *LR* 11, no. 10 (Dec. 1931): 1012.

30. Joe Berg, "Convention Recollections," *LR* 12, no. 5 (July 1932): 407: "The quiet day before the convention. Most of the first arrivals are dealers. The first to greet you with a smile, Abe Martin. Hello Joe—when do you open up? Got anything new? A customer already. Here comes Mr. Durbin. The first thing he says to me, 'well, sue me.' Francis Durbin with the same bunch of keys. Hardly any magicians on the street.

In a few hours dozens of magicians have gathered in the magic store showing tricks. Say, Joe, watch this one!"

31. *The State of Ohio v. William W. Durbin,* Case No. 2699, Court of Common Pleas of Crawford County, Ohio (Clarence U. Ahl, Judge).

32. *Bucyrus Telegraph-Forum,* August 1–3, 1932. The indictment was reported in the *Telegraph-Forum,* June 1, 1932. The trial was also covered in *Cleveland Plain Dealer,* August 2–4, 1932.

33. "That Million Dollar Episode," *LR* 12, no. 5 (July 1932): 406.

34. *Bucyrus Telegraph-Forum,* Aug. 3, 1932.

35. State of Ohio v. William W. Durbin (Decision on Motion for a New Trial, Nov. 9, 1932, Judge Thomas).

36. Durbin was recommended by Henry Rainey, the Speaker of the House, for commissioner of Internal Revenue in a letter to Louis Howe. Henry Rainey to Louis McHenry Howe, March 20, 1933, FDRL. Josephus Daniels wrote a letter to FDR on behalf of Durbin, "speaking of my knowledge of the loyalty of Mr. Durbin and his son, Francis, at a critical time." Josephus Daniels to FDR, March 17, 1933, FDRL.

37. "An Honest-to-Goodness Magician Holds Office in Washington," *Philadelphia Public Ledger,* August 2, 1933. See also "Jim Farley Puts Bill Durbin, the Magician, Into the Treasury," *New York Evening Post,* August 2, 1933; and "Durbin (Rabbits from Hats) Turns Magic Art to Politics, Lands U.S. Treasury Job," *Washington Press,* August 2, 1933.

38. "Presto! Magician Durbin Pulls a Treasury Job Out of Political Pie," *New York World Telegram,* August 10, 1933.

39. "Notables Wait in Vain for Durbin's 'Black Magic,'" *Marion Star,* August 5, 1933. See also *Columbus Citizen,* August 3, 1933, and *Cleveland Plain Dealer,* August 6, 1933.

40. "Notables Wait in Vain for Durbin's 'Black Magic,'" *Marion Star,* August 5, 1933.

41. WWD to FDR, August 21, 1934, FDRL.

42. Eugene H. Roseboom and Francis P. Weisenberger, *A History of Ohio* (Columbus: Ohio State Archaeological and Historical Society, 1973), 367.

43. WWD to FDR, August 21, 1934, FDRL.

16. Undaunted by the Deep Menacing Dirge

1. FDR to Francis Durbin, February 5, 1937, FDRL.

2. Office memo dated February 4, 1937, FDRL. Mary Kelly was Durbin's secretary in Washington. Known as "Mame" Kelly, she was the subject of a memo in June 1937 from McIntyre to Mogenthau. "T. T. Ansberry, 1317 F St., Washington, D.C. Miss Mame Kelly, private secretary to the late Colonel W. W. Durbin. Trusts President can see his way clear to take such steps as will insure Miss Kelly staying in her present position as Secretary to the Register of the Treasury. President's penciled notation: 'Mac to handle.'" McIntyre to Morgenthau, June 19, 1937, FDRL.

3. Andy Durbin to FDR, February 9, 1937, FDRL.

4. Tec Huber, "Why? When? Where?" *LR* 13, no. 12 (Feb. 1934): 841, 854. Durbin reported that he had been sick at home in Kenton since December 28, "Ill in bed most of the time with a bad case of bronchitis." He rallied but got sick again. "Along about the 24th of January we were able to get up and out," he wrote, "but some how or other, got a backset and have been in bed ever since, but by the time the Linking Ring is issued we hope to be about again in our usual good health."

5. Birthday Greeting Western Union telegram, WWD to FDR, January 30, 1935, FDRL.

6. Grace Tully, *F.D.R.: My Boss* (New York: Scribner's, 1949), 153–54.

7. McIntyre to Miss LeHand, February 15, 1935, FDRL.

8. FDR to McIntyre, February 18, 1935, FDRL.

9. McIntyre to WWD, February 19, 1935, FDRL (to the Lee House, Fifteenth and L Streets).

10. WWD to McIntyre, February 23, 1935, FDRL.

11. Tully, *F.D.R.,* 94.

12. WWD to McIntyre, May 6, 1935, FDRL.

13. FDR: Day by Day—The Pare Lorentz Chronology, Stenographer's Diary, FDRL. Roosevelt wrote that he wanted to see Durbin. FDR to McIntyre, June 16, 1935, FDRL.

14. Confidential Memorandum for the Secretary of Treasury from FDR, August 19, 1935, FDRL.

15. Morgenthau to FDR, August 21, 1935, FDRL.

16. Andy Durbin to Irene McKenna, September 9, 1935, FDRL.

17. Andy Durbin to Irene McKenna, September 9, 1935, FDRL.

18. FDR to WWD, September 16, 1935, FDRL.

19. *Washington Court House News,* April 30, 1935, FDRL: "Now, at the close of half a century in politics, it requires large figures to number Durbin's political friends in both parties and a few score is the sum total to enumerate those who still hold a grudge against the 'fightin' man' from Kenton way, who has known defeat as well as victory, and always accepted both philosophically, forgotten the bruises and hurts sustained in battle and is ready to enlist in another political war. He has helped many men to high positions in public service."

20. WWD, "My Life in Magic," *LR* 15, no. 7 (Sept. 1935): 602. Henry Ridgely Evans described Durbin's writings as "extremely interesting." Henry R. Evans, "Bill Durbin's Life in Magic," *LR* 15, no. 8 (Oct. 1935): 667: "Some of Mr. Durbin's adventures in magic as a small boy are worthy of Tom Sawyer—that boy of boys."

21. "Colorful, Brilliant Career Suddenly Is Brought to a Close," *Kenton News-Republican,* February 5, 1937.

22. WWD, "My Life in Magic," *LR* 15, no. 8 (Oct. 1935): 704–6.

23. *Washington Court House News,* Apr. 30, 1935, FDRL.

24. FDR to Morgenthau, May 20, 1935, FDRL.

25. Morgenthau to FDR, May 21, 1935, FDRL.

26. FDR to Morgenthau, June 5, 1936, FDRL.

27. Unidentified newspaper clipping attached to a letter from McIntyre to Charles Thomas of the National Colored Democratic League. McIntyre to Charles M. Thomas, February 25, 1937, FDRL. "The recent death of W. W. Durbin," the author wrote, "white, register of the Treasury, recalled the fight said to have been waged by Virginia's Senator Carter Glass, with the consent of Andrew Mellon, then Secretary of the treasury, against the appointment of a colored Ohioan to the post during the Harding administration."

28. Ibid.

29. FDR to Morgenthau, February 19, 1937, FDRL.

30. W. B. Francis to Farley, February 23, 1937, Presidential Appointment-Application File: Francis Durbin, Loc: 10E4 6/2/1/ Box 57, National Archives. Fourteen letters

are contained in the file marked "Brief—Candidate for Presidential Office," all addressed to Farley as the chairman of the National Democratic Committee.

31. Farley to Morgenthau, April 10, 1937, Presidential Appointment Papers.

32. Andy Durbin to Irene McKenna, March 1, 1937, FDRL.

33. Paul Mallon, "News Behind the News," *Philadelphia Record,* June 27, 1936.

34. Ted Morgan, *F.D.R.: A Biography* (New York: Simon and Schuster, 1985), 370.

35. *Lima News,* December 11, 1949.

36. Western Union telegram, Margie Durbin to Diane and Sally Durbin, July 17, 1940 (Chicago, Illinois), author's private collection. The telegram was sent to 82 North Resch Street, Kenton, Ohio, Durbin's home. My aunts Diane and Sally were with their grandmother listening to the convention on the radio.

37. Tully, *F.D.R.,* 238–39: "'Well, damn it to hell,' he barked at Hopkins, 'they will go for Wallace or I won't run and you can jolly well tell them so'"; Doris Kerns Goodwin, *No Ordinary Time: Franklin and Eleanor Roosevelt: The Home Front in World War II* (New York: Simon and Schuster, 1994), 130–31.

38. *New York Times,* July 19, 1940; *Cleveland Plain Dealer,* July 19, 1940; *Lima News,* July 19, 1940; *Official Report of the Proceedings of the Democratic National Convention Held at Chicago, Illinois, July 15th to July 18th, inclusive 1940,* 231–33; 238–39. David M. Kennedy, *Freedom from Fear: The American People in Depression and War, 1929–1945* (New York: Oxford Univ. Press, 1999), 457: "But old-guard Democratic Party regulars deeply distrusted [Wallace] as an apostate Republican and as a doe-eyed mystic who symbolized all they found objectionable about the hopelessly utopian, market-manipulating, bureaucracy-breeding New Deal"; Goodwin, *No Ordinary Time,* 129–34.

39. Francis Durbin to FDR, July 29, 1940, FDRL.

40. Edwin M. Watson to Francis Durbin, August 5, 1940, FDRL. MEMO FOR PA [WATSON], August 2, 1940, FDRL.

41. *Lima News,* December 11, 1949. See also *Lima News,* July 20, 1944.

42. Mary Durbin to Margaret Durbin, November 6, 1948, author's private collection.

43. *Kenton Daily Democrat,* February 6, 1937.

44. Judge Thomas Dowd to author, August 7, 1995, author's private collection.

45. *Lima News,* February 5, 1937.

46. Ibid.

47. FDR to Francis Durbin, February 5, 1937, FDRL.

48. FDR to Mrs. W. W. Durbin, February 5, 1937, FDRL.

49. Andy Durbin to FDR, February 9, 1937, FDRL.

50. FDR to Andy Durbin, February 28, 1937, FDRL.

51. "Trouping with George Marquis," *LR* 16, no. 4 (June 1936): 310.

52. WWD to Inez Blackstone Kitchen, July 18, 1935, author's private collection.

53. WWD to FDR, September 28, 1936, FDRL (poem "Roosevelt" attached). Durbin said his sister's poem "states the issue in this campaign as well as anything I have seen." He hoped FDR agreed. "I trust you will like it."

54. Francis Durbin to FDR, March 3, 1937, FDRL.

17. Crossing the Bar

1. WWW, "From the President's Chair," *LR* 5, no. 4 (Dec. 1926): 119.

2. "Many Attend Rites for W. W. Durbin," *Kenton Daily Democrat,* February 9, 1937: "Beautiful and appropriate were the tributes paid to the deceased by Rev. H. J.

Schumacher, pastor of the church of the Immaculate Conception, and Rev. John Kelly of Yellow Springs, brother of the late Mrs. Francis Durbin, in their funeral orations. They spoke of Mr. Durbin as a man among men, a leader and one who won the esteem of all."

3. "Rituals," *LR* 9, no. 12 (Feb. 1930): 1428–29; Harry E. Cecil, "He Is Just Away," *LR* 16, no. 12 (Feb. 1937): 899–900.

4. Doc Endlich, "Philadelphia Ring No. 6," *LR* 9, no. 9 (Nov. 1928): 741; Wm. M. Endlich, "The James Barton Dinner," *LR* 9, no. 8 (Oct. 1929): 852.

5. Durbin's funeral card was found in the FDR library, attached to a letter from FDR to Andy Durbin. FDR to Andy Durbin, February 26, 1937, FDRL. I also found a leather-bound reprinting of the poem in Eliza Durbin's papers inscribed by John J. Lentz, a Durbin political friend and organizer with Durbin of the Ohio Progressive League for Wilson in 1912. The lithographic gift is dated December 25, 1910. "With Christmas greetings," Lentz wrote, "and hope that there may be many and many Happy New Years before you 'put out to sea.'"

6. "Blackstone Bares Spiritualism; Proposes to Duplicate Revelations," *LR* 8, no. 2 (Apr. 1928): 98–99.

7. "Magicians–Notice!" *LR* 17, no. 4 (June 1937): 276.

8. Henry R. Evans, "Flying Leaves from the Journal of an Amateur Magician and Mystic," *LR* 9, no. 8 (Oct. 1929): 779.

9. Hiram Joshua, "Dere Pres.," *LR* 8, no. 1 (Mar. 1928): 2.

BIBLIOGRAPHICAL ESSAY

My most important sources came from a mixture of publicly available collections and private and distinctly nonpublic letters and periodicals. *The Linking Ring* magazine is for magicians only. Take up magic, join the International Brotherhood of Magicians, swear an oath of secrecy, and you can get the entire collection, now on CD. My collection was purchased from George Daily, a magic dealer who lives in York, Pennsylvania. Daily also sold me souvenir programs from the early IBM conventions.

David Copperfield was kind enough to share his Durbin files with me. I spent a day with archivist Leo Behnke in Copperfield's home and warehouse in Las Vegas. This remarkable place and collection, just as I saw it, was pictured in a gorgeous spread in *Architectural Digest* in the March 1995 issue. The gun that killed Chung Ling Soo (Billy Robinson) is pictured on page 102.

Ted Carrothers from Toledo let me copy his collection of Durbin letters to Al Saal. These letters let me hear Durbin's voice. Bob and Elaine Lund provided access to the Durbin file they maintained at the American Museum of Magic in Marshall, Michigan. Teller of Penn and Teller wrote about Bob and Elaine in a nice article in the *New York Times Magazine*, April 24, 1994. The late Judge Tom Dowd gave me a box of Durbin memorabilia, including old magic programs, the "Story of Bill Durbin" brochure from the 1930 Senate race, photos, and Durbin's scrapbook, maintained in a United States Treasury ledger book. Pasted in this scrapbook were press clippings from the time Durbin was nominated to be register of the Treasury until his death. David Price and his wife, Virginia, went out of their way to make photocopies of Durbin's scrapbook from his early days in magic through the 1920s.

More public gems came from the Franklin D. Roosevelt Library in Hyde Park and the Woodrow Wilson Papers. Raymond Teichman, supervisory archivist at the FDRL, sent me the Durbin file and other letters he found in various boxes and folders relating to Ohio. John Sears, at the time the director of the Franklin and Eleanor Roosevelt Institute, took me out to dinner when I went to the library to look for more materials, and he kindly read and commented on drafts of this book. I visited the FDRL several times, a very friendly and helpful place to research, and I always found new things.

The Woodrow Wilson Papers maintained by the Library of Congress were indexed and placed on microfilm pursuant to an act of Congress in 1957, "to preserve their contents against destruction by war or other calamity." I found the microfilm in the Ohio State University Library and the library at Cornell University. The index on the Durbins (W. W., Francis, and Andy) contains references to forty-nine letters and memos, a fraction of what can be found with some more thorough digging.

The Library of Congress also maintains the Ray Stannard Baker Papers. The Durbin letters in this collection came to me from the Manuscript Division of the Library of Congress.

Durbin's Senate confirmation files came from RG 46: Records of the U. S. Senate, Sen73B-A4 Nomination File for William W. Durbin. Francis Durbin's application to replace his father as register is found in RG 56: Records of the U. S. Senate, Presidential Appointment/Application File: Francis Durbin, 10E4 6/2/1/Box 57.

The Civil War and pension records of Timothy Patrick Kelly and Jacob Born are from the National Archives Trust Fund Board. To order veterans' records, one needs to know the unit of the soldier and company if possible. Inquiries can be made of the National Archives and Records Administration in Washington, D.C.

For information about John Brown, I used:
Banks, Russell. *Cloudsplitter*. N.Y.: HarperFlamingo, 1998.
Du Bois, W. E. B. *John Brown*. Ed. David Roediger. NewYork: Modern Library, 2001.
Finkelman, Paul, ed. *His Soul Goes Marching On: Responses to John Brown in the Harpers Ferry Raid*. Charlotteville: Univ. Press of Virginia, 1995.
National Park Service, U.S. Department of Interior. *John Brown's Raid*. Washington, D.C.: U.S. Government Printing Office, 1973.
Oates, Steven B. *Our Fiery Trial: Abraham Lincoln, John Brown, and the Civil War Era*. Amherst: Univ. of Massachusetts Press, 1979.
Scott, John Anthony, and Robert Allan. *John Brown of Harper's Ferry: With Contemporary Prints, Photographs, and Maps*. New York: Facts on File, 1979.

For information about William Jennings Bryan, I used:
Ashby, LeRoy. *William Jennings Bryan: Champion of Democracy*. Boston: Twayne, 1987.
Bryan, William J., and Mary Baird Bryan. *The Memoirs of William Jennings Bryan: By Himself and His Wife Mary Baird Bryan*. Philadelphia, Pa.: United Publishers of America, 1925.
Glad, Paul W., ed. *William Jennings Bryan: A Profile*. New York: Harold and Wang, 1968.
Herrick, Genevieve, and John Herrick. *The Life of William Jennings Bryan*. Chicago: Buxton, 1925.
Koenig, Louis W. *Bryan: A Political Biography of William Jennings Bryan*. New York: Putnam's, 1971.

Readings on Woodrow Wilson:
Baker, Ray Stannard. *Woodrow Wilson: Life and Letters*. 8 vols. Garden City, N.Y.: Doubleday, 1927–39.
Freud, Sigmund, and William C. Bullitt. *Thomas Woodrow Wilson, A Psychological Study*. Boston: Houghton Mifflin, 1966.
Grayson, Cary. *Woodrow Wilson: An Intimate Study*. New York: Holt, Rinehart and Winston, 1960.
Link, Arthur Stanley. *Wilson: The Road to the White House*. 5 vols. Princeton, N.J.: Princeton Univ. Press, 1947–65.

————. *Woodrow Wilson: Revolution, War, and Peace*. Arlington Heights, Ill.: Harlan Davidson, 1979.

MacMillan, Margaret. *Paris 1919: Six Months That Changed the World*. New York: Random House, 2003.

Shachtman, Tom. *Edith and Woodrow: A Presidential Romance*. New York: Putnam's, 1981.

Smith, Gene. *When the Cheering Stopped: The Last Days of Woodrow Wilson*. New York: Morrow, 1964.

Tumulty, Joseph. *Woodrow Wilson as I Knew Him*. Garden City, N.Y.: Doubleday, 1920.

Wilson, Edith Bolling. *My Memoir*. Indianapolis: Bobbs-Merrill, 1938.

Wilson, W. *The Papers of Woodrow Wilson*. 69 vols. Ed. Arthur S. Link et al. Princeton, N.J.: Princeton Univ. Press, 1966–94.

For information about Warren G. Harding, James Cox, and Newton Baker, I used:

Anthony, Carl Sferrazza. *Florence Harding: The First Lady, the Jazz Age, and the Death of America's Most Scandalous President*. New York: Quill William Morrow, 1998.

Britton, Nan. *The President's Daughter*. New York: Elizabeth Ann Guild, 1927.

Coffee, Thomas. *The Long Thirst: Prohibition in America, 1920–1933*. New York: Norton, 1975.

Cox, James M. *Journey Through My Years*. New York: Simon and Schuster, 1946.

Cramer, C. H. *Newton D. Baker: A Biography*. Cleveland: World, 1961.

Daugherty, Harry M. *The Inside Story of the Harding Tragedy*. New York: Churchill, 1932.

Downes, Randolph C. *The Rise of Warren G. Harding, 1865–1920*. Columbus: The Ohio State Univ. Press, 1970.

Johnson, Tom L. *My Story*. Kent, Ohio: The Kent State Univ. Press, 1993.

Means, Gaston B. *The Strange Death of President Harding*. New York: Guild, 1930.

Mee, Charles L., Jr. *The Ohio Gang: The World of Warren G. Harding*. New York: M. Evans, 1981.

Russell, Francis. *The Shadow of Blooming Grove: Warren G. Harding in His Times*. New York: McGraw-Hill, 1968.

Sinclair, Andrew. *The Available Man: The Life Behind the Masks of Warren Gamiliel Harding*. New York: MacMillan, 1965.

Franklin Roosevelt books I found most helpful:

Acheson, Dean. *Present at the Creation: My Years in the State Department*. New York: Norton, 1969.

Alsop, Joseph. *FDR: A Centenary Remembrance*. New York: Viking, 1982.

Collier, Peter, and David Horowitz. *The Roosevelts: An American Saga*. New York: Simon and Shuster, 1994.

Davis, Kenneth S. *F.D.R.: The Beckoning of Destiny 1882–1928*. New York: Putnam's, 1972.

Farley, James A. *Jim Farley's Story: The Roosevelt Years*. New York: McGraw-Hill, 1948.

Fromkin, David. *In the Time of the Americans: FDR, Truman, Eisenhower, Marshall, MacArthur—The Generation That Changed America's Role in the World*. New York: Knopf, 1995.

Gallagher, Hugh Gregory. *FDR's Splendid Deception*. Arlington, Va.: Vandamere, 1994.

Goodwin, Doris Kearns. *No Ordinary Time: Franklin and Eleanor Roosevelt: The Home Front in World War II*. New York: Simon and Shuster, 1994.

Hunt, John Gabriel, ed. *The Essential Franklin Delano Roosevelt*. New York: Gramercy, 1995.

Kennedy, David M. *Freedom from Fear: The American People in Depression and War, 1929–1945*. New York: Oxford Univ. Press, 1999.

Lash, Joseph P. *Eleanor and Franklin: The Story of Their Relationship, Based on Eleanor Roosevelt's Private Papers*. New York: Norton, 1971.

Morgan, Ted. *F.D.R.: A Biography*. New York: Simon and Shuster, 1985.

Polenberg, Richard D., ed. *The Era of Franklin D. Roosevelt, 1933–1945*. Boston: Bedford/ St. Martin's, 2000.

Roosevelt, Franklin Delano. *The Public Papers and Addresses of Franklin D. Roosevelt*. 13 vols. New York: Random House, MacMillan, Harper, 1938–50.

Roosevelt, Eleanor. *The Autobiography of Eleanor Roosevelt*. New York: Harpers and Brothers, 1949.

———. *This I Remember*. New York: Harpers and Brothers, 1961.

Tully, Grace. *F.D.R.: My Boss*. New York: Scribner's, 1949.

Ward, Geoffrey C. *A First-Class Temperament: The Emergence of Franklin Roosevelt*. New York: HarperPerennial, 1989.

———. *Before the Trumpet: Young Franklin Roosevelt 1882–1905*. New York: Harper and Row, 1985.

Magic books I relied on are:

Christopher, Milbourne. *The Illustrated History of Magic*. New York: Crowell, 1973.

Doerflinger, William. *The Magic Catalog: A Comprehensive Guide to the Wonderful World of Magic*. New York: Dutton, 1977.

Evans, Henry Ridgely. *History of Conjuring and Magic from the Earliest Times to the End of the 18th Century*. Kenton, Ohio: William W. Durbin, 1930.

———. *History of Conjuring and Magic*. Kenton, Ohio: International Brotherhood of Magicians, 1928.

Gibson, Walter. *The Master Magicians: Their Lives and Most Famous Tricks*. Garden City, N.Y.: Doubleday, 1966.

Hoffman, Professor. *Modern Magic: A Practical Treatise on the Art of Conjuring* (ca. 1877). Reprint Biblo-Moser, n.d.

Price, David. *Magic: A Pictorial History of Conjurers in the Theater*. New York: Cornwall, 1985.

Randi, James. *Conjuring*. New York: St. Martin's Press, 1992.

Ohio readings I found most helpful are:

Lamis, Alexander P., ed. *Ohio Politics: A Historical Perspective*. Kent, Ohio: The Kent State Univ. Press, 1994.

Powell, Thomas E., ed. *The Democratic Party of the State of Ohio*. Columbus: Ohio Publishing Company, 1913.

Roseboom, Eugene H., and Francis P. Weisenburger. *A History of Ohio*. Columbus: Ohio Historical Society, 1973.

Warner, Hoyt Landen. *Progressivism in Ohio, 1897–1917*. Columbus: Ohio State Univ. Press, 1964.

Wittke, Carl., ed. *Ohio in the 20th Century, 1900–1938*. Columbus: Ohio State Archaeological and Historical Society, 1942.

INDEX

DATE DUE